In Beauty May She Walk

In Beauty May She Walk

Hiking the Appalachian Trail at 60

by

Leslie Mass

Rock Spring Press
Jacksonville, Florida

© 2005 Rock Spring Press Inc.
6015 Morrow Street East, Suite 106
Jacksonville, Florida 32217
www.rockspringpress.com

First Edition
ISBN 0-9765686-0-8

Library of Congress Control Number: 2005929226

The following publishers have generously given permission to use quota-
tions from copyrighted works. From *Writing Down The Bones,* by Natalie
Goldberg. ©1986. Reprinted by arrangement with Shambhala
Publications, Inc., Boston, www.shambhala.com. From *How We Become
Human,* "Fire", by Joy Harjo, ©2002. Reprinted by permission of W.W.
Norton & Co, N.Y. From *A Woman in Love with Herself,* by Patricia Lynn
Reilly, with permission of Conari Press, an imprint of Red Wheel/Weiser,
Boston, MA and York Beach, ME. To order please call Conari Press at
1-800-423-7087. From *Pilgrim at Tinker Creek,* by Annie Dillard, ©1974.
Reprinted by permission of Harper Collins. From *Steps Toward Inner Peace,*
by Peace Pilgrim. Reprinted by permission of Friends of Peace Program.

For all those who hike with me
  — as dreamers
  — as doers
  — as readers
  — as life-givers
With grateful appreciation
  and love
    Gotta Hike!

Contents

Introduction

"In the end, what is interesting is not the plot of a story,
but the way in which it is enacted."
Natalie Goldberg, Writing Down the Bones

My hike of the Appalachian Trail is an odyssey of physical, social, mental and spiritual change: a pilgrimage towards symmetry and self-fulfillment. I write about my journey in hopes that other women will recognize me as one of their own: a woman engaged in balancing the needs of others with a dream no one else shared; a woman who found the courage to act on her dream, not knowing if it could, but that it should be done.

Since childhood, I have kept journals, diaries, and written records of my thoughts, feelings, activities, and insights. The years preparing for and then hiking the Appalachian Trail were no exception. My journal entries, set apart from the text, are included in the narrative of my hike so that my voice at the time of writing can be heard.

> "August, 1999. I've always taken to the woods loving to walk towards a destination with only essentials strapped to my back. Without a canopy of tall trees and the brief sanctuary they afforded me to be alone with my thoughts, I would have enacted my story differently. The woods help me center myself. It's the place I go to be by myself, the place I can be most myself. I feel at home in the woods."

It seems that I have been taking to the woods all my life. As a girl growing up with three brothers and a baby sister in the Connecticut countryside, I would often take a snack and, with my dog, go exploring after school, hiking the low hills and woods surrounding our small neighborhood until dark sent me home to dinner, music practice, or homework.

As a young mother, first with one daughter, then with two, I remember strapping each girl into her seat on the fenders of my bicycle and heading for the woods. We lived outside a small Ohio town then, in a neighborhood as yet undeveloped, still surrounded by woods. When my daughters were older, I discovered solo hiking and used their five-week summer camp time to hike the woods in England, New England and Ohio.

> "May, 2001. The woods have always given me quiet to reflect, helping me focus to resolve. Now they inspire me to rediscover and empower my self."

It has taken some courage and trust to reveal the self I was before I began my Appalachian Trail thru-hike, the exhausted self I was during some parts of the hike, and the self I became as a result of the journey. My family has also been impacted by the perceptions of them that I have chosen to share with the world as part of my story. I am deeply grateful for their courage and grace in letting me share them.

Prologue

My dream to hike the Appalachian Trail began in 1986 after a summer sabbatical to England when life was good: my daughters, Amy and Megg, were safe, healthy, and thriving in an independent girl's school where I taught; my husband, George, a psychologist, was strong, active and rewarded by his profession, and the early childhood literacy program I had created had just been named by the National Council of Teachers of English as a "Center of Excellence." I was living well, with impossible optimism and naiveté.

During that summer's sabbatical I hiked by myself in England, from one bed and breakfast to another, collecting folk songs and children's stories. I learned to chart my course using the ordnance survey maps of public footpaths that crisscrossed the English countryside. For several months I lived the romantic idyll of walking as an act of creating espoused by William Wordsworth and the journals of his sister, Dorothy, as I tramped the lush valleys and rocky mountaintops of the English Lake District.

When I returned to the United States, I looked for similar walking opportunities and tried to find long-distance trails where I could hike toward a destination, stay overnight in modest but comfortable lodgings, and not have to retrace my steps. I remembered my father's enthusiasm for the Appalachian Trail, which was conceived and first articulated in his generation by Benton MacKaye, a New England visionary.

MacKaye wanted to create a trail system to make the mountains from north to south along the eastern coast accessible to all. He dreamt of combining the existing foot trails of New Hampshire, Vermont, New York, and New Jersey with Pennsylvania, the central Appalachian states from Maryland through Virginia, and the southern Appalachian states from North Carolina to Georgia.

By 1937, the year my father married, MacKaye's dream of linking the fourteen states into a continuous hiking trail from Maine to Georgia had become a reality.

My father experienced that reality during the 1940s and '50s when he took his young family camping throughout New England, occasionally stopping at crossings where signs or blazes marked the AT. He knew the trail, but only in bits and pieces, from signs and maps, and only through the eyes of others. He was a dreamer, not a doer, a responsible parent, not a hiker. However, somewhere during those car camping trips, his longing for wandering MacKaye's "mountainous hinterlands" was passed on to me.

His dream sparked my interest in walking the AT as one long hike. The journals of Dorothy Wordsworth and my summer trek on the footpaths across England fanned that spark.

I began to read about the AT and look for long-distance trails I could hike on weekends near our home in Ohio. I discovered the Buckeye Trail around the perimeter of the state, and on an organized hike one weekend, learned about the huts run by the Appalachian Mountain Club in New England. These alpine huts connect the Presidential Mountain Range in the White Mountains of New Hampshire, serve breakfast and dinner, and provide a bunk with blankets to hikers with advance reservations. This was just what I was looking for. That summer, at the age of forty-eight, I hiked seventy-five miles of the AT in a group led by veteran hikers, using the hut system in the White Mountains. Difficult though the hike was for me, it ignited a flame to someday hike the entire trail in one continuous journey.

Ten years later, on a long drive down the Blue Ridge parkway in North Carolina, I remembered my dream to wander the Appalachian Trail from end to end.

When I told my father of my plans, he was lying tired and weak against the white sheet of a hospital bed.

"Dad, I'm going to do a thru-hike of the Appalachian Trail," I said, hoping to cheer him.

He squeezed my hand and smiled. "You do that!" his stroke-garbled speech replied. "You do that!"

That was our last conversation. He died several days later while I was driving through the Blue Ridge Mountains, tears streaming down my face in grief for my perception of his life: well-dreamt but actively unfulfilled. I resolved that I would not die with my dreams unlived. I determined that I would hike those trails through New England that my father so loved but was never able to connect. It would be my memorial to him.

In Beauty May She Walk

1. Preparation

In August 1999, I began to think about the conditioning I would need to do in order to be physically capable of hiking with a pack every day all day for 2,164 miles. I was so green, I didn't even know how many miles it was customary to walk every day, or how many months it would take to reach my destination. I only knew that my comfortable daily walk on park trails, casual working out on our basement weight machine, and intermittent laps in the university swimming pool would probably not suffice. My daughter Amy, a runner, suggested that I start running again.

"Here's the formula, Mom: Buy a cute little running outfit; spend some money. Get really good shoes. Start by running and walking half a mile each day. Gradually do more running, less walking. By the time you've invested one hundred and fifty dollars and a month of sweat, you'll be a runner."

I hadn't run in twenty-five years, and soon discovered that running shoes had changed a lot since my last sprint. Also, that cute little running outfit for a fifty-eight-year-old body did not come cheap, but I made the investment and followed Amy's advice. I discovered I really liked running.

> "August, 1999. I like to run by the river. Every day I run about 1.3 miles and walk between three and five miles... I swim or work out on weight machines for half an hour three times a week... At night, my body is tired but flexible and I'm beginning to feel more fit."

By early October 1999, I had considerably increased my exercise program. I was hoping to trim the ten pounds I had gained over the past few years and firm up, as well. Even when the crisp days of autumn forced me into long black tights, I kept running. On Thanksgiving Day, Amy and I ran a five-mile Turkey Trot before cooking and serving the traditional family feast. I didn't qualify for the free pumpkin pie awarded to the first 100 finishers, but I was proud that I finished.

Luckily, over the next few months I could continue to run, walk and swim every day, even when the early sunset of Ohio winter turned the afternoons cold and dark and snow made the trails slippery. Because I worked at a university with long winter and spring breaks, I was able to spend even the darkest, wettest days running and swimming, either outdoors in Florida, or at the indoor pool and track in Ohio. I ran and swam through the winter and early spring of 2000, comfortable in both environments.

> "My body looks better than it has in a long time, though I haven't lost any weight and I still can't squat very well. But, I am more limber and trimmer and I know I have more stamina. Running makes me feel more alive and alert, so I'll keep running."

In May, just before school finished for the year, I heard about a course to be taught the next semester at Ohio Wesleyan, my university. It was a ten-week training progression for balance, stability, and core body conditioning. The instructor was polite, if skeptical, when I asked if I could join the course in the fall. However, she gave me a large blue ball and several pages of exercises to do over the summer to prepare for the class.

All summer I practiced standing with one leg off the ground for fifteen to forty-five seconds, squatting at forty-five and ninety degrees on a stability board and balance beam, lying on the floor in a supine position doing a "dead bug" march, crunching my abs while inclined on the ball, extending my back while draped prone over the ball, squeezing my shoulder blades together while balancing on the ball, lunging across the floor with my knees aligned not to cross over my toes, and lying on the ball like a table, slowly dropping my hips to the floor and pushing them back up. And that was only the preparation for class!

That fall I was the oldest one in the agility class by forty years. At first I felt foolish, clumsy and out of shape. But I held my own, and when the beginners class ended, I signed on for Intermediate, and then repeated the sequence in the spring, wearing my backpack filled with weights on some of the routines. It occurred to me that no matter how silly I looked, if I could keep up with eighteen-year-olds and the football team while wearing a twenty-five pound pack, I would probably be fit enough to hike by spring.

Ray Jardine, in *Beyond Backpacking*, advocates that long distance hikers begin to train at least five months prior to their trek. So, in addition to running and swimming and balancing during that summer, I was eager to try a few day hikes with a pack. I spent one hot, humid August day traversing the hills in a state park near our home using a dry tree branch as a hiking stick. In an old, external frame pack Amy had used in college, I carried two seven-pound dumbbells, an old camp sleeping bag, some food and water, my journal, and my husband George's old Gore-Tex raingear.

On my seven-mile loop hike through the woods, I encountered paths threaded by spiders, mosquitoes, rain, sweat, and a troop of Boy Scouts sprawled at a picnic area, waiting for their water to boil.

"Can we help you, ma'am?" one politely inquired as I came straggling out of the woods, sweating and batting bugs away with a grimy bandanna.

"No thanks, I'm just looking for the trail," I said, squinting at the poorly marked map, trying to look like I knew what I was doing.

The Boy Scouts pointed me in the right direction, and I hiked on while they ate lunch. It wasn't long, though, before I was overtaken by their boisterous shouts as they burst ahead of me, with full packs and robust adolescent energy.

I felt diminished, old, and foolish. And tired. The hike convinced me that I needed a sturdier, lighter pack, waterproof boots, a lightweight sleeping bag, and a better hiking stick.

In late August 2000, George and I drove to Freeport, Maine to check out the hiking gear at L.L. Bean, my childhood reference for outdoor clothing and equipment.

But what to buy? The choices were endless and making the decisions agonizing. I knew from my reading that backpacks were finally being made for women with frame sizes proportional to a woman's body (mine measured to be extra small) and narrower shoulder harnesses (again extra small). I had read that it was important for women to carry the weight on their hips rather than their shoulders, so the fit and cant (tilt) of the waistbelt is important. My waistbelt measured as a medium, and was secured so that the angle of the belt mirrored the angle of my hip structure with no gaps at the top or bottom of the belt. I was advised that the top edge of the waistbelt should ride about one inch above the top of my hipbones.

I tried several packs, loaded, and walked around L.L. Bean, self-consciously trying to decide which one felt more natural. The Gregory Shasta won, and even though it was a bit heavier than I wanted, at six pounds, four ounces, it fit beautifully. I wasn't quite sure what to do with all the straps, but was pleased to discover that the sternum strap could be adjusted so that it neither strangled my windpipe nor acted as an armored breastplate over my chest. A pack capacity of 4,456 cubic inches made sense to me as I intended to carry only thirty-five pounds, or one-fourth of my body weight. And I liked the feature of separate top hood that could convert to a fanny pack.

Choosing boots was a matter of trying on several models of leather and Gore-Tex hikers, walking around L.L. Bean up and down a simulated rock incline, and kicking my toes against a wall before deciding on a pair of Gore-Tex lined Cresta Hikers, a bit larger than my normal shoe size. Even though I had read of hikers doing the trail in running shoes (Grandma Gatewood, the first woman to complete a thru-hike, wore sneakers), I felt most comfortable in boots with plenty of ankle protection.

I was persuaded to buy a two-person tent. My L.L. Bean salesperson convinced me that I would come to appreciate the extra room afforded by a difference of only eleven ounces, or thirty dollars more, so I purchased a micro-light hoop style tent with waterproof rain fly and vestibule. I also purchased a protective ground cloth designed to fit under the tent. I rationalized that the extra room would come in handy when (if) any of my women friends or daughters joined me on the trail.

Finally, I ordered a mummy sleeping bag of "the finest goose down" rated at twenty degrees, weighing only two pounds thirteen ounces. (I eventually discovered that the twenty-degree rating means the feathers will keep you alive, not warm and toasty, when the temperature is twenty degrees). I also purchased a long, ultra-light inflatable Therm-A-Rest mattress to place under my sleeping bag for extra warmth and comfort. This I replaced with a three-quarter-length mattress of the same make before I began to hike, a difference of ten ounces and less bulk.

I was ready to do some pre-hikes with my weighted pack and new, Gore-Tex lined boots. I preferred to train by hiking in the woods by myself.

"September, 2000, Tar Hollow State Park, Ohio. This is more like it! Beautiful day – sunny, blue sky, middle of the woods. I've just climbed a fairly steep hill and am at that point when a cheese sandwich and water taste great! I just had to note the beauty of this moment before doing anything else. I'm sitting against my pack, feet on a hollowed out tree stump, journal open. My gear is working well, though it is nice to get the pack and boots off and let the cool air bathe my back and feet! I wonder if the trail will be like this – tough moments of sweat and toil rewarded by blessed relief, quiet beauty and a cool breeze. I hope so."

I experienced my first taste of "trail magic" after one of my pre-hikes.

"When I got to school this morning, one of the roofers repairing our building noticed that my trunk was full of hiking gear. He asked about the dry branch I was using for a hiking stick and we chatted, briefly, about hiking. He told me he'd once hiked a lot in North Carolina but now had to have an operation on his knees and would be 'just sittin' around for six weeks.' He offered to whittle me a stick while he was off work."

Several days later, when he came by to measure my arm, my staff mistook him for a bum and would not let him into our building. I assumed that was the end of my walking stick.

And then the magic: The first day back after spring break, the roofer, looking much better than he had in the fall, reappeared at our school door; in his hand was a polished hardwood walking stick. He had whittled and smoothed the stick during the long winter months while he was recuperating and dreaming about hiking.

The stick was beautiful and I accepted with appreciation and admiration. I was not prepared, however, for the folded piece of notebook paper, soft with much fingering, which he pulled from his pocket.

"I wrote you a poem to go with it," he said, bashfully holding it out to me.

> "May your walks be as wonderful as the beuty (sic) of natures gift you have seen. You will stand in awe at the end of your jurney (sic) you will understand what I mean.
>
> – Happy Trails. D.R."

I read with choked emotion: a roofer and university professor sharing each other's worlds. And even though I hiked, in the end, with Leki adjustable trekking poles, I hoped I would 'stand in awe at the end of my journey', and meet others like the roofer on my way.

As I prepared for the AT, I began to realize that the hike would be more than just a physical endeavor. It would be an odyssey, a meandering journey of many changes, some spiritual, some mental, some social, some logistical. I wanted to be open to them all, and to be able to learn whatever the trail had to teach me.

> "The woods help me transcend myself. Looking to the tops of tall straight trees on a cool morning, my feet firmly shod in hiking boots, the rest of me dressed for whatever the weather might require, I find my own cathedral to worship within. Sometimes I listen to sacred choral music while I walk; more often it's just birdsong and early morning insects, leaves fluttering in the breeze or rain softly falling on my hood that I hear. I like best to listen to the quiet."

Although raised in the Christian tradition, I left organized religion after a required Bible course in college and two years as a Peace Corps volunteer in Pakistan, a Muslim country. As an adult, I consciously worked towards spiritual growth in my own way: by trying to be empathic and responsive to others' needs, by meditating and reading widely, by writing and painting, and by walking in the woods. My journals at the time reflect some initial concerns:

> "December, 1999. I'm still committed to my long-distance hike, but my reasons for going have begun to shift. Initially, it was to be able to revisit the good part of my childhood and reconnect with my parents in their beloved mountains of New Hampshire and rocky New England woods. Now I see it as an opportunity to begin to take off the robes of responsibility that have clothed me for so long, to see if I can become lighter and more visible without so many cloaks and garments. I would like to shed all the layers that no longer fit, that no longer serve me, that prevent me from bringing my naked self to the light."

Without really knowing it, I was longing for the simplicity and the purposefulness of the pilgrim.

That first Christmas after my father died I sent a donation, in his memory, to the Southwest Indian Foundation to buy a wood-burning stove for a family who needed that more than the cookies I would no longer bake for him. In return, I received a card with the enclosed prayer:

> *"In beauty may I walk.*
> *All day long may I walk.*
> *Through the returning seasons may I walk*
> *In beauty will I possess again.*
> *Beautifully birds*
> *Beautifully joyful birds.*
> *On a trail marked with pollen may I walk.*
> *With wild flowers about my feet may I walk.*
> *With dew about my feet may I walk.*
> *With beauty may I walk*
> *With beauty before me may I walk*
> *With beauty behind me may I walk*

With beauty above me may I walk
With beauty all around me may I walk.
In old age, wandering on a trail of beauty,
Lively may I walk
In old age, wandering on a trail of beauty,
Living again may I walk.
It is finished in beauty."

Adopting this prayer as my own spiritual beacon, I decided to begin each day on the trail saying it to myself.

�֍

Whenever I told anyone of my plan to thru-hike the AT, the first question, invariably, was more of a statement:

"You're not planning to hike it alone, are you?!"

My usual answer was, "No, I will be joined by my daughters, and other women friends along the way. And George will meet me every few weeks to clean me up and feed me." Although George had the early stages of Parkinson's disease, he was still easily able to go out and about. But I always meant to hike my own hike, expecting to spend long periods alone on the trail if no one joined me.

A well-meaning acquaintance, hearing of my plans to hike the AT without my husband, brought me a Stun Gun to ward off bears and other unpredictable predators. I thanked him, politely, for his concern and put the weapon in a closet.

Worry about bears and other predators did not weigh heavily, but in the back of my mind, I harbored a fear that walking alone might be construed by some as an invitation for attention or worse, permission for sexual harassment. From my reading, I knew that crimes of sexual violence, as well as murder, had been committed on or near the AT. According to the Appalachian Trail Conference, five incidents that resulted in death have taken place on the trail. Of those attacked, only two – one woman, and one man – were hiking alone.

The reports of violence were unsettling but not overly alarming. I planned to follow the precautions of other women hikers: avoid staying in shelters near road crossings, keep my itinerary to myself, and when meeting strangers, behave as though my partner were just behind me on the trail.

I did not take a weapon, not even pepper spray. My best protection, I concluded, would be to walk with vigilance, not fear. I determined that I would hike smart and not be tethered by strings of doubt and indecision.

✻

My pre-hike reading of thru-hiker's journals and books was replete with stories about the AT community itself: a community established on shared determination and dream; a community that recognizes and looks out for one another; a community of men and women, hikers and trail maintainers, townspeople and trail angels who really care about the trail and the people who traverse it. I trusted that I would find this community.

However, I continued to search for hiking partners among my friends and acquaintances. I approached the American Youth Foundation of St. Louis, Missouri, with an idea to open my trek to women participants from the Summer Seminars for Women. A group of resourceful, adventurous women would be good hiking partners, I thought, and the AYF agreed. However, even though the AYF was willing to extend the "Women's Trek: A Thru-hike of the Appalachian Trail" possibility to like-minded women through their web page, I didn't have any takers. No one, it seemed, could commit the better part of five months to being away from home, family, or job, much less to hiking and camping all that time.

I looked further. At a weekend reunion of women college friends, my stalwart buddy, Lura, agreed to join me for a few weeks at the beginning of my hike. An avid outdoorswoman, Lura had her own computer firm, consulted via small plane with clients in Alaska, and had been hiking the trails in her home state of New Jersey for many years. She had much more backcountry camping experience than I and was eager to participate in my adventure. We planned to begin the trail together and possibly meet again when I hiked through New Jersey.

Other friends at the same reunion agreed to supply me with CARE packages along the way and treat me to a shower and weekend of pampering when I reached Pennsylvania, the state of our alma mater, Gettysburg College.

I did not try to find a partner through the Appalachian Trail Conference, though I knew that prospective partners often advertised in personal ads in their publications. I preferred the companionship of my friends or family and, failing that was prepared to hike by myself.

I was eager to hike my own hike.

"Hiking your own hike" refers to the tradition of defining how, when, where, and why you will hike, tailoring the hike to your own needs and special circumstances, and then doing it. Sometimes, hiking your own hike becomes the most challenging task you will face. The definition of hiking your own hike often changes as you gain experience and make adjustments on the trail.

"Touching every blaze" refers to the idea of hiking every mile on the designated white-blazed trail without deviating from the path each club has laid out. Someone who hikes this way is referred to as a "purist."

"Blue blazing" refers to hiking an alternate route adjacent to or crossing the AT, leading to the same destination but perhaps traversing easier, more scenic, or shorter distance terrain. Circumventing the summit of Lehigh Rocks on the blue-blazed trail is an example of this kind of hiking.

"Yellow blazing" refers to hitchhiking or walking along a road to one's destination, skipping sections of the trail rather than hiking them. Hitchhiking to town and picking up the trail farther along on return is another version of yellow blazing.

The AT Conference in Harper's Ferry, West Virginia, was helpful in guiding me through the itinerary-planning phase. Initially, I read every book I could find on AT thru-hikes, particularly those written by women. In the summer of 2000, I purchased the complete Guide Set (eleven books and all the maps) of the AT and Christopher Whalen's *Appalachian Trail Workbook for Planning Thru-hikes*.

Then began the real work of mapping out a reasonable hike for each day, in each state, noting trail crossings, shelters, campsites and mail-drop towns. At first, it was completely overwhelming. The maps all looked the same and the guidebooks went from front to back, and back to front depending on the direction of the hike (south to north or north to south). Most thru-hikers begin at Springer Mountain, Georgia, and hike north to Mt. Katahdin, in Maine. Because of weather conditions, most north-bound thru-hikers begin in March and hike until early October when Baxter State Park closes access to Mt. Katahdin. Conversely, southbound thru-hikers begin at Mt. Katahdin in June when Baxter State Park opens, and hike until they reach the southern terminus at Springer Mountain just as the snow begins to fly in Georgia. By most definitions, a thru-hike is completion of the trail within one year of the starting date, no matter where you start or finish.

My university work schedule would permit me to hike from mid-May until the end of August. This was not enough time for a traditional end-to-end thru-hike of fifteen miles per day, my estimated hiking pace.

I decided to ask for release time from teaching in the fall and do a "flip-flop" hike, starting in May at a point in the south which would allow me to reach Mt. Katahdin by the end of August. Then I would return to my job for three weeks of administrative tasks and rejoin the trail at my original starting point and hike south to finish at Springer Mountain by the end of October.

A flip-flop would allow me to do a thru-hike within the confines of my work schedule and the weather restrictions at each terminus.

"April 27, 2001. Trail preparations have consumed the last two weeks: I re-worked my itinerary, adding road crossings and map markers; I re-worked my mail-drops and sent updated copies of my plans to everyone who has expressed an interest; I re-wrote my request for release time and met with the provost and my staff to clarify details of my absence-from-campus, the newly-named, non-precedent-setting status I will now enjoy. Somehow I've still managed to work out in the gym and to schlep my full pack around the park for daily training hikes. I find it hard to stay asleep at night with so many details swirling around in my head.

George has been wonderful – very helpful and supportive. He is impressed with my mail-drop preparations – twelve boxes full of food, toiletries, maps and stuff that he will send to me at various points along the trail. I think he is proud of my organization – in fact he seems buoyed by the pre-hike flurry. He is planning to drive me to Virginia and meet me after the first week – both long interruptions for him in the middle of his busy work schedule. I hope he will have the energy; even without the drain of Parkinson's disease, the behind-the-scenes support is a major undertaking. It would be impossible to do this without him."

My plan was to begin at Rockfish Gap at the southern tip of Shenandoah National Park in Virginia on May 13, 2001, hike north to Mt. Katahdin by August 22, return to Ohio for three weeks at my job, and then depart again from Rockfish Gap and hike south to reach Springer Mountain by October 30, 2001.

At the end of April, just two weeks before I was to begin, my college friend Lura wrote that she needed to undergo radiation treatments in May for the breast cancer she had thought was in remission. She would not be able to hike the first three weeks of the trail with me after all.

I was distressed for her, and disappointed for both of us. So many of my friends had been through this breast cancer scenario – it just didn't seem fair for Lura to be one of them. But who would it be fair for? I reminded myself. What's fair about any of it?

Lura was not defeated by the change in plans. She would follow my hike at home, she said. In fact, instead of hiking the AT, she would spend the summer building her strength and stamina for a sixty-mile walk for breast cancer in October. Eventually, we vowed, we would hike the AT together -- just at a different time, in a different place.

Then George read about a women's Appalachian Trail hike workshop, organized by a freelance photographer from southern Ohio named Mimi Morrison, creator of Earth Touch Workshops. The workshop was to be the following weekend at Bear's Den Hostel on the AT in Bluemont, Virginia.

"I'm really too busy to go to a workshop," I demurred at first. But the more I thought about it, the better I liked the idea of shaking out my pack and last minute worries and actually trying out my hiking feet on the AT. I called and talked my way into the group and happily discovered that Mel Blaney would lead the workshop. I had just finished her book, *A Journey of Friendship,* an account of her '96 thru-hike, and knew I would be in good hands.

> "Friday, April 27, 2001, Bears Den Hostel, Bluemont, Virgina. Everyone has gone to bed in this large, sparse bunkroom. My head is spinning. After lugging my pack around all day and listening to Mel talk about the hike tomorrow, my doubts are back. Tonight I'm so aware of my age, sixty, and the eccentricity of trying to do a thru-hike all by myself. Women travel in groups! What can I be thinking? Can I actually set off on the trail alone, for five months, with just my wits and backpack for company? I'm no Grandma Gatewood! She was from pioneer-stock – born and bred to a rough life outdoors. Hiking the trail at sixty-seven, for her, was just more of the same. I'm a middle-aged, middle-class, suburban dreamer. What do I know about survival? What if I can't even do tomorrow's hike?"

The next day was like taking my general examinations to qualify as a candidate for a Ph.D. Mel hiked with me all day, grilling me about my preparation and resolve and watching me hike. We left the other women in our dust and, unbeknownst to me, I was passing my exams and earning my trail name.

At the end of the day, we all gathered on Bear's Den Rocks to watch the sunset. Mel made an announcement and presentation:

"You burn for the trail," she said to me. "You're ready! And I have your trail name: *'Gotta Hike!'* I've been hiking with you all day, looking at the back of your hat. It says *'Gotta Hike!'* and you do!"

And just like that, I became *Gotta Hike!*, my very own trail name. I had joined the league of thru-hikers who don a new identity when they are "named" by another hiker, usually for some aspect of their personality or trail-self that may never be revealed in everyday life.

I was surprised and delighted that this veteran hiker had found me acceptable and had welcomed me into the cadre of thru-hikers, class of 2001. I had passed my exam and could go on to write my dissertation or, hike my hike.

Then Mel presented me with a copy of her book with a personalized inscription:

> *4/28/01, Leslie, GOTTA HIKE! And you are about to! You are going to have a wonderful adventure. Enjoy and savor all of the magic the trail has to offer. I'd wish you luck, but there's no need to. You're prepared, focused, determined and your heart and head are in the right place. You'll make it!*
>
> *– Melody*
> *Ga.-Maine '96*

"I'm thrilled. I guess I'm ready. And Mel's right: I Gotta Hike!"

2. *Getting Started*

Rockfish Gap, Va., to Dahlgren Campground, Md., 173 miles

May 12, 2001, to Waynesboro, Va., 10 miles

George, Amy and I set out on a sunny, cool morning to drive from our home in Ohio to the southern tip of Shenandoah National Park, the starting point of my flip-flop hike. We planned to meet my youngest daughter Megg, her husband Jim, and our twenty-month-old grandson Nemo for the weekend. As a surprise, my friend Lura and her husband, Vince, also met us in Waynesboro. Despite her treatment, Lura would hike the first day with me after all. It was her Mother's Day present.

Early Sunday morning, we started out. We all hiked together for the first five miles, through meadows full of wildflowers and woods of newly green trees. At Beagle Gap, Lura, Vince, Jim, and Nemo stopped for lunch and naps. Amy, Megg, and I continued on for another five miles, enjoying the early afternoon sunshine. We paused only once, to investigate the Calf Mountain Shelter, my original destination for the night. There was a lone thru-hiker stretched out in his sleeping bag on the shelter floor, recovering from town, he said. I took note and filed his comments in the back of my mind.

By late afternoon, tired and thirsty, we reached the Sawmill Run Overlook and, sprawled on the grass, boots off, feet propped on a rock wall, waited for a ride back to the motel for a shower and dinner. George, right on schedule, drove up in his new mini-van, with sub sandwiches and ice-cold water. What a way to begin a two thousand-mile journey, I thought. I didn't really expect the rest of my hike to be like this.

May 14, 2001, to Blackrock Hut, Shenandoah National Park, 10 miles

The next day, returning to the trailhead on Skyline Drive, I began my trek for real. My family was there to see me off.

I postponed the final moment of goodbye as long as I could, taking pictures and readjusting my pack. When I could delay no longer, I hoisted the forty-five pound pack to my shoulders, buckled the hip belt as tight as it would cinch, gave my trekking poles a final twist and everyone a second hug, and then, I headed for the woods.

Stepping through an opening in the trees that would lead to my adventure, I looked back, grinned, and waved. With a lump in my throat, I began my thru-hike.

In beauty may I walk,
all day long may I walk...
In beauty will I possess again...
I trusted I would find my way.

I walked all day in late spring sunshine and leafy green woods, and once spotted a red, yellow, and green bird preening just ahead of me on the trail.

Beautifully joyful birds...

I reached the shelter about six-thirty. It was full of robust-looking thru-hikers, cooking and trading trail stories. Nearby, a young couple had pitched their tent; they indicated a narrow, rocky strip of dirt next to them as my home for the night. I set down my pack and began to assemble my tent poles, sure every eye was on me as I pulled my tent into shape, circled the site, and pounded the stakes in place with a rock.

Pulling out my shiny titanium cooking pot, I set up my new stove and tried to light the fuel tablet without burning my thumb. I'd only tried to ignite the stove once before, on our patio, to boil a cup of water for coffee the previous week. It hadn't seemed so complicated then. Tonight, sitting on a log in front of the shelter, it was more difficult.

Too shy to ask the hikers gathered around the picnic table to make a space for me, I finally got my stove started and set some water to boil for dinner. As promised in the stove description, within three minutes the water reached a rolling boil. I blew out the flame, added the noodles and cheese I had packaged at home, and waited for my dinner to re-hydrate. When I dipped my plastic spoon into the pot, ready to eat thru-hiker style, I realized I wasn't very hungry after all. The noodles were still hard and the water that I had carried up from the stream had chunks floating in it. The dried tomatoes never did plump up, and the powdered cheese retained a slippery, lumpy consistency.

I looked around to dump my disappointing dinner. I couldn't throw it in the woods because of bears and critters; I couldn't throw it into the privy because of moldering-privy etiquette. I would have to eat it – or talk someone else into eating it for me. Self-conscious as I was about cooking, I knew better than to give my slimy meal to anyone else. I ate it, all of it, without acknowledging taste or texture. And then I stayed on my log and waited for someone to set his food bag on the bear pole so I could see how it was done.

The bear pole was a twenty-foot high steel pole topped with several ten-inch metal spikes at forty-five degree angles, about twenty feet from the hut. To hoist a food bag and keep it safe from bears overnight, one must hook the strap at the bottom of the food bag on the end of another, shorter steel pole, reach up to one of the protruding spikes, and snag the food bag strap over the spike. The bag hangs there, suspended and upside down until rescued by the same steel pole in the morning. If the food bag weighs ten pounds (as mine did that night), and the steel pole another five pounds (at least!), it's a fifteen-pound aerial task to maneuver at the end of a tiring hiking day. I didn't want to ask anyone to do lift my bag for me, but my arms were unequal to the challenge. A taller, stronger hiker than I volunteered to master the pole for everyone. I gladly accepted.

> "And now, to bed. I hope there are no bears tonight! Even though I only walked ten miles today, I feel that I did accomplish something. I said goodbye to my family, found the shelter, began my trek! Everything I own that either smells good or is edible is hanging from that bear pole. I hope it doesn't tempt anything and is in one piece in the morning. Tomorrow night I'll have to remember to brush my teeth before hanging up my stuff."

May 15, 2001, to Pinefield Hut, 13.2 miles

The next day was another beginning. A whippoorwill alerted me, and then a gray, misty sky nudged me awake when I unzipped my tent flap and scrambled out to pee. Luckily it hadn't rained overnight. But today, I thought, it might. Since I had stashed several garbage bags into the bottom of my pack before I left, I quickly pulled one out and lined the large middle compartment with it.

I kept my tent and rain gear in the lowest section of my pack, the one designated by the manufacturer to be for a sleeping bag. My reasoning was that this compartment, with its own zipper, would be more accessible in bad weather and, therefore, the most sensible place to keep the things I needed quickly. The large compartment in the middle of the bag, I thought, should be drier for my sleeping bag and extra clothes, both of which I kept in compression stuff sacks, inside the plastic garbage bag.

On top of the sleeping bag and clothes, in that same middle compartment, I kept my compressed Therm-A-Rest mattress, food bag, and cooking pot that also contained my stove and fuel. The top compartment of my pack was detachable and also had its own zippers. In this I kept toiletries, journal, watercolors, guidebooks, flashlight, first aid kit, Walkman tape player and snacks. Two side straps held my water bottles, and initially, I hung my camera from my sternum strap.

Since I didn't have a routine yet, I waited to see how others broke camp. The thru-hikers rose early, packed up their stuff, ate a cold breakfast, and headed out. Hikers doing only a section of the trail at a time (section-hikers) or hikers just out for the weekend, slept longer, cooked a hearty breakfast, and then leisurely gathered their gear. Section-hikers took more time around camp and were more likely than thru-hikers to build a campfire, either at night or in the morning.

Thru-hikers, I noticed, were more task-oriented and didn't bother with the amenities of camp. But then, if 2,164 miles is your ultimate goal, standing around and smelling the bacon, especially in the morning, is not a helpful routine.

That night I wrote about my day:

"I'm glad I remembered to line my pack; it rained all day. Being out in the rain all day puts a premium on keeping your stuff dry. It's not easy with only dripping trees for shelter.

Though my jitters and social shyness from yesterday are gone today, I haven't quite found my pace or place and don't have my trail legs yet. It was hard for me to do thirteen miles today. I got tired going uphill. My pack began to be very heavy and my legs felt weak. I think I was trying to go too fast at first and didn't have enough food to keep me energized… I'll have to be careful to eat more tomorrow.

Tonight I've pitched my tent on a moss-covered, spongy piece of land next to a noisy, frothy brook. The brook is loud, the mosquitoes plentiful. The rain has stopped but it's damp and chilly. Tomorrow should be easier – only eight miles.

Twenty-four hours is a long time when you are out, all day, in the weather."

May 16, 2001, to Pocosin (locked) cabin, 17.9 miles

My eight-mile hike the next day started in a gentle rain and brought me to my destination, a dripping, dirty, and empty hut, about noon – much too early to stop for the night. I ate a tortilla-wrapped cheese and walnut sandwich, drank some water, stashed some dried fruit in my pocket for later, and decided to push on to the next shelter, fourteen miles away.

The trail was quiet but for the steady drip of rain and loud breathing echoing inside my rain hood. I labored through wet underbrush, over slippery rocks, up and down muddy hills, with the view all at my feet.

After I had gone another eight miles, ascending and descending five hundred to seven hundred feet three more times, I could feel myself getting tired and knew I would need to find a place to camp, soon. My map showed a (locked) cabin and stream about a mile north of me, three and one half miles closer than the next shelter. I aimed myself toward the cabin, wondering what "(locked)" meant, hoping I could at least find some shelter for cooking.

The woods grew darker and wetter, and I was beginning to worry that I might not find the cabin after all. To keep my mind occupied, I began to fantasize about Goldilocks and the three bears – me being Goldilocks, looking for a snug, dry cabin to put my wet self into for the night – hot steaming porridge on the table, dry socks on my feet.

Within an hour, I came out of the woods into a clearing of tall wet grass, a cloud-shrouded missed opportunity for a view, and the (locked) cabin of Pocosin.

I had read that *pocosin* is a word of Indian derivation and originally meant dismal. Dismal I was, rain-soaked and weary. But, as I crossed in front of the cabin, I looked up to find four men seated on either side of a picnic table on the porch of the cabin. At the end of the table, closest to the outer cabin wall, was a large green Coleman camp stove, steaming with their supper. Flanking the other wall of the porch was a stone fireplace and snapping, flickering firelight. Okay, so it's Goldilocks and Four Bears, I thought, and tried my charm:

"Is it okay with you if I pitch my tent for the night?" I asked, hesitantly.

Uncharitably, one answered, "Well, this is a locked cabin and we have it reserved for the week."

So that's what (locked) means, I thought, dismayed. "Gosh, I just don't think I can walk another two miles to the next hut, in the dark," I said, trying not to whine. "You won't even know I'm here," I promised, hopefully.

The four bears held a small conference. "All right, go ahead and see if you can find a level place for your tent," they relented.

Relieved, I didn't waste a second. Over by a tree stump, waist high in wet grass, on an almost flat incline, I crawled around on hands and knees, trying to pitch my tent with the rain fly attached to keep the interior as dry as possible. It must have been a sorry sight. Certainly a pitiable one for, just as I crawled into my sagging space, one of the men appeared and called through my zippered wall:

"How about some food? We have some Dinty Moore beef stew and hot chocolate over here – much more than we can eat. Why don't you come over, get dry, and have some."

Not wanting to intrude, my first inclination was to decline his friendly offer. But when I surveyed my other dinner options, a soggy tortilla wrapped around wet cheese and walnuts or dried fruit and a Power Bar, I gratefully accepted, reassured by his manner and tempting menu.

Sitting at their fire, steaming and eating my fill of hot stew, my hosts told me a little about themselves. They were four friends from Pittsfield, Massachusetts, who used to work together and now camp together every year, somewhere along the AT. The steady rain of the past few days had discouraged their hike, however, and they were spending most of their time cooking and eating all the food their cars and coolers had brought them. They actually apologized that the cherry cheesecake for dessert was from a mix!

The next morning, there were Aunt Jemima pancakes, maple syrup, hot coffee and dry, fire-warmed, socks, gloves and hiking boots. And unlike in the Goldilocks story, the Four Bears did not chase me away. In fact, we traded real names and addresses; I planned to call them when I reached Pittsfield, Massachusetts in July.

For me, it was an instance of trail magic: magic of food, shelter, and companionship on the one hand; magic of memory on the other. One of my father's favorite places to take us camping was Berry Mountain, in Pittsfield, Massachusetts, and two of his favorite camp meals, by green Coleman stove, were Dinty Moore stew and Aunt Jemima pancakes. I hadn't eaten this hearty conglomerate since I was ten years old. It had never tasted so good.

May 17, 2001, to Big Meadows Campground, 11.8 miles

As I left next morning, I noticed the "wildflowers about my feet" – pink lady slippers, trillium, wild purple iris, blue and white wild orchid, pink azalea, mountain laurel not quite in bloom, yellow butter-cups, and yellow yarrow; a parade of color in a steady cold rain. The expanded view of the beautiful Shenandoah Valley was hidden behind thick, opaque clouds. All day, I hiked in rain, rain, and more rain – and wildflowers.

During my first week, I wore all of my clothes, sometimes all at once, just to be warm. I had spent a lot of time trying to predict what kind of clothes I would need. All of my reading suggested that whatever I took, it needed to serve more than one purpose and that if I didn't wear some-thing every day, I didn't need it. I had also read that hikers often make the mistake of carrying too much – the ratio being in direct proportion to the amount of fear they harbored about themselves on the trail.

At the beginning of my hike, I packed too much. I hiked in moisture-wicking underpants, tee shirt, hiking socks, sock-liners, sports bra, and hiking shorts, with my Gotta Hike! cap on my head. At first, I carried far too many extras – long pants and rain pants, a long- and short-sleeved shirt, a pair of moccasins, two bandannas, and a set of long underwear. Keeping these clean and sweet smelling was tricky.

> "Tonight I finally had an opportunity to wash at the camp-ground washhouse. After dropping all my clothes into a coin-operated washing machine, I went next door to the slimy shower stall provided to campers. It took two quarters to turn

the water on, and two more to keep it flowing. The water was tepid, the pressure, minimal. And at the end, there were no towels – not even paper ones. I had to dry off with my wet bandanna. Clammy!

The commercial-sized dryer was intimidating. It felt weird to be sitting naked under my raingear, checking and rechecking the progress of my miracle moisture-wicking clothes. I prayed that the super-sized dryer wouldn't melt them.

When everything was finally done, I slipped into my long underwear, still warm from the dryer, and darted back through the wet evening, hugging clean clothes under my rain jacket.

Whew! Was that really worth the struggle?

Ahh... but it does feel good to be clean and dry – snuggled into my sleeping bag, listening to rain on my roof – warm and safe and cozy for one more night on the trail."

One nice feature of hiking in Shenandoah National Park, besides campgrounds with showers and laundry facilities, is the accessibility of food. For those who have been hiking since Georgia, Shenandoah is a tableland of good eating. For me, having just begun, it was only a glimpse into a future of trying to keep my body hydrated and nourished with trail food while striving towards the variety and sustenance of fresh, nutritious meals off the trail.

"I had a massive breakfast at the Big Meadows lodge this morning before heading out. I must admit, real food, and plenty of it, seems to be the key to sustained energy on the trail. Nine miles with a sopping tent and a still-too-heavy food bag didn't bother me at all today. Must be the sausage-eggs-pancakes-orange juice-coffee-hash brown breakfast under my belt, digesting with every step."

Before leaving for the trail, I had assembled twelve packages of food, toiletries, maps, guidebooks, film, fuel tablets for the stove, tapes, books and extra clothing to either be brought or sent to me c/o general delivery along the way. At first, I planned to carry five or six days supply of food at a time, supplementing with restaurant or snack-bar cooking when/if it were possible and seemed like a good idea. Although not a vegetarian, I prefer to eat grains and rice, vegetables, fruit, cheese, and nuts in my everyday diet. I expected to eat in a similar way on the trail.

Within three days of beginning my hike, I realized that I would need more nourishment to be able to hike between six and eight hours every day. I discovered halfway up a hill one morning that my body just couldn't take another step without something to eat. It was more surprising than alarming, because I had eaten a breakfast of oatmeal, milk, coffee and dried fruit before starting out. It was much more than I would have eaten at home. But, that morning it wasn't enough, and I quickly supplemented with a granola bar and dried fruit, the novice hiker's staple. It pushed me up the hill that day and made me re-evaluate my food supplies.

In the beginning my food bag consisted of five days worth of food, weighing just over twelve pounds; it was nourishing but clearly too heavy.[1]

I didn't think about food with every step, but I did think about how to lighten my food bag and still get the nourishment I needed. In fact, lightening one's load is the predominant preoccupation of beginning thru-hikers. That first week I spent a lot of energy thinking about how to lighten my pack without sacrificing nutrients, water, shelter, safety, comfort.

1.Breakfast: Five cups instant oatmeal, four cups instant milk; five packets instant coffee; five tea bags. Lunch: 10 oz.chunk Swiss cheese; 10 tortillas; 8 oz. log of dried beef. Dinner: two cups instant beans and rice; two cups macaroni and cheese; one cup instant rice noodles and miso soup; one cup instant hummus; one cup instant cous cous; five packets hot chocolate; five packets instant pudding mix. Snacks: five cups dried fruit; five cups nuts; five granola bars; five power bars; one 15 oz. Hershey bar.

May 18-19, 2001, to Skyland Lodge (via Thornton Gap), 18 miles

I hiked most of the next two days in heavy rain and fog, listening to tapes of Shenandoah folk songs to block out the rain. I thought about the old mountain families who had lived in Shenandoah for generations until the 1930s, when the government condemned their land and relocated them so the national park could be established. It made me wonder how the earliest settlers acquired their land in the first place, and I thought about the broken treaties with native tribes.

Hikers and tourists own the land now, with lodges, campgrounds, and backcountry huts located at convenient stops along the hundred-mile stretch of the AT. I hoped the land was in the hands of good stewards. I was beginning to feel a real kinship with the forest, at home with the animals whose territory I was visiting. It occurred to me, for perhaps the first time, that buying land really meant purchasing the privilege to take care of it, to be a responsible steward. The owner of two properties, I was beginning to question just what that ownership meant. How can land be the property of anyone, I wondered. Aren't we all responsible for all of it?

May 19 marked my first full week on the trail. George drove in from Ohio to meet me at the Skyland Lodge, three-tenths mile from the AT, accessible by the Skyline Drive through Shenandoah National Park.

He was surprised, I think, that I was really all right and that nothing had happened to dishearten or frighten me. I was elated that he was willing to spend his weekend driving to Virginia to lend his support to me. It was comforting and reassuring to see him.

Sunday morning began a routine I would repeat each time I received a visit from home or a mail drop: winnowing old stuff, repacking new stuff, and making decisions about what to send back, what to send on to the next mail-drop, and what to trash.

I was reluctant to give up the potential comforts I carried in my pack: my Walkman and several music tapes, a book of poems, the guidebook to Shenandoah National Park, my journal and watercolors, some shampoo and toiletries. It didn't occur to me that my camera case, wallet, address book, film, and extra clothing were extra weight. My orientation was still "what if" for the future rather than "what now" for the present.

That Sunday, in our room strewn with drying tent, sleeping bag, clothing, boots, maps, cookware, and boxes full of dehydrated food, I agonized, debated, repackaged, and in the end, didn't eliminate anything. I just re-supplied my heavy food bag with new food.

May 20, 2001, to Gravel Springs Hut, 5 miles

When George dropped me at the trailhead Sunday afternoon to drive back to Ohio, I found that saying "goodbye" and disappearing into the dense fog was even harder this time than last.

"With dew about my feet..." I sighed, and set off resolutely in the opaque mist. My destination was the Gravel Springs Hut, five miles away.

I reached the hut earlier than expected and was surprised and pleased to find another hiker, Wonder, already established, cooking his dinner. Wonder, I learned, was from Connecticut, and was taking a year off to hike before starting his residency in medicine. Of slight build and quiet, low-key demeanor, he reminded me of my son-in-law, Jim. He was safe, I thought.

Leaning my hiking poles against the wall, I slipped my shoulders out of their straps and sat down on the wet floor.

"Mind if I join you?" I asked. "I've had enough camping in the rain. Tonight looks like a good night to stay in a hut... my first."

He shrugged. "We're the first ones here – pick a spot."

Wonder had been on the trail since Georgia and was happy to explain hut etiquette: Introduce yourself by your trail name; survey the hut (clean, safe, full, dry); read the trail register for any hints about your stay (resident mice, rampant snakes, leaky roof, proximity to water); claim your space.

"You just can't put your pack down and expect that that space will be yours," he explained. "Trust me, I was burned in Georgia. I left my pack where I thought I'd sleep and went to get water. When I got back, my pack was in the dirt and some guys had taken over the shelter. Since then, I spread out my sleeping bag first, and then do everything else. The guys who come later will respect that."

Following his advice, I spread out my Therm-A-Rest and sleeping bag on the elevated platform which was just wide enough for my body to lie straight, feet towards the hut opening, head mere inches from the sloping roof.

I hung my food bag on a stick dangling under an overturned tuna can attached by a thin rope to the cross beam at my feet. Theoretically, the tuna can would discourage mice from crawling across the beam, down the rope and into my food bag while I slept. Mice, it seems, are the official residents in every shelter. They are notorious for scurrying across the floor and over hikers' sleeping faces, looking for treats in carelessly attended food bags, empty boots, or opened packs.

At home, I would have been squeamish about a mouse encounter. Perceiving myself as a visitor to mouse-domain on the trail, however, it never occurred to me to be wary.

Nevertheless, I was careful to loop my food bag on an upside-down-can-contraption at every hut stay thereafter. I never noticed anything missing.

When I visited the privy at Gravel Springs, I was surprised to see a transparent roof and four solid walls; inside it was light (and dry) enough to read, if I were so inclined. My experience with trail privies, thus far, had been fairly pleasant. Unlike the outhouse of my childhood camping days, or the port-o-pots and latrines of contemporary public parks and recreation areas, backcountry privies don't smell. In fact, they are quite clean. Many are compost privies, and require a handful of dry leaves or forest duff from each visitor to accelerate the decaying process of underground waste. Privy etiquette discourages the use of toilet paper or sanitary supplies in favor of leaves, water, or antiseptic toilettes that can be packed out in a Ziploc bag. I used all three toilet paper alternatives without the slightest inconvenience.

Trail maintaining clubs are responsible for hut and privy maintenance along each section of the trail. Each club's work and dedication are much appreciated by hikers, and the practice of "leave no trace" is respected and proselytized by all. Consequently, huts and privies, with neither plumbing nor electricity, are usually unsoiled, well maintained and open to anyone free of charge on a first-come, first-served basis. In addition, most hut-sites also provide a small camping area nearby for overflow hikers or hikers who prefer a tent.

It is possible to hike the entire trail and stay in a hut or shelter every night. Most thru-hikers use both tents and shelters, depending on circumstance. By carrying a tent, I could do either; it was always nice to have the option.

When I returned from the privy, the rain had begun again in earnest and two wet hikers had joined us in my absence. Soon four more, wearing plastic trash bags, sloshed in. Wet boots and raingear turned the un-swept shelter floor into a sty of mud. Dripping packs hanging on hooks and wall pegs added to the slop.

As the late afternoon fog deepened to evening gloom, the inside of the hut became dark but almost cozy. I strapped on my flashlight, a three-inch aluminum tube with a LED technology bulb attached to a headband, and found my journal. While others cooked and settled in, I occupied myself by sketching the interior of our damp three-sided bungalow.

Push and Shove, a couple my age, were the last hikers to straggle in. They chose to sleep under the lowest bunks, home to spiders, mice and other critters, rather than out in the rain in their tent.

"Webbier, dirtier, but definitely drier tonight," they chuckled.

Now the hut was completely full of grubby hikers and wet, smelly gear, exemplifying the unwritten rule that thru-hikers are always welcome overnight and, in bad weather, there is always room for one more.

I snuggled into my sleeping bag and turned out my light. So this is hut life, I thought. I liked having company in the rain and it was particularly nice to meet another woman hiker. I wondered if Push and her husband might become my hiking mates since they were doing the same "flip-flop" hike as I.

In the pitch-black lair of snoring hikers, I listened drowsily to the steady drip of rain on the roof just above my head. I was warm, snug, dry and safe. I slumbered dreamlessly all night.

May 21, 2001, to Front Royal, Va., 13.4 miles

In the morning, it was still raining. I scrambled around in my sleeping bag, putting on a hiking bra, shorts, and raingear, all to make a privy stop before breakfast.

I was gone by seven-thirty. Push and Shove were ahead of me by fifteen minutes, so I was surprised when I passed them on the first ascent. They really were pushing and shoving each other up the hill.

"We're going into Front Royal tonight to dry out," they said.

I didn't see them again all day. In fact, I saw very few people. I spoke briefly with two German men who were day-hiking south, and one hiker at the Tom Floyd Shelter who was leaving just as I got there. He had spent the night in his tent set up inside the shelter, wet, cold and frightened. He mistakenly thought I knew what I was doing, causing me to wonder if I had begun to look trail-hardened. Probably just dirty, I concluded.

❋

One AT tradition is signing the register provided at each hut, campsite, or trailhead by the club that maintains that section. Hikers use the register, usually a notebook wrapped in a Ziploc bag with pen or pencil attached, to keep track of each other, to record their thoughts as they've been hiking, to ask rhetorical questions, or to complain. Sometimes the entries are esoteric; sometimes they are poetic; sometimes they are annoying. The majority of register entries are cursory:

> "In for lunch/a break/the night. Great/wet/lousy/cold/hot/ thirsty/buggy day to hike. Pushing on to _____."

Hikers are careful about trail registers. They look to register pages for entertainment, information, consolation, and affirmation. Within a few weeks, I began to recognize names of hikers I had met or merely heard about. Occasionally a hiker several days ahead of me would fall behind and we would meet. Sometimes a hiker behind me, having read my entries, would catch up and "recognize" me from the register.

I was a bit self-conscious at first about signing the register, noting my location, time, and date of entry, but I did it anyway because I thought it a good way to make my whereabouts known every day; it was a safety precaution for my family.

To my knowledge, register entries are not an official record of anyone's thru-hike. I have wondered, however, if collecting a hiking year's register entries along the entire trail would reveal patterns of thru-hiker personality, motivation, endurance, energy level, or humor.

Most of my own entries were rather mundane. Occasionally, I would leave a poem, insight, or Burma Shave-like ditty.

At Tom Floyd Shelter, where I stopped for lunch on the seventh consecutive day of rain, my thoughts ran thus:

"To be damp in a swamp is a romp;
To be damp on a tramp is a vamp;
To be damp in a camp
Soaking butt in a hut
Ain't no fun!
Where's the sun?
Gotta Hike!"

Later, I wrote more personal thoughts in my journal:

> "It was a long, green, wet, soaking day. I found myself thinking of my father a lot today. Actually, grieving for him, thinking about how he loved to camp and about all the camping trips to New England and New York State that he planned so carefully while we were growing up. I remember looking at maps and talking to him about routes as we drove and everyone else slept. Lots of those days were wet and cold, too. I wondered what he would think if he could see me now. I wondered if he would be proud of me."

I pushed on towards the next shelter and reached US 522 within an hour. There, at the road crossing, a trail angel had hung a plastic bag on a bush. Inside the bag I found cold beer, Cokes, fresh apples, and chocolate bars. I sat down in the long wet grass, snapped the tab on a Coke and bit into a tart, fresh apple.

I pulled out my trail data-book, the thru-hiker's bible, and discovered that it was only three and six-tenths miles to RGLM, data-book code for Road access, Groceries, Lodging, Meals.

I weighed my options: I could continue on another five and two-tenths miles to the Jim and Molly Denton Shelter for a wet night and trail food, or I could walk just over three miles to RGLM for a dry night with real food. At four-thirty on a dark, rainy afternoon, the decision was easy. I hoisted my pack, crossed the road, and headed west to a dry night of RGLM in Front Royal, my first trail town.

Within a mile, a mini-van pulled over and stopped in front of me. I was wary about hitching into town on my own, but was curious about who had stopped. With a pointed hiking pole in each hand I walked up to the passenger side of the van. It was a mom and seven of her eight children on a home-schooling field trip. They had stopped because I was a hiker.

"Our brother is doing his senior project on the trail," they explained. "He's in Pennsylvania now. We always pick up hikers and talk to them. Then we e-mail what they say for his project."

I breathed a sigh of relief and climbed in.

"How does your brother pick up his e-mail on the trail?" I asked.

"He goes into trail towns that have libraries and uses their computers."

I was enlightened, and impressed by his ingenuity. My data book did not have an abbreviation for "Library," and I would never have sought one to check my e-mail. But I didn't mind being part of someone else's e-mail.

And so, for my thoughts on hiking the trail, I received a safe ride to town that eliminated a long, tedious road walk. The local Super 8 Motel and special hiker rate, including breakfast, added to my sense of well being. Then I discovered that Push and Shove were staying in the next room.

"We're heading back to Florida to get our camper," they said. "We'll still do the trail, but from the car... hike the trails with road access... stay in our camper at night."

So much for my potential hiking partners, I thought. We'd only been on the trail for a week... They must have been a lot colder and wetter than I was. And I thought my logistics were complicated. But, everyone hikes their own hike – who was I to say what they should do. I was still too new to it all to be discouraged by the weather, though I was tired of being wet.

When I said goodnight to my new friends, it seemed an abrupt end to something that had just begun. It felt like a loss, though I hardly knew them. I was sad that they were leaving the trail, leaving me to "flip-flop" on my own.

May 22, 2001, to Dick's Dome Shelter, 15.1 miles

The next morning I awoke to clouds, but no rain. I scrambled out of bed, ate a quick breakfast and was ready to go by seven-thirty. Several other hikers had planned to share a taxi back to the trail with me, but when the taxi arrived, they were still asleep. I was stuck for the taxi fare, ten dollars cash. Although I had expected to need money in towns, I only carried about a hundred dollars in cash, along with a credit/debit card, driver's license, health insurance card, and small address book. On the trail, I stashed these valuables in my pack; in town, I belted them around my waist in a hip pouch so I could leave my pack on the doorstep without abandoning my identity. I learned, later, to wrap the cards, cash and address book with a rubber band and keep them in a baggie in my pocket. I eventually sent the hip pouch home, in an effort to shed superfluous weight.

Back on the trail, I hiked past the Jim and Molly Denton Shelter and mentally kicked myself. The shelter was beautiful. Until now I had only experienced the shelters of Shenandoah National Park, originally constructed in the 1930s by the Civilian Conservation Corps. These shelters were typically three-sided stone or wood structures with dark and dreary interiors, an outside picnic table, and a bare wood floor for sleeping. The Denton Shelter, in contrast, had a large wooden front deck, a picnic table under roof, wood benches with backs, and a sleeping loft inside a light, spacious interior. It would have been a lovely place to spend a rainy night.

I'm still learning, I muttered to myself as I passed it by.

Five miles farther, I stopped at the Manassas Gap Shelter for lunch. Both the data book and trail register warned, "home of a wood rat and several copperheads, so be careful." I wondered where I would be on the food chain if I were to stay overnight. I decided to move on five miles to the next shelter.

Up the trail I passed Wonder sitting on a tree stump, eating some trail mix from his latest mail drop and reading a book.

"No matter how fast I walk, uphill or down, I still only hike two miles an hour," he said.

"Does that include reading stops?" I wondered.

He grinned and kept reading. I liked the way he was hiking his hike. He was not competing with anyone and seemed to be enjoying his own company. He told me that his trail name was a combination of 'wonder' and 'wander'. I liked that, too.

I walked on, becoming aware of increased bird chatter all around me, both louder and more persistent than it had been before. In the distance, I heard the first faint rumbles of thunder and ahead on the trail, the leaves began to blow backwards. Thunderstorm – about an hour away, I thought. It'll hit just about the time I reach the shelter, if I hurry.

I practically ran the last two miles to the shelter. When I reached the trail to the shelter, the rain had started and the wind was blowing so hard I couldn't see the trail. I scrambled through the wild underbrush and snapping tree branches and, just when I expected the shelter to appear, the trail disappeared. I turned around and frantically retraced my steps back to the AT. It looked as though the trail ran right through the streambed. I charged back, running through the stream, with thunder crashing overhead, lightning flashing in front of me, and branches and leaves scratching my face. Sloshing and thrashing up the trail, I tried to remember what to do if caught in a thunderstorm. I think I read somewhere to stay off the trail, put your pack with its metal frame off your body, and move away from swaying trees. Impossible.

I shouted into the rain.

And then I saw the shelter, just ahead: a three-sided dome, shingled in gray plywood, on the bank of a swiftly running, wide stream on the other side of a rickety wooden footbridge. I ran across the bridge and threw all my stuff, and myself, onto the floor of the dome.

A huge clap of thunder and bright sharp bolt of lightning followed me. I was soaked and trembling and out of breath. But I was safe. I sat on the floor and watched the storm above and the rushing stream below, too stunned by noise and adrenaline to move. This was no pastoral symphony by Beethoven. This storm was deafening and frightening. This storm was real.

Within a few minutes, more wet but less-flummoxed than I, Wonder wandered in, followed, eventually, by another hiker named Moto. The three of us sat on the floor and waited for the storm to move on, recovering in the aftermath of dripping woods and overflowing stream just below our feet. Eventually I changed into dry clothes, set my cooking pot outside on the picnic table to collect rainwater for breakfast, and boiled some black bean soup and hot chocolate for dinner. Moto, self-named for his enthusiasm for bikes, I think, talked to Wonder about his dirt bike. Wonder listened politely. I crawled into my sleeping bag, wrote in my journal, and eventually put my head inside my bag and went to sleep. It had been a harrowing day, my first thunderstorm in the woods with no place to hide and all the elements crashing, uncaring, around me.

May 23, 2001, to Rod Hollow Shelter, 9.2 miles

In the morning, a beam of sunlight was shining on my rainwater-filled cooking pot. This was more like it. I was thrilled. The picnic table had some dry spots and the sun looked as though it would be around for the whole day. I packed outside on the picnic table, had a leisurely breakfast of oatmeal, powdered milk, dried fruit, and coffee and was ready to hike by seven o'clock. Wonder was already gone; Moto was still asleep. Only nine miles to go today, one slight elevation of five hundred feet and the rest fairly small ups and downs. Maybe I would even go farther than Rod Hollow Shelter – start the roller coaster (ten ups, ten downs in ten miles) to Bears Den, arrive a day early. I felt healthy and successful and relieved to see the sun again. I had big plans for the day.

I hiked all morning in dazzling sunlight, delighted when the trees briefly parted at a pipeline clearing, and then cleared again across Ashby

Gap. The dense woods and dark skies of the past two weeks had been a long green tunnel. It was nice to see the sun in the blue sky. About eleven o'clock, as I crossed US 50, I met another hiker, heading south. We talked for a minute, and then sat on the grassy bank next to the highway to eat a snack. He was bothered because a mouse had gnawed a hole through his sock at the shelter the night before. I was just happy to sit in the sun and soak up the warmth for a minute. I offered to sew up the hole in his sock and did, as cars whizzed by spraying us with dust and fumes.

"Not quite what I had in mind for a break," he said, "but definitely okay."

We chatted for a bit longer, then got up, hoisted our packs, and went our separate ways. I never did find out his name nor give him mine.

Around one o'clock I began to feel really tired and decided to take a side trail two-tenths of a mile away, to a PATC (locked) cabin. There I found an enclosed stone structure with a wide front porch of wood, a picnic table, and a porch swing. The cabin was deserted, so I took off my boots, socks and tee shirt and lay back on the porch in a sudden diagonal of sunlight slanting through the trees towering above. I think I fell asleep for a few minutes. That, plus a Hershey bar, was enough to revive me for the last two miles to the Rod Hollow Shelter.

When I reached the shelter, I set up my tent, splashed water on my face and neck beside the stream, and changed into long pants, shirt, and moccasins. I hung my sweat-soaked clothes on low branches around me. Tidy, I thought, and such a contrast to arriving wet, scrabbling around to make a place for myself without getting everything in my pack wet and filthy, and trying to stay warm and dry when everywhere around you is cold and dripping.

"I hope there are more sunny, warm days ahead of me, and that I can begin to take my time and not feel I have to hurry. I think I got so tired today because I really pushed those last five miles yesterday. And then there was the fear and uncertainty of being out in a thunderstorm. Unnerving. But, the more experiences I have, the more my confidence grows!"

May 24, 2001, to Bears Den Hostel, 10.1 miles

The next day's hike, though long and hard with many steep ascents and descents, was fragrant with the aroma of wet leaves, dirt, and the delicate scent of yellow tulip poplar flowers scattered on the trail and clinging to the branches overhead. I crossed several rushing streams, picking my way over slippery rocks with my trekking poles that helped me balance. The sun stayed in place, shining through the trees, drying the underbrush. I loved it!

> "I think I like hiking best in the early morning when I have lots of energy, the day is new, and nothing seems too much. Though there are not so many knee-high wild flowers here, the highest elevations have sandy soil and some kind of white flowering bush that smells divine! There are dozens of caterpillars, and this afternoon I saw a red fox! The path under my boots is rocky and root-strewn – like the veined backs of my mother's (my own?) hands. My eyes are constantly surveying the path in front of me, deciding just where to put each foot so as not to fall, not to strain a knee, not to move too far, too fast."

Bears Den looked very civilized, well organized, and clean when I reached it in the late afternoon. I found my way to the hiker room, put in the special code (a mileage note from the data-book), and entered a bunk-room with a couch, refrigerator full of soda, and a shower supplied with soap, shampoo, razors, bath mat, wash cloth, and towels. Next to a washer/dryer, a rack held a selection of tee shirts and pants – something to wear besides raingear while washing my clothes. It was clear that this hostel was run by former thru-hikers.

A steamy, cleansing shower later, I climbed the back stairs to the main lodge where I had stayed with the women from Ohio only a month earlier. Patti, my mentor Mel's partner, was ready with a big smile to welcome me. She thrust a pint of Ben & Jerry's ice cream in my hand and invited me to use the phone to call home. Bears Den was a friendly hostel, indeed. And when I called home, I discovered that George, Amy, Megg, Jim, and Nemo were planning to meet me in Harper's Ferry for the weekend, just a day's hike away.

May 25, 2001, to David Lesser Memorial Shelter, 11.1 miles

The morning was overcast and windy with sun occasionally peeking through the trees and rain late in the afternoon. My hiking pace was picking up. I arrived at the shelter early enough to sit on an Adirondack-style bench built into the deck and paint a watercolor of the view in front of me: trees, trees, and more trees soaring upward, blocking the foggy gray sky, protecting me from rain slapping the roof and picnic table.

Only nine miles from Harper's Ferry, this shelter is a popular overnight stop for short-term hikers, especially on Memorial Day weekend. I wasn't prepared for their noise and confusion. Or their dogs! I left early the next morning before anyone was up. Even the dogs slept in.

May 26, 2001, to Harper's Ferry, Va., 9 miles

The approach to Harper's Ferry through the woods was steep, dramatic and everlasting. Reaching the four-lane bridge across the Shenandoah River, I was disheartened to discover another two miles of steep woods remained before town.

Harper's Ferry is the home of the Appalachian Trail Conference and the psychological midpoint between Georgia and Maine. Hikers generally sign in at the conference center, have their picture taken for the yearbook, and receive affirmation from whoever is staffing the desk when they arrive. I registered: "Gotta Hike! 5/26/01."

It was only a short walk to Hilltop House, the hundred-year-old stone inn perched on a hill overlooking the confluence of the Potomac and Shenandoah rivers. George had reserved two rooms for our family at the inn.

When I checked in at the desk, I tried to camouflage my healthy odor and trail dirt. The clerk agreed that a shower before lunching in the main dining room might be refreshing, and gave me a key to the only room ready for us.

Lunch in the glass-walled dining room, above the two rivers roaring silently below, was spectacular. I was clean and hungry and quickly relaxed in the early afternoon sunshine, eavesdropping on other diners' conversations. Sitting in a chair, with a white linen napkin, silverware, and plate at my disposal, I felt a bit out of place. Though I had only been in the woods for two weeks, it seemed that I had been gone a lifetime.

My family arrived late in the afternoon, after I had explored the restored village of Harper's Ferry, stopped to look at the nineteenth century merchandise displayed in the store windows, viewed the slide show about John Brown's raid, and bought a small paperback of Walt Whitman's Civil War poetry and war correspondence.

At the outfitter in the center of town, I also bought some lightweight raingear to replace my heavy Gore-Tex parka and rain pants. The outfitter seemed to have everything that a thru-hiker might need, but I was not interested in buying any more stuff. My new perspective surprised me. In the past, I might have been interested in the array of tantalizing gear displayed on the shelves, but after carrying everything I owned on my shoulders all day, every day, for the past two weeks, none of it even tempted me. I was much more pleased at the respect and admiration the staff gave me for being a thru-hiker, even though I hadn't gone very far, yet. Their high positive regard was the only kind of extra weight I was willing to carry. That didn't weigh much at all.

While awaiting my family, I returned to the front lawn of the Hilltop Hotel to paint a watercolor of the historically marked rivers, railway trestles, and valleys below me. The scene was peaceful and remote, under purple clouds of sunset and a gathering storm.

As I painted, I scanned every car that pulled into the circular drive in front of the old-fashioned hotel, until I finally caught a glimpse of my family. Amy and George pulled up first in the Odyssey, closely followed by Megg, Jim, and Nemo in their little VW. I was overjoyed, and swept off the porch, arms outstretched, to catch them all in one big embrace.

"Amy, as usual, looks like a fashion plate and is in good spirits. She brought all kinds of goodies: my favorite coffee cake, home-baked toll house cookies, cheese and crackers, veggies and fruit, a bottle of Pinot Grigio.

George, wonderful and calm, set about opening the wine and we quickly put a cocktail hour together while we waited for Megg, Jim, and Nemo to settle into their rooms.

Tomorrow we will hike to Weverton Cliffs. It will be a pre-view hike, a chance for Megg and Jim to try out some of their new gear.

Amy and Megg are planning to hike with me later in the summer, at different times. I'm really surprised and pleased. I'll have plenty of company at this rate.

I so wish George could hike, too. But, it's enough for him to whisk me away to food and showers whenever he can. He seems to be thriving on that role. He's wonderful.

Tomorrow I'll slack. Yippee."

To "slack pack" refers to the practice of hiking with a loose (slack) pack loaded only with the provisions needed for a day hike: lunch, snacks, water, rain gear, first aid kit, map, flashlight. The hike covers the same trail but, unencumbered, the "slacker" can go faster and therefore hike more miles, or reach the predetermined destination sooner. Some thru-hikers refuse to slack and define their hike as one of walking every mile of the AT carrying a full pack.

Other thru-hikers define their hike as one of walking the AT most often with a full pack but occasionally with a loose one. If the day's hike ends at a road crossing, it is sometimes possible to arrange for heavy packs to be ferried to that crossing at the beginning of the day and picked up later at day's end.

The longer I hiked, the more relaxed I became about slacking, particularly over very steep or rugged mountains. For me, hiking was the important part; it never made much sense to me to carry a full pack when a lighter one would suffice.

May 27, 2001, to Weverton Cliffs, 5 miles

Nemo rode in his new backpack for the first time, and I happily hiked with a slack pack until an unexpected afternoon thunderstorm sent all of us scurrying for shelter at a road crossing. We called George, and he used the global positioning tracker in the Odyssey to retrieve us and take us back to Harper's Ferry for another night of fine dining at the hotel.

We took turns helping Nemo discover all there was to see and do in an old-fashioned hotel after bedtime.

> "While we all sit around the table, Nemo plays on the floor with his trucks, or climbs on the chair, or sits in George or Amy or Megg or Jim's lap to eat. He doesn't much care for the high chair, and no one insists that he use it. He amuses himself and the adults at the table with good-humored playfulness... I like how attentive Megg and Jim are to him. They do have consistent limits... but never mete them out in a harsh, abrupt or angry way – just firmly. It is so rewarding to see your children parent. They are so much better at it than we ever were.
>
> Amy is wonderful with Nemo. She plays with him, talks to him, takes him on little excursions around the hotel; he runs to her happily, and she adores him.
>
> It's easy to see that George had a loving and playful grandfather when I see him interact with Nemo. He talks and plays with him with such ease. They have a real bond.
>
> I'm very pleased with my family, even though Megg still irritates Amy and vice versa, especially after a tiring day of hiking and thunderstorms. They do seem to care about each other and try hard to be clear with each other; it was even fun crowding under that improvised roof this afternoon, eating lunch during the worst of the storm.
>
> My hike is beginning to reap benefits I never even anticipated. I certainly didn't expect it to revive family vacations. What a gratifying turn of events!"

After dinner, there was a lot of food repackaging to do before I could sleep. My athletic, health-conscious daughters had brought me a variety of energy bars, freeze-dried meals, protein supplements, and electrolyte-replacement drinks to replace some of the heavy food I had been carrying and eating for the past two weeks. But it was exhausting to try to anticipate weather, energy, and appetite needs, eliminate weight, and re-package everything into Ziploc baggies.

I did the best I could, and eventually organized all the boxes, envelopes and bags of food I might need until the next visit from George in three weeks. Then I collapsed into bed, hours later than my usual trail bedtime of sunset.

> "It's been a wonderful weekend and I'm eager to continue my trek, especially now that Amy and Megg will be joining me during different weeks this summer... I'm looking forward to our hikes, but I still dread saying 'goodbye' again in the morning."

Next morning, Megg, Jim, and Nemo left for Philadelphia, and George and Amy took me to the trailhead. Always careful to watch me go, George never drove away before I had started back, once again, on the trail.

The picture I carried with me every time I disappeared through a break in the trees was George's smiling face and encouraging wave behind me. Though a small gesture, it symbolized his steadfast support and belief in me. I appreciated his subtlety, and though it could never quite eliminate the ache in my throat when I set out, it helped keep me going once I began.

May 27, 2001, to Dahlgren Campground, Md., 14.2 miles

The next night I stayed at the only backpacker campground that has free hot showers, flush toilets, and gravel camping squares, each with its own picnic table.

There were several other tents set up when I arrived: Heckle and Jekyll, section hikers enroute to Pennsylvania, Texphar, a thru-hiker pharmacist from Texas, and someone else whom I had not yet met.

As I was cooking the heaviest food in my pack, Texphar stopped by to talk. "There's someone else here from the Midwest – Indiana – on his second thru-hike. You should talk to him."

I wasn't sure I wanted to talk to anyone on a second thru-hike. But a bit later, when a bearded, muscular young man ambled by and introduced himself, I made an attempt to be friendly.

"I'm Jed," he said. "I hear you're from Ohio."

"Texphar tells me this is your second thru-hike," I said, impressed.

"Yep. You?"

"I just started two weeks ago – at Rockfish Gap – doing a 'flip-flop' to Katahdin, then back to finish on Springer in October. I just picked up a food drop and my pack weighs a ton. Got any good advice?"

Jed looked at the picnic table strewn with all my stuff, including my two-inch by five-inch mini watercolor set.

"You probably won't be needing that," he said indicating my watercolor set. "I'd send that on, if I were you."

So much for expert advice. I laughed. Little did he know that my journal and watercolors were the soul of my hike.

"Thanks," I said. "Maybe I'll pitch some of this food, instead."

Jed continued on to his tent, and I gathered my stuff in mine. When I got up next morning, he was gone. I thought that would be the last time I ever saw him.

3. Finding My Trail Legs

Dahlgren Campground, Md., to Gardners, Pa., 65 miles

May 29, 2001, to Ensign Colwell Shelter, 13.8 miles

In the morning, hiking across low hills of laurel, chestnut oaks, and American chestnut shoots on unpaved, rocky forest roads, I passed a stone cylindrical structure soaring against the blue and white sky. It was the first monument built to the memory of George Washington, and reminded me that I was traveling on ground that had been trod many times before, just another set of footprints passing through lands that would endure long after I was gone.

I descended through woods of silent hickory, oak, maple, sassafras, and dogwood trees, and entered the noisy twenty-first century via a footbridge covered with curved chain-link fencing. The footbridge crossed Interstate 70 between Hagerstown and Frederick, Md. Halfway across the bridge, a semi honked and gave me the trucker's ninety-degree elbow hello. I raised my hiking stick in response, remembering all the times I had driven under this bridge myself, dreaming about the trail. I'd never seen a hiker passing overhead, though. That would have made my day... I wondered if it made the trucker's.

Later, I took a blue-blazed trail loop to a rocky overlook on Black Rock cliffs and paused to read a new cardboard sign posted on a tree. It warned that just a week ago someone from the town below had climbed up the cliff, walked too close to the edge, and plunged to his death.

The footing was precarious and the cliff steep. I sat well in from the edge to eat my lunch.

May 30, 2001, to Deer Lick Shelter, 14.7 miles

The day was beautiful and sunny, but not warm. My arthritic bare knuckles, wrapped around the exposed handles of hiking poles, were cold. I climbed several wooded hills of new growth saplings before beginning the long, steep, rocky ascent and descent of Quirauk Mountain.

It seemed to take forever to pick my way over the boulders, and I was careful not to put too much weight on either knee, stumble over loose rock, or fall. I was willing to bet that a giant once stood at the top of the mountain and threw rocks of all sizes down the slope, arbitrarily slapping white blazes here and there to mark the path. What path? Up, down, over, through – the longer I hiked, searching the rocks for the trail, the more irritated I became. By the time I reached the grassy knoll of Pen Mar Park, I was tired and grumpy.

As I sat with my back against the warm shingles of an outbuilding, eating my lunch, I tried to envision the park's heyday when excursion trains brought picnickers on Sunday school outings and carried vacationers from nearby Chambersburg and Waynesboro to the resort hotels. The park had once accommodated a fun house, a roller coaster, a miniature railroad, two resort hotels, and several restaurants. Today, only a few outbuildings and a snack bar remain, spread out over acres of newly mowed grass and mature leafy trees. It was breathtakingly beautiful in its quietude.

After lunch I crossed the Mason-Dixon Line into Pennsylvania and wondered if the old "Mason-Dixon Roadhouse" of my college days was still there. While innocent residents of nearby Gettysburg College, a campus still dry in the early 1960s, my friends and I had daringly driven, on occasion, to the "old M-D" whose dining rooms straddled the state line between Pennsylvania and Maryland. Younger than my friends by at least a year, I was of legal drinking age in Maryland, but not Pennsylvania. My friends, considerately, drank beer with me in the Maryland dining rooms.

That night, after pitching my tent on a grassy patch of dirt at the twin huts at Deer Lick, I discovered that the spring at the shelter was dry. My choices were to hike on to the next shelter, two miles farther north and uncomfortably near a road crossing, or to hike down a side trail to a stream a quarter mile away. I chose the quarter mile downhill slide. It was a long walk down and a longer one coming back up.

At the beginning of my hike, I carried my water in an old scout canteen and a half-liter water bottle. Rather than pumping or filtering water each time I refilled my bottles, I purified my drinking water with iodine crystals during the day and boiled water for cooking in the evening.

However, my system for fetching water and staying hydrated was unwieldy at first. In the evening I often found myself scrambling up a hillside with a cooking pot of water in each hand, my plastic water bottle seeping into my pocket, and my canteen hooked to the back of my shorts, splashing my legs and backside and wasting the water intended for my evening meal, teeth brushing, and breakfast. Eventually I replaced the canteen and plastic bottle with two Nalgene liter bottles for drinking, and a vinyl, two-liter bladder for cooking.

Before starting out in the morning, I drank as much water as I could hold and treated a fresh supply of water before I left camp. As I hiked, whenever I crossed a stream, I drank each bottle of treated water, refilled, re-treated, and waited twenty minutes for the iodine crystals to purify my new supply while I hiked. Except for water from the highest mountain streams, I was careful to treat all my water, and I learned to drink even when I wasn't thirsty.

With this system, I remained disease-free and adequately hydrated the entire length of the trail.

May 31, 2001, to Caledonia State Park, 13.2 miles

When I struggled out of my warm sleeping bag, it was too cold to crawl back in; the only way to stay warm was to move. I hiked out early and climbed a thousand feet to the top of Chimney Rocks through leafy woods dappled in early morning sun. Unfortunately, underbrush and trees obscured the view at the top; the appeal of hiking to a view was beginning to seem silly.

I hiked on, across the rocks of South Mountain, the oldest on the Pennsylvania AT. These rocks, said to be at least six hundred million years old, are steep, rugged and capped by a spine of hard, shiny quartzite bedrock.

So these are the infamous Pennsylvania rocks, I thought, as I carefully picked my way down the spine, balancing and hopping from one to the next until I reached the bottom. I was proud that I had made it and breathed a sigh of relief, only to turn to look back up the rocky slope and lose my balance. I fell sideways onto a bed of midsized boulders and scree.

My pack took the brunt of the fall, and I wasn't hurt, or even shaken. I sat where I landed, slipped out of my pack to assess the damage, and set to work stopping the blood and applying antiseptic to the superficial scrapes on my forearms and knees.

It was my first fall and it helped me re-think and lighten my first aid kit.[2] Eventually, I discovered that duct tape was the only adhesive that would keep gauze pads or moleskin in place on my sweating, ever-damp body; that insect bites and muscle soreness were better soothed with morning, afternoon, and evening doses of Ibuprofen, the hiker's "Vitamin I"; that problems of the bowel were better addressed by hiking hard each day, drinking lots and lots of treated or filtered water, and eating a diet of grains, nuts, dried fruit, black beans and rice.

In the end, I reduced my first aid kit to: two toilettes, a baggie full of "Vitamin I;" a small vial of 100% Tea Tree Oil, a homeopathic antiseptic; a two-ounce bottle of waterless antibacterial soap; two squares of moleskin, to prevent blisters. I wrapped Duct tape around my hiking poles for emergencies. On the AT, it seemed, I was never very far from a clinic or drug store if I needed extra supplies. Until then, antiseptic cleansing, duct tape, and a cool head were first aid enough. Everything else could be improvised.

---

2. In the beginning, my First Aid Kit contained 12 Band-Aids, one tube of Bacitracin, 24 Ibuprofen pills, three sterile gauze squares, 2 oz. bottle of antibacterial waterless soap wrapped in duct tape, 10 antiseptic towlettes, a small pair of scissors, a small sewing kit with needles and matches, a packet of dental floss, 4 Imodium tablets, a tube of pills for insect bites, two squares of Moleskin Plus, two squares of Second Skin, 1 oz. of First Skin.

As I hiked on after my fall, it occurred to me that the little red Elmo strapped to the back of my pack might have tumbled out onto the rocks when I went down. Given to me by my grandson, I planned to take Elmo to Katahdin, but I didn't really want to take off my pack again just to see if he was still there. When I spotted a day-hiker coming towards me, I broke my rule of not talking to male day-hikers and asked: "Do you see a little red Elmo strapped in back there?"

"Well, I do see a little guy," he said. "But he's crying! What happened?"

"We had a little fall," I replied, laughing.

I was happy that Elmo was still with me, but surprised that I had broken my own rule of never engaging solo male day-hikers in conversation. Was I foolhardy or just becoming more comfortable on the trail?

Even though I had been hiking for only a few weeks, I was learning to differentiate between day-hikers, section-hikers, and thru-hikers, just by their appearance.

Thru-hikers and section-hikers, I noticed, wore similar expensive gear: large packs, covered in rainy weather, ankle gaiters to keep dirt and rocks out of boots and socks, a bandana tied around the head or neck, trail boots or shoes, and clothing made of micro fibers. Most carried one or two hiking poles.

Day hikers, on the other hand, often wore blue jeans and clean cotton tee shirts, sandals or running shoes, and carried small, inexpensive packs. They seldom used hiking poles.

I also noticed that the speed and focus of their pace, the look of determination on their faces, the sleekness of their packs, the dirt and grime on their gear, and the odor of their bodies could differentiate hikers.

Thru-hikers hiked purposefully and quickly; they smelled of stale sweat and body odor; their packs were streamlined, dirt-streaked, and moved with their bodies, as another body part. Thru-hikers rarely stopped to chat and often were alone, even if they had a hiking partner on the trail.

The pace set by section-hikers was usually less determined and more relaxed. Their packs, carrying more stuff, looked unwieldy. Their clothes did not have the same ground-in dirt look, and their bodies smelled of stale sweat and, frequently, campfire smoke. Section-hikers took more breaks, planned shorter days, and stopped at a shelter earlier at day's end. They usually walked together in pairs or foursomes and often used hiking poles.

Day-hikers moved at a slow pace, carried a lot of water and snacks in their small packs, and smelled of shampoo and laundry detergent. They were often friendly and eager to stop and talk. They usually hiked in pairs, usually without hiking poles.

In recent years, a Go-Lite philosophy has become popular, especially with young hikers, and their equipment, to a novice, could assign them day-hiker status. The difference to me was the kind of equipment they carried and the agility and speed of their pace. Go-Light gear is designed to be efficient, functional, and lightweight. This often means a tarp instead of a tent, a small, frameless pack, an umbrella for raingear, quick-drying micro-fiber clothing, and running shoes or sandals instead of heavy hiking boots. Go-Lite hikers often average twenty-five to thirty-five miles per day and look like serious athletes. They seldom carried hiking poles and, to my eye, were not easily mistaken for casual day-hikers or ne'er do well drifters.

June 1, 2001, to Shippensburg Road, 11.3 miles

Early in the morning, I packed my gear quickly and walked in the cold, damp mist through Caledonia State Park where I had camped overnight. Within two miles, I discovered a new, double-hut structure connected by a covered deck.

I arrived at the shelter just as two section-hikers were finishing their breakfast of sausage, hot cakes, and coffee. I tarried at the picnic table, talked to the caretaker, and sniffed the trace of campfire and sausage lingering in the air. It smelled good; I was glad I was on my way to a reunion of college friends and a weekend of slacking, sleeping inside, and eating real food.

My friends, Lura and Deni, were to meet me at three o'clock at the trail crossing on Shippensburg Road. At two fifty-five, I crossed the road to our rendezvous point. The day had been wet and cold, but in the woods I had not noticed the heavy mist all around me. However, when I set my pack, sheathed in a bright orange rain cover, beside the road to wait, I began to wonder if I would ever be found, surrounded by fog on a deserted hilltop, in the middle of a rainy afternoon. What if no one showed up? I pulled out my map to determine my location and discovered that the valley at my feet was named Dead Woman Hollow. I chuckled, dubiously.

A few minutes later, I looked up to see headlights thrusting a smudged yellow beam around the curve in the road, announcing the arrival of my rescuers. Lura and Deni shuddered to a stop, jumped out to hug me, and, laughing at our absurdity, tossed my gear into their back seat. I hopped in, hoping the warm car would not release my thru-hiker aroma.

When we reached Deni's home, I showered, washed all my clothes, had a glass of wine, and caught up with my friends from Gettysburg who were gathered for the weekend just to meet and encourage me.

"Aren't you worried about being by yourself, all alone on the trail?" they wondered.

"But I never feel alone," I answered. "I'm surrounded by good friends who will do anything for me – even pick me up in the fog in some far-away place, hose me down and shower me with treats!" I laughed, then continued more soberly, "It's true that I'm by myself most of the time, but I feel your presence on the trail. Good people who are eager to assist me, encircle me. On the trail we call you Trail Angels. You remind me that I'm not alone. You are wonderful," I choked, emotionally.

I was stunned by my own verbosity. Usually, I am more reserved and don't reveal my feelings so openly. Encountering more basic vulnerabilities on the trail, however, I had cast my accustomed reticence aside. I was truly grateful for my friends who loved me and admired that I was trying to fulfill a dream. More than trail gifts, their faith in me helped fuel my own. I was, indeed, beginning to learn from the trail; it was giving me a new perspective and courage.

June 2, 2001, Gardners, Pa. to Shippensburg Road, 12 miles

In the morning, Deni dropped a group of us at the trailhead so we could hike north to south, allowing me to begin again on Sunday without backtracking or missing any of the trail. Our trek that day taught me a valuable lesson about hiking with others.

When we set out, I suggested that we split up and meet at a shelter several miles ahead, down a blue-blazed trail. I didn't think to mention how to find one's way on the trail or that the color, shape and placement of trail blazes signaled specific information. I had become so accustomed to looking up to confirm the two- by six-inch white rectangles that mark the AT, painted on trees, rocks, or fence posts, it never occurred to me that someone on the trail for the first time might not notice them.

The night before, we had waited for Ginder, a member of our hiking group, to drive from her home in suburban New York to Deni's home in rural Pennsylvania. After many cell phone conversations, aborted routes, and changes of direction, Ginder finally found us, after midnight, six dark and rainy hours after she had begun her estimated two-hour drive.

Today, Ginder was leading the hike. Her group plunged straight ahead into the woods, talking and laughing and following the well-trod path at their feet. Lura and I followed more slowly, looking for the single white blazes at eye level every hundred yards or so, pausing to consider the meaning of a double blaze: one directly above the other – be aware, a change is coming up; one blaze above the other, top one slightly to the right – turn right; one blaze above the other, top one slightly to the left – turn left; or of a blue blaze – side trail to shelter or water. Lura and I were looking for the blue blazed trail leading a fourth-mile downhill to the shelter and water source where we would meet the rest of our group. We expected that they would be pleasantly rested and well hydrated by the time we arrived.

But when we arrived, the shelter was empty. I recognized my mistake immediately. Talking and laughing, following the path at your feet rather than the blazes at eye level, it is very easy to lose the trail and hike on without knowing you are on another path. Our friends had hiked on, oblivious to the double white blazes indicating a change, or the blue blaze to the left, indicating the side trail to the shelter.

My map showed that there were many trails crisscrossing the AT in the section we were hiking. It would be easy to get lost without a map or compass and scary to feel lost, even if you weren't far from a road cross-ing or civilization.

The best course of action when you have lost the trail or have not seen a white blaze in the last fifteen minutes is to turn around and retrace your steps until you find a white blaze. Because the trail is blazed the same in both directions, sometimes you need only walk back a few hundred yards to spot a white blaze for hikers headed in the opposite direction. The car-dinal rule, however, is to stop and retrace your steps as soon as you become aware that you have lost the trail.

Lura and I agreed that I should run ahead to find Ginder and the oth-ers while she hiked back to the AT and then continued heading south. So, I sprinted back up the side trail to the junction of the blue blazed and white blazed trails, then up another five hundred feet, ascending Piney Mountain, to find them. My hiking boots made heavy running shoes, but anxiety for possible misadventures kept adrenalin pumping through my legs and the exercise actually felt good after a morning of walking at a slower pace than usual.

Fortunately, I only needed to run to the top of Piney Mountain before I found Ginder and friends, retracing their steps to find the shelter. Naively, they had assumed the shelter would be visible from the AT and abashedly, they admitted that they had not been paying any attention to the blazes, white or blue.

But I was the one to be contrite. I had forgotten that they were new to the trail and as green as I had been only a few short weeks before. It didn't occur to them to watch out for other trail markings, or other trails. They had assumed that the AT was the only path through these woods. And I had assumed that they knew what it had taken me weeks to learn about the trail: you have to be vigilant not only for rocks and water, weather and food, strangers and animals; you have to watch for the trail and know where you are going and how you are going to get there. You have to follow the blazes and keep your wits about you. While we wait-ed for Lura, I taught them a little lesson on blazes and they taught me a big lesson on humility.

The rest of the afternoon went smoothly and when we reached Pine Grove Furnace, we took pictures of each other at the marker noting the midpoint between Springer and Katahdin. Although it was only mile two hundred-forty for me, I felt that I had accomplished something. There were only a thousand more miles to Katahdin – and only eight hundred more to Springer.

The day's hike had been good for me. It had reminded me not to take anything on the trail for granted. It had cautioned me to be humble with my knowledge. It had encouraged me to keep on learning. And it affirmed for me that I was becoming a thru-hiker.

I had found my trail legs, at last. They would get me where I needed to go.

4. Setting My Stride

Gardners, Pa. to Delaware Water Gap, Pa., 183.3 miles

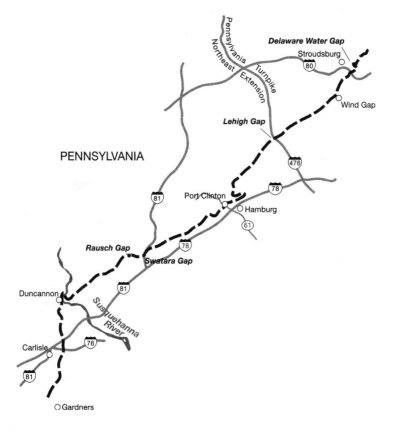

June 3, 2001, to Alec Kennedy Shelter, 6.9 miles

I bid my friends goodbye at the trailhead, and by midafternoon was jolted back to the reality of being on my own, once again. I encountered my first impossible rock climb, a boulder taller than me by half, with no footholds. After several unsuccessful attempts to climb it, I solved the problem by taking my pack off, lifting it over my head, and pushing it over the rock that had stopped me in my tracks. Not bad for an amateur, I thought, but as I scrambled up and over the boulder without my pack, I was struck again by the reality of having to solve the problem by myself.

That night, alone in a shelter for the first time, I wrote:

> "It's very quiet and growing colder. I don't think I'm afraid, but I'm not quite at ease, either. The wind is howling through the trees, cracking and banging branches against the roof. It's spooky! This may be another reason more women don't attempt this on their own."

June 4, 2001, to Darlington Shelter, 18.2 miles

I climbed five hundred feet early in the day, one thousand feet at the end of the day and fifteen miles of flat pastureland, woods, and rolling fields, in between. As I walked I listened to a tape of Civil War songs and was reminded of my own innocence at Gettysburg College, almost forty years ago. How idealistic I had been. How young. And how lucky I was that some of the friends from those days were still part of my life today. We could still pick up a conversation where it began years ago and leave it unfinished until the next time we saw each other.

My musings distracted me from the fatigue of a long, boot-lugging day – the longest I had walked, so far. When I reached the shelter, it was occupied by a grubby-looking hiker from Quebec. I decided to cook up a pot of black beans and rice, pitch my tent, and crawl inside to eat and sleep. The next morning when I crawled out, the other hiker was gone and I was again alone.

June 5, 2001, to Duncannon, Pa., 12.6 miles

It was an easy morning, hiking over fairly level terrain with only a few rocks, but by noon I was again hot and sweaty. When I reached Hawk Rock, overlooking the Borough of Duncannon, I decided to stop for lunch and sat down to take off my boots and socks and let them dry out in the sun. It was then that I discovered the itch on the back of my leg had become a ring-shaped rash, with several tiny black spots no bigger than the head of a pin at the center. I pulled out my Pennsylvania Guide to read further. My guidebook was not reassuring:

"… it is especially important to … wear long sleeves and pants… apply an insect repellent that is effective against deer ticks."[3]

3. Gross, Wayne E., ed., Guide to The Appalachian Trail in Pennsylvania, 10th edition, Keystone Trails Association, Cogan Station, Pa., 1998, p.47.

I looked down at my sweaty body. It was too hot to wear long pants and shirt and any insect repellent I might have applied would not have survived my perspiring body. I continued to read:

"Symptoms may include a ring-shaped rash... fever, chills, headache, stiffness in joints, weakness and fatigue."[4]

I'm stiff every time I try to get up, I thought, and what hiker isn't fatigued at the end of the day? I read on:

"Some cases are without symptoms... If you have any reason to suspect the possibility of Lyme disease, consult a physician promptly... In the absence of prompt diagnosis and treatment, Lyme disease can cause serious problems involving the heart, joints, or nervous system."[5]

Perhaps I should find a doctor in Duncannon, I thought. If this was the beginning of Lyme disease, I wanted to catch it before it caught me.

When I reached Duncannon thirty minutes later, I went directly to the post office to pick up my mail drop. I was a little anxious about this. It was my first post office resupply on the trail, and I wanted to have plenty of time to repackage whatever I didn't need and send it home.

As I knelt under the only shade tree on the front lawn of the post office, surrounded by my resupply, a middle-aged couple walked by and asked me if I were the thru-hiker named Butterfly.

"We're holding a package for her at our hotel," they said. "Can we do anything for you?"

I asked if they knew where I could find a doctor.

The couple introduced themselves as Pat and Vicki. "We've only been here a few weeks... but there is a clinic about four miles outside of town; they might be able to help you," they assured me. "We run a hotel for thru-hikers down the street. We'll take your pack to the hotel and run you to the clinic. Your stuff will be safe with us – and you can stay overnight if you want."

Walking four miles along a paved road on a hot June afternoon did not appeal to me. I hopped into their small packed car.

"Here's my phone number," Pat said, handing me a slip of paper when we arrived at the clinic. "When you're done, just call and I'll come and get you."

4. Ibid.
5. Ibid.

I was bedazzled by his kindness.

At the clinic, I waited for my turn to see the doctor. Looking down at my hands, sweat-soaked shorts, and muddy boots, I was suddenly struck by the dirt under my fingernails, uncombed hair, sunburned skin, scabby knees, and bruised shins. I remembered the running joke of the trail:

"What's the difference between a thru-hiker and being homeless?"

Answer: 'Gore-Tex'.

The doctor who examined my rash assured me that I had not been bitten by a deer-tick, and that my rash was probably from debris or something that was irritating my skin. I was relieved and felt a bit sheepish, as though I had wasted her time. She, on the other hand, was gracious and pleased, I think, to be of some service to me.

I called Pat. He picked me up and drove me back to the hiker hotel: The Doyle.

The Doyle Hotel is legendary among thru-hikers. Built more than one hundred years ago by Anheuser-Busch, it was run by the Doyle family for more than four decades and now, under new owners, is being renovated.

Vicki greeted me as I walked into the bar. She directed me up four flights of stairs to my room, a ten by ten-foot box with a single light bulb, sagging double bed, and wrought iron chair squeezed under a shuttered window. A hand-lettered sign on the window warned: "USE GREAT CAUTION WHEN OPERATING WINDOW DUE TO AGE AND CONDITION. WINDOWS ARE UNSTABLE. OPERATE AT YOUR OWN RISK."

Stuffy and hot as the room was, I didn't dare touch the window. I didn't want to stay overnight either, but felt beholden for the rides to and from the clinic and for the hospitality. Besides, it was getting late. I set down my pack and mail drop and went to look for the shower.

It was easy to spot the renovations in the fourth-floor bathroom. The new shower curtain, toilet seat, and paper holder gleamed. I was glad that my mail drop had included shampoo and soap, but I longed for a fluffy, dry bath towel.

That night it was hard to sleep in a hot room with a closed window and my neighbor's TV blaring through the wall. The Doyle, I discovered, was home to the down-and-out and night-trade as well as to thru-hikers.

June 6, 2001, to Peters Mountain Shelter, 12.2 miles

Walking through town in the early morning gray light, darting across a noisy railroad track still active with early morning and late night trains, passing abandoned buildings whose time had come and gone, I was filled with melancholy. The town was so forlorn and forgotten; no wonder the cars and trucks whizzing by ignored it. And hiking the first two miles up Peters Mountain, crisscrossed by switchbacks and unchanging view of the river and town below, seemed to take forever. The day was overcast and muggy, my pack was heavy with eleven days of new food, and I couldn't seem to push myself any faster.

I hiked dispiritedly all day, slowly picking my way across rocks, trying not to think of how heavy my pack felt or how much my boots were beginning to pinch.

> "I reached the shelter about four-thirty – a two-story affair with lofts in the upper level. The walk to the spring was half a mile downhill on stone steps most of the way. When I got back from the spring, another thru-hiker named Flea was settling in. Flea prides himself on hiking fast and on not shaving or cutting his reddish hair until he reaches Katahdin. He looks like a leprechaun, has a slight build and jumps about when he talks. He seems wired... Tomorrow, if I keep to my plan, I'll hike seventeen hilly miles. Flea tells me they might be too much for me in one day. We'll see about that."

June 7, 2001, to Rausch Gap Shelter, 17+ miles

I inadvertently hiked south for a mile and learned another valuable trail lesson: the importance of noticing on which side of the trail the shelter is placed. Because the AT is white blazed on both sides of the trees, it can be very confusing in the morning to remember which direction you came from. Trees and blazes tend to look the same in the early morning light. This morning, at the junction of the AT and blue-blazed trail from the shelter, I turned the wrong way. Although my gut told me that something wasn't right and my eyes reminded me that I had seen that lookout rock before, I stubbornly continued, trying to convince myself that I was headed north. Luckily, in about half an hour, I met two men and their teenaged sons hiking towards me.

"I hope you're heading south," I greeted them.

"Nope. We're going north."

"Are you sure?"

"Yep. Just started last night – we're hiking north for a week."

We all consulted my map. Sure enough, I had turned south at the trail junction out of the shelter and had been retracing my steps of the night before. Groaning, I turned around and hiked north with them, relieved to be heading in the right direction, glad I had only gone a mile out of my way, and feeling a little foolish for my missteps.

My new companions were nice. The men began including their sons on their hikes ten years before, when their sons were just big enough to trot ahead without packs. The boys, Casper and Topo, still ran ahead of their dads, Methane and Gray Bear, but now they also carried their own gear, and some of their aging dads' supplies, as well.

We talked and hiked most of the day together until late in the afternoon, when I stopped to pee and lost them. I also lost the blue-blazed trail to the shelter and ended the day as I began – retracing my steps another mile, this time following the smoke of the campfire my section-hiking friends had built at the shelter. Flea was there, too. That night I slept in a shelter with all five of them and discovered how Methane got his trail name: he was named for his gaseous adaptation to trail food. I was too tired from my nineteen-mile day to either care or be amused.

The next day, I hiked on and off with Methane, Gray Bear, Topo, Casper and Flea, and joined them at the end of the day around their campfire. I listened to their stories as they reminisced about the parts of the trail they had already hiked, and basked in their admiration for my attempt at a thru-hike on my own. I discovered I didn't mind hiking with someone beside myself. I liked being able to consult with another person when I questioned the map or number of miles to the shelter. It was interesting to learn about another person's hike, and I enjoyed swapping trail snacks (my Powerbar for Topo's fresh orange). It was heartening to have the miles seem only half as long when someone else was sweating them with me, and it was welcoming to have a friend saving me a spot in the shelter when I straggled in, last, at the end of the day.

The trade-off was hiking at someone else's pace, waiting until someone else was hungry or thirsty to eat or find water, and breaking my own rhythm of silence. I would struggle with that trade-off many times on my journey north to Katahdin.

June 8, 2001, to 501 Shelter, 17.5 miles

After a full day's hike, we reached the 501 Shelter and I met Butterfly, the second woman over fifty I would meet, and her hiking partner, Old Gazelle, a sixty-three year old marathon runner.

"Ah, so you're Butterfly," I said. "They're looking for you at the Doyle Hotel."

"I know," she replied. "I picked up my mail drop yesterday – but we didn't stay there."

"Probably wise," I observed, and left it at that.

The 501 Shelter near Route 501 is famous among thru-hikers for its pay phone, ice cream bars, cold soft drinks, and pizza delivered to the trailhead. Flea had arrived before the rest of us and had taken the liberty of ordering dinner: pizza. While waiting, I devoured two ice cream bars and a Coke, and rinsed my sweaty body under the hose in the not-so-solar shower out back. Unlike most shelters, this shelter was enclosed on four sides and had a Plexiglas skylight in the roof. Because darkness comes so early and so completely in the woods, a skylight is always welcome; it means that daylight will remain indoors much longer into the evening. The skylight at 501 enabled us to see our pizza as we ate it, sitting in chairs around a table crowded with trail food discarded by pizza-preferring hikers.

When the sky outside finally wrapped to velvet darkness, a group of students preparing for an international exchange trip to China arrived and pitched their tents next to the shelter. As I lay on my bunk, I was pleased to hear them talking quietly and singing around their campfire. Their voices evoked nostalgia for my days as an exchange student and Peace Corps volunteer; I slipped into sleep lulled by their song, under the stars shining through the skylight.

June 10, 2001, to Port Clinton, Pa., 22 miles

"I hiked in to the Union Bed & Breakfast with Butterfly and
Old Gazelle this morning. Flea, Methane, Gray Bear, and their
sons were ahead of us – "doing miles." I enjoyed hiking with
Butterfly – her pace is much like mine. And I liked her company. She told me about herself as we were hiking. She has two
daughters, 18 and 21, and started hiking five years ago. Hiking
gave her the courage to leave a bad marriage, she said. She
divorced her husband two years ago. I was curious about her
hiking arrangement with Gazelle since he's married to someone else, a non-hiker. It doesn't seem to pose a problem for
either of them."

It was a relief that the descent into Port Clinton later that morning
was via a series of steep stone steps rather than the loose rocks I had
expected. My feet hurt. The soles on my boots had lost their cushioning
protection over the past ten days, and I had developed a blister on my
right heel. Both feet were so swollen my toes bumped the end of my
boots with every step and I could no longer feel the bottoms of my feet.
Walking in or out of boots was torture; my feet would need some serious
remedies from the drug store in Port Clinton.

When we reached town, a young, self-designated trail angel named
Hikarita was parked by the side of the road, eager to drive us to the strip
mall in the next town. We stowed our packs at the B&B and squeezed in
for a ride to the Acme and Rite-Aid pharmacy. I bought bananas, a small
jar of Tang, granola bars, and self-sticking gauze wrap for my feet. Old
Gazelle treated everyone to a Frostee. It was fun, though I was dazed by
the number of choices in the grocery store and soon escaped to sit outside in the sun. I felt invisible to the townspeople coming and going on
their Sunday shopping errands.

Back at the B&B, I took an old-fashioned bath in a claw-foot bath-
tub. Then I started going through my pack, trying to eliminate weight.
Everyone agreed that my pack was too heavy, and though I didn't have a
mail drop waiting at the post office across the street, I planned to mail
home my extra stuff from there before I hiked out in the morning. I was

determined to lighten my load – but sorting and deciding what to send home was a chore.

In most towns along the trail, hostels, motels, and some post offices provide "Hiker Boxes" for donations of food and other extras for or from hikers. Upon receiving a mail drop, most hikers eliminate anything they don't want or no longer need by either donating it to the Hiker Box or sending it back home. Hiker Box items are free to the taker and, in most cases, are treated with respect and not trashed. Hikers usually look through the Hiker Box before shopping at the local grocery. I donated all of my oatmeal, cheese, and trail bologna to the hiker box at the B&B in Port Clinton.

Butterfly suggested that I establish a "Bounce Box" for anything else that I didn't want to carry but might need later on the trail. A Bounce Box is used to send gear, food, clothing or small luxuries to a post office or hostel ahead on the trail. It eliminates the need to carry the items but keeps them accessible without the cost or inconvenience of sending them back home. Bounce Boxes can be sent from one post office to another without charge, as long as they remain unopened. If opened and added to or deleted from on a regular basis, the Bounce Box system can become very expensive; if the Bounce Box's arrival does not coincide with your own arrival, waiting to retrieve it can be a nuisance. But Bounce Box goodies are also a treat.

The only items in Butterfly's Bounce Box that I envied were her red toenail polish, clean town clothes, and a soft, fluffy bath towel – everyday commodities in my old life, superfluous luxuries in the new. I created my own Bounce Box and sent my pants, long-sleeved shirt, extra fuel, film, guidebooks, batteries, foot powder, and some dried fruit and nuts ahead to the next mail drop.

That evening, Butterfly, Old Gazelle, Flea and I met for dinner on the porch of the B&B. Herman, the owner, barbequed some baby back ribs and baked potatoes on an outdoor grill. We were the only guests eating and drinking under the string of yellow lights that outlined our space. Trucks, cars, and motorcycles roared by on the four-lane highway just fifty feet from our table; we had to shout to be heard above the din. The contrast of the noisy, speeding traffic, the artificial illumination, and the shabby attempts at elegance compared to the quiet woods and dark mountain majesty that were the usual backdrops for our dinner conversation lent a dreamlike aura to the evening. Two bottles of cheap wine made the scene even foggier, more surreal. I couldn't wait to escape from the disorienting clamor for a long, restful sleep in a room of my own.

None of us slept well that night. Route 61, the main east-west artery between two interstates and the cities of Pottsville and Reading, Pa., was the four-lane highway just outside our door. The walls, floors, and light fixtures of our turn-of-the-century roadhouse vibrated with truck noise all night.

In the morning, Butterfly and Old Gazelle elected to have a day of rest in town: a "zero day," as some call a day of hiking no miles. I had not yet had a day without hiking at least eight miles, but a whole day of this loud traffic did not forecast rest to me.

I stopped at the post office to send my Bounce Box and met Push and Shove, the couple I had last seen in Front Royal, when they abandoned their flip-flop hike for a van and change of weather.

"We've skipped a few miles," they admitted. "We're going up to New Hampshire next. Hiking in the mid-Atlantic states isn't for us. Too many rocks. Too boring."

I couldn't help agreeing about the rocks, but I wasn't bored – just a little foot-sore and weary. I was glad they were still "hiking their own hike" but was eager to get going; I didn't spend much time chatting. In my head, I had moved on.

Before I left the post office, I weighed my pack. Even with a Bounce Box and Hiker Box donation, I still weighed in at forty-five pounds! Where was this extra weight coming from? What could I eliminate next? I didn't know. Perplexed, I hiked out of town, thinking I might catch up with Flea by day's end.

June 11-12, 2001, to Allentown Hiking Club Shelter, 23 miles

For the next two days, I trekked over some significant rock formations and small pointed rocks underfoot. Whatever views there might have been were obscured by low clouds and mist rising from the valley below.

Picking my way over the rocks made for long, slow hiking. Trekking poles helped, but my feet felt raw inside my now too-tight boots. In addition, I had to monitor each step and test each rock before committing my weight to it, and step carefully, mile after rocky mile, in thunder-threatened heat. By late afternoon of the second day, I was tired, sore, and anxious about finding the shelter.

> "The hardest thing for me, so far, has been to be unsure of the trail and be aware that it is getting late and I need to get to the shelter soon. I'm not afraid to camp along the trail by myself, but having one other person nearby, to commiserate, is very reassuring. And it's more fun. I like having someone to talk to at the end of the day."

At the Allentown Shelter, I found that someone.

Wilson was a tall, good-looking young marathon runner I had met before in Port Clinton. He took his trail name from Tom Hanks' volleyball companion in the movie *Cast Away*. But unlike that silent communicator, this Wilson talked non-stop and had a lot of complaints. He was having problems with his feet and was angry at "the damn Pennsylvania rocks." In fact, Wilson was angry at just about everything and belabored his troubles most of the evening.

June 13, 2001, to Palmerton, Pa., 17 miles

When I left in the morning, Wilson was still in his sleeping bag. He was one of those hikers who sleep in, get a late start to the day, and then hike hard and fast to "make miles" by the day's end. No wonder his feet hurt, I thought.

Walking out in the early morning sunshine, I reflected on Wilson's grumpiness the night before. I was startled by his negativity and wondered why he was still hiking. He wasn't really the end-of-the-day companion I had had in mind.

Then I forgot about Wilson. I encountered 'The Cliffs' – an eighth-mile of huge white rocks soaring above my head, dropping off several hundred feet on each side to ravines below. The trail was marked straight up and across the knife's edge at the top. There was no other path, no blue-blazed alternative, no other choice. Once again, I had to figure out a way to get up, across, and down those rocks by myself, with no one to notice if I fell, no one to help if I stumbled.

Interestingly, I wasn't scared, just challenged to figure out how to get over safely.

I took a sip of water, tightened my pack straps, and slowly began to pick my way up and over each rock, thrusting first a pole, then a foot, the other pole, the other foot, balancing each step. At times, I abandoned my poles and, hand over hand, pulled myself to the next crevice. At the top, I very slowly and very carefully continued my pole-foot-pole-foot method as I made my way across to the other side. I concentrated on my progress and never looked down on either side.

When I reached the far side, I sat down and scooted off one rock to the next until I was down. Then I turned around and looked back. Impressive! And I had done it! I took some pictures of the rocks, knowing that a photograph could never do justice to the feat I had just accomplished.

Within a mile I had another chance to polish my foot-pole-foot-pole system over a rock scramble not quite as big, requiring the same slow picking with poles and hand-over-hand pulling. Rocks are hard on the feet and ankles, but harder on the knees, especially descending. I was glad I had spent so much preparation time last winter, lunging across the gym floor and squatting on a balance board with a loaded pack strapped to my back; that had made the difference today. I was proud of myself and surprised that I hadn't been frightened by the day's challenges. Too busy strategizing, I concluded, and wondered if this knife-edge were a forecast of the rock-faced summits to come. If they were, I decided, I would just figure out a way to deal with them when they happened. I hiked on, with calm assurance, energized by my newly earned confidence.

In the late afternoon I walked a sunny path through tall grass, mountain laurel, daisies, and pink wildflowers all in bloom. A cool breeze ruffled my hair. I was tired but looking forward to reaching the shelter, stretching out on my inflatable mattress, and resting up for the steep rock climb out of Lehigh Gap in the morning.

I heard a rustling on the path behind me and knew I was about to be overtaken by another hiker. It was Wilson, my unhappy companion of the night before.

"I'll wait for you at the bridge over the Lehigh River and we'll hitch into town for the night," he shouted as he strode by. "We can stay for free at the 'jailhouse hostel'."

He continued his pace, arrogantly, not waiting for my answer.

"This is probably the dumbest thing I've done so far. Wilson talked me into coming to the hiker hostel in the basement of the old police station in Palmerton, two miles from Lehigh Gap. I was headed for a different experience, but when I wound down the sinewy trail to the bridge, there he was, waiting for me. We crossed the bridge and stood at a busy Y intersection to catch a ride into town. A beat-up flat bed truck finally stopped; we threw our packs on the bed and climbed up after them. The driver took us directly to the police station. The policeman at the desk looked at our identification and, in a friendly manner, showed us to the dungeon – a dark cavernous room lined with double bunks, underneath a gym in the former town hall. The janitor at the hostel was grouchy. He said we couldn't use the showers on the third floor because a group might be coming in to play basketball and, for some reason, showering while they played was unacceptable."

But Palmerton, where I had landed, had some of the nicest people I would meet on the trail. That evening, walking down the quiet main street looking for a meal, I found a coin-operated laundry, turned around, and went back to the hostel for my dirty clothes. Dumping everything I wasn't wearing into a washer, I continued my dinner quest, but neglected to note the Laundromat closing time. Although Wilson had disappeared, I discovered several other hikers at the local pizzeria. We sat together, talking and swapping stories of The Cliffs and the trail until dark.

Strolling back to the hostel, I remembered my laundry. Too late. The doors were closed and locked and wouldn't reopen until nine a.m. I was dismayed. Not only was I staying in a dump, now I would be delayed in the morning – with the toughest rock climb of Pennsylvania just two miles away – all because my clothes were locked in a washing machine.

"How stupid I am. Why didn't I just tell Wilson to hitch to town by himself? I never planned to come here in the first place. And, besides everything else, I have to hitch out in the morning – by myself! Because he sure won't be up. Damn," I thought.

And then the door to the Laundromat opened and a middle-aged woman attendant motioned to me. "When you didn't come back," she said, "I put your clothes in the dryer. Here they are." She handed me my clean, folded clothes with a smile.

I was so grateful, I wanted to dance around the block. I gave her a hug and big thank you instead. Much relieved, I crossed the street to the hostel, no longer minding the basement's solitary overhead light or lack of ventilation.

Early the next morning, suited up with pack, poles, boots and clean hiking shorts, I walked along the sidewalk to reach the road back to the trail. A retired postman parking his car identified me as a hiker. "It's a long walk on tarmac," he said, "and then a long steep climb up the Lehigh Rocks. Let me give you a ride to the trailhead."

I accepted without hesitation and wasn't the least bit worried about hitching alone with him. Enlightened self-confidence, I thought later. Well-earned, enlightened self-confidence, enhanced by several random acts of kindness. They made all the difference.

June 14, 2001, to Leroy A. Smith Shelter, 17 miles

The Lehigh Rocks are a straight-up climb of one thousand feet in one mile. As I approached the stony face, I saw two dots slowly progressing up the trail in front of me. Hikers, I speculated. Someone to witness my rock-climbing success – or failure.

I began to climb. About halfway up I spotted a blue-blazed trail to the right; it was an alternative path to the top, designed for foul weather or the faint-hearted. But I was emboldened by yesterday's success and the presence of the other hikers. I spurned the path and trod on, catching up with the hikers when they stopped on a ledge to eat a snack. They were another father-son team named Darth Vader and Luke Skywalker.

We climbed together. Once, all of us had to take off our packs to scramble up a boulder. This time, someone was there to help me. That added assurance turned a scary challenge into an off-hand success. Amazing what a little help from a friend could do, I thought.

When we reached the top of the rocks, my friends sprinted ahead and I was left to walk alone in thick swirling mist, low-growing vegetation, and twisted knobby trees silhouetted against bare rocks. It was a landscape from the netherworld. It reminded me of Dante's Inferno.

I pondered the significance of encountering hikers named Luke Skywalker and Darth Vader, light and dark, just when I needed them.

I met Virgil in the Netherworld, I thought. Amazing.

As I continued, the sun began to burn off the morning mist, leaving the exposed rocks hot and glaring. Toxic fumes from a zinc-smelting plant below, over many years, had killed the plants and polluted the water where I walked. Although the area is being reclaimed, hikers are still warned to avoid drinking the metallic-tasting water or touching the vegetation. After the hot climb, however, I was sweaty and thirsty. I took a sip of the extra water I had carried up the rocks and looked longingly at the only vegetation at my feet: ripe blueberries. I dared not eat them and reluctantly hiked on.

As I began the next ascent, something in a low branch caught my eye. Stopping to investigate, I discovered a trail angel had visited and left a plastic bag full of ripe peaches, round, firm and juicy, hanging in a tree. I grabbed a peach and smacked it with a big wet bite. Delicious. But I was still thirsty.

I hiked on, at a slower pace. My water supply was almost gone and it would be seven miles, or three and a half hours before I would reach a safe spring. The effects of dehydration – low energy, headache, decreased hiking motivation and performance – were beginning to claim my body.

Some trail maintainers, finished with their day's chore of removing dead branches, hiked towards me.

"How're you doing?" one asked.

"Okay. But I could use some water. How much farther to the spring?"

The trail maintainer reached behind his back and thrust his bottle of water in my direction. "I'm hiking out," he said. "Take mine."

I accepted his bottle with thanks and drank thirstily. Only another thru-hiker or a trail maintainer would be on this mountain on such a hot day; but only someone hiking out could afford to give up his water. My trail maintainer was another trail angel, watching out for me.

I hiked on and finally, in late afternoon, reached a road crossing and a sign that announced: "Water, 1.0 miles" with an arrow pointing down the road. I debated.

Should I hike a mile down a winding tar road at the end of the day? Then I would have to hike back up, and then hike on to the shelter, at least three and a half miles farther. But this might be my only chance for water; there was no guarantee that water would be available at the shelter.

I hoisted my pack and started down the paved black curves, the longest mile I had ever walked. Nary a car or truck passed by.

Within half an hour, however, I encountered another set of trail angels and my destination, Blue Mountain Dome, the rustic home of John Stemp and Linda Gellock. John and Linda's dogs greeted me, barking loudly as I approached, but John and his three-year old son came out to quiet them and welcome me with water from the long green hose snaking across the yard. Linda came home shortly thereafter and insisted that I eat and drink something more nourishing. I gratefully accepted some iced tea and two hot dogs slathered in ketchup, relish, and mustard – my all-time favorite meal.

After dinner, Linda and John dropped me back at the trailhead. Hydrated, nourished and full of appreciation, I headed for the shelter, and hiked those three and a half miles in just over an hour, the fastest I had ever hiked with a full pack. It was also the first time I had hiked through the woods at dusk. I was charmed to watch the deer watch me. Unlike my invisibility at the supermarket, I felt at home among the deer, as though they accepted me because they knew I would do them no harm.

When I reached the shelter, I decided to pitch my tent in a grove of trees rather than join Wilson and several hikers already bedded under the roof for the night. Retreating to my sanctuary, I stripped off my sweaty clothes and slept naked inside the privacy of my tent, caressed by a cool breeze, under a canopy of stars. Although it had been an arduous day, I was content and humble.

I had had my full share of trail angels today, I reflected. Without their grace and help all along the way, today's hike would have been impossible. Pennsylvania, though infamous for its rocks, unstable water supply, and overabundance of road crossings, could not be surpassed for the generosity and timely help of its trail angels. The magic of the trail continued to surprise and sustain me.

June 15, 2001, to Kirkridge Shelter, 13.5 miles

Hot, muggy, buggy silence characterized most of the hike. I draped a bandanna over my face and neck, trying to outsmart the mosquitoes diving at my exposed, sweaty body. It was a relief to reach the shelter in the late afternoon, but I was loath to exchange its dark dreary interior for the bright clear sky of remaining daylight. I pushed on.

As I hiked up a hill, the woods opened onto the top of a grassy hillside and I encountered two men parasailing.

Their graceful vivid beauty mesmerized me. They were like giant eagles cavorting and gliding against the early evening sky. Their colors of bright orange, blue, red, and yellow, were breathtaking; their sense of adventure, competence, and courage were awe-inspiring. I felt as though I were in a sacred place, watching a spiritual dance, re-enacting a faith. I sat and watched for the remainder of the day.

At dusk I set up my tent in a nearby birch grove, laid out my sleeping bag, and fell asleep under stars of fiery beauty. My spirit soared as I dropped off, listening to the wind rustle through the tops of the trees.

June 16, 2001, to Delaware Water Gap, 6.4 miles

The morning began with another kind of wildlife. As I was hiking out in the early morning mist, completely surrounded by silence and dripping trees, I looked up to see a very large bear on all fours across the path in front of me. He was about fifty yards ahead, with his head swung around in my direction. I froze. I hoped his eyesight was bad. I wished my camera was more accessible. I realized, quite suddenly, that he and I were alone.

I remembered that when encountering a bear one should avoid eye contact, stand still, and make lots of noise. I did all three. In fact, I made a colossal racket. Nothing happened. The bear didn't budge.

I stepped back behind a tree, trying to regroup. I could just see the tip of the bear's nose, so I knew he was still there. How could I get him to move? Nothing came to mind.

I tried again. Stepping out from behind the tree, I banged my metal poles together, blew my whistle, yelled, shouted, and sang as loud as I could. This was no time to feel foolish or shy about my sense of pitch.

The bear looked back at me for a long, long minute... and then slowly and deliberately picked up first one foot, then another and finally continued his way across the path. There was no question about who was in charge.

I waited a fraction of a minute, and then walked as quickly and directly as I could, down the path and as far away from him as I could get. It occurred to me that I hadn't been scared – only very aware that I always needed to have a strategy. The suddenness of the encounter was a real surprise.

Later I surprised a rattler stretched out on a rock. Luckily, he was not worried about me and didn't even coil. I walked on, unfazed, but gave him wide berth. I would have a good story to tell my family when I met them later in the morning. Megg, Jim, and Nemo would be meeting me at Delaware Water Gap to hike for the rest of the day. George had agreed to meet me this weekend, as well, to bring all my remaining food and some extra boxes so I could reorganize.

Making the arrangements to meet had been complicated. On a busy summer weekend high in the Poconos, the only reservations George could find for all of us were at the High Point Country Inn, forty-four miles north of Delaware Water Gap. Trail-savvy as I had become, I knew this would be a long two-day hike for me; with Megg, Jim, and Nemo along, I would only be able to walk a fraction of those miles.

As I walked, I tried to sort out the dilemma this presented: the importance of reorganizing my food drops, the logistics of coordinating Megg and Jim's hike with George's long drive and work commitments, the importance of keeping to my own schedule so that I could continue to meet people and still get to Katahdin by August, the disappointment of "blue blazing" or "yellow blazing" as I hiked, rather than "touching every blaze" as I had planned, the adjustment I would need to make to my definition of "hiking my own hike."

For me, hiking my own hike meant to complete the trail in one continuous trek within one calendar year: a thru-hike. To do this, it was important for me to keep to the schedule I had worked out pre-hike. However, it was equally important for me to honor my women friends' and daughters' interest in hiking with me. I began to realize that I would need to be flexible about *how* I would hike, and accept the fact that I might need to include occasional blue- or yellow-blazing as I thru-hiked.[6]

So far, I had hiked every day for a month, four hundred thirty-one miles, with only minor changes to my original schedule.

When I decided to meet Megg, Jim, and Nemo at Delaware Water Gap, hike with them for the day, and drive the rest of the way to meet George at the inn, I knew I would have to yellow-blaze, or skip, those miles of the trail. It disappointed me. But I could come back and mop up those miles at a later time, I reassured myself. The total number of miles walked, I decided, was less important to me than the manner in which I would walk them.

6. The idea of thru-hiking began with Earl Shaffer in 1948 when, returning from WWII, he took to the woods in Georgia and kept hiking along the entire trail until he finished some months later, in Maine. Since then, several thousand people each year plan to complete the trail in one year. Only several hundred actually do it.

5. One Foot in Two Communities

"Then we all walked together down the state line road
One foot in Ohio and the other
Walked another time zone."
Beth Lodge-Rigal, "Family History"

Highpoint, N.J. to Salisbury, Ct., 142.6 miles

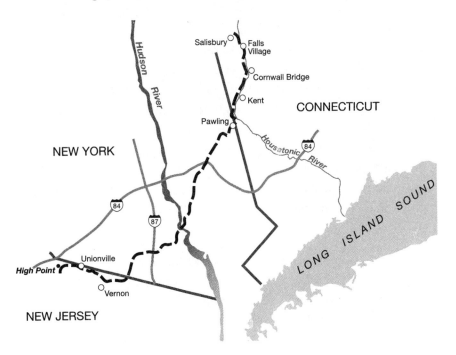

June 17, 2001, Highpoint, N.J., 0 miles

By the time Megg and Jim met me in Delaware Water Gap, a series of thunderstorms had rolled into the valley and it was too late and too wet to hike. Instead, we drove directly to Highpoint, New Jersey, to meet George at the High Point Country Inn. The inn was furnished with garage sale couches, faded overstuffed chairs, red velvet drapes, and riotous houseplants. Megg and Jim loved it for its 1970s retro look; Nemo liked the pool and backyard swing set; George and I, remembering the 1970s, appreciated its romantic nostalgia.

It was fun to be with my family again, even in the rain. I put aside my worries about yellow blazing and keeping up with the trail community, and prepared to enjoy our time together. This would be one of the last times we would be able to meet. Our next rendezvous would be in Vermont, and then we would not see each other again until the end of the summer at Katahdin.

True to his word, George had brought all my resupply boxes so I could reorganize my mail drops. Sunday morning, while he slept, I redistributed my food, maps, and clothing. Everything that no longer appealed to me was sent back home. I was determined to carry only those items that I would eat, wear, read, or listen to every day before my next mail drop. I successfully trimmed my pack weight to thirty-five pounds.[7]

George also brought me my old hiking boots to cushion my swollen feet and blackened toenails. Though not as water-repellent as my Gore-Tex lined boots, I hoped my old boots would provide more toe space and give my aching feet some respite on the long trail ahead. In addition, he surprised me with a new, more reliable cell phone. I had many miles to walk and many people to meet before I would see him again; a good cell phone and comfortable hiking boots were his way of making sure I had the essentials.

> "I am to meet Ginder in New York on Wednesday, Megg & Jim in Connecticut next week, and Happy in Massachusetts the week after that. In July, Robin & Tammy want to hike with me, and then Amy will join me in Vermont. I'm beginning to wonder if meeting people isn't more than I can handle: much as I'm looking forward to their company it makes for a lot of logistical coordinating. It is hard to be at a certain place at a certain time when all I have to rely on are my feet."

June 18, 2001, to Wildcat Shelter, 20.4 miles

The weekend was over all too soon, but when George dropped me at the trailhead Monday morning, I was comfortable enough to think about

7. For food, I eliminated everything except a box of breakfast granola bars and Tang, a bag of bagels, a 4oz. tub of cream cheese, a large Hershey bar with almonds, two cups each of instant beans & rice, couscous, and polenta, five envelopes of hot chocolate, and an assortment of complex carbohydrate and protein energy bars.

things other than logistics and trail food. The trail had begun to feel like home. As I walked, I listened to Kathleen Battle singing German Lieder, and reflected on the role of music in my life.

My father had introduced me to classical music through his extensive collection of 78-rpm records, Saturday afternoon broadcasts of the Metropolitan Opera, and the Monday evening television program of the Firestone Hour, which we always watched together. Beautiful music still calms me. It gives me hope and reminds me that others have trod my path, and survived.

On this beautiful summer day, hiking through dense green woods and up over flat rock outcroppings, I thought about other journeys I had walked, listening to this same music. When Megg was in college, recovering from a date rape that led her into depression and attempted suicide, I walked through numbness, pain, guilt, and agony, not knowing how I could help her, and devastated by my inability. Kathleen Battle's music connected my emotions to reality; walking and listening, I learned how to forgive myself for being powerless.

Walking the trail now, far away from that time of noise and confusion, I could finally put that era of our lives to rest. Megg was becoming the beautiful, resourceful woman she was meant to be. These last few weeks, meeting her on the trail, watching her reconnect with the strength she had once garnered from challenging experiences in the wilderness, I knew she was, at last, remembering a different self. I had a strong sense that she would reconnect with that self as we hiked together in the weeks to come.

I continued to ponder deep thoughts in my journal that night while I sat alone in a shelter, burning two small buckets of citronella candles provided by the trail maintainer to keep the mosquitoes away.

"Is this a spiritual journey that I am on? I heard a discussion about spirituality today on the local NPR station. One participant defined a spiritual experience as being a meaningful experience — but one that encompassed more than just the intellectual. He emphasized that one's whole being must be involved in the present moment: intellectually, emotionally, and physically.

I was definitely involved with my whole being during those years of Megg's recovery. But I would hardly call it a spiritual experience, unless spiritual presupposes a search. I was searching, then, to understand. Now my search is for wholeness, for a sacred component that uplifts my soul in the present.

Hiking certainly does encompass my whole being in the present moment. I am emotionally, intellectually, and physically totally present with each step, each sound, each thought. I scan before me, beside me, above me, behind me, monitoring every leaf-rustle, noting every turn, elevation change, rock, stream. I am aware of every muscle and organ of my body, aware of what I need to nourish myself to move on. I know when I'm tired and when I'm refreshed. I feel fully alive and alert and aware of my surroundings, my physical self, and my emotional self. I engage my brain with thoughts of the past and future but I am wholly caught up in the present. Does this make my hiking every day a spiritual experience? Is it reverently dedicated to some purpose or object? Does it, somehow, uplift my soul? I believe so."

June 19, 2001, near Fingerboard Shelter, 17 miles

I hiked hard all day to get to the William Brien Memorial Shelter by sundown so that I could meet my friend, Ginder, the following day at the Bear Mountain Bridge near her home. But try as I might, I could only manage to hike seventeen miles over several steep, rocky, hand-over-hand ascents and then descents. The day was hot and sultry and I hiked in sports bra and running shorts; mosquitoes annoyed my face and neck and left my bare skin speckled with their bites.

It wasn't much fun, even though the trail through Harriman State Park, blanketed with tall swaying grass and shaded by well-spaced pine and hemlock trees, was beautiful. I was hot. And tired. And aware of pushing myself, trying to get to a destination rather than enjoy the journey.

I did not like hiking just to get to a destination, hurrying my journey. Perhaps I should re-think this part of my adventure: pushing to reach the next trailhead for a pre-arranged meeting; straddling two communities, one foot in each. Hiking just to get somewhere was keeping my thoughts far from lofty, was fending off rare emotion from touching my spirit. I was a little off-balance.

Nearly out of water, I noted the shore of a small pond down an overgrown gravel road and decided to change my course. I hurried to the edge of the pond, set my pack down, and took off my hot boots and socks. The pond was isolated and larger than I had thought, surrounded by trees on all sides with several small islands in the center. I filled my water bottles, dropped in iodine crystals, and dipped my bandanna into the clear, cool water, wiping my face and the back of my neck. It occurred to me to dip myself into the pond, as well. Though hot and sticky, I was probably no dirtier than any other animal at the shore, I reasoned, and probably would not contaminate the water supply.

As I was about to take off my clothes, I heard the unmistakable purr of a small engine. Around the island just in front of me trolled an outboard motor with two fishermen aboard. Eyes fixed on their lines, they weren't paying any attention to me. But then again, I was not yet a mermaid lolling on a rock. So much for a nude interlude in the wild, I thought.

I sat a few more minutes, waiting for my water to become safe so that I could drink up and refill my bottles before hiking on. If I had been hiking with someone else, we could have dipped in safety. But by myself, remote and quiet as the scene was, skinny-dipping in front of two fishermen only forty-eight miles from New York City did not seem wise.

Instead, I drank some water, laced up my boots, and moved on, never acknowledging the intruders, and only slightly restored for my journey to Ithaka.

Within a mile, I reached the base of the Lemon Squeeze, a steep rock climb through a narrow passage between boulders. It wasn't as bad as I had anticipated and I squeezed through in minutes and began to look for a place to pitch my tent. I didn't have the energy to walk five more miles to the next shelter.

As I crossed a grassy knoll dotted with yellow buttercups and tender new grass, I found a thick carpet of lush green moss – the perfect spot to spread out my ground cloth and pitch my tent. My bed that night was so soft, there was no need for my Therm-A-Rest mattress, and the moon was so bright I did not need my led-light to write in my journal.

In the morning, I was surprised to discover that I had pitched my tent beneath a white-blazed tree. Luckily, no one was behind me, hiking under that bright moon; or maybe, luckily, there had been so much light from the moon that night hikers had seen me and stepped aside. In any case, I had slept all night, au natural, in comfort, unaware that I was sleeping right on the trail.

June 20, 2001, to Bear Mountain Bridge, 14 miles

I spent most of the next day drenched with sweat, and thirsty. Although I had filled my bottles at the spring-fed well at the William Brien Memorial Shelter early in the morning, by midafternoon, my bottles were empty. The stream I had looked forward to reaching was dry. To make matters worse, the trail to the summit of Bear Mountain followed a winding, exposed, asphalt road. In the hot afternoon sun, this looked like a blistered, oily river. I groaned when I realized I would have to walk it, more than six hundred feet up, parched and dizzy with exhaustion.

Then I heard a loud pick-up truck grinding its gears behind me. As it gained altitude and clattered past, a young man yelled, "Want a ride?"

Irritated and hot, I yelled back, "No, just water."

A few minutes later, the same truck came barreling back down and braked just ahead of me. The young man leaned out of his window and thrust a small bottle of cold water into my unresisting hands. I was completely taken aback. Though only thirty-four miles from New York City, this was the first person I had seen in three days. He was a knight in battered armor. Once again, trail magic had come to my rescue.

I thanked the chivalrous gentleman, opened the bottle, and raised it in salute. My Lancelot smiled, waved, and motored on.

Bear Mountain, one of the highest points on the AT in New York, is part of the Palisades Interstate Park Commission, created from land donated by the Harriman family in 1910 for development into a park. I remembered Bear Mountain from my childhood; we frequently crossed it on family vacations, but never without singing all three verses of 'The

Bear Went Over the Mountain' as loud as we could. Under my heavy pack that afternoon, climbing up to go over the mountain, I felt like that bear.

On the top of Bear Mountain there is a stone monument, a restroom with a Coke machine, and a water fountain. When I finally reached the summit, I drank as much water as I could hold, then went into the restroom and rinsed my face, arms, and clothes under the tap of a small sink. I filled my water bottles at the fountain and then, from the machine, bought an ice-cold Coke.

Never had anything tasted so right.

A ranger came up to talk to me and told me that several thru-hikers, one by the name of Flea, had hiked up earlier in the day, and were headed into the city for several days of civilization. That civilization didn't even tempt me; New York City in June is hot, crowded, noisy and expensive. It was part of the world I was glad not to straddle. But I was happy to hear that Flea was still hiking and only a little ahead of me.

The ranger also told me that the gates of the Trailside Museum and Wildlife Center, the zoo through which the AT is routed during regular business hours, would close at four-thirty. That seemed early on this long summer afternoon. I didn't want to take a chance on missing the statue of Walt Whitman sheltered within the gates. I quickly descended the mountain, and arrived at the gate just at four-thirty. It was still open but no one was there to take or sell tickets. I walked through, unannounced.

The zoo features plants native to the Bear Mountain area, and serves as a refuge for disabled animals. I passed several cages containing small animals, but wasn't interested in stopping to stare at them, imprisoned. I wanted to see the famous Walt Whitman memorial with its excerpt from the *Song of the Open Road:*

"Afoot and light-hearted I take to the open road

Healthy, free, the world before me,

The long brown path before me leading wherever I choose."

I paused to consider Whitman's words. I would agree, I thought, that the trail had lessons for me to learn, but I wasn't yet afoot light-hearted.

"I feel as though I am afoot in two different worlds, with one foot in two communities: the community of the trail where the decision to hike from point A to point B is the only weight I carry, and the community of relationships and responsibilities, built up over a lifetime, that travel along with me."

Bemused, I snapped Walt's picture and hurried on, anxious to reach the Bear Mountain Bridge to meet someone from that other lifetime: my college friend, Ginder, and her husband, Rick.

I crossed the half-mile long bridge on a narrow concrete sidewalk, inches from the five o'clock traffic whizzing past. My shins protested the cement and steel tread underfoot.

Ginder and Rick weren't on the other side to greet me, but they arrived shortly in their four-wheel-drive SUV, with two Jack Russell terriers inside. I couldn't help noting the contrast in our appearance. My friends, dressed in matching golf shirts and khaki shorts, looked like the comfortably well-off suburbanites they had become. They had crossed the bridge looking for me but hadn't recognized me, the dirty hiker poling along, squinting and sweating under a grimy pack, buffeted by the backwind of trucks.

After Rick drove us away from the traffic on the bridge, Ginder and I walked to Graymoor Friary where we planned to spend the night. Ginder, a New Yorker, was nervous about being at the Friary where "they take in men from the drunk tank for the night and dry them out," she whispered.

Reassuringly, I told her what I had read about the Graymoor Friary: that it would have rolling green lawns, manicured flower gardens, an ambiance of contemplation and reverence, cell-like rooms, showers, a hot dinner of thick stew, and monks looking very monk-like, dressed in dark robes.

We walked down a paved drive and found, instead, a four-sided cinder block structure next to a ball field, and a middle-aged man wearing a denim shirt, talking to two hikers.

"You can stay overnight," the monk told us, "but the monastery does not offer cooked meals until after the first of July. I can get you some submarine sandwiches if you're hungry, and you're welcome to the shower in the wash shed."

I was, frankly, a little embarrassed by the contrast between my expectations, the picture I had painted for Ginder, and the reality we found. Ginder, however, was just relieved that no drunks were lurking behind the bushes. We politely accepted the monk's hospitality and began to settle into the shelter for the night.

No sooner had we spread our sleeping bags on the gray cement floor, however, than the wind began to gust across the ball field, through the openings in the waist-high walls of our bunker. We quickly rolled down the curtains, pulled our sleeping bags off the floor, and scrambled to reposition our packs away from the flapping bamboo. Deafened by rain pelting the tin roof over our heads, we sat on a picnic table and watched the ball field disappear and then shimmer alive again in sudden flashes of light. Rivulets and runoff crisscrossed the once dry floor.

We congratulated ourselves on being under roof before the rain hit, and toasted our good fortune with plastic cups of wine – a pleasure from my old world that Ginder produced from her gourmet-stuffed foodbag.

June 21, 2001, to Canopus Lake, Fahnestock State Park, 12.2 miles

We were up early. It had not been a particularly comfortable night, but Ginder was a good sport and the day, though damp, was clear. We hiked out early, careful to avoid the blue-blazed trail looping around the Friary, looking for the white blazes that would take us to Fahnestock State Park and Route 301, our rendezvous point with Rick.

It was fun to have someone to talk to while I hiked, and we talked steadily all morning. Ginder told me about her love of being in the woods, her experiences in New Hampshire at camp when she was a child, her family summer home in the Adirondacks, and their new log cabin retirement home on Lake Champlain in New York State. I mostly listened, enjoying the companionship. I told her that being outside, for me, was the "essence of reality." She liked that well-turned phrase. I liked having her company.

About ten o'clock it began to rain – at first only a little drizzle, then a steady downpour. We stopped, covered our packs, and put on rain jackets. But the rain never let up and in no time our boots and bodies were soaked. Ginder plodded on, carefully picking her way across rock streams and up and down boulders. She never complained. I was impressed, and though our pace together was slower than my pace alone, we were having a good time and making good time. Ginder had put a lot of thought into her preparations and carried about twenty-five pounds of gear – mostly gourmet food for me. At lunchtime we sat in the open rain on a wet rock, ate canned chicken wrapped in tortillas, fresh fruit, and chocolate, and tried to ignore our dripping sandwiches. Ginder graciously offered a dry bed at her house for the night and ride back to the trail in the morning.

"It will be on my way," she insisted, "and you can take a real shower, wash your clothes, and be out of the wet for a few hours."

Ginder was heading to Vermont the next day for a three-day bike trip, planning to stay overnight in small country inns. She was going from the ridiculous to the sublime, I thought, envying her small inns ahead. But a dry bed tonight would be nice.

"I accept," I said with a smile.

We packed up our lunch and trod on, descending through dripping mountain laurel and cloud-darkened hemlock groves, over log bridges and across grassy swamps. By late afternoon, the rain gave way to heavy humidity and large, hungry mosquitoes. We battled on, joking about our jungle-like appearance and soggy socks, looking forward to meeting Rick and spending the night in suburban comfort.

Rick met us at the trailhead, as planned. That night I dried my soaking boots with Ginder's hair dryer, washed all my clothes, and let the steam of a long, hot, shower permeate every pore. Civilization, I admitted, did have its advantages.

June 22, 2001, to Telephone Pioneers Shelter, 23 miles

When Ginder dropped me at the trailhead, I was forlorn. It wasn't about leaving Ginder; it was about being alone again, on the wet, lonely trail, close enough to see the world I usually called home. I wondered what on earth I was doing out here in the wet woods. I should be biking inn-to-inn with Ginder, or planning for George's and my retirement, or carrying out acts of charitable kindness. Instead, I was out in the woods alone, like Medusa, an eccentric old woman with snakes in her hair. I hiked on, out-of-sorts.

In midafternoon I reached the edge of a small crystal lake and waded in to splash my face and arms with cool water. As I sat by the shore, eating a bar of chocolate and drinking in the beauty of the quiet seclusion, I wondered how a lake this close to New York City could be so isolated. There were no cottages built along its shores, no motors or voices breaking the stillness of the afternoon, no litter or signs of mankind anywhere. Only the steady lapping of waves at the shoreline and gentle movement of beavers' logs floating nearby gave any indication that the scene before me was not a still life.

Looking through my guidebook, I discovered the reason: thirty years ago this lake had been the site of a facility that processed low-level radioactive materials. Contaminated and then cleaned up by the National Park Service, it is today free of radioactivity and, though it looks and feels like unspoiled wilderness, it retains the name from its unfortunate past: Nuclear Lake.

I thought about the inter-connectedness of civilization and the importance of balance, about how imbalance, like nuclear waste, affected the entire ecological system of the secluded lake. I was grateful for that seclusion but wondered at the cost to the environment. I thought there must be a better way to provide seclusion in a natural setting, a way not based on destruction. That night, alone in a shelter I wrote:

"How do I solve my dilemma of balance? Of staying connected to the world of people and the world of wilderness?

These woods, in summer particularly, are my spiritual home, a place where I can be completely centered and focused, all encompassed and present. I feel at peace here, sitting by a lake, crossing hot flat rocks strewn with sun-drenched pine needles, surrounded by bird song and insect hum and woodpeckers.

But I want my real-life family and friends, too. I miss them terribly. I miss civilization. I miss being able to bathe when I'm sweaty and dirty; being able to use a clean bathroom instead of a privy; being able to comfort and be comforted. I miss being held.

Virginia Woolf instructed me long ago to create a 'room of my own,' a place she meant for writing but a place I mean for being – just for me. In a sense, this hike, these woods, are that room of my own, and I love it. But I love the other rooms in my life, too.

I want both worlds, both rooms.

Is achieving balance on the trail any different than achieving balance anywhere else? Does finding time and space for one's self require being disconnected from the time and space of others? Is this just my dilemma or is this the quandary of all women?"

Unable to do anything but pose the questions, I fell asleep listening to wind in the trees.

June 23, 2001, to Ten Mile River Lean-to, 15 miles

The day began overcast and windy. Storms coming in, I thought as I gathered my gear, ate a quick granola bar, and started out, with a stiff breeze in my face and trees swaying overhead. In less than two hours, I came upon a railroad track in a clearing. Next to the track, just ahead, I was surprised to see a wooden bench.

Crossing the track, I sat down on the bench, unwrapped a granola bar, and began to eat. A long slow whistle announced the approach of a train from the southeast. Within seconds, a train pulling several passenger cars came hissing and braking out of the morning, preparing to stop in front of my bench. I was sitting at the only train station on the AT. The Metro-North Commuter train into Grand Central Station was stopping for me. I could go into New York City for nine dollars and be home by midnight.

But I didn't really want to go home. Never had it been so clear. My homesick musings of the day before vanished in the split second it took for me to wave the engineer on. I wanted to hike. But how startling to see the denouement of my homesickness present itself with such clarity in the early morning mist.

Back on the trail, the wind soon turned to rain, then thunderstorms. By noon I was soaked. I crossed a road and a woman passing by in her station wagon stopped, rolled down her window and shouted, "I'd offer you a ride, but there's a shelter nearby, about half a mile."

I waved and sloshed on up the muddy trail. I hoped my hiking poles would not attract lightning. Just as I reached the shelter and swung my pack inside, the rain began to let up. Intending to settle in for lunch and wait for the rain to stop altogether, I took off my boots and socks. My old boots were definitely not waterproof. In fact, I poured the water from them as though from a pitcher. My socks were equally wet and the skin on my feet had withered and turned bluish- white. My feet felt clammy and looked dead. Fortunately I had a film canister full of rubbing alcohol and another of baby powder. I set to work, rubbing my toes and massaging my soles and heels back to life.

I still had one pair of dry socks in my pack and debated about whether I should put them on now and hang the wet ones on my pack to dry, or hike all afternoon in wrung-out-but-still-wet socks and save the dry ones for later, when I stopped for the night. The sun came out briefly, so I decided to take a chance and changed my socks. With a bagel and cheese sandwich, I stretched out on the dirty floor of the shelter to read the trail register, looking to see if I knew any of the hikers ahead of me.

The register reported that indeed, there were other hikers ahead of me, but no one I recognized. I guessed most of the ones I knew had made a detour into the city for the weekend and would catch up in a few days.

Ready to go again, I pulled on my pack, picked up my poles, and set out for the Ten Mile River Lean-to across the New York state line near Kent, Connecticut, hometown of the summer camp I attended as a child.

No sooner did I begin to hike, however, than the sun dipped back behind a cloud, the wind picked up and another thunderstorm rolled in.

This time there was no shelter to duck into. I was caught, and drenched within minutes. So much for hanging out my socks to dry on my pack, I grumbled and sloshed on, wet leaves blowing in my face, rain and mud slipping into my boots. Crossing another road, I spotted a house with a small side porch sheltering the doorway. I ran to the porch, dripping, rang the doorbell, and waited through several loud crashes and slashes of thunder and lightning. When it was quieter, I peered through the glass-paned porch window into a dry, old-fashioned kitchen and knocked, loudly. Finally, a thin, middle-aged man appeared.

"Do you mind if I wait out the storm on your porch?" I asked.

"Not at all," he answered in a clipped British accent. "I was upstairs working on my computer and didn't hear you over the storm. Nasty weather, isn't it? Would you like a glass of water?"

I accepted the water, longing for an invitation into his dry kitchen. I could see myself sitting at the table, eating a sugar cookie, perhaps sipping a cup of tea, and talking with him about my hike in England, my childhood in Connecticut, and my present hike on the AT. Instead, my host closed the door, went to fetch me some water, and came back to hand it to me through the partial opening. Then he disappeared, back to his computer, I surmised.

A few minutes later, a car drove into the driveway and parked. Quickly, its driver, a middle aged woman, stuck out an umbrella, pushed it open, and ran up to the porch were I was standing.

"Oh, hello," she greeted me perfunctorily, in matching British inflection.

I moved aside to let her pass.

"I'm just... "

She didn't wait for me to finish but instead, opened the door, closed her umbrella, and shook off the rain – all over me. When she disappeared, I couldn't help being surprised. Granted, I was already wet and probably looked wetter, in my glistening and dripping rain parka and pants, carrying an equally dripping rain-covered pack. But what had happened to the British sense of hospitality I had found again and again on my hike across England? And in Connecticut, I was a native daughter. Where was my welcome home? I seem to have come a long way from my suburban Connecticut roots, I thought ruefully. But am I really the wet dog they take me for?

I decided to paw on through the rain. Wet dog or not, I suddenly felt unwelcome on that porch. Disgruntled, I hiked on.

Four miles later, I reached the Ten Mile River Lean-to, a newly built wooden structure on the edge of an open meadow. After the gloom and wet of dripping woods, the lean-to was bright and dry. In one corner, a ridge runner named Lump had set up camp and was busy priming a stove to cook his evening meal.

Glad to have some company, I was delighted to be in a dry shelter with its prospect of deer and other wildlife appearing across the meadow at dusk and early morning. I changed into my only dry clothes, the long underwear kept just for sleeping, and chatted with Lump while we cooked and settled in for the night.

The design of the lean-to was a little disconcerting; the floorboards stopped three feet from the front edge, creating a four-foot drop-off between my sleeping bag and the exit of the shelter. Lump explained that having this space between the floor and the front edge of the shelter discouraged porcupines and skunks from nocturnal visits. I wondered if it would discourage my need for a nocturnal visit to the woods to pee. I didn't want to fall through that gap in the middle of the night.

In the morning, I awoke to a meadow misted with dew and early morning fog, but no deer or other wildlife. Nocturnal visitors had been absent, as well, and I had managed to pee without falling through the floor.

June 24, 2001, to Silver Lake Campsite, 19 miles

Even though it was Sunday, Lump told me the outfitter in Kent would be open for business later in the morning. I decided to stop there and try to replace my wet socks and gaiters and get some advice about my leaking boots before hiking on.

Kent, on a sleepy summer Sunday morning, seemed bustling and lively to my blinkered trail eyes. The main street was lined with small cafés, quaint village shops, upscale restaurants, and specialty grocery stores. I strolled down the street, looking for breakfast. The Villager Restaurant was just what I had in mind. It reminded me of those Sunday mornings when my parents picked me up from camp to feast on French toast and maple syrup, bacon, orange juice, and fresh fruit. Later when George and I visited Amy at her college in New London, we found similar fare in equally prepossessing places.

I sat at a corner table, plugged my cell phone into a nearby outlet to charge the battery, and watched the ebb and flow of local diners, casual in their weekend attire. George and Amy would feel right at home here.

It occurred to me that I missed my family most when I found myself in places I knew they would enjoy. Sleeping on the floor of a three-sided hut, struggling up and down mountains with a heavy pack, and eating re-hydrated food in the rain reminded George of his army training; he avoided that and I never missed him then. But sitting in a quaint café, surrounded by people we might know, savoring a hearty brunch and gourmet coffee, would appeal to him. That's when I missed him most.

I considered a new remedy for homesickness: I would think of my family when I was swatting mosquitoes and eating dirt, and avoid think-ing of them in places like this. Simple, I thought, the trail is making me simple. But I did miss my family when I knew they would enjoy the good stuff. This café was some of the good stuff.

Absorbed in my coffee and ruminations, I failed to notice two men, obviously hikers, at a nearby table preparing to leave. As they passed my table, one stopped and greeted me:

"We've met before… at the Dahlgren Campground in Maryland. I'm Jed. I met you with Heckle and Jekyll and that pharmacist from Texas."

I did remember the campground – the only one on the trail with a free hot shower – and I also remembered Heckle, Jekyll, and Texphar because I had met them several times after that in Pennsylvania. But I couldn't place Jed until he reminded me that he was from Indiana and that this was his second thru-hike. Ah yes. The muscular young guy who wanted me to ditch my watercolors, I remembered.

Jed introduced me to his friend, ET, a tall, angular man with a short white beard, about my age. ET told me he was from Virginia and was fin-ishing the thru-hike he had started last summer. He and Jed had been hiking together for several weeks and had spent last night in town.

I introduced myself as Gotta Hike! and chatted with them briefly while I waited for my check. I told ET my flip-flop thru-hike would go back to Virginia in the fall to finish the trail by late October.

"But first," I said, "I'm on my way to the outfitter to replace my socks and gaiters, and see if he can shore up my old boots. They have a chronic seepage problem."

After they left, a preacher from Virginia came over to my table. "I couldn't help overhearing your conversation," he said. "I've walked some of the AT myself. I'm up here with my church to do some missionary work. When you get back to Virginia, give me a call. Maybe I can be of some service to you there. I'm always interested in hikers and their stories, and our church has a mission to help them however we can."

He gave me his card. I thanked him, and headed down the street to the outfitter.

It was the most social interaction I had had since I said goodbye to Ginder.

I felt a little dizzy from the townspeople swirling around me, the caffeine in the expensive coffee beans, and the intimacy of the brief conversations in the café. It felt as though I had metamorphosed in the space of a few hours. Just yesterday I was mistaken for a wet dog; this morning I was a credible human being with a story to tell. It was a curious feeling to suddenly be recognized and remembered by someone I had forgotten. Becoming visible once again, I felt reborn.

When I reached the outfitter, he was ready for my business and supplied me with some new thick, dry Smartsocks, polypropylene and Spandex blend liner socks, a pair of low gaiters to keep my new socks free of rocks, dirt, and ticks, and some half-inch thick Superfeet insoles to line my stiff, leaky boots and cushion my tired, swollen feet. I also bought some environmentally friendly, Deet-less insect repellent and considered my town visit complete. I was ready to hike.

With dry pampered feet, warm full belly, and newly re-established visibility to think about, I hiked out of town to continue north. I was a bit uncertain of the direction because the map for this section of the trail was in my next mail drop. However, I did have the trail guide and knew I would soon be climbing. To double-check my bearings, however, I knocked on the door of a little blue house whose front yard was dotted with scraggly flowers and children's toys. The man that came to the door was friendly and confirmed my route to the AT, pointing to the place where I would pick it up. Following his directions, I soon reached the trailhead and began to climb.

Ascending Caleb's Peak I could see the Housatonic River below, prettier and more peaceful than the Housatonic River that I had known growing up on Long Island Sound, its estuary. Power and manufacturing plants belching smoke and chemicals into that river's flow had polluted the water; speedboats and yachts had disturbed its silence.

This Housatonic River didn't look or sound like that river at all. This Housatonic River, winding its way from the west side of the mountains, across farmlands and meadows, was bucolic and quiet. This Housatonic was the river of my adulthood, pastoral and healthy. It was, I thought, separated from the Housatonic of my turbulent and noisy childhood by as many years as miles. We had both come a long way since then.

I descended from the St. Johns Ledges, a five hundred-foot drop through a steep granite cliff via a well-engineered staircase built by a trail crew from New Hampshire. At midafternoon I stopped by the side of the river for a snack and watched a fisherman across the cove cast his line into the water.

When the trail turned off the dirt road to ascend Silver Hill, I ran into ET and Jed again. They had accepted a ride into town and back and were sitting on the hillside eating big sandwiches. The person who gave them the ride had also given them some home-brewed wine, which they were saving for the cocktail hour at camp. We talked for a few minutes and then hiked up the hill together. I was planning to stop at the Silver Hill Campsite just below the summit; I didn't need to be in Salisbury until Tuesday and was in no hurry to hike any farther. By the time we reached the side trail to the campsite, they had decided to join me.

Silver Hill boasts a wooden deck, swing, several picnic tables, and a magnificent view overlooking the valleys and villages below. We each found a level spot under the pines, pitched our tents, and met again on the deck for drinks and hors d'oeuvres to welcome the evening. Jed poured a little home brew into each of our water bottles. It was strong and sour, but warming. I donated some cheese and ET found some crackers. We each cooked our dinners and sat in the gathering dusk, laughing and telling stories until a slight, bright crescent moon gradually appeared in the sky.

> "I'm glad ET and Jed decided to stay. They are fun. It is so nice to have someone to laugh and joke with at the end of the day. Having company makes a big difference."

June 25, 2001, to Falls Village, Ct., 15 miles

I was up, packed and ready to go before Jed and ET had finished their breakfast. We had agreed to hike to Salisbury together since we all had mail drops waiting for us at the post office. I had arranged to meet Megg and Jim and Nemo in Salisbury, as well; they were planning to hike with me for a few days.

Feeling a little antsy, I sat on the swing and watched the sun begin to burn off the mist in the valley below. I was unaccustomed to waiting for anyone else in the morning and eager to start hiking. We finally set out about eight o'clock at a pace just a little faster than my usual two-plus miles per hour.

"We're gonna hike slow for awhile," ET assured me. "We've been hiking with a guy whose been pushin' and pushin' us. It's no fun. We finally lost him in Kent, but we'll have to hike real slow to keep behind him so's he'll move on without us. He was really beginnin' to get on my nerves."

Jed was in no hurry, either. This was his second thru-hike and hiking fast was not as important, this time.

"Initially, I was planning to do the photographs for a book," he said. "A professor contacted me last year to see if I would be interested in shooting his thru-hike for the book he planned to write. I thought about it and decided, 'why not?' But then, after I'd quit my job and made the commitment to hike, his plans fell through. I decided to go ahead anyway."

"I guess that explains all that extra stuff I see strapped to your pack," I replied, noting the black tripod, cameras and assortment of lenses he carried.

"Yep. At least fifteen extra pounds in camera gear, no telling how much in film."

The three of us hiked north together in the early morning sunlight, through dark green hemlock groves, across dirt roads and over clear-running brooks. As I hopped from one stone to the next crossing Guinea Brook, swatting at the mosquitoes swarming and unmercifully biting my face and neck, Jed sprinted on ahead, threw down his pack and scrambled up the muddy slope.

"Sit down right where you are," he commanded. "Don't move!"

"Why?" I wondered, casting about for snakes and finding a suitable rock on which to perch, instead. And then, looking up, I knew.

Just ahead, over the crest of the hill looming dark in front of me, the sun was streaking through the hemlocks, promising brilliant light. I sat motionless for seconds that seemed like hours, while Jed composed his shots, adjusted his lenses, rearranged his vantage point, and clicked his shutters.

The longer I sat, the easier it became to ignore the insects swirling around me. The scene was magical, worthy of Tolkien. I sat stunned and silent, grateful to Jed for making me stop, mosquito-bothered and rushing, to sit and look at the beauty of the light before me.

Not only is he an accomplished hiker, I thought, he is an artist as well. What an interesting young man.

We hiked on. Jed pulled ahead and I found myself hiking with ET. Not to be outshone, ET told me a little about himself. Married, with a daughter and son a little older than Amy and Megg, he had recently retired from teaching and coaching, in a rural school system in southwestern Virginia. After hiking regularly for years in Virginia and North Carolina, he finally, last year, began a thru-hike in Georgia, hiking as far as Pine Grove Furnace, Pennsylvania.

When he hiked behind me, I wasn't always able to understand ET's drawl; when he hiked ahead of me, I lost most of what he had to say. But ET sure could hike. His long legs seemed to start at his ears, and each of his strides was longer than mine by half. I was surprised that I was able to keep up with him, "slow" as he claimed his pace to be.

ET talked most of the way, telling stories about the South and stopping, occasionally, to remark on the wildflowers or plant life at our feet. He was tickled to be hiking and pleased to have someone with whom to share his observations. The miles passed quickly, and about lunchtime we reached a rocky outcrop called Hang-Glider View, overlooking Bear Mountain and Mt. Everett.

Sprawled on the rocks, Jed was waiting for us. I pulled out my food and began to fix my lunch, but Jed was ready to move on. Hastily, I stowed my food back in my pack, stuffed some snacks in the pockets of my shorts, and, surprising myself, moved on with him.

Jed was full of stories about his military days and life at boot camp. He and ET joked about their escapades in college, ET as a three-sport athlete, Jed as a renegade pre-law student looking for adventure. They were curious about me hiking the trail by myself, and I told them I was meeting my daughters, Amy and Megg, and various friends along the way and that my husband, George, was managing my food drops and life at home while I was gone.

"You'll have a chance to meet Megg in Salisbury," I said. "She and her husband, Jim, and twenty-month-old son, Nemo, are planning to meet me there and hike with me for a few days. And Amy will be meeting me in Vermont in a couple of weeks. She's a lawyer and hasn't taken much time off lately."

We hiked on, me listening, Jed talking, ET contributing to the easy flow of conversation. By six o'clock we had reached a road crossing, not far from the Hotchkiss School where I had spent several teenaged summers.

"Only two more miles to Falls Village," Jed said. "When I was here before, I stopped there for hamburgers and beer! Ice cold beer!" He and ET quickened their steps.

I struggled to keep up. For me, it was two hours past my late afternoon stopping time, four hours past a lunch that had been snacks instead of real food. I was tired, hot, and beginning to feel grouchy. I didn't want to walk two more miles on a road. I began to fantasize about hot dogs and cold water and eventually relaxed, resigned to turning the responsibility of decision-making to someone else.

Falls Village is a sleepy New England town of a bygone era. The old white-frame inn at the village center is now a pizza restaurant with a full menu. Instead of a train depot, there is now a liquor store/garage, and an exhibit featuring a rebuilt caboose that fascinated ET.

We set our packs on the front porch of the old inn and went inside to use the washroom. I was embarrassed to be so grimy; I hadn't washed or combed my hair in days and my clothes smelled of sweat. I needn't have worried. Though the patrons at the bar were no cleaner than ET, Jed, and I, we were the only hikers in the after-work crowd.

I ordered a large sandwich, French fries and a liter of iced cold Coke.

"I'm surprised you drink Coke," Jed said.

"Why? It's wonderful!" I replied, slurping. "Nothing like a cold Coke on a hot day, especially after a long hike. It's just what I need."

What I really needed was the caffeine.[8] But I didn't say that to Jed. I simply added, "I like the way it tastes!" and left it at that.

After dinner we reluctantly pulled our packs off the front porch, tightened them onto our shoulders, and hiked out, back the way we had come, to the iron bridge overlooking a power plant and a 1850s-era canal. We crossed my river, the Housatonic, for the last time and headed north through a small park. Dusk was turning to dark and ET and I were tempted to pitch our tents in the little park. However, Jed saw a "NO CAMPING" sign nailed to a tree and convinced us that we wouldn't want to move at midnight when the local patrol discovered our tents.

We trudged on, walked past a spring, and began to ascend Prospect Mountain. We hadn't climbed far when we crossed a meadow of long grass and tall wildflowers overlooking Canaan Mountain and the Housatonic valley.

"This is as good a spot as we'll find," ET declared. "I'm pitchin' here though it's likely to be wet as all get-out in the mornin'."

"I'll join you," I replied and began pulling stuff out of my pack.

Jed continued up the slope to a small grove of trees, "within whistlin' distance," he said.

---

8. Caffeine releases the free fatty acids stored in muscles for use as glucose, and releases the hormones epinephrine and norepinephrine that increase blood sugar and enhance muscle strength.

"ET's tent is next to mine. He snores, but makes me feel safe – so – I'll put plugs in my ears. I don't know what the next few weeks will be like – meeting Megg tomorrow and Happy this weekend. I may hike with ET when Jed leaves to hike ahead in Vermont. It's all very fluid. I like hiking with these two. They're interesting and funny and good company.

There's a beautiful crescent moon over the field tonight. The meadow is crowded with crickets and insects and I'm enveloped in tall grass and wildflowers. The view in the morning will be magnificent! I think I'll sleep well tonight."

June 26, 2001, to Salisbury, Ct., 7 miles

The tall grass was wet and shining in the morning sunlight. When I couldn't find any of my breakfast food, I made do with a Hershey bar and some dried apples.

After I ate, ET joined me for breakfast, sitting on my pack.

"Did you hear that buck last night?" he asked. "I woke up to some sniffin' and pawin' around my head. Couldn't figure out what it was, at first. I hollered and shook my poles at him. Guess I scared him 'cause he didn't come back once I run him off."

"Maybe that's who ate my breakfast," I replied, laughing at the picture of skinny old ET chasing off a deer in the middle of the night.

In due time, ET packed up his gear and we joined Jed for the seven-mile trek into Salisbury, skirting fields heavy with hay and darting under trees ripe with dark purple mulberries. The morning shone with promise. I was eager to retrieve my mail drop and organize it before meeting Megg and Jim and Nemo in the early afternoon. Megg had made reservations for us at a nearby inn and we planned to hike from the inn to Lee, Massachusetts, where I would meet my friend and former colleague, Happy, on Saturday.

Walking down the road behind ET and Jed, passing by old-fashioned gardens, barns converted into guesthouses, and lawns surrounded by white picket fences, I felt a tug of nostalgia for my New England roots. But this wasn't the New England of my childhood; it was, rather, the

New England of storybooks. It was clean, prosperous, and well balanced, like a painting. There was no mud in these pastures.

In the center of town Jed knew right where to go for groceries and lunch: LaBonne's Epicure Market. Typical of the genre, LaBonne's shelves overflowed with expensive natural foods, organic vegetables, imported biscuits, cheese, wine, choice meats and mouthwatering in-store baked goods. I wandered the aisles, stepping out of the way of serious shoppers with grocery carts and wicker baskets. I was bewildered by the array before me. Finally, from the deli counter, I chose melted Swiss cheese and asparagus on a multi-grained croissant with a side order of fruit salad and a tall glass of lemonade.

To my surprise, I had packages from two college friends, George, and myself (my Bounce Box) plus some assorted letters and postcards. I was overwhelmed as I staggered back to the green behind the post office to sort through all the goodies.

I also wanted to dry my wet gear. Several other hikers joined me with the same idea and we littered the fence, stone wall and lawn adjacent to the brick sidewalk connecting the shops and village services. I was aware of foot traffic along the sidewalk, but no one stopped to talk, and I concentrated on eliminating and re-packaging my supplies.

When I finished repacking my gear and replenishing my food bag, I sat under a tree, back against the stone wall, to write notes to my friends for my windfall. CARE packages had become a double-edged sword, I realized, looking that gift horse right in the mouth. I appreciated the thought that went into my friends' food and music selections, but I had found carrying the extra weight a real burden. In the end, I stashed the books, music and chocolates into my Bounce Box and sent everything else home.

ET and Jed were engaged in similar maneuvers. In addition, Jed was eager to look at some slides he had received from his photo studio, and ET wanted to visit the outfitter across the street. Although I expected Megg and Jim to arrive at any moment and was ready to be on my way, ET and Jed didn't seem to be in any hurry to leave.

The afternoon blazed on. At two-thirty when Megg and Jim still had not arrived, I began to pace around the town. I visited the drug store, card shop, ice cream shop, and the outfitter. By three-thirty I began to worry. I called Megg on her cell phone but she was out of range. In half an hour, I tried again. This time, we were connected.

Megg was driving, and described her location, which sounded lost to me. Jed and I went back to the card shop, bought an automobile map and tried to pinpoint the route Megg might be on. Indeed, she had turned in the opposite direction in Danbury and was headed due east and quite a bit south of our meeting point in Salisbury. It would take them another two hours to arrive.

I was relieved to know where they were and certainly familiar with turning in the opposite direction and losing the way, but I was also dismayed by their delay. With some disquiet, I began to re-calculate our itinerary for the week so that we could hike reasonably and still reach Lee, Massachusetts, by Saturday.

Seeing my perturbation, Jed decided that imported beer on the village green would be a good way to pass the time. He bought a six-pack at LaBonne's and the three of us sat on the steps of the post office sipping water bottles full of brew. I knew he and ET were trying to make me feel better, and I tried to be a good sport, but I was weary with waiting.

By the time Megg and Jim arrived, downtown Salisbury was deserted and we were the only three left on the village green. It was dinnertime. Megg drove ET and Jed back to the trailhead while Nemo and I played run and catch-me. Jim made a beeline to LaBonne's for the last deli sandwich before the store closed. Everyone was tired.

When Megg returned from the trailhead, we drove to the inn where we had reservations for the night. The inn was a luxurious contrast to my usual outdoor arrangements. In addition to nostalgic New England ambiance, my room had its own pristine bathroom and state-of-the-art modern plumbing. I took a long, elaborate shower, washing my clothes in the oversized porcelain vanity, and then spoiled the tidiness of my four-poster bed by stringing a clothesline and hanging my wet clothes to dry overnight.

"This inn certainly is a different world from the trail. It's still amazing to me that these two worlds – the world of ease and privilege and the world of discomfort and hardship – can exist within miles of each other. I'm glad to have the respite from the trail, but after today's wait and worry I'm beginning to appreciate what the difficulty of joining my two worlds – the world of home and the world of trail – is for everyone. The pace in each world is very different. These little towns and trailheads are hard to find – and hanging around all day waiting to be found is a lot harder for me than it used to be. I've grown accustomed to moving at a certain pace, in my own rhythm. Even adjusting to another thru-hiker's pace is difficult. Trying to accommodate to the pace of the outside world and also meet the exigencies of the trail is a bigger challenge than I thought it would be.

I've really been looking forward to hiking with Megg and Jim and Nemo – and I want them to enjoy it – but the trail is hard – it's not just a walk in the woods.

After this week with Megg and the week hiking with Amy in Vermont, I probably won't meet or hike with anyone else from home. This might be a good thing... much as I'll miss their company."

I was beginning to understand that if I were going to realize my dream of hiking the whole trail, I would have to keep both feet on the path in just one community, the community of the trail.

6. Hiking With Family

South Egremont, Ct. to Lee, Mass., 37.1 miles

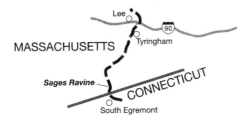

June 27, 2001, to Mt. Wilcox North Lean-to, 17.1 miles

It seemed strange to wake up in a bed, with sunlight streaming through a window and dust motes dancing in the air. Although it was early, Megg, Jim, and Nemo were already up. I found them in the parking lot trying to reorganize their gear, food strewn at their feet.

"I had planned to do all this yesterday," Megg said. "I pictured us arriving in time for a hike and a swim before dark, and then getting your help with a final pack check before starting out this morning. As it is, I don't think we'll ever be ready. There's just too much stuff."

"Let's see if we can rearrange some of it," I tried. "Why don't you put Nemo's stuff in his pack where you can reach it easily, and your things in the other pack… You probably won't need this," I said, tossing a packet of biodegradable toilet paper back in the trunk. Noting the look of disbelief on Jim's face, I had a brief flashback to Jed telling me to ditch my watercolors. Too late, I realized my gaffe and put the packet back, sorry that I had been so tactless.

Recalling my first few weeks on the trail, I could appreciate the dilemma before them: Jim had never camped overnight in the woods and, though he wanted to help, did not have much practical advice to offer. He was worried about comfort and about having enough food; his tendency, understandably, was to over-pack.

Megg, on the other hand, had had many backcountry experiences, but never with the added responsibility of caring for a toddler, much less a husband who was uneasy about being in the woods. Trying to anticipate her family's disparate needs for four days, and eliminate non-essentials was a daunting task. I could see why she might feel perplexed and overwhelmed.

My agenda was to get packed and be off. I felt responsible for reaching the shelter before sundown; the itinerary we had agreed on the night before did not allow for too much time reorganizing packs in the parking lot. Impatient to start hiking before the morning slipped away and the sun grew too hot, I expected our pace to be slow.

Finally, after many pack revisions, we were ready to hike. We drove to the trailhead near South Egremont to leave the car until Saturday. Jim, in a jaunty white Stetson, settled Nemo on Megg's back, hoisted his own unwieldy pack, and led the way.

It was a beautiful day to hike: clear, sunny, slight breeze, no threat of rain. I thought the first mile of level terrain and log walking over low, wet swamp would be a good introduction to the more demanding, but still moderate climbs ahead. Megg and Jim were in good spirits; Nemo loved sitting in his seat, humming and sipping water from a tube attached to the water bladder in his pack. This will be all right, I sighed, thinking that they would have their trail legs in no time.

Our first ascent was a gradual climb of five hundred feet in one mile to the ridge around the top of Blue Hill. We climbed slowly, stopping to rest several times, drinking lots of water, feeding Nemo dry cereal, and singing silly nursery songs to keep him entertained. The path was smooth and even, but ascended steadily. Jim was carrying an old, external frame pack that had been fitted to Megg when she was in college. Unaccustomed to the weight on his shoulders, he tried several times to adjust the straps so that the weight would ride on his hips. With sleeping bag, mat, tent, small stove, water, and the extra food and clothing, he carried about forty pounds. Megg's load, with sleeping bag, mat, diapers, snacks, water bladder, food, clothes, and Nemo – was about thirty-five constantly-shifting pounds.

After our first ascent, Jim decided to trade loads with Megg. Nemo didn't mind; he was content on the back of either parent and rode quite happily up and over the soggy ground, noticing the woods, trees, sunlight, rocks, and bugs around him. But it was a long, slow walk for his dad in gathering heat and steady sunshine.

We reached the blue-blazed trail to Benedict Pond about lunchtime and walked the half-mile loop to some picnic tables sheltered in a grove of tall, cool pine trees. A sandy beach adjacent to the grove was noisy and crowded with children just released from school for their summer vacation. We had not yet escaped civilization.

Jim and Megg couldn't wait to plunge into the icy water and eagerly took Nemo to the beach for a swim. I was cool enough under the pines and sat at a picnic table to sketch and catch up on my journal. I missed the quiet of the woods and needed some time to be still.

Reflecting on the long wait yesterday and the unexpected delays today, I could feel myself becoming uneasy about the next few days.

> "Putting this all in perspective, lugging a forty-pound pack up and down mountains with your mother-in-law, in the heat of the noonday sun, swatting bugs and eating trail food, is probably not the ideal summer vacation."

We stayed in the pine grove for a while, alternately swimming, eating, and watching Nemo run through the pine needles and climb on the benches. He liked best to grab my trekking poles and hike stiff-legged across the dirt. Collapsed to their shortest length, the poles were just a bit taller than the top of his head and made good spears for the rocks and twigs at his feet.

"He has the makings of a hiker, Jim," I said, nodding in Nemo's direction.

Jim gave me a wry smile, but said nothing.

Knowing that the last miles of the day often seemed to be the hardest, and that we were not yet halfway, I began to gather my gear to resume hiking. If we stayed in the grove much longer, I worried, we might not make our destination before dark. My general rule of thumb was to hike the steepest, longest miles before lunch, and save the easier, level or descending terrain for that after-lunch lull. Today we had stopped a little too soon.

After lunch, our packs seemed even heavier, the miles longer. Luckily, we had only two fairly small ascents in the three miles ahead of us. We stopped several times to rest. When we reached Mt. Wilcox South Lean-to, we took the blue-blaze trail to the shelter to see if we could camp overnight. Megg lowered Nemo's pack to the wood-planked floor and pulled out the kickstand.

Nemo woke up from his nap, spotted a broom with a broken handle in the corner, and ran over to claim it for his own. For the next ten minutes he busily swept the mouse droppings across the floor, then climbed down to tackle the hard packed dirt in front of the shelter.

I could see that Jim was hungry, tired, and disappointed in the shelter. Perched on rocky ground, in the middle of the woods, there were no clear, level areas for tents; we had no choice but to push on to the Mt. Wilcox North Lean-to, one and a half miles farther along the trail. To Jim, an artist whose entire life had been spent in the city, this was not good news. We trod on.

To his great credit, Jim revived when, through the woods just over a small rise, we came to a secluded beaver pond, magnificent in the slanting rays of the afternoon sun. It was a glass-smooth pool rimmed with stacks of branches and sticks, punctuated by tooth-sharpened tree stumps. We stopped at water's edge, marveling at this masterpiece of engineering. Jim whipped out his Polaroid to capture the desolation of the forest, the starkness of the trees still standing, the quiet, remote beauty only to be found in the backcountry.

I breathed a sigh of relief and, happily, we reached Mt. Wilcox North Lean-to a short time later. Two hikers had already settled in for the night: a section hiker going south and a troubadour named Tacoma heading north on his second AT thru-hike.

Tacoma was charmed and bashful with Nemo: when Nemo found the shelter broom and began to tidy the floor, Tacoma quietly cheered him on, not seeming to mind the intrusion; when Tacoma lit his stove, Nemo, watching carefully, started to sing "happy birday happy birday happy birday happy birday," Nemo language for "flame"; when Tacoma reached for his guitar and strummed another chorus, Nemo laughed and sang along with him.

I watched them both, fascinated. As a professor of early childhood education, I was impressed; as a grandmother, I was enchanted.

Megg, Jim, and I set up our tents beside a stream near the shelter and Jim gathered sticks for a campfire. The tents, particularly the zippers, intrigued Nemo. He ran from one to the other, zipping the flaps up, then down, then up again, captivated by the sound and his magical powers.

Finally all was quiet. Under the trees we could just see the stars and waxing moon above. The night sounds were calming. I hoped everyone would sleep well and be ready to hike again in the morning. *"In beauty will I possess again,"* I murmured before falling asleep. *"In beauty may we walk."*

June 28, 2001, to Tyringham Woods, 7 miles

We awoke to beautiful sunshine, low humidity, and a cool breeze riffling the leaves above our tents. I was energized and full of plans. This would be a perfect day to hike, I thought, with only thirteen miles to Upper Goose Pond. We could easily do that today – a level walk, mild climb, lunch at the top, and then only four and a half miles of fairly level terrain to the cabin.

I knew Megg and Jim would like the cabin. It was on a glacial pond and had a caretaker, indoor bunks with mattresses, a canoe for hikers to use, and swimming. We would be able to spend all the next day taking a backcountry mountain break before hiking out on Saturday morning. It would be the perfect way for Megg and Jim to finish their hike, I thought. And Nemo would love the canoe.

I sprang out of my tent, eagerly anticipating the day ahead. Even the weather was cooperative. As I began to roll up my sleeping mat and stuff it into its sack I looked over to the other tent and could see Nemo's head poking up the underside of their roof.

"How about some breakfast," I called.

Nemo came bounding out of his tent and over to sit with me on a log next to the fire pit. We shared a granola bar and traced twig tracks in the cold ashes at our feet. Megg soon joined us.

"How was your night?" I asked. "Isn't this a beautiful day?" I barreled on without pausing. "I think we can get to Upper Goose Pond cabin this

afternoon and have all day tomorrow to swim, canoe, hang out – look!"
I said, pointing enthusiastically to the map on my knees. "What do you
think?"

"Looks great," Megg agreed, glancing over at the map. "But I'm not
sure Jim will want to go that far today. He didn't sleep at all last night.
He's pretty tired."

"Oh," I replied, deflated by her tone. "Well, okay. We can do it in two
days, half today and half tomorrow, and still have some time to swim and
hang out at the cabin tomorrow afternoon."

I began to reconnoiter. Clearly, in my enthusiasm for the day, I had
forgotten how hard the first few days of a hike could be and had seriously overestimated Jim's endurance. Megg was more realistic, having had
the benefit of his uncensored comments over a long sleepless night. We
continued our breakfast preparations.

"Does Jim want to go back today?" I finally asked, anxiously.

"Well, he really can't," Megg replied. "He doesn't want to hike back to
the car from here… even if he could find the car… I most certainly don't
want to go back. I've been looking forward to this hike all summer… He
knows how important it is to me. He'll just have to go on with us.
Besides, 'It's a mark of leadership…'"

"To adjust," we both said together, chuckling at the motto of Megg's
camp director during her teen-aged adventure years.

"Or," she continued, "as my mother would say: 'When the going gets
tough, the tough get going.'"

I agreed, ruefully. "We'll go slower… and stop sooner," I said. "It will
be okay," I said, hoping it would be.

"Are you sure, Mom? I don't want to slow you down. I know you usually hike a lot more miles in a day than this."

"I'm sure. Hiking's hard – especially at first. We'll try to make it more
fun for him – though it's probably not going to get easier." It was the best
I could offer.

We talked a bit longer, played with Nemo, and began to break camp.
Dismayed that it was so unpleasant for Jim, I anticipated a
challenging day.

The first twenty minutes of the day's hike are often difficult: legs need to stretch, feet need to bend and wake up, back and shoulders need to readjust to carrying a pack.

I had learned to give myself this time to get my hiking legs in order and give the endorphins in my brain a chance to kick in, raise the pain threshold of my body, and remind me of that euphoric feeling of a "runner's high" that was my usual reward. During this time, I say my Navajo Prayer and look at the beauty before, behind, above, and around me. I notice the sky and the air and the world at my feet. I keep going. In the time it takes for my hands to warm up and the sweat to gather in the middle of my back, I am ready to hike.

But Jim didn't know these tricks, these mental strategies to begin the day. AT thru-hiking veterans will tell you that hiking the AT is a mostly mental endeavor; the physical aspect is challenging, but not problematic if mental stamina is sufficiently developed. Thinking that the hike ahead is primarily a physical feat is misleading; the physical must be tempered by mental preparation and strategies for endurance. My way to prepare, mentally, was to give my body permission to warm up, to know what to expect from the general terrain ahead, and to center myself with ritual.

I would eventually learn that though the trail would never become any easier, it would become easier to bear when I expected it to be hard.

On his second day out, Jim didn't know what it had taken me weeks to discover. Why should he, I reminded myself; he's never done any of this before. I was still surprised, though, when I looked back twenty minutes after we had begun to hike and discovered him sitting on a log, totally discouraged and miserable.

I dropped back, sympathetic but frustrated with the situation. Jim's giving up so quickly perplexed me, and I was beginning to feel desperate. Cutting the day's hike in half might still not be enough, I realized.

We traded packs and walked on, slowly. Nothing seemed to help for long, but I knew we had to keep going. We couldn't just sit in the woods and wait for the trail to get easier.

Eventually we came to a campsite crisscrossed by several brooks and tenting platforms, the site of an old Shaker homestead. We stopped for lunch and rested while Nemo played on the tent platforms. Jim suggested that we stop for the night, but Megg and I both knew we had to move on. We still had an eight hundred-foot ascent in front of us; it seemed better to conquer it today rather than wait until morning. Perhaps with energy renewed from sustenance, it would be less daunting.

It wasn't. After lunch, I carried Nemo, asleep and blissfully unaware of the tensions weighing us down. We climbed Tyringham Cobble, a four hundred-foot hill, and descended gradually to the base of Baldy Mountain, the eight hundred-foot climb that I had naively planned as our lunch stop early this morning.

"This will be a long ascent," I told Jim, holding out the map for him to see. "But we can do it." I tentatively suggested that we hike steadily, like a truck in first gear, until the halfway point, then stop only long enough to catch our breath, and then continue to the top. Having a metaphor, a strategy, gave me the illusion of being in control of a particularly troublesome climb; the truck metaphor had proven to be a good one for me.

With Nemo still on my back, I started to climb, slowly, steadily, and purposefully. Megg dropped behind to hike with Jim. I'm not sure what, if any, strategy they used, but when Nemo woke up, our strategy was to play "huff and puff and blow your house down," singing, "the wheels on the bus go round and round" all the way to the top.

It was hot, sweaty, buggy, grueling, and steeper than I had anticipated – but we all made it. At the top we began to look for a place to camp. Megg wanted a pine grove, Jim wanted water for a bath, and I searched for level ground and balance.

Jim saved the day and found a pine grove with two level places for tents. Then he went off to scout for water. Not much farther along the trail, he found a small stream off to the side, in the woods. Megg and I pitched the tents and started our cook stoves.

"The mosquitoes at least respect smoke," I observed, lighting a smudge fire to keep them away while we cooked.

Jim came back with a tote bag of water, refreshed and revived from his bath, and we all sat on logs and ate under the protective smoke of the smudge fire.

After dinner, in the growing dusk, Nemo and I played inside my tent and Megg visited the stream for a bath. She came back chuckling.

"Picture this," she reported. "I'm sitting on a rock, naked, pouring water over my hair, watching the moon rise just above the trees. It's almost dark. The trees are black. I'm Hiawatha, with night sounds all around me. And then I hear a man's voice, clear through the trees: 'How far is the Pennsylvania Turnpike?'

"Just visible through the woods, there's a wild looking man – long bushy beard, long bushy hair, skinny legs, hiking sticks – but no pack! Rumplestilskin? I just kept quiet and hoped he would keep going. He did. I sat there trying to recapture the mood, but then I decided I'd better leave the moon and come back. Scary-looking guy! Was I dreaming?" Shaking her head, she gathered Nemo and his things and crawled into her tent, zipping the mosquitoes out. Jim was already asleep.

I wrote in my journal for a bit and listened to Megg's voice and the muffled strains of her old camp songs, softly disguised as lullabies for Nemo.

> "It's comforting to hear Megg sing those old songs, strong connections to her roots at camp. She showed gutsiness today. I'm proud of her. I'm resolved to learn from her example. I need to learn patience. It's been a trying day."

June 29, to Upper Goose Pond Cabin, 6 miles

We broke camp a little earlier and were on our way by nine o'clock. It was, unfortunately, a repeat of the day before, with many rest stops and water breaks. By eleven o'clock I decided to hike ahead so that I could reserve bunks at the cabin for all of us. I expected that weekenders might arrive by midafternoon and I wanted to be at the cabin before that happened. I was also, despite my resolve of the night before, impatient with Jim's discouragement and need for rest. I pulled ahead, settled into my own stride, and began to feel more relaxed.

In about half an hour, I lost the trail. A large tree with many leafy branches had fallen across the path and, in my haste to get around, I bushwhacked too far and couldn't find the trail on the other side. I followed several minor paths, probably made by deer or other hikers in the same predicament, but to no avail.

When I finally found the trail, it occurred to me that I was acting very irresponsibly. I had left Megg with a baby and an unhappy hiking partner to fend for herself, without a map, trusting that they would all make it to the cabin. If I could get lost, so could she.

I sat down on a leafy branch to collect myself. Maybe I could leave Megg a note on the other side of the tree, telling her how to find the rest of the trail. I opened my pack to look for a pen and paper, realized that that was no solution, and started to cry. The events of the last few days caught up with me; I cried disappointed, frustrated, weary tears. Our hike was almost over and I was dismayed that it had been so difficult.

I indulged myself for a few minutes, then took a deep breath, and started back around the blow-down to wait for Megg.

In the distance, I heard Megg's voice, singing and laughing as she tramped up the trail with Nemo on her back; he was waving a stick and slurping his water tube. Jim was not far behind. All was well. And, once again, I was proud of my daughter – strong and cheerful when I had given in to weariness and regret. Good for her! We hiked on together, and soon came upon the cabin, a lovely spot to finish our hike.

Goose Pond Cabin is a two-story enclosed structure with a kitchen, common room and front porch downstairs, with a large sleeping loft with bunk beds upstairs. A long wash table and pump out back is set up for hikers to clean dishes, gear, and clothing, and signs posted in the composting privies behind these give specific directions for use by each gender.

A caretaker couple and their dog were on site, and their welcome, as I wound my way up the path, was both reassuring and jovial.

"Don't mind the dog," they shouted over his fierce bark, "he only bites hikers."

But as I hiked in, the dog stopped barking and trotted up to me.

"That's unusual," the man said. "We usually have to put him inside. He won't really bite, but he keeps barking and making a nuisance of himself until he gets used to you. You must be a gentle creature."

Hot and irritable, I didn't feel gentle, only happy to be nosed and not bitten by their dog. At midafternoon, we were the first hikers to arrive.

We climbed upstairs, claimed our bunks for the night, and headed downhill to the water's edge for a swim and paddle in the clear lake below.

We borrowed paddles from the cabin and strapped Nemo into a life jacket for his first canoe ride. As I plunked him down in the middle of the canoe, he began to sing: "rowrowrowboatrowrowrowboat," another Nemo-use of language to name an event.

"Where does he learn these things?" I asked.

Megg just shrugged and joined him for the chorus, breaking the stillness but not the serenity of the water, woods, and mountains surrounding us on all sides.

We canoed and swam, then read paperback books until late afternoon, glad for a break from hiking. When it was time for supper, we pulled out our stoves and the last of our food.

The porch filled with other hikers. Nemo was drawn to Waco, a tall, lanky young man from Texas, and his hiking partner, Joel from Japan, known for being able to hike more than thirty miles every day. I listened to their trail stories with attention; I doubted that our paths would ever cross again.

As the mosquitoes emerged full-force and we prepared to find our bunks, Jed and ET hiked in.

"We've been hiking hard to catch up with you," Jed said. "I'm not doing the Long Trail to Canada after all. ET and I are going to hike with you and meet Amy in Vermont. That okay with you?"

"Sure," I replied, surprised at his change in plans and pleased that they wanted to hike with me. "But I'm not meeting her until next weekend. Tomorrow I'm hiking with an old friend for a couple of days. I'll see Amy in Manchester Center next weekend."

"Jed's got all cleaned up now," ET interjected. "It'd be a shame for Amy to miss his new haircut," he laughed, and pointed his chin towards Jed.

I had wondered about the orange baseball hat perched on Jed's head. Must be hiding a small-town haircut, I guessed.

"Nah," Megg teased. "Amy needs a good reason to hike and camp again. She'll borrow your orange hat, Jed."

Later, after Nemo fell asleep, Megg and I sat on the stairs leading to the loft, looking up at the dark sky flooded with stars.

"I've really liked hiking with you this week," I said quietly.

"It's been great," Megg agreed.

"Well, not so great for Jim," I added. "How could we have made it better?"

"I don't think we could have done anything, Mom," she replied. "He just never did any of this growing up. When it gets hard, he gives up."

"I've noticed that you pick up the slack. Seems to me that you're doing everything yourself – including all the arrangements and driving and navigating to get here."

"This was sort of my last attempt to get him to do something that I wanted to do. I've been feeling like such a bitch. You're right. I've been trying to fill out graduate school applications for a long time now – I really want to get started. I'm glad to hear you say what I've been thinking."

"On this hike, Megg, you've shown a lot of strength and resilience. Even when you're tired and discouraged, you don't give up; you always seem to find another way. The thing that really impresses me is that you do it with good humor."

"Not always," she demurred, listening.

Encouraged by her attention, I carefully moved forward. "If you want to go to graduate school, I think you can decide to find the time to fill out the applications... and once you know where you will study... "

"Yeah, I know. We might need to grow in different directions for a while. The trees and stuff," she laughed, alluding to the metaphor I sometimes quoted for marriage: that trees must first establish their own root system to grow tall and strong; that their trunks must be pliant and woody, their branches many-leaved and nourishing so they can bend with the storm and recover; that offspring need two strong parents who can shelter them from the elements as they grow, not two trunks twisted around each other, or one tree tall and straight, the other weak and strangling.

I winced at the metaphor and chuckled with her.

"Thanks, Mom, I'll think about it," she whispered, falling silent in the starlight.

We sat quietly for a few more minutes, until Jim came down the stairs, ready for a moonlight swim.

"I'll go up with Nemo," I said. "You two go ahead." I climbed the stairs and crawled onto my bunk to write and think about the events of the last few days. Somehow, twenty-four hours in the woods seems like a much longer day than one framed by the usual routines and pastimes at home. For me, the last eighty-six hours together had been surprisingly comprehensive and thought-provoking. I couldn't help wondering about the impact of the hike on Megg and her family. I sensed that they had reached a turning point, and hoped it had been a growing experience for all of us.

June 30, 2001, to Lee, Mass., 7 miles

The next morning, with the caretaker's help, I arranged for a taxi to meet Megg, Nemo, Jim, and myself at the junction of the trailhead and US 20, seven miles ahead, to take me to the post office in Lee, and my family back to their car in South Egremont, just over the Massachusetts line.

We hiked out with ET and Jed. Just before reaching US 20, we approached the AT footbridge over the Massachusetts turnpike.

"Ah ha," Megg cried gleefully. "The Massachusetts Turnpike. I did see a wild man the other night – but he was looking for the Massachusetts – not the Pennsylvania Turnpike. I thought it was Rumplestilskin," she exclaimed, relaying her story to Jed and ET about her moonlit bath in the woods. "But unlike Rumplestilskin, he didn't have a pack."

"Oh, so you've met Wildman," Jed confirmed. "That really is his name: Wildman. I met him in Georgia. He's a real one-of-a-kind. A retired entrepreneur. Unpredictable. Always appearing where you least expect him, he sometimes doesn't know where he is. He's constantly upgrading his gear – packs, tents, boots, clothing, and he's always hungry for advice. Scary-looking – but harmless." He chuckled. "You've had a full hike. You even met Wildman."

While we talked at the trailhead, an outdated sedan drove by, spotted us and circled back to take us to town. Jed and ET meandered away down the trail; Meg, Jim, Nemo, and I stowed our packs in the oversized trunk and tucked into the back seat of the taxi.

We reached the post office in bustling Lee, Massachusetts, well before the noon closing hour. I pulled my pack out of the trunk, hoisted it onto my hips, gave my family a quick hug, and waved them on their way. In less than a minute, they were gone and I was on my own once again. I hoped that their trip home would be more relaxing than their trip to and through the woods.

I went to the post office and joined a long line of patrons stopping and starting their vacation mail. A young woman thru-hiker "wannabe" accosted me with a barrage of questions about my pack, my gear, and my hike. For the next hour, I sorted out my mail drop, responded to her questions, and tried to organize my supplies.

Then I looked up and saw my old friend, Happy, striding across the tarmac, arms outstretched to meet me, unfazed by my dirty, smelly appearance. I was really glad to see her.

"We're booked into my cousin's condo for the night," she greeted me. "Do you have a bathing suit? They have a wonderful pool and this weather is beastly. I've got to have a swim."

Our first stop was a sporting goods store for something to make me decent for a swim in polite company. Trying on bathing suits in the small dressing room at the back of the store, I tossed aside one baggy suit after the other. I'll never use this in the woods, I murmured to myself, pawing through to eliminate the most garish Spandex.

Since adolescence, a bikini, for me, has been a state of mind, not body, and trying on bathing suits is an ordeal I would still rather avoid. But, looking in the full-length mirror for the first time in six weeks, I was shocked at the reflection staring back at me. I couldn't believe my eyes. Where was the potbelly I had carried around since Megg's birth twenty-nine years ago? Those couldn't be my slim hips! Whose shapely calves and thighs were these? Could this be the well-guarded secret of hiking? I had read that men usually lose excess pounds hiking the AT, and that women firm up but stay about the same weight. That certainly had been my experience training – tauter muscles, but no weight loss. But I couldn't argue with the image of the lithe, slender body staring back at me. Could that really be my body?

"Hey, Happy, this little black bikini actually fits," I held up my prize in triumph.

"What an exercise program," I said as I tumbled exultantly out of the dressing room.

"Let's see what we can do about that," she grinned and took me straight to a sandwich shop for a huge lunch.

Happy's cousin, Becky, and her husband, Tim, live in Concord, but spend weekends in a condo near Williams College with the amenities afforded by the surrounding summer arts festival community. Becky had made dinner reservations for all of us in Bennington, followed by a summer playhouse performance of *Panache* in nearby Williamstown.

Happy, with gracious thoughtfulness, had brought a long skirt, tank top and flat-heeled shoes for me to wear to dinner. I slipped the clothes over my new black bathing suit and felt dressed up and slinky for the first time all summer. I wondered if it would be hard to stay awake if our candlelit dinner extended past sundown and whether I would be able to keep my eyes open during the play. I was so entertained, however, that neither was a problem. I thoroughly enjoyed myself – quickly resuming a role I had not practiced in months.

July 1, 2001, near Lee, Mass., 0 miles

In the morning, a table lay with fresh fruit, orange juice, bagels, cream cheese, coffee, and the *New York Times Book Review,* all waiting for me next to the colorful napkin set at my place. I learned that Becky was a Unitarian chaplain and had worked with my father's cousin, Dana, a liberal Unitarian minister in Boston, until his death ten years ago.

I had been chastising myself for being too focused and goal directed in my mission to hike the trail. I talked to Becky about my concerns over breakfast. She helped me understand that focus and goal orientation were a form of discipline; that discipline, from the word "disciple," meaning "to teach," was a necessary guide for any endeavor.

"Without discipline," she reminded me, "one cannot reach one's destination, be it spiritual growth, enlightenment, or Katahdin. You are on a quest, and you must be disciplined in order to accomplish it. Never mind those who don't understand, who may interpret your way as rigidity or lack of flexibility.

"Your hiking days, and nights, sound very disciplined to me; discipline is a necessary part of the journey, an important part. Keep on with your quest," she counseled, "and do it your way. You'll find what you're looking for."

I listened gratefully, and felt better. *On a trail marked with pollen may I walk.*

7. The Community of Hikers: Hiker Family

"... every unhappy family is unhappy in its own way."

Leo Tolstoy, Anna Karenina

Dalton, Mass., to Manchester Center, Vt., 88.6 miles

July 2, 2001, to Mark Noeple Shelter, 19 miles

I was eager to get back on the trail after a week of slow hiking and tending to other's needs. Happy drove me to the trailhead south of Dalton, Massachusetts, and mailed my Bounce box home to George. Learning my lesson from Jim, a gift gratefully received from our days of hiking together, I now carried only the barest essentials: my journal, watercolors, camera, led light, cell phone and charger, driver's license, several traveler's checks, Visa and insurance cards, and only the maps and pages from the guidebook I would use until the next mail drop. I kept an extra pair of hiking socks and liners, a lightweight polar fleece shirt, my long underwear, hat, gloves, and rain gear and wore hiking shorts, socks and liners, hiking bra, underpants, bandanna and tee shirt. I trimmed food, as well, discarding any meals that I might replace by restaurant or town food. My pack, fully loaded, now weighed only thirty pounds, a little less than one-fourth my body weight, which had also decreased by twelve pounds.

It felt good to be in the woods again, striding along at my own pace, listening to early morning birdsong. Weekend thunderstorms had chased away the heat of the past week; the morning was cool and crisp. I passed two women in ski parkas, heading south; one was celebrating her fiftieth birthday, feeling good about her age. I didn't tell her I was sixty, but we did comment on the temperature. The morning sun had not yet penetrated the trees.

"Now that I've sent my long pants and shirt home, the thermometer dips," I whined good-naturedly, knowing that I would be sweating within the hour.

Presently, several thru-hikers passed me: Tacoma, Waco, Joel from Japan, Flea, whom I had not seen since Pennsylvania, and his brother, now recovered from the surgery that had taken him off the trail.

"Meet us in Cheshire," Flea shouted as he raced by me. "It's right on the trail – there's a pizza place and ice cream store, too."

I doubted that Flea and his brother would still be there by the time I reached Cheshire, but I agreed to join them if they were.

Cheshire, Massachusetts, is a quiet New England village with several white-steepled churches, a post office, a general store and a pizza parlor. It also boasts a monument commemorating a block of cheese, created in Cheshire when Thomas Jefferson was president. Jefferson, the story goes, was so impressed by the size of the cheese that he put it on exhibit in the East Room of the newly built White House, giving that room its nickname, the Mammoth Room. The cheese was so large it took more than six months of nibbling for it to finally be consumed, thus earning the town of Cheshire a permanent place in annals of historical trivia, and the town square, a proud monument.

Only one booth in the pizza parlor was occupied, and that was a long one, crowded with thru-hikers, Flea and his brother among them. I left my pack outside with theirs and joined them. I was the only woman in the group.

After lunch Flea and his brother hiked out with me, stopping for ice cream at a gas station five hundred feet from the trail. I had been right about the temperature: by early afternoon I was once again hot and sweaty and a Dove Bar, even for the exorbitant price of three dollars, tasted good.

I was sitting on my pack waiting for Flea and his brother to check baseball scores when it occurred to me to wonder why I was waiting on them. Their hiking style, fast and hard for short periods of time, interspersed with long breaks equal to the time they had been hiking, was very different from mine. My style was slower, steadier and dotted with only a few short breaks to drink, snack, or pee. At the end of the day, I would usually have hiked as many miles, but arrive at the shelter later. As expected, when we resumed hiking, Flea and his brother pulled ahead and I, once again, was left to hike alone. I didn't mind at all.

The shelter that night was crowded with thru-hikers and a group of international high school students planning to sleep in the loft above. Flea had saved me a space with the hikers on the floor below so I felt compelled to spread out my sleeping bag rather than camp. After hiking almost twenty miles, I was tired and happy to change into long underwear and fleece and set up my stove on the picnic table to cook and eat. A sense of camaraderie and accomplishment, sprinkled with jabs of lighthearted banter, sweetened the evening.

As I finished my meal and prepared to brush my teeth, Jed and ET hiked in. They had stayed in Dalton the night before and had had a late start to their hiking day. I was happy to see them, but too tired to talk in the now-quiet shelter.

It still surprised me that a shelter full of hikers could have everyone in their bags, either asleep, writing, or reading, before the sun had set for the day. I inserted two foam plugs into my ears, turned out my light, and drifted to sleep surrounded by the muted metronome of snores.

July 3, 2001, to Seth Warner Shelter, 16.5 miles

At five-thirty, the unmistakable sounds of someone zipping open his sleeping bag, riffling for food, and igniting a stove signaled every thru-hiker that the day had begun. Joel from Japan, the daily thirty-plus miler, was the first to get up, waking everyone else; by six-thirty only the international students were still tucked in above our heads.

My destination before breakfast was the summit of Mt. Greylock, a climb from the shelter of seven hundred feet. At 3,491 feet, Greylock is Massachusetts' highest peak and has been the inspiration for many writers, among them Hawthorne, Thoreau, and Melville. A lodge and restaurant is located at the summit.

For me, Mt. Greylock had always inspired mystery and fear. When I was five years old, my father bought a WWII-era camp trailer full of army surplus gear and took us to the top of Mt. Greylock to try it all out. Sleeping under a moldy canvas tent on wooden folding cots, inside scratchy mummy-style sleeping bags and voluminous mosquito nets, my brothers and I were shaken awake in the middle of the first night. Whisked out to the back seat of the car, we were ordered to keep the windows closed and go back to sleep. By the light of a kerosene lantern, I watched my parents take down the tent, put away all the cots and sleeping bags, and kick the campfire ashes into the fire pit. The no-see-ums, they explained when they joined us, were too fierce for anyone to sleep. Confused and frightened, I huddled on the floor until dawn, a sharp image of dark angular silhouettes against a bright yellow light playing on my tightly closed eyelids. I was much older before I discovered the actual size and threat of the tiny biting flies.

This morning, the mountain was cold, gray and hard-edged. I put on all my clothes, even my rain gear, and hiked out with ET, blowing visible puffs in the frosty air. We agreed to meet Jed, Waco, Flea and his brother, Joel from Japan, and Tacoma at Bascomb Lodge on the summit. Within the hour, we reached our destination, a large stone structure of bare wood floors, an open fireplace, cavernous dining room, and a small gift shop run by the Appalachian Mountain Club.

The others had saved ET and me a place at the long table and were busy devouring French toast, scrambled eggs, bacon, coffee, orange juice, muffins and cereal. It looked and smelled scrumptious. The dining room was not open to the public, but, as a special favor to our group of thru-hikers, the lodge maintainers had agreed to cook breakfast for all of us for the nominal fare of seven dollars each. I'm not sure how much food we consumed, but I know I ate my seven dollars' worth, and then some.

After breakfast, content and warm, I wandered out to the reception area to use the pay phone. But Waco was talking to his mother, and it was a long, long conversation. While I waited, I meandered into the gift shop to look at the wares offered by the Appalachian Mountain Club.

As I poked through the tee shirts and guidebooks on display, I looked up to see a man staring at me. "You look familiar," he said. "Were you hiking in Virginia earlier this spring?"

"Oh my gosh," I gasped. "You're one of the Four Bears. Of course I remember you. You practically saved my life in the Shenandoahs – you and the other Three Bears. What are you doing here?"

And then I remembered. Pittsfield, Massachusetts, their home, is within a days' hike to the base of Mt. Greylock. Dave, the leader of the Dinty Moore stew crew, was a volunteer at the AMC gift shop.

"Are you surprised to see me still hiking?" I asked. "I hope I've learned a few things about camping since I saw you last. I really had no idea what I was doing that rainy night, trying to get my tent up without getting everything inside soaked."

"We noticed," he grinned. "You may not have known what you were doing, but you sure were determined. We had no doubt that you would stay the course. I'm not surprised to see you still hiking at all." Then he added, thoughtfully, "You're one of the dreamers who actually do something about their dream. You hike the trail; we keep it open and try to protect it. When you finish, I know you'll return to the trail, same as we do. It's good to see you."

His words brought back my father in a flood of memory. About the same age as my father when he died, Dave could have been him, understanding and affirming me for doing what he had only dreamt about doing. I vowed that I would give back, someday, so that others could discover the woods and live their dreams, just as I had been given the opportunity and resources to live mine.

Out in the cool morning sun, Jed and ET were impatient to move on. It was nearly eleven o'clock, and Jed wanted to shoot some photos of hikers crossing the trail in front of the war memorial atop Mt. Greylock before the clouds dissipated. He wanted ET and me to be those hikers.

With a lump in my throat, I hugged Dave and reluctantly said goodbye.

"In old age, wandering on a trail of beauty, living again may I walk," I chanted as I hiked up the hill, ready to continue my trek, inspired by memories of my father and Dave's generosity.

ET and I hiked out together, promising to catch up with Jed at a campsite nine miles north. As we hiked, ET entertained me with a string of southern folk tales, drawled out slowly over the descent from the summit of Greylock, across the summit of Mt. Fitch to the ascent of Mt. Williams. The climb up Mt. Williams seemed easy, laughing and talking as we were, and at the top we were rewarded with a view and the company of a retired professor, eating his lunch and gazing at his college in the valley below. The professor was full of advice about hiking Mt. Williams; he had been hiking its many trails for fifty years.

It was hard to move on graciously. By the time we left, I couldn't remember which way we had hiked in. I knew we should descend, but the white blazed trail in both directions headed down. Had I been by myself, I would have consulted my map. However, in the presence of a local "expert" and a hiker I assumed to be more experienced than I, I listened to them, instead. ET and I turned back in the direction we had just come and descended the five hundred feet we had just climbed. At the base, we met the hiking couple we had passed an hour ago.

We recognized our mistake immediately, turned around, and abashedly, hiked back up to the summit of Mt. Williams. This time, we crept by the rocks at the top, but the professor had finished his lunch and vanished.

"I guess that's the drawback of gettin' advice from the locals," ET drawled, "they don't know beans about a thru-hike or the difference between hikin' north and hikin' south. To them, the AT is just another trail. We'd best pay them locals no mind in future."

"And not talk so much," I added, kicking myself for being distracted instead of paying attention, for assuming the men around me knew more than I did, for following rather than leading my own hike.

Late in the afternoon, we came out of the woods and followed a residential road between North Adams and Williamstown. A man sitting in his backyard spotted us.

"Hey, come have a beer," he shouted.

I had forgotten that the next day was the Fourth of July; he was celebrating early.

We chatted with our benefactor for a few minutes before moving on to meet Jed at the campsite a mile or so up the trail.

We reached the campsite by five o'clock. ET, reading his data book, noted that the next campsite was only five miles farther. He wanted to keep going.

"We can leave a note for Jed and tell him we're goin' on," he said. "He's probably not far behind, fast as he hikes. He can meet us at Seth Warner. It'll only be another two hours or so."

Instead of looking at my map to determine what kind of hours they would be or type of terrain those five miles would cross, I simply agreed to push on. Had I realized that we would ascend thirteen hundred feet over large rocks and loose scree, straight up through dense woods and uneven footing in twilight and gathering darkness, I would have balked. But, without thinking, I deferred to ET. Sixty years of being socialized as a woman, acceding to a man's judgment, was more deeply ingrained than I realized.

I scrambled on behind ET who, like a horse heading to his barn, left me panting just to keep the back of his pack in sight. We had hiked a long way since breakfast and though I was not particularly tired, I was hungry; my muscles and brain needed glucose. I pulled several granola breakfast bars out of my food bag and snacked as I hiked, but I was losing energy faster than I could replace it.

At sunset, we reached the twenty-three hundred foot summit, the marker for the Massachusetts/Vermont state line and the southern terminus of the Long Trail. The Long Trail extends two hundred sixty-five miles north to Canada and shares its first hundred miles with the AT. Until the AT turned northeast at Killington to cross the White Mountains of New Hampshire, we would share shelters and campgrounds with Long Trail hikers as well as weekend and youth camp hikers. "We'll have plenty of company in these Green Mountains," I said to ET as we hurried to get to the campsite before dark. Indeed, when we reached the Seth Warner Shelter almost three miles later, the shelter was crowded with hikers. As we pitched our tents in a nearby pine grove near the shelter, Jed hiked in.

"I've busted my butt to catch up with you," he greeted ET. "When I got your note, I couldn't believe that you would be climbing a mountain this late in the day. That was quite a push!"

"Yeah, I didn't think it would be so steep, or so rocky," ET agreed, spreading out his stove and supper on the ground in front of his tent. "We probably should have stayed at that last campsite and waited for you."

By now it was pitch black outside. Using the beam of the light strapped to my head, I finished setting up my tent and crawled inside to spread out my sleeping bag. Tempted, I stretched out full length on my bag, thinking I would find something to eat in a few minutes. In the darkness, from the depths of my tent, listening to Jed and ET rustle about cooking and making camp, I drifted off to sleep. It was the only night on the trail that I did not have dinner. It was a bad idea.[9] But at the time, I didn't know enough about nutrition and endurance activity to realize the effects it would have both the next day and in the long term. I slept fitfully that night.

July 4, 2001, to Bennington, Vt., 12 miles

The next morning, I woke early, dispirited. I didn't think I would be able to hike the twenty-one miles Jed and ET were planning for the day. Guess I'll be saying another goodbye, I lamented, feeling sorry for myself. I was sitting on a tree stump eating my last oat cracker and the little bit of almond butter left in my food bag when Jed unzipped his tent.

"What happened to you last night?" he asked.

"I guess I just was too tired to eat. I fell asleep on top of my sleeping bag. And I ate all my granola bars yesterday," I admitted, chewing on the oatcake, mixing some powdered Tang into the last of my water.

"Here, eat this bagel," he offered gruffly, "and some peanut butter. You can't hike all morning on an oatcake and Tang."

"Thanks," I accepted, gratefully. More nutritious food did help, and by the time I was ready to leave, Jed and ET were too.

"We're only going thirteen miles today – not push the twenty to the Goddard Shelter after all," Jed said. "That okay with you?"

"Sure," I replied, relieved. "I expect I can do thirteen miles today." I pulled on my pack and decided quickly to join them.

---

9. Not only does the body need nourishment for warmth through the night, it also needs to be replenished so that it can hike the next day; when depleted, muscles need at least twenty hours to replenish their glycogen stores. I had seriously depleted the glycogen in my muscles and I was exhausted.

As we were heading out, several hikers from the shelter approached us. One, an older man with long hair, a long beard, hiking sticks and a very small pack was talking non-stop in a deep, loud voice to the young woman walking behind him. I waited for them to pass as Jed greeted them. "Hey, Wildman. How's it going? Hey Megan." Waco, Tacoma, and Joel from Japan followed them.

"So that's Wildman," I said when they were gone.

"Yep. And his daughter, Megan," replied Jed. "She's just hiking with him for a few days – has a car somewhere nearby."

We fell into line behind them, hiking out under low clouds and oppressive humidity, passing and re-passing them all morning. About midmorning, at a rocky overlook, I was surprised to come upon a hiker stretched out, gazing off in the distance. It seemed early to be stopping. Taking a closer look, I discovered it was Joel from Japan. He was so quiet I passed by without disturbing him. At his usual speed, I would have expected him to be much further ahead; I never imagined I could catch up with him.

I had agreed to meet Jed and ET at Congdon Shelter and arrived just about lunchtime. The area was strewn with packs and hikers, all engaged in either cooking or eating or both. Wildman was still talking – pontificating actually, in a loud voice, about university affirmative action policy decisions. I put my pack as far from him as possible, irritated by his voice and topic of conversation, and rustled around in my food bag for something to eat. I had no patience for Wildman and talked quietly with Waco, instead.

"I saw Joel from Japan stretched out on a rock this morning," I said. "I thought you two were hiking together."

"We are. Well, maybe not now. He hikes faster than I do, but this morning he had a sort of epileptic seizure on the trail. My sister has epilepsy, so I knew what to do. I stayed with him 'til I could see he was okay. He said he just wanted to rest for a while. That's probably when you saw him. He'll be okay, but he's going too fast for me; I want to slow down a little and enjoy these mountains. They're what I came here for."

After lunch, no one was in a hurry to move on. Then it started to rain. We all scrambled to put rain covers on our packs, grousing, when someone suggested that an early dinner in Bennington, an "easy hitch" from the trailhead five miles north, would be a good idea. Someone else, reading his guidebook, suggested a night at the Knotty Pine Motel might be even better. ET pulled out his cell phone, called the Knotty Pine and reserved a room for four: himself, Jed, Waco, and me. Tacoma said he would pass.

"Ask if they have another room for me and my daughter," Wildman shouted, "and we'll join you."

By the time we reached the trailhead at four-thirty, there were seven of us. Jed instructed us about hitching: "First, we need to split up. The women go with the scruffiest men – much easier to get a ride if a woman is with you. Take off your pack and lean it against your hiking poles – so you don't look too massive to the driver – and stand where a car can pull over without getting hit. Be prepared to move fast when a car stops and throw your stuff in the trunk or keep it on your lap. Look friendly and like you're having a good time.

"Smile and wave if they can't pick you up. Keep smiling 'til the next car comes along. If they can take more than the two of you, motion how many more, and we'll join you. When you've gone, the next pair will try their luck."

The car that stopped for Jed and me was littered with pop cans and candy wrappers. The young driver knew the Knotty Pine Motel, on the edge of town, and dropped us at the office within half an hour. Wildman, his daughter, and Tacoma were right behind us. ET and Waco were not so lucky. Their teenaged drivers decided it would be fun to take them in the opposite direction from the motel. By the time they found another hitch across town, it was almost dark and they were furious. Theirs was an unusual occurrence; people who pick up hikers in trail towns are usually hikers themselves and eager to be of assistance.

Already used to sleeping mat-to-mat, sharing cooking space and privy use in the shelters, it is customary for thru-hikers to share living space in town, as well. Most small motels appreciate hiker business and encourage hikers to sleep four to six in a room, using the beds, floors, porches for sleeping space, splitting the cost and the towels and leaving the room in orderly condition when they move on. I had read about this custom, but this would be my first actual experience in a motel room with three guys.

We checked in, bought cokes from the vending machine, and took turns in the shower, rinsing the mud and grime from the afternoon's rainy hike down the drain.

"I'll be washing these the way a guy does," Waco warned when he stuffed my clothes into a garbage bag with everyone else's, heading for the laundry. "All in one load. Okay?"

"Sure," I replied, way beyond caring about separating whites from colors.

Waco, laundering his only pair of shorts, was wearing my rain pants to the public Laundromat down the street. Taller than I by six inches, they came to just below his knees. He grinned, did a little jig, and hurried across the parking lot, arms akimbo, looking like an over-sized elf. ET and Wildman went to find dinner; Jed and I headed to the local supermarket for beer and groceries.

The clouds overhead were massing for a major storm, and the wind lashed across the parking lot, nudging the metal outdoor furniture and flapping unlatched screen doors. The sky grew darker and meaner.

"I'm glad we're not still on that mountain," Jed observed as we pushed into the fluorescent brightness of the supermarket. "This could be a brutal one. We'll have plenty of fireworks tonight – all from Mother Nature," he chuckled.

"Probably," I laughed too. "But I don't really care, as long as I'm not sleeping in it. I'd rather listen to the rain surrounded by four dry walls," I added, choosing some peanut butter and bagels for my food bag. We continued down the aisle looking for beer and soda, and then pushed our way out into the wind, ahead of the rain.

Back at the Knotty Pine, everyone was crowded into one room. ET and Wildman had bought several large buckets of Kentucky Fried Chicken, mashed potatoes, rolls and coleslaw. Jed and I contributed the drinks, and thunder and rain provided background music. Lightning slashed the darkness outside our screen door while rain swept across the parking lot.

By ten o'clock, all that remained of our buckets and beer was a strong greasy barroom odor lingering above the beds. After the storm blew away, we pulled lawn chairs into the parking lot to watch the scheduled fireworks. Against the mountains and the black backdrop of sky and rising mist, a wild palette of red, white, blue, green, and yellow bursts of light flaunted and cracked. Muted pops of gunpowder in the distance juxtaposed with loud, steady drips of rainwater in the gutters behind our heads.

When the fireworks were over, we folded our lawn chairs and crashed, early for townspeople, late for hikers. I slept in my sleeping bag and had more space on my shared bed then in any backwoods shelter so far. Wildman was still outside on a chair tilted back against his room, continuing a one-man party. I predicted a late start for his morning hike and fell asleep listening to my roommates' snoring and rain falling gently outside the window. We all slept soundly and woke early, ready to hike in the misty, wet morning.

July 5, 2001, to Goddard Shelter, 10.1 miles

Even though we were in a motel, we were up by six o'clock, packed our gear, and went to a nearby diner for breakfast. Although we were the only customers, the waitress wouldn't let us make any substitutions on the menu or draw up an extra chair to the table. Behind her back we called her the "Breakfast Nazi" and didn't linger, even though it had started to rain again and we were waiting for Wildman to return with his daughter's rental car. I wasn't sure that Wildman would find his way back to us but he did, and soon his daughter dropped us at the trailhead. We began to climb Woodford Mountain, a sixteen hundred-foot climb in two miles. The rain stopped, but it was overcast and dreary. Everything – leaves, bushes, rocks and ground, was slippery and wet.

We ascended fairly quickly, reaching the blue-blazed trail to the Neuheim-Melville Shelter in about an hour. Waco went up to the shelter to check on Joel from Japan and came back to report that no one was there but two women looking for Gotta Hike!. Jed and I looked at each other, stashed our packs, and climbed quickly up to the shelter.

Sure enough, my friends Robin and Tammy, from that pre-hike women's weekend at Bears Den so many months ago, were drying their tent and repacking their gear. They had driven in from Ohio the day before, hoping to meet up with me to hike for a week. Their climb to the shelter in last night's storm, however, had dampened more than their gear; this morning they had decided to go back down the mountain and see Vermont through the windows of their car. I couldn't really fault them. The trail in Vermont is tough, and they were not prepared, as I was, by seven weeks of hiking.

We chatted at the shelter for a few minutes, and then walked down to the trailhead together. Robin gave me her trail spoon (I had lost mine the day before) and Tammy had some goodies for me from Mimi: candy, film, stamps and a wonderful letter. We shared the candy under dripping trees before ET, Jed, Waco, and I turned north, Robin and Tammy, south.

I was relieved. To hike with them, I would have had to drop back, hike at a slower pace, and probably lose the hiking family that I had just found. While I was disappointed that their plans had proved unrealistic, I couldn't help applauding the changes in me: having realized the importance of keeping both my feet in one community, I had chosen the community of the trail. I was no longer trying to accommodate to both worlds and had firmly committed myself to the discipline I had worked so hard to acquire. Even though my friends from home might interpret my way as rigid or inflexible, I would continue my quest, my way, confident that because it was correct for me; it was right.

I hiked through trees blurred by lifting mist for the next two hours, meeting Wildman and Tacoma from time to time along the trail. I could always hear Tacoma before I saw him. He composed songs and sang them at the top of his voice while he hiked. Deep in the woods, if he didn't see you, he would keep right on singing, guitar slung on his pack, poles thrashing through the bushes in time to the beat in his head.

At Little Pond Lookout we all met for the last of the beer ET and Waco had carried up the mountain. It was fun to talk and laugh and relax for a few minutes before heading down, then back up another thirteen hundred feet in five miles to the Goddard Shelter.

Hiking together after lunch, the men insisted that I set the pace, which, though slower than theirs, was not really slow. My legs were strong from the extra food and rest in town and I felt that I could hike forever across the puncheons, through the low growing bushes, under the tall green trees.

Waco, walking behind me, observed, "Those Frenchmen sure had it right when they named this state Ver-mont, "green mountain." This is the greenest place I've ever seen. It sure is different from Texas!"

I liked Waco. Just out of college, he had been hiking north since February, first with one partner, then another. Tall and lean, he grinned slowly when I asked him how he had come by his trail name.

"Well, one night when I just started out from Georgia and it was cold and dark and still winter – snowin' like you wouldn't believe – I lit my stove to cook inside the shelter. Somehow, I lost track of the fire. Pretty soon, flames were snakin' across the floor – I guess I spilled some fuel, and somebody yelled 'watch out!' I had a regular inferno goin' there. I smacked it with my sleeping mat and kicked and stomped with my boots – finally stopped it – but when the others found out I was from Texas… well, they just started callin' me Waco. I've been Waco – and real careful with fire ever since."

A gentler, more unassuming cult leader would be hard to find.

I hiked a little faster, the others a little slower than their usual individual paces, and the afternoon passed quickly.

We reached the Goddard Shelter about six o'clock. A large shelter with a front porch and sleeping lofts overlooking Greylock to the south, it was crowded with weekenders and thru-hikers. Jed convinced us to eat there and then hike a half-mile farther to the summit of Glastenbury Mountain to camp overnight near the fire tower.

I put on my long underwear, fleece shirt, hat and rain gear and was just warm enough while I cooked; the wind was fierce. Up at the fire tower we camped in a circle under a canopy of tall pines, out of the wind where it was warmer. Unfortunately, as soon as we pitched camp, it started to rain again, so there was no point in climbing the tower to see the stars.

Inside my tent, dry and warm, I wrote in my journal:

"A world of difference today. It's fun to be hiking with people who are adventurous and knowledgeable, even though I get a little tired of the chatter, I do enjoy the camaraderie. I like Waco and I'm glad he's joined us. He's looking forward to meeting Amy, but I think Jed has claimed her for himself.

We've been teasing Jed because he doesn't have a cell phone. He says it's because he doesn't have anyone to call – so I told him he could call Amy – she loves to talk on her cell phone. I think he is looking forward to meeting her.

Two more days until we meet up in Manchester Center. Meanwhile, it's cold and rainy, but I'm dry, warm, and comfortable. Sleeping in a pine grove on a cushion of thick needles tonight – it cannot be surpassed."

July 6, 2001, to Stratton Mountain warming hut, 17 miles

It was a clear, sunny day, but cold. We were up early to hang our tents on the fire tower to dry in the wind that was still blowing strong. I climbed, shakily, to the top of the tower and saw a beautiful view of mountains all around: to the north, the White Mountains of New Hampshire, always visible from the summer cottage of my mother's childhood on Lake Winnipesauke, and to the east, Mt. Monadnock, the first mountain I ever climbed and always visible from the summer cottage of my childhood on Laurel Lake. I would be hiking home!

On our first camping trip to Mt. Greylock, my parents stopped in Fitzwilliam, New Hampshire, at the summer home of my father's cousins, Dana, Deb and their four daughters, the youngest two just my age. My parents pitched our tent in their field, and by the time my father's vacation was over, they had decided to have a cottage built down the hill on the shores of Laurel Lake, just below. For the next six years, Fitzwilliam, Laurel Lake, Mt. Monadnock and my wonderful cousins would fill my days all summer and my letters to Boston, all winter.

At the top of the fire tower I could feel the energy surge through my body, like sap returning to a tree in spring. I was hiking home. For me, it was an epiphany.

"Welcome to my childhood," I shouted to the sky, blue and clear and sunny. "Welcome to the best of my childhood," I amended, recalling the despair I felt when the cottage was sold several years later, without consulting my eleven-year-old heart. "Welcome to the best part of me," I whispered descending the rickety stairs, holding tight to the handrail, watching my feet, eyes blurred with tears and wind and memory.

In the early morning sun, we broke camp wearing everything we owned; Waco even wore his sleeping bag. When we started hiking, we began to warm up and within an hour had removed the "long handles" (ET's term) covering our legs, but kept hats, gloves and fleece on our upper bodies. We hiked all day in temperatures in the low forties, in and out of sunshine, stopping to put on, take off and put back on clothes as the wind and cloud cover dictated. I hiked on and off with ET, Waco, and Jed, occasionally catching the sounds of Tacoma singing somewhere behind me.

It was a long, beautiful, mostly solitary day, ascending via a series of switchbacks to the summit of Stratton Mountain, a climb of sixteen hundred feet in three and a half miles. From his first thru-hike, Jed remembered a side trail from the summit of Stratton to a nearby warming hut, free for thru-hikers. We had agreed to meet at the warming hut for the night. It was a good decision.

The warming hut was one room with overhead fluorescent lights, a stove, several tables and one bare bed frame next to the door. When we arrived, ET, always the southern gentleman, insisted that the others let me have the bed frame. I quickly accepted and found some cardboard boxes, which I flattened and put on top of the springs, under my Therm-A-Rest and sleeping bag. I recalled the story about the Princess and the Pea but doubted that this comfort would spoil me for the hardships ahead.

I cooked my supper on the hut stove and heated some canned hot dogs for Wildman, who couldn't figure out how to cook them. I could have helped him eat one of those dogs, I thought, but he didn't offer, so I didn't ask.

Later, we called Amy and George on my cell phone. We were scheduled to meet them in Manchester Center in two days.

"They both sounded a bit stressed getting ready for their trip. I hope Amy will like hiking with me. Everyone is looking forward to it – especially me. I think having her join us will be fun. When she asked what she should bring, I handed the phone to Jed and he said 'Bring liquor!' and then joked with her for a few minutes. I think they'll get along. She is probably the reason he's hiking with me. But I'm glad he is.

I would never have found this hut, nor thought to stay in it if I were hiking by myself tonight."

I was well aware that the mountains ahead would be harsh and difficult, and I was glad to be climbing them with other hikers. But I was also aware that my hiking style did not quite match theirs. I was not sure that I could keep up with them, or that I would always want to.

"There's no doubt that Jed, ET, and Waco hike faster than I do. They all have the advantage over me – strength, experience, testosterone, not to mention age (except for ET) – and I often feel that they are pushing me to hike too fast for myself. On the other hand, no matter how I urge them to hike ahead of me, they seem reluctant to do so, fearing that I might not catch up by the end of the day, I suppose. I like having their company but I don't like feeling that my pace and style are wanting. I sometimes wonder why they are hiking with me."

When we finally turned out the hut lights, Tacoma sang us to sleep: a medley of his own and others' folk songs. I was lulled by his voice and the pull of the wind, muffled but still howling around the corners of the hut, trying to get in through the windows. It was warm and safe and friendly inside.

I couldn't imagine hiking alone in elemental conditions such as these.

July 7, 2001, to Manchester Center, Vt., 14 miles

The morning began with an exquisite sunrise seen from the top of the mountain. The wind was still strong, but not as cold. I had the luxury of a hot-water wash in the sink before heading out with the others.

Our first stop was the fire tower, a little less than a mile away. I climbed the stairs and took in the view all around me: the White Mountains, Somerset Reservoir, Mt. Pisgah, Glastenbury Mountain, the Taconic Range, Ascutney Mountain, and, at last, my beloved Mt. Monadnock. Impressive! I couldn't wait to hike. We soon began our descent via a series of switchbacks to Stratton Pond, a beautiful secluded body of water about halfway down the mountain.

A caretaker tenting nearby talked to us briefly about the site. Legend has it that it was on the slopes of Stratton Mountain that Benton MacKaye first imagined the long-distance trail that would link the high peaks of the Appalachian Mountains. I sat on my pack and gazed out at the water, trying to see what MacKaye had seen, before any warming huts or ski lifts or tenting sites dotted the landscape. The view from Stratton was still beautiful, but MacKaye's vista had truly been one of unspoiled wilderness, I reflected, envying him.

After that, I hiked for long stretches by myself, at my own pace, eleven miles mostly downhill. My pace felt good. I had agreed to meet the others at the trailhead and routes 11 and 30, and hitch with them to Manchester Center where George had made reservations for all of us at a motel outside of town.

The last few miles ET caught up with me and hiked on my heels, pushing me faster than I wanted to hike, talking non-stop about the farmsteads that had graced the area in a bygone time. I could hear traffic on the road unseen, parallel to the trail. The sound of civilization and ET's drawl made the distance to the trailhead seem that much longer. I was glad to finally reach the hiker's parking area and see Jed and Waco waiting patiently for us by the side of the road.

A pickup truck drove by, stopped, and invited us to hop into the back for a ride to town. In the course of introductions, I discovered that our driver was Ranger Bob, one of the first thru-hikers I had encountered in Shenandoah. Still hiking the trail, today he was with his girlfriend, Kathryn, who had driven from Virginia to meet him for the weekend. They drove us right to our motel, a cluster of one-room cabins just beyond the center of town.

ET, Jed, Waco and I took turns showering, then hitched a ride to the Laundromat and Friendly's restaurant conveniently located across the road from each other. We may have looked unkempt, but we fit right in with the thru-hiking community wandering the streets of this factory outlet town.

Jed spent the evening mapping out a four-day hike for Amy's visit. He showed us the itinerary when he was finished and announced that we would divide the food so that she wouldn't have to carry too much. I was surprised that he had taken over responsibility for her hike. I'll wait and see, I decided, knowing that if Amy didn't like him we could make our own plans. To quote my friend, Happy, from our time together as teachers: "Whatever happens, happens." That's just how I felt about Amy and Jed. I knew she could take care of herself.

I fell asleep to the persistent pounding of the TV just inches from my feet. This would be my last night sharing a room with three guys. Tomorrow, George and I would have some privacy. I couldn't wait.

8. Whatever Happens, Happens

Manchester Center to Killington, Vt., 48.9 miles

July 8, 2001, Manchester Center, Vt., 0 miles

We spent the morning wandering the streets of Manchester Center. I was drawn to the used bookstore and spent a long time looking for something lightweight to read on the trail. I finally found a slim paperback volume of *Pilgrim's Progress,* which I hadn't read since college, and bought it to read aloud to Waco in the shelters. We straggled back to our cabin to clean up for George and Amy. They arrived in the late afternoon, just at cocktail time.

I ran up to the van to greet them. Amy stepped out in a tank top, shorts, and sandals; her toenails were painted hot pink. I thought Jed would faint.

"She's so clean," Waco exclaimed when I introduced him. She was, particularly to a hiker unaccustomed to bathing. Waco had been in the woods a long time.

We were a merry group. The narrow railing in front of the door to our cabin was just wide enough to balance a cooler-lid tray of cheese, crackers, and assorted chips. ET, with a motel towel draped over his arm, served wine to the guests assembled on the driveway in lawn chairs. It was the first time George had met any of my hiker friends; they were eager to please him.

The hiking poles propped against the door of the next cabin belonged to a young woman named Jessica, hiking the Long Trail. She joined our party and we shared drinks and snacks as twilight faded to evening. The eight of us packed into the Odyssey and drove to a local diner for supper, laughing and telling trail stories all the way. Amy and George fit right in, parrying wisecracks with dry jibes of their own.

Back at the cabins, Amy, Jed, Waco, and Jessica finished the beer, and then went scouting for more. George and I finally had some time together without other people around. We grabbed it while we could.

July 9, 2001, to Peru Peak Shelter, 9.7 miles

George dropped us all at the trailhead the next morning, promising to meet us at the forest service road crossing Mad Tom Notch at lunchtime. This enabled us to hike the first five miles of the day, with a thirteen hundred-foot climb and descent, without our packs. The plan was for him to bring our packs to us and then drive back to New York for the week to help his mother sell her house. His project for the summer was to help her relocate to Ohio and, while we were hiking, help her decide which things to leave behind after fifty years of living in the same town. I wouldn't have traded places with him for the world, but it was really hard to say goodbye when he brought us our packs and some extra food at lunchtime.

We did say goodbye, though, and he drove away, taking some hikers hitching from the trailhead to town with him. Amy, Jed, ET, Waco, Jessica, a bearded hiker named Snowman, and I headed out into the bright sunshine, blue sky and puffy white clouds. It was a beautiful day to hike, though I didn't trust the puffy white clouds. By midafternoon they grumbled with distant thunder.

We entered the Peru Peak Wilderness and ascended steeply to the ridge of Styles Peak, a climb of nine hundred feet in one and a half miles, and then over several knobs to the summit of Peru Peak, two miles farther. Amy hiked very well, particularly for her first day out. Jed was careful to have me set the pace so that we could all hike together and, even though his knees were badly damaged from previous hiking abuse, he gave up his hiking poles to Amy before we had ascended the first mountain. She gratefully hiked with those poles all week. I was impressed.

Although the use of hiking poles has been the subject of a mock controversy for the past few years (noise made from scratching their tips on rocks, holes poked in soft dirt on either side of a narrow trail), hiking poles are extremely helpful for balance, particularly in steep, rocky terrain. Most thru-hikers use them to help distribute the weight of the pack and put less stress on knees and ankles. Hikers don't give up their gear, especially gear as important as hiking poles, without a good reason. For Jed to offer his to Amy, I thought, was above and beyond the call of chivalry. But he was not to be dissuaded, and I was not about to interfere.

After a short break at the wooded summit of Peru Peak (3,429'), we hiked to the Peru Peak Shelter. As expected, it was crowded, but Amy and I found spaces on the floor and quickly spread out our sleeping bags, hung up our packs, and went to find some water. ET, Jed, and Waco were tenting behind the shelter. Snowman found a fairly smooth spot on the ground under the shelter overhang.

When Amy and I returned with water, we discovered Jessica had hiked in and spread her things next to ours on the floor of the shelter. Amy was not happy to see her, and I wondered if Amy thought of Jessica as competition.

That night was cool, but not cold. Amy and Jed stayed up to talk while I fell asleep to the sounds of their laughter and Jessica's snore.

July 10, 2001, to Greenwall Shelter, 14.7 miles

The morning dawned clear and cool. We ate breakfast, broke camp and headed out in a large group: Amy, Jed, Waco, ET, Snowman, Jessica and I.

The first ascent of the day was fairly easy, and together we all reached the flat white rock summit of Baker Peak, comfortably warm in the bright sunshine. Amy had already pared down to a tank top; I soon joined her and we relaxed in the sun, snacking and joking, greeting other hikers as they scaled the rocks and hiked on.

It was a much longer break than I would have taken had I been hiking alone, but no one seemed eager to leave. Watching Amy, Jed, and Waco frolic amid tiny wildflowers poking through the crevices in the rocks, I tossed poetic license to the winds: Ah, the boisterous capers of carefree merriment, the light-hearted playfulness of budding attraction, the innocent spirit of mountaintop summer. I reflected on the beauty way: "in old age, lively may I walk," the wind at my back, the future unfolding. Why hurry? I was content in the sunshine.

Eventually, we put our food and water bottles away, strapped on our packs, and rejoined the trail. I was intoxicated by the heady pine scents all around me. It was a perfect day to hike in the Green Mountains, I thought as I looked around at the soaring emerald foliage before, behind, above, and all around me. Though high, these mountains were easily ascended by switchbacks and graded paths with only minor descents over roots and wet logs.

This is hiking paradise, I mused, practically dancing to the edge of the Big Branch River. The river was strewn with large boulders tossed haphazardly across clear, rushing white water. Shallow and cold, this river reminded me of the Lost River of my childhood.

The vision kept alive by a home movie of me, age five, eating a peanut butter sandwich while climbing over similar boulders, was my childhood vision of heaven. I could feel again the smooth stones under my bare feet, the fish darting through my legs, the frothy water chilling my toes to numbness. I saw the same afternoon sun dappling and warming the flat granite and intensifying the shimmer of blue, gold, green, and silver all around me. I was, once again, home.

It was lunchtime. ET, Waco, and Snowman had already claimed rocks to sit on when I hiked in, hungry. Amy and Jed soon joined us. Jed lay flat, horizontally shooting photographs of us while we ate and cooled our feet in the bubbling current of Big Branch. The lunch hour lazed on into early afternoon. Reluctantly, we laced up our boots, hoisted our packs, and hiked out, committed to going eight more miles before stopping for the night.

Those miles were relatively easy with little change in elevation until the thousand-foot ascent of White Rocks Mountain. We hiked along its ridgeline just west of the summit and, at about six o'clock crossed a grassy meadow dotted with large piles of stones, called cairns. They must have been placed by other thru-hikers. We walked around the statuary admiring each lopsided collection, looking for stones to embellish our favorite. It was a bit of whimsy at the end of the day.

When we reached Greenwall Shelter, it was crowded with novice Long Trail hikers. We knew they were novice because, when we hiked in, no one greeted us or made eye contact, afraid that we might try to usurp the shelter space. We knew they were Long Trail because they were still clean-shaven and over-packed with new-looking gear.

Since we all had tents, it made little difference to us whether these hikers shared the shelter, but their attitude annoyed ET. He stomped around, cussing, to find level ground to pitch his tent. Amy was also testy, but I knew it was because she was really tired. I set up our tent and gave her some time to relax. She was fine again soon and went off with Jed to find water for cooking.

When they returned, we sat on our packs on the rocky ground behind our tents, spread out our food, and fired up our cook stoves. Food calmed ET and renewed his spirits. Soon we were all laughing again, and we chatted and joked under the stars until a slight drizzle sent ET and me to our respective tents.

I fell asleep to the quiet murmur of Jed and Amy, still finding something to say after a long day of talking and hiking together. I was glad they were enjoying each other's company and that Amy was having a good hike. It pleased me that she was able to leave her professional self behind to enjoy camping and hiking in the woods again.

July 11, 2001, to North Clarendon, Vt., 7 miles

We rolled out early, with a threat of rain nudging us to stuff our packs and eat before the clouds broke loose. On the trail by eight o'clock, we walked steadily all morning to reach the Whistle Stop Café a half-mile from the trailhead, just past Clarendon Gorge. The gorge is spanned by a suspension bridge dedicated to the memory of Robert Brugmann, a young hiker who drowned there during a flood in 1973; we crossed without incident and walked to the Whistle Stop.

Jed remembered the Whistle Stop for its huge hamburgers, fries, and friendly faces. It was, in reality, a caboose converted to a diner. We stowed our packs at the picnic tables on the attached porch and greeted the Long Trail novices from last night's shelter, deliberately making eye contact. As we ordered, the clouds that had been threatening all morning gathered and darkened, the wind picked up and thunder rolled overhead. We moved our packs closer to the caboose and huddled under umbrellas to ride out the storm. It was fierce but we didn't care – we were too busy eating oversized burgers and onion rings, and getting up to order more. Since it was still raining when we finished eating, Waco pulled out a deck of miniature playing cards and challenged us all to a rousing game of Hearts.

In an hour, the heart of the storm blew elsewhere, but the temperature dropped and the rain continued. The thought of hiking all afternoon uphill against a running stream of a trail and camping in the rain or spending the night in either the Clarendon Shelter (near the road) or Governor Clement Shelter (an old stone shelter near another road, used frequently by partying neighbors) did not appeal to anyone. It would make a long hike up Killington tomorrow, but on this cold, gray, rainy Vermont afternoon, the decision to stay overnight at the nearby Country Squire Motel in North Clarendon was unanimous. A van of trail maintainers gave us all a ride and we booked two rooms, splitting the cost six ways – four dollars each.

By evening, the rain had settled into thick wet mist framed by gloomy mountains. I was glad to be sharing a room with Amy, away from the beer and the grungy smell of four guys and their dirty hiking gear next door. I looked in, at one point, to see ET slumped dejectedly in a chair trying to get a signal on his cell phone.

"Homesick?" I asked.

"Yeah. I guess it's the dreary weather. I really miss my wife today," he said.

ET hadn't talked much about his wife, a retired teacher and amateur doll collector.

"Here, try mine." I handed him my phone. "It can usually get a signal ... and I don't have to plug it into a tree to recharge it here."

Returning to my room to write in my journal, I was soon joined by Waco and Snowman; they sat on the floor and cut pop cans into alcohol stoves to replace the heavy, more complicated stove systems they had been carrying for cooking. They offered to make me one, too, but my Esbit fuel cube system worked beautifully for me: it boiled a pot of water in less than three minutes, weighed three ounces, cost an initial six ninety-five, and averaged about forty cents a day for fuel. But then, I had been cooking for almost forty years – I wasn't intimidated, or bedazzled, by stove systems.

Later that evening, Jed and Amy went for a walk, both carefully brushing their teeth before they left. Waco kept me company until I could keep my eyes open no longer. I was happy to be sleeping in a motel, though it made me homesick, too.

> "Tomorrow we've decided to slack the eighteen miles up, then down Killington Peak. George is driving in from New York and meeting us at Sherburne Pass at the end of the day; we can pick up our packs with the Odyssey. George is half-expecting me to come home with him, I think, and sometimes I'm tempted. I'm tired of camping and reorganizing and being uncomfortable. But I love hiking in Vermont and I'm really looking forward to New Hampshire and Maine. I miss him, but I love being in the New England woods in the summer."

July 12, 2001, to North Clarendon, Vt. via Sherburne Pass, 17.5 miles

The day began by hitching from the Country Squire in the early morning mist.

Jed had planned our day: Snowman and Waco would hike the AT relocation trail to Maine Junction for their mail drops; Jed, Amy, ET and I would hike to Killington Peak and descend via the old AT to Sherburne Pass, meeting Waco and Snowman at the trailhead to wait for George. First we would split up, three and three, to expedite the hitch back to Clarendon Gorge and the trailhead to Killington.

In the cold morning mist, only a few cars passed us. I had my doubts that we would get a ride and dreaded walking extra miles along a road in the rain. I continued to stick out my thumb and smile, however, and the next car that passed almost ran us down before stopping in the ditch next to the road.

"I'll give you a lift if you don't mind the smell of pot," the driver said.

Waco and Snowman jumped right in. I was dubious but followed them into the back seat, daypack on my lap, heart in my throat. As soon as we were in, our driver pulled out his pipe and offered us all a toke.

"A little early for us," replied Snowman, shaking his ponytail. Waco and I also declined, and we drove on, weaving down the empty mountain highway. Ahead, Amy, Jed, and ET were still trying to hitch a ride.

"Know these hikers?" our driver asked, swerving into the ditch to stop for them. "Hop in," he offered, before we could answer.

Amy, Jed and ET slid in and slammed the door. The six of us, plus the pot-headed driver, continued our journey at, to my hiker perception, top speed. In my head, I read the obituary column, saw the headline: "Mother and Daughter Done In By Pot-Smoking Mountain Boy" or "Car Crash Along Deserted Mountain Road Probably Drug Related."

In the end, nothing happened and we all reached the trailhead without a mishap, including our driver. But I was a wreck and happy to get my daughter, and myself, out of that car. Grudgingly, I also had to admit that I was glad we hadn't had to walk the extra five miles to the trailhead.

We crossed the road to begin our climb up Shrewsbury Mountain. Just behind us Luke Skywalker and Darth Vader crossed the trail and disappeared into the mist, heading to the Whistle Stop for breakfast. I remembered this father-son duo of light and dark from the Lehigh Rocks in Pennsylvania. They had appeared and disappeared into the mist just as suddenly on that day, after helping me hoist my heavy pack up the rocks. Odd that I should see them again today, I thought. Was their appearance an omen? A harbinger of the hike ahead?

Since we were slacking, we only had snacks, rain jackets, and water with us. This, I later realized, was unwise because, as the elevation increased, the weather grew colder, windier, and wetter. Amy and I, dressed in shorts and tee shirts, were unprepared for an emergency or bad weather in the mountains. Letting Jed plan the week's hike, I had somehow abandoned responsibility and forethought for my own preparation. Weather in the higher elevations was unpredictable. I knew that.

As we hiked up Killington, I shivered in the cold, windy rain and told myself that this was a good lesson in hiking and would remind me later how to slack in the Whites.

More than forty-two hundred feet high, Killington is the second highest peak in Vermont, with commanding views of the Green Mountains in Vermont, the Adirondack and Taconic ranges in New York, and the White

Mountains in New Hampshire. All we saw that afternoon, however, were dripping evergreens and thick gray clouds overhead. On the top of Killington, my bare legs, hands, and head were wet and I was freezing.

Ducking into a four-sided stone hut to escape, for a moment, the howling wind and chilling temperatures, Jed put his arms around Amy to keep her warm. I was looking forward to George, a motel, and hot water at the bottom of this mountain for the same warm comfort.

Descending, the trail was slippery and treacherous from the recent rain but, without our heavy packs, we were able to hike quickly. Even though it was steep and wet, we expected to be down the mountain in less than half an hour. With ET ahead and Jed and Amy behind me, I trod confidently on pine needles, leaves, and rocks, until, with no warning at all, I slipped on a wet root and fell, crashing onto the rocks in front of me, striking my left temple on a sharp pointed stone.

Through closed eyes, I could hear Amy and Jed catching up.

"Uh oh, she's down!" Jed exclaimed when he reached me, squatting down to survey the damage.

"Mom! Mom! Are you all right? Mom! Say something," Amy cried.

"Get her over here, get her off the trail," ET shouted, crashing back to see what happened, thrusting his arm under my shoulders.

"Mom, say something!" Amy pleaded with real fright.

I could hear them, but it hurt too much to move or to answer. I could only lie, face down in the dirt, whimpering and trying to will myself to talk. Finally, clutching the side of my head, I managed to roll over and sit up. The pain at the juncture of my cheekbone, jaw, and left ear was exquisite – sharp and flashing, dull and throbbing all at the same time. Blood was everywhere: dripping from my face, smeared across my fingers and wrists and down the sleeves of my rain jacket, splashing on the rocks.

"It hurts it hurts it hurts it hurts," I managed to moan, cradling my head, trying to make the pain stop.

Amy put both arms around me and held me like a child. I couldn't stop shivering or crying. But I did stop moaning.

ET squatted on his knees in front of me to look at the pupils of my eyes.

"Old coaches never quit," I tried to laugh, hiccuping and gulping, instead.

Jed thrust a candy bar in my face, ET wrapped his wet rain jacket around me, and I, gradually, brought my shivering and hiccuping under control, poking and checking my legs, feet, arms, and hands for other injuries. Nothing else seemed amiss.

"I'm okay, really," I said, sensing that it was important to convince us all.

"That was some fall," exclaimed ET. "I could hear the crack from where I was. You must have hit that edge, there," he said, pointing to the tip of the most offending rock.

"Yeah. We should have stuck to the rerouted AT," admitted Jed. "This trail isn't used enough anymore. It's too steep to descend in the rain. We should have used the other trail."

"It's okay. It's not your fault – or the trail's fault. It happened so fast, I don't even remember going down – only the crack."

They helped me up and we descended the rest of the mountain slowly, with ET just ahead, Jed just behind, ready to catch me, I supposed, if I fell again. I appreciated their concern but was too badly shaken to concentrate on anything but walking. It seemed to be taking a long time to descend, and I was concerned that George would be waiting at the trailhead only to see me all bloody and goofy. Step by step, I pulled myself together, picked up my pace, and hiked out.

George and Waco were waiting for us in the Odyssey, chatting about graduate school, oblivious to my mishap on the mountain. No one else mentioned the blood-crusted hair under my rain hood or my filthy knees and face. I couldn't wait to get to the motel and its promise of a steaming hot shower.

Back at the motel, clean and warm, wrapped in wool blankets and nestled in couch pillows on the sofa bed in our room, I watched the clouds roll over the mountains just outside the wide picture window. I told George about our week's adventures, including the fall. He was solicitous and comforting but not overly concerned.

"I would like to sit here forever," I said, dazed and weary from the events of the afternoon. "I don't want to move from this place. I don't want to hike anymore."

"Any time you want to stop," he said, "I'll come get you. No matter where you are, all you need to do is call."

George always said this. It was his version of that old psychology experiment featuring aversive conditions and a panic button. Those subjects with a button to push to stop the aversive conditions of the experiment were always able to endure more than the subjects who had no way out, no button to push. In fact, the subjects with access to the panic button never pushed it at all. George's accessibility was my panic button. I knew I could call him from anywhere and he would find me. It was reassuring, but not always helpful. It always left the decision to me.

"And you'll probably feel better in the morning," he added with a smile.

When Amy and Jed returned from fetching our packs at the Country Squire, we all went out to dinner at a nearby Italian restaurant. Seated around a large round table with my family and hiker friends, I felt comforted and safe. I hoped I would be ready to hike after a good night's sleep.

July 30, 2001, North Clarendon, Vt., 0 miles

I awoke on a bloody pillow with a huge headache. I washed down several Ibuprofen tablets with a tall glass of orange juice and looked outside. It was still raining and I didn't feel at all like hiking.

George and Jed proclaimed a day of rest and Waco rented four movies from the motel office. Amy, George, and I took everyone's clothes to the laundry while Jed, ET, and Snowman slacked the four miles they had missed the day before. I spent the rest of the day wrapped in a blanket by the side of the motel pool until rain drove me inside to the comfort of the couch cushions, once again.

Dinner that night was hearty lamb stew and Guinness Stout around dark wood tables in McGrath's Irish Pub at the Inn at Long Trail in Killington, Vermont. Beer flowed freely and spirits were high. Through the mist of my throbbing head, I watched and listened to the boisterous laughter of those I had come to depend on over the past few weeks: Jed, ET, Waco, Snowman, Tacoma, Joel from Japan, Flea and his brother, Darth Vader, Luke Skywalker and others. I was proud to be accepted in this incongruous group of determined hikers.

Gazing at the rugged faces surrounding me, scarred and bruised as I felt, I decided that I would hike out with them in the morning. Although I wouldn't see my own family again until I reached Katahdin, I knew I would be among friends even if I were to be by myself for most of every day ahead. I could count on my own wits and intuition, my panic button, and this new quasi-family of like-minded thru-hikers to sustain me on the rest of my journey.

"I'll be ready to hike in the morning," I declared, "fit and willing."

George gave my hand a squeeze and we said goodnight to everyone assembled at the bar. We walked out into the clear cool air of mountains freshly washed with rain.

"The night renews itself for morning," I breathed in with release, and remembering Happy, "whatever happens… happens."

"And all you need to do is call," George reminded me, giving my hand another squeeze, "but it probably won't be necessary."

9. The Going Gets Tough

North Clarendon, Vt. to Glencliff, N.H., 84.6 miles

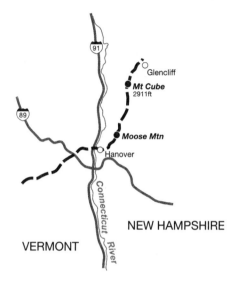

July 14, 2001, to Chateauguay Rd., 8 miles

The next morning I awoke to sunshine and some good news. Amy
had decided to join us again in two weeks for a weekend in Gorham,
New Hampshire, on the other side of the White Mountains.

"Things must be going well with Jed," George observed dryly, driving
us all to the trailhead before he and Amy left for Ohio.

We stopped at a deli for sandwiches and cokes, then said goodbye at
the trailhead on River Road. Amy and George drove away as Jed, ET,
Waco, and I hoisted our packs and started up fourteen hundred feet, by
switchbacks and former logging roads, to the north shoulder of Quimby
Mountain. The day was relatively mild and my recovering body was equal
to the hike along ridge crests and across muddy brooks. Other than feeling light-headed and bruised, I was able to hike at my usual pace – slower than Jed, but about even with ET and Waco. Jed occasionally dropped
back to hike with me; sheepishly, awkwardly, he wanted to talk about
Amy.

At dusk we decided to camp on a flat dirt road next to a stream. The mosquitoes were daunting, but as soon as we had eaten, Jed and I climbed a steep knoll to try to get a signal on my cell phone. I said a brief hello to George, still en route to New York, and handed the phone to Jed; he was eager to reconnect with Amy.

A discreet distance away, I waited for another turn at the phone, batting mosquitoes in the gathering dark, wondering how long my cell phone battery would last. Finally, Jed clicked off and we descended the knoll back to camp together. I asked him how Amy was doing and he replied, looking bashful, that she was fine. Remembering how important phone calls were when George and I first started dating, when Peace Corps training and ROTC summer camp separated us, I decided not to tease him about using my cell phone. But next time he talks to her, I thought, I won't wait around.

Jed's headlamp shone late into the night, writing a letter, I guessed, the first of many in the weeks ahead.

July 15, 2001, Bluejay and Wild Rose Farmhouse on Vermont Route 12, 17+ miles

I awoke to see Jed and ET dancing in the middle of the dirt road. What was silence to me was bluegrass music to them through their earphones. It promised to be a sunny day and after breakfast we all set off. The early morning grass was still wet when we descended, crossing pastures of wildflowers over the rolling green hills. I stopped with Jed while he placed another phone call to Amy at the top of a small rise, waited a short distance away, then gave up and hiked on in the bright morning sun, catching up with ET and Waco.

"Must be true love," ET said, shaking his head when I told him Jed was sitting in a field of buttercups, talking again on my cell phone.

We descended gradually for the next four miles through old fields and woods. Stone walls and cellar holes, evidence of former homesteads, fascinated ET. He poked around looking for artifacts from bygone farming days, excited by some old metal barrel hoops at the base of a crumbled chimney.

By early afternoon, Jed caught up with us. "There's a farm at the next road crossing," he said, "where some hikers I know are staying for a few weeks. I'd like to stop there for lunch and see if they're home."

Not only were Blue Jay and Wild Rose home, they were eager to welcome us to their barn for the night. Jed had met them both in the south, before Wild Rose injured her knee and came north to recover at her uncle's farmhouse, greeting and assisting thru-hikers as they crossed the trail just east of their barn. They suggested that we leave our packs at the barn, slack south from the trailhead five miles north, and join them for a hearty home-cooked supper at the end of the day.

It was an offer too good to refuse. Eight of us squeezed into Blue Jay's small battered car and careened with unbelievable speed and levity around curving backcountry roads to the trailhead. This time the headlines in my head were silent.

Blue Jay and Wild Rose continued on to Woodstock, Vermont, for provisions for our dinner. Jed, ET, Waco, Snowman, Morpheme, a hiker from England staying at the farmhouse, and I hiked south, across pastures rippled with swaying hay and framed by green hills shimmering in the distance. Without my heavy pack, I practically floated along the crest of Thistle Hill, through open woods and around a field brilliant with wildflowers and brown Jersey cows chewing sleepily in the afternoon sun. It was a perfect way to spend a summer Sunday: hiking carefree under a cobalt blue sky, breathing in clean air heavy with the aroma of raspberry bushes and hay-scented ferns. I was glad I had decided to hike on with the group.

Back at the farm at day's end, I spread my sleeping bag in the dusty loft of the barn and waited my turn for the outdoor hiker shower below. I was impressed that Dr. Bronner's Magic Soap was available for me to lather suds onto my hair and body.[10] To save weight, I no longer carried soap or shampoo.

Clean and refreshed, I changed into long underwear and fleece, and joined the bonhomie of hikers around a massive picnic table on the farmhouse porch. Two additional hikers, the first southbounders I would

10. Dr. Bronner's amazing soap is the only choice of soap-carrying hikers: 100% vegetarian pure castile biodegradable soap, made of all natural ingredients… with outstanding water softening and cleansing powers… used as soap, shampoo, mouthwash or for shaving.

meet, had joined us. The ten of us, plus our hosts, did justice to the reputation of thru-hikers' appetites, eating through several banquet-sized platters of lasagna, fresh bread, corn on the cob, and chocolate chip cookies.

"In the morning," Blue Jay offered, "why don't I take your packs to
the Outing Club at Dartmouth College so you can slack to Hanover for
your mail drops."

It sounded like a good idea to me. I fell asleep that night feeling happy
and relaxed. It was only fifteen miles to Hanover; it would be an easy hike
without a pack. I was looking forward to seeing Dartmouth again and
planned, with the others, to spend the night in one of the fraternity houses, a thru-hiker custom I anticipated with mixed feelings.

July 16, 2001, to Hanover, N.H., 15 miles

The day dawned sunny and warm. We gathered on the front steps of
the farmhouse to cook and eat before hiking. When I pulled a stale bagel
out of my pack, Wild Rose asked if I might like to use her toaster to make
it more edible. I had stopped expecting anything more than nourishment
from my trail food. That small gesture made a big difference to my taste
buds and, smeared with her fresh raspberry jam, my first carbohydrate of
the day became sixty grams of sublime nectar. I was ready to hike.

Blue Jay once again drove us all to the trailhead five miles north, and
we began our hike with a steep ascent into the woods of Bunker Hill. At
the very first opportunity, Jed borrowed my cell phone and began another conversation with Amy. I hiked ahead through a red pine plantation
and across several hilltop pastures to catch up to Morpheme, Waco, and
ET. At eleven-thirty we stopped for a break and Jed caught up with us.

"We'll meet for lunch at the Country Store where the trail crosses the
road in West Hartford," he greeted us curtly. "And Waco, you hike with
Mom," he added, pulling ahead to set an increased pace for the others.

I was puzzled by his gruffness and annoyed that he had assigned Waco
to hike with me. I wasn't his mom. Besides, I was hungry right then. I
didn't want to rush on to a soda fountain lunch, though I knew I would
probably eat again when the opportunity presented itself.

We picked up our packs and hiked out. Waco hiked behind me and
talked continuously all five miles to the crossroad. By the time we arrived,
I felt pushed and tired.

Jed, ET, Morpheme, and Snowman were sitting at the lunch counter in the back.

Smoke seemed to be coming out of Jed's ears. He neither looked at us nor spoke. He glowered. I was hot and hungry – but puzzled, too. What had happened to our jovial hiking group? I sat at the counter and ordered a hot dog. When the teenager behind the counter pushed it towards me a few minutes later, it was still raw. Fond as I am of hot dogs and hungry as I was, I asked her to grill it a few minutes longer. At that, Jed got up from his stool and stormed out of the store, mad as hell. ET and Morpheme followed him. Waco and I looked at each other, shrugged, and finished our lunch. No one had said a word.

Later, as we set off on the tarmac road to the trailhead, Waco wondered about Jed's behavior.

"He sure does get bossy," Waco observed. "Must be from his days in the military. I don't get it."

"Me neither," I agreed. "He's pretty grouchy all of a sudden. I guess he's in a real hurry to get to Hanover." Unprepared for Jed's surprising moodiness, my feelings were hurt. Somehow, I thought, I've done something to displease him, and I had no idea what it might be.

We hiked down the road in sticky afternoon heat. I wondered what the hurry really was, all of a sudden. We were just going to Hanover to pick up our packs and spend the night. Before ascending the ridge of Griggs Mountain, Waco and I crossed a small stream with a big sign declaring its name: Podunk Brook. I started to laugh at the absurdity of the situation. Podunk was my mother's word for "little bit of nothing" – and it seemed, on that hellishly hot afternoon, that we were, indeed, in a little bit of nothing, letting cranky people lead us to perdition. Podunk! It sure was.

Wry laughter lightened my mood. The rest of the afternoon passed quickly as the trail turned from pastures overgrown with pines, to country lanes lined with well-bred New England frame houses and local traffic. By late afternoon we reached the bridge over the Connecticut River that marks the state line between Vermont and New Hampshire. At rush hour, it was noisy, hectic, and hot. I couldn't wait to pick up my mail drop and get back to the woods.

But first, I had to go to the Dartmouth Outing Club to pick up our packs, visit a pizza parlor for dinner, and settle in a fraternity house for the night. Jed, ET, Snowman, and Morpheme had already arrived when we hiked in.

The fraternity house was awful. Littered with empty beer bottles from a bash the night before, the hiker facilities consisted of mattresses strewn about the floor of the main hallway. The bathrooms and kitchen were cluttered with dirty dishes, food, and discarded clothing. I was repelled by the sight and smell. This is one bathroom that is dirtier than I am, I thought, passing up the shower stalls on my way to the laundry. But the only alternatives were several expensive tourist inns or a shelter a mile north of town on the trail. I didn't want to hike out of town and then back in again in the morning to pick up my mail.

That night as I lay on a stained mattress surrounded by a rainbow of sleeping-bagged bodies, both north and southbound, I vowed to wake up early, find some breakfast, pick up my mail drop and leave town as soon as possible. Uncomfortable on my lumpy mattress, I drifted asleep to the sound of rain gently falling on the romantic campus, lit by converted gaslights just outside my window, blurry in the evening mist.

I spend my professional life on a privileged college campus, I reminded myself drowsily. No wonder I feel out of place sleeping on the floor in this trashed fraternity house. It feels incongruous because it is.

July 17, 2001, to Etna-Hanover Road, 6 miles

In the morning, Waco had an appointment to talk with someone from Dartmouth about graduate school, and Jed and ET promised that if I would wait, they would soon be ready for breakfast and an early start out of town.

First I waited for them to gather their gear. Then I waited while they initiated south bounders with tales of hiking prowess and the number of miles they had already walked, and how tough those miles had been. Discussing miles and how fast you hike them, I had observed, seemed to be a preoccupation of some male hikers when they met other male hikers. I wondered if this were the human male version of marking one's territory, keeping the other males of the species at bay.

When we finally went to breakfast I tried to take advantage of the extensive menu and nourish my body to hike, but I wasn't very hungry. My face, still swollen from my fall, prevented me from opening my mouth very wide and my stomach and intestines were out of sorts; greasy eggs and bacon had little appeal, no matter how heartily prepared.

Jed was all business; he had talked to Amy for over an hour the night before and was eager to reach Gorham to meet her. In fact, he wanted to hike the hundred forty-four miles from Hanover to Gorham, over the White Mountains, in less than eight days so that he would have time to clean up before her arrival. He planned to hike fast and hard. He was a man with a mission.

But after breakfast he didn't seem to be in much of a hurry to leave town. At the post office, we waited a long time for him to reorganize his pack and send his film home to be developed. I sat on the post office steps writing letters, then went across the street to the outfitter where Jed helped me purchase some gear replacements more suited for the White Mountains and Maine: a warmer fleece shirt, some stream-crossing aqua-sox, and a new pack belt, sized extra small.

It was nearly two-thirty before we were ready to hike. The delay and the blistering heat of the afternoon sun exasperated me; we still had a long hike ahead of us and I wanted to be off. But the trail in Hanover goes right through the center of town, and on the way out we passed a Ben & Jerry's ice cream store, featuring White Blaze milkshakes (white Russian ice cream, chocolate sauce, and whipped cream), free to thru-hikers. Of course we stopped. Of course we posed for pictures around the Ben & Jerry's cow. Of course we drank free milkshakes while the afternoon whiled away.

When we finally pulled out of town, sluggish from too much food, town frenzy, and ice cream, it started to thunder. We debated about stopping at the shelter just north of town, but Jed pushed us on, and we hiked several miles through dark woods just ahead of the storm. I hiked as fast as I could, worried about hiking in a thunderstorm and arriving after dark, at a shelter crowded with already settled hikers.

The thunderstorm hit about seven o'clock, nine miles shy of our destination. Partially sheltered from the rain by tall pine trees, we hiked halfway up the next hill and discovered a fairly level overgrown logging road in the middle of a pine grove. ET, Waco, Morpheme, and I decided to pitch our tents. Jed dropped his pack but continued on to the top of the hill. He returned just as I pushed my last tent stake into the wet ground.

"I'm going to hike on tonight," he announced. "I'll meet you in Gorham in ten days. I can hike fast and get there sooner – before Amy gets there."

This time, I wasn't surprised at Jed's change in behavior. No longer gruff and glowering, he had once again become jovial and good-natured. I suspected that his moodiness of the past two days had come about while he was trying to make up his mind about hiking on without the rest of us. Once he made the decision, he was pleasant again – and eager to get moving.

"Go for it," I said. "But saying goodbye makes me sad." I gave him a quick hug and watched him hoist his pack and adjust his poles.

With a tug on the brim of his orange hat, he turned, waved, and was gone.

I didn't really mind that Jed was hiking on, and I think ET and Waco were relieved. Unlike Jed, they didn't have any reason to race through the Whites, and I didn't want to miss any of it by rushing, either.

But I was sad that our hiking family was breaking up. At the same time, I thought that without Jed we would have a less pressured hike. His hiking expertise had made me, at least, hesitant to insist on my own hiking goals for the day, and several times I had been frustrated at the pace and destinations he had set for us. His leadership style, learned in the Marines, could be overbearing. I suspected that ET and Waco would be easier to hike with, though perhaps not easy to catch if they wanted to stretch their legs and hike fast. But, I was willing to hike with them for however long it would last, eager to resume responsibility for my own hike, making decisions based on my own best understanding of the maps and data book.

July 18, 2001, Dartmouth Skiway, 12.6 miles

Early in the morning we hiked out of our pine forest, leaving

Morpheme behind with diarrhea and stomach cramps. He planned to hitch back to Hanover and sleep the day away.

"Now we are three – me, Waco, ET."

We hiked, initially, at my pace, ascending gradually across abandoned farmland shoulder-high with wet grass. Luckily I still had my rain pants on; ET, in shorts and tee shirt, was drenched.

"This is a sorry excuse for trail maintenance," he grumbled, thrashing his poles through overgrown bushes, releasing a shower of dew. "I'm goin' to write them a letter. This is the worst so far."

We climbed steadily at first, crossing and following woods roads to the summit of South Peak of Moose Mountain, and then along the ridge through a col between the south and north peaks. Our hike was definitely more leisurely and less pressured, though we were hiking at a good pace. I thought about the difference in our hiking without Jed. No one was competing to get to a certain place by a certain time, to hike faster than their natural pace; Waco was taking more responsibility for using the maps and ET seemed freer to stop and stretch out with his hands behind his head, just drinking in the view. I just liked hiking without worrying about keeping up.

We stopped twice. The first was at midmorning on the rocky top of the South Peak. Lolling about, we dried our tent flies in the sunny breeze and ate chocolate bars. The second stop was for lunch about noon, at the top of the North Peak, overlooking mountains in the distance and valleys below. We talked to a southbounder, took off our boots, and ate leisurely. After lunch, we moved on, deciding to hike at our own paces and meet up again later in the afternoon.

Hiking by myself, I was happy to be alone in the quiet and was surprised at how much better I felt with a midmorning snack, midday lunch, and steady pace of my own choosing. Descending the North Peak after lunch made sense to my body; it made the steep ascent of one thousand feet to Holts Ledge an hour later much more manageable. I passed ET on the ascent and we met Waco at the viewpoint.

Waco was sitting with his back against a rock, eating wild blueberries. We joined him and talked about the view of the valley below us.

We seemed to have the mountains to ourselves on this quiet, sunny afternoon.

The Trapper John Shelter, named for the fictional Dartmouth character in the movie and TV show, M.A.S.H., was halfway down the mountain about two-tenths of a mile off the trail. We decided to meet there for the night. ET and Waco headed out ahead of me.

Descending through the woods, aware that the blue-blazed trail to the shelter was within a mile, I kept a close watch for the turnoff. When I saw two hiking poles stuck in the dirt on the side of the trail, I assumed they were Waco's poles, signaling me to turn. But there was no trail, no turn off, no blue blazed marker – nothing but overgrown bushes and trees. I continued to descend, searching for the trail crossing, remembering that this was the part I hated – trying to find the shelter at the end of the day, never quite knowing where it was, worrying that I'd miss it altogether and have to camp on the trail or grope my way to the next shelter in the dark. I kept descending.

When I could hear a highway ahead of me, I realized with dismay that I had gone too far and had missed the shelter. The base of the mountain was just below.

I took off my pack, and, because I was within hearing distance of a road, stashed it behind a leafy bush. I turned around and hiked back up the mountain, looking for ET and Waco. I passed the abandoned hiking poles about halfway up and realized that they were just abandoned and didn't signify a trail marker. I continued up.

Just before the summit, I saw ET, coming towards me with his pack still on.

He told me the shelter was full, and I admitted that I had missed the turn-off and left my pack at the bottom of the hill. We agreed to camp farther on, and waited for Waco to catch up with us.

When he arrived, we all walked back down the mountain, picked up my pack and within fifteen minutes found a fresh meadow by a pond at the base of the Dartmouth Ski-way. We pitched our tents underneath a stand of pines, fetched pond water for cooking, and ate dinner in the lengthening shadows of the mountain at our back.

Settling into our tents, comfortable on a bed of newly mown sweet hay, I reflected on the day just passed. It had been good: no rush, no pressure, and no displeasure, even when I missed the trail to the Trapper John Shelter.

The day matched the mood of the night to come: calm and still with touches of brilliance in the sky.

July 19, 2001, to Mt. Cube Sugar House, 16 miles

I scrambled out of my tent at six a.m. to hang my sleeping bag and tent fly to dry in the early morning sun. After a hurried meal of dried fruit and instant breakfast we set out, still wet from the dewy meadow, and were soon overtaken by some hikers from the Trapper John Shelter, Flea and his brother among them.

As the hikers passed us, our pace quickened; ET and Waco did not want to be out-hiked by Flea or his brother. At first, ET hiked right behind me, almost stepping on my heels to speed me along. Finally, stopping to pee, I took off my pack and urged him to hike on.

"I'll catch up with you," I panted, not yet having found my trail legs.

Grudgingly, ET hiked on and I did my best to hike faster so that I could catch up with the others. I knew ET and Waco would be taking a break at the top, but their new pace, matching Flea's, was just too fast for me. We had a long way to go today. With two ascents over twenty-eight hundred feet, I didn't want to use all my energy before the first climb.

My stamina and the resources provided by my skimpy breakfast were not enough to sustain me. By nine o'clock I had already hiked four miles, two of them a steep ascent, and by the time I reached Lambert Ridge, I was spent. ET and Waco were sitting on a rocky ledge outcrop fifty feet in front of me taking a break.

Slipping out of my pack I sat down on a rock to use my cell phone. George and I had begun a new custom of checking in with each other in the morning after my first ascent, before he went to work. By then I usually had found my trail legs and had climbed high enough to get a phone signal. It was a running joke that I had to climb a mountain to talk to him and all he had to do was eat breakfast and wait – but the ritual pleased us both and assured him every day that I was still all right.

This morning, I was not all right. As soon as I heard his voice, I started to sob, surprising both of us.

"I just can't do this," I wailed. "It's too hard. I don't have enough energy. I can't get the right kind of food and I'm exhausted and it's only nine o'clock in the morning and I have two more mountains to climb before tonight and I can't do this."

I was taken aback at my outburst. In the past few days I had begun to notice that my emotions were close to the surface and erupted easily: anger, exasperation, joy, and sadness, all were quick to escape my usual composure. Sometimes I would catch myself crying at the top of a hill, just from the exertion of the climb, or more often, from the beauty of the moment.

Hiking fast to catch up with ET and Waco this morning had taken all of my reserves; I couldn't hold back the tears of exhaustion and helplessness the scramble had cost me. I didn't even try. I felt so inadequate and weak, as though something were the matter with me because I couldn't hike as fast, as easily as the others. I could hear the taunting voices of my brothers from a childhood long ago: "you're just a girl; girls can't run; girls can't throw a baseball; girls can't… girls can't…." I still believed them. Composed and reassuring, as usual, George listened to my lament and offered, without patronizing, to come and get me. My panic button. I could see ET and Waco on the rocks across from me, aware of my discomposure, disapproving of my behavior. I looked at the mountains around me, the valleys below me, the blue sky above me. Short of a helicopter, the only way out was by foot.

"I'll be all right," I assured him. "But it's just so hard. I had no idea that it would be this hard."

We talked a few minutes longer. I dried my eyes, ate a power bar, and drank some water. Then I hoisted my pack. Looking at my map, I resolved to hike to the summit at a pace comfortable for me, no matter how long it took. I lifted my head and began again.

Heading out across the rocky ledge, I deliberately attended to the view below, above, before and behind me and remembered: "with beauty all around me may I walk."

With beauty all around me, there was no way out but to hike. With beauty all around me, calmly, and with sure steps, I hiked out.

The climb was steep and when I reached the fire tower just east of the summit, Waco and ET were having lunch on the rocks. Two women and a teenaged boy were sitting on the fire tower steps. I climbed to the first level of the tower to hang my rain fly to finish drying in the wind, and one of the women helped me tie it down. Too tired to be sociable, I sat on a rock to pull off my boots.

"How's your foot?" Waco asked.

"My Achilles tendon is a little sore," I replied, "but I'm okay. Just tired and thirsty. How far is water?"

"About a quarter of a mile down the other side," he replied. "The stream up here is dry."

I groaned and lay back on the rock.

Overhearing our conversation, one of the women said, "My son and I are going for water. Give me your bottle. We'll bring some back for you, too."

Her friend, Brenda, approached me diffidently. "Are you ready for your foot massage now?" she asked.

I nodded yes, handed over my water bottle, and with thanks, lay back down on the rock and, spread-eagled, surrendered my feet to a massage.

Brenda kneaded and rubbed my dirty, numb toes and pressed life back into the soles and heels of my feet. Close to tears once again, I lay in the noonday sun, paralyzed by kindness.

"Are you a trail angel?" I finally asked.

"No, we live nearby and hike on our day off," she said. "I like to help hikers… give them what they need." She continued to rub, soothing me with quiet words as much as muscle relief.

"Do you think I can make it?" I asked, trying not to sob.

Feeling the backs of my calves, Brenda nodded in assurance. "You'll make it," she said. "Know how I know?"

I didn't.

"Your muscles are strong," she said. "And so are you. I'm taking the miles out of these feet. You'll make it."

As they were leaving, Brenda gave me a hug and asked if I had any trash she could pack out for me.

"Only a trail angel would get me water, massage my feet and spirit, and offer to carry out my trash," I exclaimed in grateful appreciation. "This is true trail magic," I said, hugging her back.

"We just like to help hikers," her partner answered. "Especially women hikers. There aren't many of us out here." With that, they disappeared down the trail in the opposite direction, towards town.

I hiked out soon after, reflecting on their appearance and help just when I needed it most. This had been the most trying day, in a series of trying days, so far. I couldn't figure out what was wrong, but something was definitely out of balance. It occurred to me that ever since I had teamed up with ET, Jed, Waco, and the others in our rather transient group, I had been trying to blend into their style of hiking. Their style was one of competition: hiking the fastest or the longest each day, reveling in the challenge to conquer or collect each peak as a trophy, using the metaphor of "kicking butt" as they climbed, never admitting to fatigue or discomfort at the end of the day. By hiking with them, I had begun to judge myself in terms of distance covered, mountains climbed, hardships endured rather than in terms of balance, and of hiking well while still being connected to my surroundings. I was beginning to devalue and lose my awareness of kinship with the natural world.

As a woman, I wanted to hike in harmony with the world through which I was passing and celebrate my kinship with it. As a woman, I knew myself to be a life-giver, not a conqueror; I knew my hiking style was equally legitimate and strong.

Today, I had needed the understanding of other women who accepted my gender and hiking style. More than the foot massage and the water, their acceptance and words of comfort gave me ease.

George and I had often joked that the difference between men and women trying to help each other was that men offered solutions while women gave support and sympathy. My trail angels today were women: life-givers. Their metaphors were right for me. Unable to conquer Smarts Mountain by kicking butt, I was able to reach the summit by hiking smart, by taking the miles out of my feet, and by listening to the mysterious language of the life and beauty all around me.

Indeed, I felt so much stronger that the next climb of twenty-nine hundred feet in three miles was actually enjoyable. Instead of being brutal, the rocks were smooth and life affirming; the sun, the sky, the breeze, the wild blueberries could not have been sweeter. It took me over two

hours to reach the next summit, Mt. Cube, and I was tired when I met
ET and Waco on the ledges near the top. But I was not exhausted. In fact,
I was exhilarated by the climb and liberated by the peak. My perspective
from the top was unsurpassable.

When we began our descent of Mt. Cube, a hand-lettered sign on a
tree directed us to the Mt. Cube Sugar House at the base of the mountain. The Sugar House was owned by former New Hampshire first lady
Gale Thompson, and provided overnight barn accommodations and a
pancake, maple syrup and sausage breakfast to thru-hikers hungry
enough to hitch the two miles from the trail.

Even the name "Sugar House" was promising. With ET and Waco, I
stood by the side of the road next to my pack, thumb in the air, big smile
on my face, tasting pancakes and maple syrup. A station wagon stopped
and took us to the front door of a well-kept farmhouse across the road
from the Sugar House.

Blackberry bushes, heavy with lush, ripe fruit, surrounded the front
door of the farmhouse. I kept my hands in my pockets and waited for
Mrs. Thompson to answer our knock. Within minutes, an elderly
woman came to the door and graciously invited us to pitch our tents or
sleep in her hayloft for the night.

"But," she apologized, "I no longer cook pancakes for breakfast. My
husband died last April and I promised my children that I wouldn't do
breakfasts at the Sugar House this summer. You are welcome to take
whatever you would like from the refrigerator, and make yourselves at
home in the barn," she added.

I ducked my head to hide my disappointment about the pancakes,
and listened as Mrs. Thompson told us her family's history at the farm.
She was lovely and loquacious but I was eager to eat. I had to concentrate
on not stripping the blackberry bushes and stuffing my face in front of
her startled eyes.

One look at the bird-crusted hayloft in the barn convinced us to pitch
our tents on the lawn in front of the Sugar House. Inside, the refrigerator held cold juice and water, and there were several cans of maple sugar
paste on the dusty shelves. I pulled out my stove, lit a fuel cube, and
boiled some water for my instant beans and rice dinner.

The evening was cool and clear with millions of stars shining vibrantly overhead. While ET and Waco tried to name the constellations outside, I lay in my tent, writing and thinking about the day that was just ending.

> "I feel savage – preoccupied with thoughts of food, easily brought to anger or tears. It's a curious feeling to know what I need and to pursue it without fear and accept it without apology. How fragile are the social threads that keep us civilized."

July 20, 2001, to Glencliff, N.H., 10 miles

In the morning our tents were soaked from dew rising off a nearby pond. I did my best to not think about food as I swallowed reconstituted powdered milk, dry granola, and some orange/pineapple juice that I found in the refrigerator. I had forgotten about the blackberries by Mrs. Thompson's front door and used my time to hang my tent on a nearby fence to dry in the early morning sun. ET and Waco were in no hurry to gather their things, even though we needed to hitch a ride back to the trailhead before we could begin our trek to Glencliff, New Hampshire, where we all had mail-drops.

We finally set out and began walking down the road, thumbs ready to catch a ride. The road was deserted. We walked about a mile, dejectedly resigning ourselves to walking the rest of the way to the trailhead, when a shiny new Mercedes approached and passed.

"Don't bother with that one," ET counseled, "Mercedes don't stop for nobody – 'specially the likes of us!"

I stuck out my thumb and smiled anyway. The Mercedes braked, stopped, and made a U turn just behind us. I walked up to the passenger side of the car. A gentleman from India or Pakistan greeted me politely and asked if we would like a ride to the trail.

"Ha-ji. Bahot Acha! Mere Bahni, Shukri-ah," I said, a reflex from my Peace Corps years in Pakistan. It occurred to me only later that I had answered in Panjabi: "Yes, please. Very good! Thank you." ET and Waco didn't even notice, but slid onto the leather-upholstered seats with their packs on their laps. We rode to the trailhead in style, chatting with our benefactor, a local businessman and non-hiker. He was a very proper trail angel, I decided.

Our hike proved to be fairly easy, with three rather gentle ascents and only one sharp descent, down Mt. Mist, seventeen hundred feet in less than one-tenth mile. ET was moving slowly, stopping often to outsmart the stomach cramps and diarrhea that had plagued both Morpheme and me earlier in the week. When we reached the marker announcing the official boundary of the White Mountains National Forest, we stopped to honor the passage.

"These Whites are what I hiked all this way for," ET drawled. "I'm gonna just hike slow and *enjoy* them."

ET had confided in me that when he crossed the Mason-Dixon line, he had been wary of Yankees stalking and harassing him. At the time, I thought he was pulling my leg. As we became better acquainted, I realized he really did harbor misgivings about "damn Yankees." For him, the Civil War was still very real; he had never before been in Yankee territory and, as far as he knew, it was still hostile land. When Waco and I stopped for lunch, ET wanted to continue, on his own, to the hiker hostel in Glencliff.

"You sure you'll be okay alone in these Yankee woods?" I teased him.

He shot me a look but said nothing, feeling too shaky for a snappy retort, I supposed. We met him at the hostel an hour later, stretched out and recovering in the early afternoon sun.

Glencliff consists of a post office, two hiker hostels, a home for the elderly, and several houses along a two-lane country road. We opted for the Hikers Welcome Hostel across the road from the post office. Run as a business, this hostel provided a mattress on the floor for six dollars, a shower with towel for two dollars, the use of a washer/dryer for four dollars and a ride to a nearby convenience store for five dollars. It was furnished with chairs, picnic tables, a fairly clean sleeping loft, and a new outdoor solar shower with free use of flip-flops for my hot, sore feet. It seemed the perfect place to rest, clean up, and resupply before entering the White Mountains in the morning.

I walked up to the hostel porch to drop my pack before heading to the post office. A thin, lively woman greeted me.

"Hey! I'm Dare," she drawled. "I'm from Texas, taking a zero day and restin' up for the Whites, finishin' a thru-hike I started last summer. I had to get off because my daddy got sick. Just got back on two weeks ago," she explained. "Who're you?"

"Gotta Hike!" I introduced myself. "And this is Waco – he's from Texas, too."

"I met a guy two nights ago," Dare said, "Jed. He told me there were some more Texans comin' along. 'Hey!'" she repeated, greeting us as fellow-Southerners.

"Actually, I'm not from the South," I replied. "I'm just hiking with ET and Waco. Jed was with us for awhile, but he's eager to get to Gorham, so he pulled on ahead."

"Yeah, he's movin' fast," she agreed. "He spent most of his time here talkin' to his girlfriend – on the pay phone up the road. Silliest grin on his face ever' time he mentioned her name – which was a lot. He's ahead of you by two days. You probably won't catch him."

"Not expecting to," I offered. "We'll meet up in Gorham on the other side of the Whites next weekend. Jed's silly grin is for my daughter. She's planning to meet us there, too."

"Oh," Dare said, pausing only a moment to register this new information. Then she continued, "Say, mind if I join you through the Whites? I'm hikin' on my own – not fast, but steady… and I don't have a tent. I'm sorta hopin' to stay in the AMC huts and work for stay – whenever possible. How about y'all?"[11]

"ET is planning to take a day off tomorrow and then hike slowly through the Whites," I answered. "And Waco has some friends nearby and hopes to meet them in the next few days. I think our little group is about to become just me – and I'd love to have your company across the

11. The Appalachian Mountain Club maintains the AT and other trails from the southern end of the White Mountain range at Kinsman Notch, to Grafton Notch in western Maine. Because so many hikers and campers visit this backcountry each year, the AMC, the US Forest Service and the NH state park system have established a number of shelters, tent sites, and huts to accommodate them. Thru-hikers are permitted to tent or stay in the shelters on a first-come, first-served basis, but many of the sites are tended by a caretaker and charge an overnight fee. The AMC also provides accommodations for hikers, by reservation, at full-service huts at various locations along the trail. These huts sleep from thirty-six to ninety people and provide bedding, dinner, and breakfast for an additional fee. Thru-hikers can sometimes avoid this fee by arranging to work for stay.

Whites. I have a tent and a reservation for one hut stay – but otherwise, I'm game to try some work-for-stay with you. I've stayed in the AMC huts before. The food is awesome."

We agreed to hike out together in the morning.

"At last, a woman hiking partner," I wrote later, in my journal. "Woman: life-saver!" I fell asleep early and woke refreshed.

10. The Whites

"Take the breath of the new dawn and make it part of you. It will give you strength." Hopi

Glencliff, N.H. to Mt. Washington, N.H., 66.4 miles

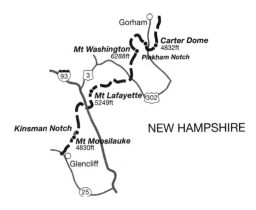

July 21, 2001, to Gordon Pond, 13 miles

The next morning, ET felt better and Waco decided not to join his friends. They both decided to hike with Dare and me.

"For five dollars each," the hostel owner said, "I'll slack your packs to Lost River Gorge. You can pick them up tonight at the concession stand. They'll be safe there."

We gave him our packs and the four of us set out to climb Moosilauke, "a high bald place," an ascent of 4,820 feet, through steep woods and sharp cliffs, in just under six miles. Without our heavy packs, we expected to summit by noon, have lunch, and pick up our packs by late afternoon. We spread out along the trail to hike at our own pace.

Moosilauke, on the southwestern edge of the White Mountain range, would be our first ascent above treeline. I was looking forward to a three hundred sixty-degree view from the summit of bare rock, my first. Because I had not yet hiked the balds south of Shenandoah, the only all-around view I had seen so far had been from the top of a fire tower. For me, the AT had been a long green tunnel with occasional one-direction views from a rocky ledge or tree-covered summit. Climbing Moosilauke, I expected to see more.

After the first four thousand feet, I began to notice some changes in the trail that I had not seen before: underfoot, the soil turned sandy; beside the trail, the spruce and fir trees became shrubby and gnarled. These dwarfed trees, I later learned, are the result of windborne ice destroying their growing tips, creating a forest that grows laterally rather than vertically. Known as krummholz, the appearance of this vegetation signals that treeline is close.

I took advantage of the blueberry bushes lining my path as I hiked through the krummholz, eating my fill and remembering the blueberries I dared not eat on the Lehigh Rocks in Pennsylvania. I doubted that these blueberries were contaminated; small, sweet and vibrant, they were delicious.

As I climbed higher, the temperature began to drop and the wind increased in velocity. I had been alone for more than an hour. At 4,700 feet, the krummholz disappeared and was replaced by bare rock and low-growing alpine vegetation. I noted the delicate sturdiness of the plants, trying to remember what I had read about the "snow bank communities" of mountain heath, dwarf willow, and moss that grow in depressions and behind rocks. I was looking for a plant called sundew, which was known for its small round leaves covered with a sticky substance that slowly folds over unsuspecting small insects and digests them for nutrients.

I never found the sundew, but I did see many tiny plants growing horizontally in rock crevices. Their tenacity was impressive. If they could maintain themselves through harsh snow, wind, and freezing temperatures year-round, I could do my part by staying on the designated trail, keeping my big heavy boots from their fragile faces.

I hiked on, transported by the climb. The wind was in my face and the sun suddenly broke out in full force overhead. I felt alone at the top of the world. It was exhilarating.

Tapping the points of my hiking poles against the mica-schist and gneiss rocks under my feet, I was surprised when I reached the summit to find that I was, indeed, not alone. In fact, the summit was crowded with small groups of colorfully clad hikers, families with young children, and several dogs.[12]

It was an experience that would become familiar to me in the White Mountains: hiking by myself for hours, thinking I was the only person on the trail, and then reaching the summit and finding myself surrounded by other people. Even when I anticipated them, other hikers at the top always surprised me.

When I hiked below treeline in New Hampshire, I usually forgot about the other trails through the mountains. These trails draw thousands of hikers each summer. Below treeline, hikers cannot be seen and the illusion of a solo hike can be maintained, sometimes all day. Above treeline and on the summit, however, hikers are not only visible, they are flamboyantly visible. On the trails they look like brightly colored snakes winding their way up and down the bare, gray rocks; on the summit they look like models in outdoor magazine advertisements; turned-out, fit, and exuberant.

I stood with my back against a boulder and shouted into the wind, just for the glory of being, intoxicated by the beauty of the moment. Waco and ET came out from behind some rocks, where they had been taking in the magnificent prospect of the high peaks of the White Mountains to the northeast, ahead of us.

"Look what we're going to!" Waco shouted, pointing in that direction.

"It's even better than the southern balds," ET added, disloyally for him.

Giddy and excited, we pulled out our lunches and sat out of the wind to eat and wait for Dare. When she arrived, someone snapped our photo. Clutching bagels and cream cheese, we posed at the Mt. Moosilauke 4808'/ Benton Trail sign, looking energetic, happy, full of life, and skinny – four faces, one big grin.

Cairns marked our descent of the north ridge. When the trees reappeared at treeline, the familiar white blazes on the trees replaced the cairns.

12. Mt. Moosilauke had once been a logging and resort center, with a hotel, several bridle paths, and a carriage road leading to the summit. In 1922, Dartmouth College assumed ownership of the hotel and the summit for recreation and education of its students. A popular climb, Moosilauke is still the destination of thousands of hikers and outdoors enthusiasts year round.

The trail was moderate at first, climbing a low ridge with views to the east. Coming down this ridge, however, was difficult. The stone ledges were exposed and wound around a steep wooded ravine. The path underfoot was jagged with roots torn out of the ground in preparation for a new path. I was glad it wasn't raining; the soil under those roots would have been treacherous.

We reached a col between Mt. Blue and Mt. Jim and then began the steepest descent yet: straight down flat rock face that was slick with loose dirt and pine needles. Trekking poles helped us control our descent, as did grasping the saplings and overhanging branches on either side of the trail, but each step was a considered decision.

We poked, grabbed, slid and scooted as best we could, keeping our balance by sheer concentration. The rewards, when we could afford to look west through the trees, were humbling: towering white-frothed cascades, crashing down the cliffs in a torrent of rushing water and incandescent spray. The noise was deafening.

I could have spent the rest of the afternoon under one of those falls, but playing in the water, deliciously tempting as it was, was not possible on this sticky afternoon. I have "miles to go before I sleep," I reminded myself, and "promises to keep," the discipline of the thru-hiker.

Dare and I kept descending, hand-over-hand on metal rungs riveted diagonally down and across the rocks. Hanging onto the metal rung at my shoulder, one foot reaching for the next rung a good leg stretch away, I was surprised by a large dog bounding recklessly up towards me. Startled, I shouted back to Dare, "Watch out! Big dog coming!"

Dogs on the trail can really be a problem – not just for hikers, but also for the environment – particularly unschooled dogs that were not accustomed to trail-hiking. I had encountered several dogs on my hike so far. The ones accompanying thru-hikers were generally well-behaved and wonderful hiking companions. Dogs like this one, accompanying weekenders and day-hikers, often seemed to be out of control, creating a potential hazard for themselves and others.

It wasn't the dog's fault, I knew. He was just out for a romp. But I wish his owner had been more considerate.

Shaken, I continued and eventually the descent began to level out. I passed the final cascade and reached the base of the mountain within half an hour.

Walking across a large wooden bridge, I looked down at the clear glacial water below. Here was a milestone in my wilderness pilgrimage. I raised my poles, quickened my pace, and crossed the source of my childhood vision of heaven: the Lost River.

ET and Waco were waiting at Kinsman Notch, looking for the receptacles usually provided in parks and parking lots for trash.

"We don't have trash bins in New Hampshire parks," said a woman stowing her day pack in the back of her station wagon. "We expect people to minimize their trash and pack it back to wherever they came from. Where are you from?"

"We're thru-hiking the AT," Dare answered. "On our way to the Lost River Gorge concession stand to pick up our packs, heading north to Katahdin."

The woman's expression softened. "Hop in and I'll take you up the road to the concession stand."

Always grateful for an off-trail ride, we accepted and squeezed into her over-packed car.

She waited while we picked up our packs and visited the snack bar. When the server behind the grill discovered we were thru-hikers, she slashed the prices for our food and drinks in half. I ate two large hot dogs and drank a liter of ice-cold Coke. The server came over to our table.

"I can't sell you beer," she said, "but I bet I could find some for free." She thrust four beaded cans of local brew in my direction. I accepted them for ET and Waco; I knew they wouldn't mind carrying the extra weight for the taste.

Back at the trailhead, we decided to head up Mt. Wolf and find a camping place for the night. Putting on my heavy pack after a day of exhilarating freedom was the lesser challenge; the greater challenge was climbing nine hundred feet in six-tenths mile, straight up from Kinsman Notch, trying to digest two oversized hot dogs and one large Coke with the late afternoon sun beating directly on the back of my head.

We hiked for two and a half hours, climbing steep ups and steep downs, squishing through bogs, alternately batting and trying to ignore the swarms of bugs looking for dinner behind our ears and knees. By this time of the day, I was usually tired of hiking; today was no exception. To me, ET and Waco seemed to be competing to see who could hike the fastest as they stretched their long legs farther and farther ahead of me. I could feel myself becoming grumpy and, not wanting to spoil the magnificence of the day, concentrated on the hike at my feet, deliberately not thinking of how tired I was. It was a relief to finally reach the trail to Gordon Pond and see Waco's hiking poles stuck at the trailhead, indicating that we had finally reached our destination.

Taking the trail three-tenths of a mile through dense trees and scratchy brambles, I was surprised to find a sheltered grove with a fire ring by the edge of a pond, black and smooth, streaked with the pink afterglow of sunset and blanketed with lily pads whose blooms had closed up for the night. Although the bugs continued to harass me, I walked out through the marsh anyway, drinking in the stillness of the twilight, hoping to spot a moose or hear a loon on the distant shore. I waited in the silence as dusk slipped into evening, surrounded by mountains and darkening firs, at peace in the calm, cool air.

Quietly I walked back to camp to set up my tent and cook. Waco built a fire to discourage the bugs, and together we ate and planned our next day's hike in the flickering firelight. Later, under the protection of the tall firs, sharing my tent with Dare, I fell asleep with a sense of deep contentment, as though wrapped in a cocoon, listening for the call of a loon across the pond.

July 22, 2001, to Lonesome Lake Hut, 10 miles

We headed out about eight o'clock. ET and Waco planned to hike ahead of us so they could be the first to arrive at Lonesome Lake Hut and garner the work-for-stay positions. Dare and I both had a reservation at the hut and, since we were expected, knew we could take our time hiking, as long as we reached the hut by dinner time.

Before starting out we looked at the map. The hike promised two major and one minor elevation change totaling three thousand feet in ten miles; doable, we thought, by dinner. Although we had heard that the hike up Kinsman South would be a rock scramble and would take more time and effort to climb, Dare and I hiked all morning at a moderate pace, talking about our relationships: fathers, husbands, daughters, sons. I marveled at the contrast between my hiking conversation with Dare and the hiking conversations I usually had when I hiked with men. Dare and I took turns talking and listening to each other; we asked questions for clarification and offered related topics for further dialogue.

Hiking conversations with men, in my experience thus far, had been about their exploits and accomplishments, or the activities they were interested in pursuing. Seldom had my male companions discussed relationships and never had I been asked to clarify my opinion or expand my point. Hiking and conversing with a woman hiker was a novel and welcome turnabout.

At lunchtime we crossed a rushing brook scattered with midsized boulders. We sat on the rocks to eat and talk. In about fifteen minutes, we were ready to hike again. Like me, Dare kept a steady pace, stopping long enough to eat or rest but not so long as to become stiff or sluggish. I was enjoying my female hiking companion.

Dare and I hiked for about a mile, ascending beside an inviting two-tiered cascade. We reached the promised rock scramble in the early afternoon.

> "We moved very slowly up Kinsman South. Dare is shorter than I am and we both found the footholds on the boulders too wide apart for our legs. My pack was too heavy to allow me to place all my weight on my thighs and knees and climb by stepping up. I discovered, eventually, that hanging my poles on my wrists or tossing them ahead and pulling myself up on my knees or the seat of my pants was the best way to climb. Not pretty."

It took us about two hours of hand-over-hand pulling and pushing up twenty-five hundred feet to reach the exposed summit of Kinsman South, but we both did it without falling or losing our poles. Heady with accomplishment, the descent of four hundred feet through scrub and evergreen forest to the col between Kinsman South and Kinsman North seemed close at hand.

"Only one more 'cupcake' and we're there," I informed Dare when we stopped at the beginning of the next ascent to consult our map. "We'll be at the hut in time for a swim before dinner."

But the "cupcake" up ahead was instead a three hundred-foot climb up and a long sixteen hundred-foot descent over loose rock and "snatch-at-cha" roots. We threw our shoulders back and hiked on.

An hour later, instead of the mountain tarn of Lonesome Lake as expected, there was a sign that read: Lonesome Lake Hut 1.2 miles.

We struggled on, hopping from the top of one boulder to the next, up and down small rises and big rocks, legs shaky from bearing our heavy packs. At the estimated arrival hour we still had not reached the hut.

"These darn PUDs! They're killin' my knees," Dare protested.

We were still over a mile away. And those Pointless Ups and Downs (PUDs) were discouraging.

"Pursuing Unknown Destinations is more like it," I elaborated for Dare's benefit. "Never mind. As long as we're there by dinnertime the croo[13] will save us some food."

We trekked on through growing evening shadows.

Finally, about half an hour before sunset, we encountered the sign for Lonesome Lake Hut and followed it through the woods to the welcome sound of human voices and clattering plates and silverware. A very welcome din, we agreed, and hurried up the path to claim our place at the table.

We found ET and Waco stretched out behind the hut, tired and waiting to eat. They had secured the work-for-stay and offered us the two extra bunks in their room. We took them up on their offer, as the room assigned to us was full of weekend trippers and too much gear.

---

13. The croos (crews) of the high huts are typically a group of college students full of energy, humor and pranks. One such prank is the on-going raid of a wood propeller from whichever hut captured it last. The propeller was the only thing to be recovered from a small plane, crashed by three drunken men dressed as Santa Claus, in 1968. Each summer, the croo from one of the huts tries to capture or recapture the propeller for their hut. Since the high huts are at least a day's hike from each other, this is not an easy task. In 1989 when I stayed at Mizpah Spring, the propeller found its way to our hut by means of a stealthy croo-hike of twenty-eight round-trip miles in the wee small hours of the night.

Too hungry to swim, we went straight to a hearty meal of lasagna, soup, salad, vegetables, rolls, blueberry shortcake, and coffee.

Lonesome Lake Hut was surprisingly large: two horizontal wooden buildings of bunk rooms connected by a long wooden deck and outdoor stairs to a bath house at one end and a dining area/common room at the other. The croo was all women: wonderful cooks and affable hosts. Both dinner and breakfast the next morning were mouth-watering, ample, and nutritious, boding well for good hiking.

> "After dinner we tried to make plans for the rest of the week but were really too tired to concentrate. Tomorrow is a short day to North Woodstock in Franconia Notch for mail drops, laundry, and lunch; after that, its only forty miles to Mt. Washington where Amy and Jed will meet us. I can't wait."

July 23-24, 2001, to Garfield Campsite, 13.2 miles

We hiked three miles to North Woodstock and spent a hot and lazy afternoon organizing our mail drops and laundry. Rather than hike out, we decided to spend the night in a hiker hostel on the main road leading to Franconia Notch and ascend to Franconia Ridge in the morning.

In retrospect, this was a poor decision. We would have been better rested had we spent the night at the tent site; the hostel was hot, dirty, depressing and noisy. On a two-lane highway lined with tourist motels, restaurants, and souvenir shops, under the steady whir of an electric fan that only played with the humid air and mosquitoes, we hardly slept.

The four of us were up early the following morning to begin our ascent of Franconia Ridge via a steep three-mile switchback trail below treeline.

"The best part of this trail," ET observed, "is that, once you're up, you're up."

He was right. Once we reached treeline at forty-two hundred feet, we continued along the high ridges of the Franconia Ridge Trail, then the Garfield Ridge Trail overlooking the western and northern edges of the Pemigewasset Wilderness.

Dare and I hiked together over four major peaks: Little Haystack, Mt. Lincoln, Mt. Lafayette, and Mt. Garfield, ascending and descending on narrow, steep, rough ledges all day. The trail brought back memories of my hike in the White Mountains in 1989, just twelve years ago to the day when, as a participant in a group hike, the illusion of hiking on my own had been made possible by the expertise of trained leaders. Then, I had been free to enjoy the hike, leaving the responsibility of safe hiking decisions to the leaders.

During that hike, we were caught in a storm on Mt. Washington and forced to spend an uncomfortable, crowded night with several hundred other hikers, all stranded by the weather. That experience taught me about the real hazards of hiking the high peaks, particularly for novice hikers who are unprepared and/or disrespectful of the weather.

This time, I had to be vigilant about the weather; I was responsible for my own safety. Romantic as it might have seemed to be hiking alone, I knew that I was not alone in the mountains, nor should I be. The trail is made possible by a large community of maintainers, guides, emergency rescue teams, and environmentalists – people who love and want to preserve the wilderness for everyone to enjoy and be safe within. This time, I was aware of my very small place in the grand scheme of mountains, weather, and trail community.

Gathering clouds and overcast skies quickened my steps over the ridges on this day. Though I did not want to spoil Dare's experience, her first in the Whites, I was apprehensive about the weather. I suggested to Dare that we hike a little faster to be off the ridge before any weather materialized. Luckily, it never did, and we arrived at the Garfield Ridge Campsite by late afternoon.

The evening was clear, but cool; the shadows were blue. A new crescent moon rose just at twilight, illuminating the silent mountains across the wilderness expanse in front of the shelter. Our hike in the morning would traverse those mountains. It was a privilege to fall asleep in their quiet, imposing presence.

July 25, 2001, to Zealand Falls Hut, 10 miles

It was a beautiful day for looking at distant mountains: clear, blue sky, light wind, and no haze. Dare and I hiked out early, climbing down steep boulders, some flat-faced and vertical. While descending, I decided to experiment with a different hiking technique: rather than scooting down on my bottom or coming to a complete stop at the conclusion of each downward step, I decided to stay upright and keep moving with a forward motion, relying on the soles of my boots to give me sufficient traction to keep me from slipping. I continued to use my hiking poles for balance, but put more trust in my knees and feet to keep upright.

This method worked particularly well descending dry rock face. It helped me hike more quickly and with more confidence. I found that even with a heavy pack, I was better able to keep my balance and not put undue strain on my knees and ankles. And it was fun.

About midway up the next ascent, South Twin Mountain, I took a side trail to Galehead Hut. The renovated hut was beautiful and, at mid-morning, empty. The croo invited me to finish the leftover French toast from breakfast and take a look around. What I saw pleased me. The bunkrooms, common room, and bathrooms were clean, light, spacious, and wide enough for my father, in his later years, to have been able to maneuver in his wheelchair.

I wondered who and when the first wheelchair-bound hiker would be. No doubt someone would accept the challenge to make his or her high-hut dream a reality. I wished them Godspeed and hiked on, pulling ahead of Dare to hike by myself for a few hours.

The mountains were quiet in the early afternoon light; the silence was sublime, the view exquisite. In front, behind, and all around me the mountain peaks appeared as ocean waves, yellow-green in the foreground, dark green behind and smoky blue and hazy gray in the distance, blending into a light white horizon of clouds and sky looking level at over six thousand feet above the sea.

When I reached the Zealand Falls Hut, ET and Waco had already claimed the work-for-stay thru-hiker positions. The hut would be full with paying guests but, the croo assured me, Dare and I were welcome to any food left over after the guests, croo, and work-for-stay hikers had eaten. For ten dollars, we could also sleep on, or under the tables, as long as we were up before breakfast.

I was willing to gamble that there would be plenty of food left over; Dare and I agreed to wait for leftovers and sleep on the tables.

It was the longest wait of my life. While six long tables of well-nourished men, women and children cheerfully helped themselves to platters of roast pork, fresh vegetables, potatoes, whole-grain bread and butter, juice, milk, coffee, blackberry cobbler, and jovial conversation, Dare and I sat by the wall and watched.

As I watched I could feel myself growing more irritable. I knew I would feel better if I could go outside to wait, but I could not move. I physically could not get up from my bench by the wall and leave that food, close but not close enough, to satisfy my ravenous appetite. Even being aware of what I was doing and feeling, I could not move.

Finally the paying guests were satisfied and it was ET, Waco, and the croo's turn to eat. I continued my vigil. No one offered to share his food with me, nor did I ask. I continued to watch; I could not leave my bench. I was paralyzed with hunger.

At last, Dare and I were the only two who had not eaten. When, finally, it was our turn, I ate with both hands, stuffing three large helpings into my mouth as fast as I could. I'm not sure I even tasted the food, such was my rush to fill my stomach.

The experience gave me a new perspective on being hungry in the presence of food and not allowed to eat. For the first time, I was able to understand why people go to war: while I watched everyone else eat, I begrudged them every bite and hated every diner and his benign indifference to my need. Had I been denied, in the end, I think I would have fought like an animal to have my share. Luckily, that night I never had to fight. But I was surprised at how angry I became while I watched others eat, totally unresponsive to my presence or my need.

Once I had eaten, however, I cheered up, and that night slept warm and satisfied on top of the table that fed me, next to three screened windows open to the high mountain air.

I never heard the snores of hikers jammed into the two airless compartments of bunk beds lined up three to a row, on either side of the dining room.

Thursday, July 26, 2001, to Mizpah Spring Hut, 14 miles

In the morning, under the supervision of the hut croo I created *The Sandwich:* two thick slabs of homemade whole-grain molasses bread liberally smeared with chunky peanut butter and swirled with thick honey. It was a masterpiece in nutrition, taste, and eye-appeal.[14] For miles, while Dare and I hiked, I fantasized about this sandwich. Every now and again I would remind her about *The Sandwich* waiting to be withdrawn from my pack at the proper time; my anticipation of epicurean delights kept me hiking and drooling all morning.

Although the day began with rain, by midmorning we were splashed instead by sunshine and deep blue sky. Hiking through the green and leafy woods, I noticed many other trails crisscrossing our path. I remembered hiking several of those trails in 1989, and sunbathing au natural at Thoreau Falls. Today, as we passed the falls, I would have loved to lie on the rocks again, letting the sun drench my bones. But Dare and I were on a mission. We needed to be the first thru-hikers to arrive at Mizpah Springs Hut in order to secure work-for-stay jobs for the night.

In my pack, far away from the food bag in which I carried *The Sandwich*, I bore a prank gift from the croo at Zealand Falls to the croo at Mizpah. With much ceremony, just before leaving, they had presented me with a "little something to sweeten the pot," they said: a baggie of dry moose turds. I was certain that if our timing were right, we would be able to secure the coveted work-for-stay positions at Mizpah. Moose turds could not fail to convince, I thought.

It was a great day to hike: sunny, cool, and breezy. When we reached Crawford Notch, Dare and I stopped for lunch at a picnic table and I, with ceremony equal to that of the Zealand croo presenting us with our hostess gift, opened my pack, reached into my food bag, and withdrew *The Sandwich*. With great reverence and respect, I unwrapped the plastic, eased open the layers, and set each half on the table, spread apart to eat open-faced in deliberate, long-lasting appreciation.

I chewed each bite, letting the peanut butter crunch between my teeth, the honey melt around my tongue, the bread slide down the back

14. Female endurance athletes need between 65 and 90 grams of protein per day and, during exercise, foods with a high glycemic index (i.e. food that enters the bloodstream rapidly after ingestion to produce a faster rise in blood sugar). My whole-grained molasses bread, peanut butter and honey sandwich provided at least 48 grams of complete protein and had a glycemic index of 73% (pure glucose is 100%). My sandwich gave me almost a full day's supply of complete protein and a healthy jump start for the energy I would need to climb the high peaks ahead.

of my throat. After eating *The Sandwich,* I was ready to go again, full of energy and good spirits within minutes.

Ascending Mt. Jackson after lunch, Dare and I hiked as old friends, companionable in our silence, truthful in our conversation and acceptance of each other. We were two women, doing what few women have the opportunity to do. As we climbed, she told me a little more about herself.

A pharmacist and EMS provider, she said she had grown up in a dysfunctional home. At home and in her first marriage, she had assumed the role of co-dependent rescuer.

I remembered that when we met, Dare had told me her thru-hike had been interrupted last summer when her "daddy got sick." At the time, I assumed she was a spoiled little "daddy's girl." I was curious about Dare's story and asked her to elaborate.

"On the trail in Vermont, I received word that I had an emergency at home. My dad's cancer had spread and this time, there were no treatment options. I flew home to help. It was an awful six months watching my dad die. I realized I still had emotions that had to be 'walked out' back on the trail. I returned to finish this last five hundred miles and sorta sort myself out."

She went on to explain that she had, unwisely, married as a teenager. Her parents' marriage was the only example she had; it was the kind of marriage she expected. It was the kind of marriage she got. Unlike her mother, who chose to stay, she was able to change her path. Times were different, she said. As an adult she found the courage to recognize her mistake and to accept the support she needed to escape. She broke the cycle of abuse she had thought normal, divorced her husband, and made a different life for herself and her young son on her own.

"It never was easy and I did marry again," she continued. "The trail can't teach me much about hard, but it has taught me other life lessons. I learned that hard doesn't have to hurt your heart; that each person is responsible for their own stuff; and I can't change anyone but myself."

We hiked in thoughtful silence after that. I thought about the nature of support.

I have always wrestled with the nature of support and how to both give and receive it. I did not learn how to recognize my need for support as a child or trust that when support was offered, it was genuine and not a disguise for control. Hiking the trail, I was learning, finally, to know what I needed, how to ask for it, and how to accept with grace; I was learning to be humble and grateful rather than ashamed when I needed help.

I had learned on the trail that it was supportive to be treated with dignity, and reassuring to know that I could refuse support that was not helpful, as well.

"I guess there are a lot of things for the trail to teach us," I said, finally. "For me, the lessons of the trail are hard."

We hiked on with our thoughts and our moose turds.

When we reached Mizpah Spring Hut, Dare and I were, indeed, the first thru-hikers to ask for work-for-stay. The moose turds secured our places: two bunks in the attic. Our job was to set and clear the tables for dinner and breakfast and sweep the bunkrooms in the morning. For that we received two free meals, two free bunks, and a warm night with convivial company.

Accessible by several trails from Crawford Notch, Mizpah is located at the southern end of the twelve-mile hike above treeline that passes over the highest Presidential summits: Pierce (4,310'), Franklin (5,004'), Washington (6,288') and Madison (5,363'). Mizpah is a popular stopping place, with bunks and meals for fifty inside and a tenting area for campers outside. On this cold, windy afternoon, I was glad we had secured bunks inside for the night; the temperature outside was dropping rapidly.

In the late afternoon sun, Dare and I sat on the exposed rocks in front of the shelter, talking to other hikers as they came in to register for the night or find a tent site next to the shelter. I pulled out my watercolors. Mizpah was just as I remembered it from my last visit: shingled, angled, set on gray rocks framed by blue-green pines. The hikers around the hut were like birds returning to the nest in early spring, I thought: colorful, noisy, and easily startled.

My watercolors were the one luxury I still permitted myself even though I did not often have an opportunity to use them. Initially I had planned to add sketches and colors to journal entries at the end of the day or when I stopped for lunch or a break. I soon discovered, however, that I rarely stopped long enough midday to even pull my journal out of my pack. At the end of the day, I was usually too tired to do anything but make camp and eat. My journal entries were most often written after dark, by flashlight, while I stretched out in my sleeping bag. Sleep usually eclipsed both the light and the energy I needed to paint.

This late afternoon at Mizpah, I took advantage of the full sunlight and vivid display of hikers and mountains and brilliant sky overhead. I painted while someone else cooked dinner.

July 27, 2001, to Mt. Washington, 6.2 miles

In the morning, Dare and I were up by six o'clock to set tables and sweep bunkrooms while we waited for breakfast. Several older women hikers were staying at the hut and interrupted us at our work, full of admiration for our hike. I admired them more for theirs. Even though they were only hiking from hut to hut, theirs was a strenuous endeavor for seventy-plus year-old women. I thought it was remarkable that they would be hiking together rather than sitting on a porch somewhere, reminiscing. I hoped I would be as fit at seventy.

The day was full of sunshine but cold, with winds of sixty miles per hour.

Dare and I hiked alone all morning in long johns under and hats, gloves and fleece over our hiking clothes. As we hiked, the summit of Mt. Washington's weather station appeared and disappeared in the distance.

"I've never seen it before," I shouted excitedly to Dare when the view first came into sight. "Every time I've climbed Mt. Washington, the summit has always been covered with clouds or snow flurries or horizontal rain. It's otherworldly from a distance."

Continuing along the ridge, wind howling in our ears, sun dazzling our eyes, I watched the weather station get closer, become larger. Finally, two broadcasting towers and a radio and television transmitter loomed in eerie silhouette against the sky. It could have been the setting for a 1950s science fiction movie, until it dissolved into two large parking lots full of cars and a long black train disgorging passengers into a rambling building housing an observatory, museum, snack bar, souvenir shop, toilet, telephone, and post office. We had reached the summit of the highest mountain in New England, 6,228 feet above sea level, and it was a busy thoroughfare of hikers, tourists, shopkeepers, and high-tech equipment mapping the heavens.

When I opened the door to enter the building, the din was cacophonous. It fell on my head, confusing and blunting my senses. Crowded with tourists and hikers, the setting was unreal; it made me dizzy.

We stowed our packs in the basement and headed for the snack bar. Waco, ET and several other hikers were already ensconced at tables by the windows, with full views of the mountains, train tracks, and auto road winding below. I called Amy on her cell phone and discovered she had just arrived in Gorham; she and Jed would be up to retrieve us within the hour.

I spent my time painting the view below me, using magenta, purple, gold, green and blue hues in undulating waves of color. I was content to rest and wait, out of the roaring wind.

Amy and Jed arrived holding hands and grinning. Our raucous greetings added to the noise and confusion of hikers and tourists all around us. We scrambled out to the "Washington Summit 1.917 miles" sign, and Jed snapped the official photo: Dare, Waco, ET, and me looking like mountaineers in our hats, gloves, long underwear, hoods, parkas, packs and hiking poles.

The ride down the mountain in Amy's rented Durango SUV was scary. The road seemed to drop off just inches from the wheels under us. I felt disconnected from the earth, suspended and out of balance. It was strange to descend without touching the soil and rocks with my boots, or feel the rush of air in my face. I wasn't sure I liked it.

But I did like the motel and shower at the base of Mt. Washington in Gorham, at a motel where Amy had booked us all for the night. Our family had stayed in this motel years ago on a college visitation trip through New England. It hadn't changed much and was a bit extravagant for hikers, but I welcomed the clean, private bathrooms and a double bed all to myself for the night.

July 28, Gorham, N.H., 0 miles

I got up early to drive Waco, ET and another hiker to the summit of Washington for their AT descent. Dare, Amy, and Jed slept in. I hadn't slept well the night before just worrying about the drive up the steep, curvy road. But the drive was all right, though it felt strange to be the taxi service, driving rather than hiking.

When I drove back down the mountain, I met Jed and Amy walking to town for food. I dropped them at the restaurant and went back to the motel to get Dare and the laundry. We joined them in town for lunch.

> "All was going well until I asked Jed if he would help me with my itinerary. Surprisingly he said 'no', and hurt my feelings. Sometimes I don't know how to react to Jed; today was one of those times. I excused myself and went into the ladies room – and burst into tears.
>
> My easy tears must be related to how tired I am. I feel pushed and pulled all the time. I would like to continue hiking with Dare, but she won't reach Katahdin until mid-September. I have to be there by the end of August. I don't really want to hike by myself – especially through the Hundred Mile Wilderness. But I can't hike as fast or for as long each day as Waco and ET and Jed."

July 29, 2001, Gorham, N.H., 0 miles

It was Sunday. I decided to take another Zero day, hike out Monday morning from Gorham, and let my memories of my 1989 hike on that part of the AT suffice for this time, as well. I remembered that hike with stunning clarity:

> "July 29, 1989. Bundled in as many layers as we could find, we climbed, huffing and puffing and grunting, against the glorious wind. At the summit, I was overcome with euphoria and dizziness and exhilaration, and almost blown over several times. We shouted and yelled and waved our arms, trying to catch the

wispy clouds scudding by. We were wild children, having the time of our lives, grasping at rare, exquisite, freedom."

But this Sunday morning, July 29, 2001, I was just too tired to hike. I opted to stay in town and taxi ET and Waco to their trailhead, then Dare to hers. I would see ET and Waco again that evening, but this was goodbye for Dare.

I waited with Dare until she was ready to board the van to the summit of Mt. Washington. I was sad that this would be the end of our hiking together. We hugged and promised to keep in touch. I knew we would, for a little while at least, and waved as I watched her van disappear into the early morning sun.

Hiking with Dare had been fun and thought-provoking. I had loved hiking with another woman and would love to have continued hiking with her. Unfortunately, now I had to move on at another pace, either by myself or with men whose hiking style and stamina were very different from my own. The prospect of the days ahead left me uneasy.

On a trail marked with pollen may I walk.

I hoped my steps would be so blessed.

11. The Going Gets Tougher
Gorham, N.H. to Monson, Maine, 182.1 miles

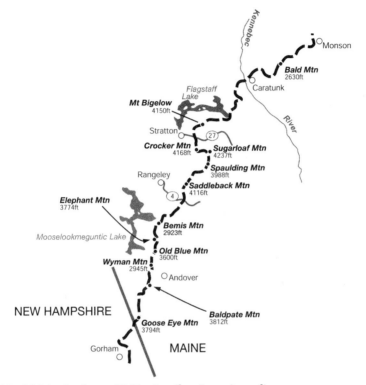

Kennebec

Monson

Bald Mtn
2630ft

Flagstaff Lake

Caratunk

Mt Bigelow
4150ft

River

Stratton

(27)

Crocker Mtn
4168ft

Sugarloaf Mtn
4237ft

Spaulding Mtn
3988ft

Rangeley

Saddleback Mtn
4116ft

Elephant Mtn
3774ft

(4)

Bemis Mtn
2923ft

Mooseookmeguntic Lake

Old Blue Mtn
3600ft

Wyman Mtn
2945ft

Andover

NEW HAMPSHIRE

Baldpate Mtn
3812ft

Goose Eye Mtn
3794ft

Gorham

MAINE

July 29, 2001, Gorham, N.H., 0 miles (continued)

That afternoon, while I sat by the pool and wrote letters, Amy and Jed came up with a plan: ET, Waco, Jed, and I would continue to hike together and summit Katahdin the third week in August. Then Amy and George would meet us in Millinocket, the town closest to Katahdin, the day after our summit, and Amy, Jed, George, and I would drive back to Ohio in the Odyssey. The plan made sense to me and I was pleased that Jed wanted to continue hiking together.

Since this would be the terminus of his second AT thru-hike, Jed also wanted to summit in style. That afternoon, he, Amy, and I went thrift store shopping in Gorham to find just the right attire to wear over our hiking clothes to mark the occasion. For twenty dollars we purchased a black polyester sheath dress with gold and black-spangled sleeves with long black string gloves and dangly earrings for me, a silver spangled long dress and earrings for Waco, and an orange-flowered Chinese shirt and flowing chiffon scarf for ET. Jed planned to wear a tuxedo jacket and silk shirt over his hiking shorts.

"We can send this stuff ahead to the ranger station," Jed said. "They'll hold packages for thru-hikers – and we can change at the summit. We'll be magnificent," he laughed.

It was fun to be light-hearted and silly again. Amy and Jed seemed to be delighted with each other; the weekend had gone well. They had not spent a lot of time together by ordinary standards, but their time together on the trail had been significant. The trail is such an intense experience, with emotions so close to the surface, I was not surprised their relationship had progressed so far, so fast. Remembering Amy's unhappiness of just a few years ago, I was pleased and happy for her. I had no reason to doubt that Jed felt as she did and, judging from the expression on his face when he was with her, he was, as my grandmother might say, besotted.

Their affection for each other, I suspected, was probably the basis for Jed's intention to continue hiking with me; he had assumed a rather protective attitude towards me. I was flattered, relieved, and a little wary. I didn't want to do anything to intrude on or interfere with his and Amy's romance, but I was realistic about the difference between Jed's and my hiking style, our ages, and our physical capabilities for the trail ahead. Compared to Jed, I was still a raw beginner, though I no longer saw myself as a novice hiker. But I was a tired hiker. Even with two days of rest, my body had still not recovered; I had grown thin and angular and could not seem to eat enough to sustain my energy. Food had lost its appeal, even in town where it was plentiful and nourishing. My sixty-year-old body was catching up with me, and I feared it was reaching its limits.

That night when ET and Waco learned of Jed's plan for all of us to hike and summit Katahdin together, they were circumspect and reluctant to commit themselves. After their twenty-three mile hike that day, all they wanted to do was rest. They decided that they would hike behind Jed and me for a day and then pull ahead and hike faster, to reach Katahdin three days sooner than Jed's more modest plan.

Jed knew the terrain ahead, and he was skeptical. The trail in southern Maine crosses twenty peaks in one hundred and thirteen miles, and there is considerable elevation gain and loss between summits. In addition, the infamous mile of hand-over-hand-over-foot-under-boulder-squeeze-and-scramble in Mahoosuc Notch is part of the challenge early on. Jed thought ET and Waco would find his timetable more realistic.

I was disappointed that ET and Waco would not be hiking with us. It would have been fun, I thought, to recapture the carefree camaraderie of our hike through Connecticut and Vermont, and summit together at Katahdin, wearing our silly clothes in celebration of our accomplishment.

Those days, unfortunately, were not to be recovered. Waco tried on his outfit at the hiker hostel in Gorham and left it there. ET never opened his gaily-wrapped package. When Jed discovered that the ranger station at Katahdin would no longer accept hiker parcels, I mailed my spangles home.

July 30, 2001, to Gentian Pond Shelter, 12 miles

Monday morning began with a hurried goodbye to Amy, who would spend the day flying home to Ohio. I would be on my own, now, to hike with Jed through the toughest terrain so far: along streams, watersheds, and wild lakes, across twenty-four mountains, through the Hundred Mile Wilderness, and, finally, up Katahdin. After that, my odyssey would continue another eight hundred miles; I couldn't even think about it. For the present, I could only put one foot in front of the other and think about the journey at hand. I was glad that I would have Jed's company.

After Amy left, Jed and I walked over to the post office to mail our high peaks clothing home. I filled the extra space in my pack with as much food as I could carry.

We hitched a ride to the trailhead and were on the trail just before noon, crossing the Androscoggin River to ascend two thousand feet in four miles to the east summit of Mt. Hayes and the beginning of the Mahoosuc Range.[15] Our goal for the day was to reach a small mountain tarn, Gentian Pond, twelve miles distant, over steep woodsy trails and old

15. The Mahoosuc Range is a long, southwest-to-northeast mountain chain extending from the Androscoggin Valley of New Hampshire to Grafton Notch, Maine. It crosses eight major mountain peaks with the total climb in either direction of approximately 8,000 feet.

logging roads, through dried gullies and along small ledges and ridges. The day was gold and blue, hot, humid, and sweaty. Drought had dried up much of the bog and swampy woodland underfoot, so that the anticipated wet hike along log walkways and across bog bridges was dry and uneventful.

Jed hiked ahead of me most of the day, though I usually caught up with him when he stopped at a stream for water. When we did hike together, he listened to a small radio plugged into his ears. I appreciated the quiet and lack of pressure to converse.

We reached the Gentian Pond Shelter early in the evening and discovered Wildman had set up camp on a nearby tent platform. I hadn't seen him since the Fourth of July in Bennington, Vermont, though he had run into Jed and Amy in Gorham.

"I met your lovely daughter," Wildman greeted me, "and I can see why Jed is so taken with her. They make a handsome couple."

I agreed, but was too preoccupied with setting up my tent on a slatted platform to engage in much conversation.

"Let me give you my shoelaces for that fly," Wildman offered, seeing my consternation and flopping tent fly. I had not yet encountered a tent platform and didn't know how to tie, rather than stake, my tent.

"Jed showed me how to do this in Georgia," Wildman continued. "He showed me everything I know about the trail. I wouldn't still be here without him."

Wildman was in high spirits. That evening, his goodwill was infectious and, supplemented by the flask of LLBeam (sic) he carried in his pack, his generosity was helpful and very much appreciated.

After dinner, Jed added some supplement to my spirits, as well, and produced a small juice bottle of Bailey's Irish Cream for my after-dinner coffee.

We downed our nightcaps and crawled into our tents. It had been a long day, especially since we had started late. We were both glad to rest. The trails had been rougher and wilder today, I thought, but I was glad to be out of the White Mountains with the steady stream of hikers and tourists at every trailhead, hut, and campsite. I understood why the New Hampshire trails were so well graded and the huts so regulated, but I much preferred the ruggedness and solitude of trails less traveled.

I fell asleep with hope that the rest of the hike through Maine would be stress-free. I had always liked the independent resourcefulness of spirit in Maine. This is a place I could live, I thought as I fell asleep, snuggling into my goose down on the hard wooden slats under my bones.

"If I can keep this up, I'll be at Katahdin in no time."

July 31, 2001, to Full Goose Shelter, Maine, 9 miles

The morning was clear and warm. Jed wanted to reach Mahoosuc Notch by late afternoon, go through it, and camp on the other side for an early climb up Mahoosuc Arm the following morning.

Mahoosuc Notch is often called the most difficult mile of the AT. It is, in actuality, a deep cleft of giant boulders and caves between the walls of two very steep mountains, Mahoosuc Arm and Fulling Mill Mountain. Because sunlight reaches the Notch only at midday, it is not unusual to find ice under some of the boulders and in the caves even in the heat of summer. In order to traverse the Notch, hikers need to climb under and over boulders, squeeze between crevices and narrow rock openings, and crouch under and step over dripping and rushing white water. It is a challenge to the most fit and has stopped many a tired hiker from continuing to Katahdin.

I had heard stories of how hard the Notch would be, and was doubtful that I would be up to its challenge at the end of a hard hiking day. But, I agreed to try to reach it by midafternoon, and broke camp early to hike out with Jed.

We crossed the state line from New Hampshire to Maine about midmorning and took each other's picture next to the sign posted on a pine tree that said: WELCOME TO MAINE, THE WAY LIFE SHOULD BE. Below that sign was another that declared: Mt. Katahdin 281.4, Springer Mtn. 1877.8.

For a brief moment, I wished I had only 281.4 miles left in my journey. It was sobering to realize that once I reached Katahdin, I still had 877.8 miles to hike. I tried to focus, instead, on the beauty of the moment, which in this case was the intoxicating aroma of pine all around me. I was happy to be in Maine at last, walking under tall trees, pampering my feet with a thick cushion of soft needles and dry leaves. I loved the pungent odor of decaying wood and the stickiness of melted pine tar on my hands and elbows. August in Maine, I knew from my childhood, could be wet underfoot and cold for days on end. Or, it could be like the weather we were experiencing on this day – sunny, hot, humid, and resplendent with fragrance. As far as I was concerned, we had lucked out with the weather. I had no complaints about the heat.

The climbing was another matter. I loved hiking up, then down over sags, through woods, across long stretches of ridges topped with krummholz pine and bare rocks strewn with blueberries. Had I been without my pack, I would have flown. However, on this day of heat and diminished energy, under my heavy pack I found the hiking tough. Exhilarating, but tough.

Although Jed and I were hiking separately, I usually found him at the summit of whichever peak I was currently ascending, pack at his feet, talking on the cell phone he had recently purchased. Only in the highest elevations could he get a signal to Amy; he took full advantage of that while waiting for me to catch up, and made a lot of phone calls. I teased him that our prediction of his talking to Amy by cell phone had come true. He just grinned and kept dialing.

The peak of the afternoon, for me, was hiking above treeline on Mt. Carlo, the east peak of Goose Eye. I felt like a sparrow under the watchful eye of the universe, as though even my little speck mattered at the top of the world. Climbing above treeline has magic of its own, not to be missed in anyone's lifetime. My spirit soared.

But I was not able to hike fast enough to reach Mahoosuc Notch by late afternoon. In fact, we didn't even reach the shelter, a mile and a half south of the Notch, until almost seven o'clock in the evening, much too late to begin a climb through, even if I had had the energy.

Full Goose Shelter was crowded with hikers, both north and southbound. Jed recognized several old friends from previous hikes in Vermont and in Colorado. I was surprised when he introduced me as his mother-in-law.

Later he explained he had dated the friend of one of the women at the shelter and wanted her to be clear about his status. It didn't seem that clear to me since I was not his mother-in-law. But I was too tired to care, much, and set about making camp for myself and settling in for the night. I did agree to start early the next morning so that we could be through the Notch before noon. The other women at the shelter, young professional hikers, assured me that I would love Mahoosuc Notch.

"It's a playground," one said. "Just throw off your pack and enjoy it."

I was prepared to enjoy it – but my pack, heavy as it was, was easier to lift when it was strapped to my body. I couldn't imagine lifting it over rocks and swinging up boulders to retrieve it, rock after rock, for over a mile. I'll just worry about that in the morning, I thought, and fell asleep to the bragging and boasting of hikers much less tired than I.

August 1, 2001, to Grafton Notch, 10 miles

I was up, packed, and ready to go by seven o'clock. Jed and I left promptly and ascended the first four hundred-foot climb to the crest of Fulling Mill Mountain. At the beginning of the day, a steep ascent and descent is a good way to shake the sleep and stiffness out of your legs; it was good preparation for the rugged mile to come. When we reached the west end of Mahoosuc Notch, I thought I was prepared.

After the big buildup of the night before, the entrance to the notch was unimpressive: drooping pine branches overhanging a narrow passage-way strewn with rocks. Big deal. The air was misty, promising a day of high humidity and sunshine; the rocks were mostly dry. It reminded me of a scene from *The Hobbit* – mysteriously green and foggy, with echoes of dripping water onto shallow puddles. It was spooky.

We entered the notch. The beginning was deceptive: large boulders to pick our way across, using trekking poles, vibram-soled boots and the muscle power of quads built up from a thousand miles of hard hiking. At first, it was like a playground – or would have been had I not been toting thirty pounds on my back. The heaviness of the pack was not the problem, however; it was the pack's bulk that made the journey difficult.

As we proceeded through the notch, the boulders grew bigger, more slippery, and more hazardous. My trekking poles became useless; more of a burden than a help. Initially, sliding down the face of a giant boulder, I tried sending the poles down ahead of me so that they would not trip me up in my descent. This worked until one of the poles slipped through a crevice at the base of a boulder and got stuck, luckily, before it disappeared into the unreachable cave below. Jed instructed me to loop the poles over my wrists and climb down in spite of them. He was right, but the poles bumping into my knees and catching on rocks made my climbs even more awkward. I was cautious and careful when I had to step on wet moss. It was unpredictable and, unfortunately, covered the top and sides of most of the stepping-stones.

We entered the notch about nine o'clock. Jed told me that the first time he had maneuvered this rocky jungle it had taken him forty minutes to complete. At ten o'clock I looked at my watch. We were barely three-tenths mile from our starting point.

"Sorry to be taking so long," I commented when next I saw him with a camera looped around his neck, his eye to the viewfinder.

"It's okay. I'm getting some good shots, " he replied, clicking his shutter on my grimacing face as I tried to wriggle through the small opening between two rock slabs.

My slow pace gave him the opportunity to compose and shoot the small canyons and caves in the early morning shadows. From time to time he would pick his way back over a boulder to find me, stepping and halting, sliding and reaching over the next giant natural edifice.

By eleven o'clock we were still two-tenths mile from the east end of the notch. The light had changed for Jed's photographs, and he was eager to move on. He tried to help me by offering suggestions of where to place my feet, where to try to maneuver under a rock, how to pull myself through a small opening with my pack still on my back. I wasn't sure if his suggestions were helpful or harassing, and I was growing weary of the climb. The playground had long ago turned into a maze of phantasmagoric proportions. I tried to see the humor, the beauty, the pleasure in the endeavor. At least the water pooling around and under some of the rocks was cool and clear, I reminded myself. In fact, it was polar and, in some places, tinged with ice crystals; it tasted great.

At long last, close to noon, I emerged from the playground of my nightmares, tired, sweaty, and bloody. A line from a poem I had translated in Russian class forty years ago ran through my head like a taunt: "Then returning to his castle in far distant countryside, Tired, sad, bereft of reason, in his solitude, he died." I thought I might be blessed if I could die right there. It had been a long, slow, deliberate passage and I was "tired and bereft of reason." I was also ready for lunch, but Jed was eager to hike on.

We crossed a brook, filled up with water, and climbed again, steeply, across the southern slope of the sheer-walled Mahoosuc Mountain to the open summit of Mahoosuc Arm. After the events of the morning, that twenty-two hundred foot climb in less than a mile seemed negligible, though it took over an hour to achieve. At the top, I finally sat down to eat and rest. Jed called Amy on his cell phone.

Continuing, we reached the Speck Pond campground and shelter about four o'clock. It was already full of day hikers and groups of youth campers. I splashed my face with cool pond water and looked longingly at the level places still available for tenting. Though it was early to be stopping, I was tired; it would have been a lovely place to camp for the night. But Jed wanted to keep going. He wanted to reach Grafton Notch, five miles distant, by nightfall.

When I looked at the map, I saw a five-mile descent of three thousand feet. At least it's downhill, I thought, and agreed to trudge on.

We ascended first, through the woods and away from the pond, to the ridge at the summit of Old Speck Mountain. The summit was rocky and barren and overlooked green mountains striped with long vertical scars of forested clear-cut. Jed had hiked ahead and I was, once again, on my own. It was quite pleasant.

By seven o'clock my legs and stomach told me I should have reached the crossing of the Eyebrow Trail and the small box canyon below. I was not even close. Shakily, I continued on.

I reached the Eyebrow Trail crossing, finally, about an hour later, worried about the encroaching darkness. According to my map, I still had more than a mile to descend. Why hadn't I stayed at the campground? Descending these rocks in the dark was just plain stupid. I expected that Jed was somewhere up ahead, frustrated with my pace, and I tried to move more quickly in the gathering darkness, but try as I might, I couldn't go any faster. My legs just wouldn't follow the feet I placed uncertainly on the unpredictable rocks and roots.

When I could hear rushing water somewhere to the left and below me, I began to feel better; the brook through Grafton Notch couldn't be far, I thought. Finally, crying with apprehension and relief, I reached a break in the trees and burst through the woods to find Jed on the edge of the brook that I had been following with my ears for the past half-hour.

Without even stopping to take off my pack or drink from the brook, I scooped up some water for dinner and followed him up and over the rocks, three-tenths mile to the parking lot of Grafton Notch State Park.

We set up our tents at the edge of the parking lot and squatted, illuminated by headlamps, to cook our rations. By now it was pitch dark and I was totally whipped, too tired to talk or eat. I forced myself to be pleasant and to swallow the last of my lumpy rice and beans and instant vanilla pudding and then crawled into my tent to collapse in private. I wrote, briefly, in my journal, switched out my light, and was asleep in minutes. I was too exhausted to reflect on the day, one of the toughest I had yet hiked. I didn't know if Jed had helped or hindered my progress through the notch. I was too busy resenting him for making me hike farther than I wanted to go, and too disgusted with myself for agreeing to do it.

August 2, 2001, to Andover, Maine, 10.3 miles

Six o'clock came much too soon. I was still tired and cold when I heard Jed zip out of his tent and assemble his gear for the day's hike. A half-liter of instant breakfast, Tang, and a dry granola bar did nothing to energize my body or boost my spirits, but, when Jed was ready to go, I hoisted my pack and followed him across the Grafton Notch parking lot, sleepy and stiff in the cold morning air.

After the first two and three-tenths mile of steep ascent from the base of Baldpate Mountain, we reached a small stream and a log Adirondack-style lean-to with an open front, raised platform for sleeping, and slanted roof. The lean-to was deserted and quiet. Sunlight streamed in long narrow bands across the floor. I unbuckled my pack and curled up in a sparkle of dust motes under one of the sunny angles. All I wanted to do was lie there. I was depleted.

Jed was full of energy and eager to hike. While I snoozed, he had a snack, visited the privy, and filled his water bottles at the nearby stream.

When he was ready to go, I roused myself, hoisted my pack, and reluctantly, followed him, wishing I were anywhere else but at the base of a two-mile, twelve hundred-foot ascent. I felt groggy and listless, not my usual self at all.

After a mile, I began to notice the crooked, gnarled, and twisted trees that signaled treeline and knew the end of the climb was close at hand. My spirits began to revive. By the time I reached the summit of the west peak of Baldpate, Jed was a mile ahead of me, a tiny khaki speck on the distant trail ascending the east peak of Baldpate Mountain. I was struck by the views, magnificent in all directions. Jed and I had them to ourselves; unlike the hike above treeline in the Whites, there were no other hikers snaking ahead or behind us.

I trekked on and followed the white blazes painted on the rocks ahead of me, straight up a two hundred fifty-foot rock climb to the summit. Jed was still ahead of me and, as I scrambled to catch up, I lost my footing on a rock ledge slick with sandy pebbles. I grabbed at air, flailed my arms and, after a very long minute, regained my balance. Too late I realized the white blazes did not go directly up but had, indeed, shifted left. Somehow I had lost sight of the trail and had hiked too far to the right, onto a ledge over a dangerous drop below.

Without looking down, I spread-eagled my arms and legs against the rock face and felt my way back across the ledge, looking for the trail.

Trembling, I took a deep breath, squinted my eyes in the bright sunlight, and tried to locate a white blaze for safer passage. Finally spotting a blaze, I inched my way towards it with slow careful steps, across the narrow surface of the rock face, poles hanging from my wrists, hands at shoulder height and spread wide to guide my steps and hang on.

It seemed like forever, but was only a few minutes before I was safely back on the trail, making my way to the summit to join Jed. When I reached him, he was sitting with his back against a rock, looking at his map.

"We have to be at the trailhead by three o'clock," he greeted me, gruffly, not aware of the effort the morning had cost me.

While I had been negotiating ledges and rocks, trying to glue myself to their side rather than become a heap at their base, Jed had been busy with his cell phone making arrangements for a shuttle to a bed and break-fast hostel he remembered from his last AT thru-hike. He had decided that we would stay at the hostel and slack the next nine peaks, the most difficult on the Maine AT, all above three thousand feet. We would sum-mit Katahdin three days sooner than our original plan, he informed me, implying that I had already agreed to his plan.

Slacking the peaks sounded good to me, but ascending Katahdin three days sooner seemed impossible. This was the first I had heard of the plan and, after my harrowing morning, didn't feel I could do it. I was too over-whelmed to do anything but take off my pack and plop down on the rocks. I needed to rest, eat, and regain my composure right then. I could-n't think about meeting a shuttle by three o'clock, descending, climbing, and descending over an elevation change of thirty-five hundred feet with-in the next two hours, much less hiking faster to reach Katahdin three days sooner. Still shaky from my morning's climb, however, I was not equipped to argue. I routed through my pack for some food, and, close to tears, began to eat.

Jed tried to appease me. "Look over there," he said, pointing towards the distant mountains, wide and green and lovely in every direction. "Do you know the names of those mountains?" he asked.

"No! I don't have to name the mountains to enjoy them," I shot back, still reeling from the news that we were going to speed up to reach Katahdin three days earlier than planned.

Jed didn't say anything. In a few minutes, however, he was packed up and ready to leave.

"I'll meet you at the trailhead," he said brusquely. "Be there by three o'clock."

He picked up his poles and, without looking back, was gone down the trail.

I was stunned. Momentarily, I put away my lunch, picked up my things, and tried, once again, to catch up.

Luckily, the descent down Baldpate Mountain was easier than the climb up. When I reached treeline, I was actually able to pick up my pace a bit and soon caught up to Jed. With his earphones in his ears, he did not acknowledge my presence, so I hiked behind him in silence. At one point, when we stopped for water, I tried to talk to him. He would have none of it – or me. We hiked on. Despite my resolve to hike at a pace comfortable for me, I pushed myself to hike even faster, and kept up with Jed most of the descent. About a mile from the trailhead, however, he pushed on, saying that our ride would be waiting and he'd go tell him we were coming. It was an uneasy truce. I hiked out, hot, dispirited, and tired.

When I reached the West Branch of Ellis River, I was greeted by a happy shout through the woods on the bank above me.

It was Paul, our ride to the bed and breakfast in Andover, Maine. Accustomed to meeting hikers in grimy, sticky condition, he had parked his battered blue pick-up truck by the side of the road and was jubilantly waving his arms to get my attention.

I climbed up the bank and sank into his front seat. Waiting for me was a tall, cold, sparkling cup of lemonade. I had never tasted anything so good. I drank three more cupfuls before my thirst was quenched.

The drink had equally soothed Jed while he waited for me by the side of the truck. In fact, he greeted me as though nothing had happened on the mountaintop. Maybe nothing had. I decided to forget it.

Paul, affable and chatty, put his truck into gear. We sped off around the mountains, windows open to the wind, eyes wet with the force. It felt good to be sitting instead of hiking. I relaxed, as much as fifty miles per hour in a battered pick-up truck over curvy mountain roads would let me.

We reached the B&B in time to take a shower, do laundry, and eat a hearty small-town restaurant dinner.

> "Andover has a general store, a gas station/convenience store, a restaurant (Addies Place), a church, a fire house, a post office, a few dozen clapboard houses, and a Victorian turned-wood white gazebo perched on the village green in the center of town. Very olde Maine. Paul and Eileen, the owners of our B&B, remembered Jed from his earlier thru-hike and put us up in the little house trailer in their back yard. It's hot, screened-in, and quiet. Jed sleeps at one end, I sleep at the other, a good arrangement.

While I waited for my laundry to spin, I put on a voile Indian skirt and old tee shirt of Eileen's and reclined on a chaise on the front lawn under a large shade tree. I was very elegant... and very tired!

We ate dinner at Addies – a seafood roll, salad, and French fries. Jed bought some more Baileys for our coffee on the trail.

I weighed myself today: twenty pounds fewer than when I started, eight lost in the last few weeks. I am skinny!"

August 3, 2001, Andover, Maine, South Arm Road to East B Hill Road, 10 miles

In the morning, Paul lent us small daypacks and drove us north to the trailhead at South Arm Road in Black Brook Notch. We began our slack pack hike in mild sunshine and early morning dew. Our first climb, one thousand feet in less than a mile around the north shoulder of Sawyer Mountain, and up to the summit of Moody Mountain, seemed easy by Baldpate and Mahoosuc Notch standards. With a light pack, a good night's sleep and a hearty breakfast to start the day, I felt great. Nothing hurt, I had plenty of energy, the weather was sunny and clear, and I knew that at the end of the day Paul would be waiting in his battered blue truck with ice-cold lemonade. I would enjoy this day.

Jed and I hiked together most of the morning; he was positively chatty about himself and his life "before Amy." I was glad we were on speaking terms again. He said Paul had cautioned him to be more mindful of my hiking style and fatigue; I guessed Jed had listened. In any case, I appreciated his conversation and, without a heavy pack, had no trouble keeping up with his pace.

We crossed a brook in Sawyer Notch at the base of Hall Mountain and ascended thirteen hundred feet to a small sag between the two peaks of Hall Mountain. Stopping for lunch at the Hall Mountain Lean-to, we met someone I had first met in Shenandoah and again during a thunderstorm at Dick's Dome. He was sitting on a peeled log, known as the "deacon seat," eating his lunch and reading a book.

"Nice hiking, this Maine, eh-yuh?"

I hadn't heard "eh-yuh," a typical Maine affirmation, in years, but then remembered Wonder had graduated from Bates, a liberal arts college in northern Maine. He was hiking home, too.

Jed and I pulled out our food and caught up with Wonder's news. He was still hiking by himself, with his walking stick and pack full of books for company. He planned to summit Katahdin sometime during the third week in August, but he was taking his time, he said, and didn't want to finish his hike before he figured out what kind of residency he would pursue once he returned to medical school.

I was happy to see him. It seemed fitting that we would meet again. I remembered Wonder for his gentle humor and easy-going acceptance of the vagaries of trail life.

After lunch, Jed asked jokingly if Wonder had been on "the list."

"What list?" I asked, genuinely puzzled.

"The list of guys you had lined up for Amy," he replied. "I figure Wilson was there – and Flea. Who else?"

I laughed and told him there hadn't been any list.

"Besides, Wonder is more Megg's type. When I first met him, he reminded me of her husband, Jim – looked kind of like him before the beard. Even if there had been a 'list,'" I assured him, "you'd be number one."

We hiked on in easy silence, broken first by reaching the semi-wooded north peak of Wyman Mountain and then its southern shoulder a mile later. Although the afternoon was hot and muggy, the hiking was superb without a pack.

By midafternoon we reached an old gravel logging road near Surplus Pond, and within a tenth-mile, Burroughs Brook, an outlet of the pond. The guidebook warned we would have to ford this stream, but in the drought, the water was low and we were able to hop across stepping-stones without even getting our boots wet. I wondered if I would need the stream-crossing Tevas I had purchased in Hanover after all. Ah well, they made good camp shoes, I reassured myself – great for late-night pit stops in the woods or wearing in town after long day's hike and refreshing shower.

We reached the trailhead at East B Hill Road. Paul and his lemonade were waiting. I was hot and tired, but not exhausted. It had been a satisfying day.

Later, at the counter in Addies Place, we met ET, Waco, and another hiker eating their evening meal. They had just hitched in from the trailhead and planned to hike the trail we just finished slacking.

> "ET and Waco weren't very friendly and don't seem very eager to join us. We are still a day ahead of them but they are determined to finish ahead of us. Jed still doesn't think they can do it but he will probably want to join them if they catch up. Jed won't want to be left behind.
>
> We went to a concert on the green tonight – a 'Fireman's Muster' as the poster at the general store announced. A delicious taste of Americana: fries, seafood, lemonade, and kids of all sizes running around while their parents gossiped in lawn chairs and tapped their toes to the music. Wildman was there, too. He ambled by looking for beer and sat and talked for awhile. Gotta Hike! tomorrow – thirteen miles. We'll see how it goes."

August 4, 2001, Andover, Maine, South Arm Rd. to State Route 17, 13.3 miles

We got up early to meet ET and Waco for breakfast at Addies, but they never arrived. Paul drove us to the trailhead at South Arm Road so that we could slack thirteen miles north. I was delighted with another opportunity to slack.

This day's hike would take us to the summit of Old Blue, the shoulder of Elephant Mountain, the 4-3-2-1 peaks of Bemis Mountain, and two-thirds of the way up Spruce Mountain. It was a glorious day to hike: sunny, warm, slight breeze, blue sky, and white clouds.

Our first ascent seemed to go straight up. However, without heavy packs, the climb was easy. Descending Old Blue, six hundred feet in a half-mile, was effortless as well. The Maine woods and mountains are ruggedly beautiful, I thought: very green, very remote, very stone bald on top with good views of mountains all around and hundreds of ripe, sweet blueberries to reward every climb. The trails made sense to me; they neither meandered to obscured views, nor were they overcrowded with day-hikers or tourists. Hiking through the forests and above treeline, I had a feeling of solitude and unspoiled beauty, even though I knew the forests had been changed by the natural cycles of deforestation and man-made cycles of logging for many years.

As we continued north around the shoulder of Elephant Mountain, I looked for a col above Clearwater Brook where a forest of balsam fir and red spruce, dating back to 1620, still grew undisturbed. When I reached the col, I was not certain that the tall spruce trees around me were those mentioned in the guidebook, but they certainly were beautiful.

The forest floor, covered with balsam needles, brought to mind the pillows my cousins and I used to stitch for our dolls, on rainy summer days in Maine so many years ago. We had stuffed these pillows with balsam needles, I remembered, and enjoyed their fragrance long into the winter when the pillows found their way to Connecticut and Massachusetts and the bureau drawers of our socks and wool sweaters. Fragrances, I mused, are one of the earliest, most rehearsed patterns to be laid down in our brains; no wonder the smell of warm balsam needles evokes such strong memories and fills me with such joy. Those early years, camping in Maine and New Hampshire, had been deeply etched. Or maybe I was just getting old, I chuckled to myself, tramping on and enjoying the rustle of the tall boughs above me.

Continuing north towards the west peak of Bemis Mountain, we passed through a forest nearing the end of a natural cycle. The climb to the summit was a steady, gradual ascent to smoothly rounded rocks and beautiful views all around. Jed, talking to Amy on his cell phone when I arrived, banished me, laughingly, to the summit of the east peak, a short lateral climb away. I dutifully went "to look at the view" in a brisk afternoon wind that had begun to gain velocity and drop the temperature. When I returned, Jed completed his call and we hiked on, gradually descending the peaks ordered from highest to lowest: Third Peak, Second Peak, and First Peak, before reaching the Bemis Stream at sixteen hundred feet by late afternoon. I had been looking forward to fording this stream, which divides around an island. During periods of high water, it was a formidable crossing, but for us it was a dry, shallow river of brown rocks stretching westward to Lake Mooselookmeguntic.

Hopping and balancing from one stone to the next, arms out-stretched, I rolled the word "mooselookmeguntic" around on my tongue. In Abenaki, mooselookmeguntic means portage to moose-feeding place; as I crossed the stream, I looked, in vain, for moose.

When we reached the trailhead at the end of the day, Paul was again waiting for us in the blue pickup with a fresh batch of ice-cold lemonade. This was hiking at its best, I thought, and wished we could continue the slacking arrangement forever. Hiking without my pack, with plenty of nourishing food under my belt, I was truly enjoying myself. Was it the heavy pack, the tasteless food, or the lack of a shower that made the usual hiking so hard? Perhaps it was the reasonable destination and certainty of a comfortable bed and companionship at the end of the day that made this so much easier. Whatever it was, at the end of this day I was still ener-gized and enthusiastic about hiking in the morning.

Later, in the soft warm evening, Jed and I sat on the front porch of the B&B and talked to Paul and Eileen about hiking and hikers. Our hosts were intelligent, down-to-earth people: helpful, resourceful, unassuming, and hard working. I appreciated every nuance of my three-night stay with them – especially the lemonade.

August 5, 2001, to Gull Pond, 13 miles

In the morning, Paul dropped us at the trailhead once again. Our slacking days were over; the mountains of Saddleback, The Horn, Saddleback Junior, Spaulding, Sugarloaf, and the south and north peaks of Crocker were ahead. Before we left, Jed snapped a photo of Paul and me with the breathtaking view of blue sky, dark green forests, and the wide, island-divided Lake Mooselookmeguntic, languorous and shimmer-ing in the distance below us. It would be a good day to hike, I thought.

Jed and I began the day by finishing the climb up the broad, wooded summit of Spruce Mountain that we had begun the day before, and continued over fairly easy terrain to the north shore of Moxie Pond, an Abenaki word meaning "dark water." A mile or so farther, we climbed several hundred feet to Bates Ledge and had another view of blue, blue green, and bright yellow: blue water of Long Pond, blue green of tall pines, and bright morning glitter of sunshine over all. The day was growing hotter; when we reached a sandy beach on the northeast shore of Long Pond, I cooled off by splashing in the water for a few minutes.

We hiked up about five hundred feet to a power line clearing in the full noon sun. The heat was brutal. Jed, looking at his map, thought he remembered another trail to the road leading to Rangely, our destination. I agreed to follow him and we set off through deep Boreal bogs to an old gravel road and drier footing.[16] Our mini-bushwhack was an adventure I never would have undertaken by myself, and though no shorter than the route to Rangely by the AT, I enjoyed the derring-do and wide view of lakes and meadows our way provided.

When we reached the road, we were lucky to catch a ride into town immediately. Jed had a mail drop in Rangely that he would pick up in the morning. Meanwhile, we had the afternoon and evening to ourselves and decided, after two large ice cream sodas, that we would stay in a hiker hostel by a small pond just outside of town.

I spent the remainder of the afternoon lying in a hammock at the edge of the pond, writing and painting in my journal and talking to Megg on my cell phone.

During the afternoon, Wildman and several other hikers arrived with steaks and corn on the cob to grill at the hostel. Unfortunately, I had not had the foresight to shop for dinner when I was in town, but the hostel owner agreed to drive us to a restaurant.

Back in town, Jed and I discovered Wonder on a bench by the post office. We decided to have a meal together; Wonder was hiking on after dinner and would not be staying at the hostel.

It was relaxing to sit on the patio of a nice restaurant, overlooking pleasure boats on the lake, listening to waves lapping against the hulls while the masts bobbed in the evening breeze.

16. Boreal bogs are a distinctive type of northern wetland, common along much of the AT in Maine. They look like swamps or open meadows with a small pond at the center, but are, instead, floating mats of organic debris. Usually formed in glacially-carved depressions with restricted water flow, these bogs are highly acidic and actually preserve the organic matter that accumulates on their surfaces, providing support for Sphagnum mosses and sedges to create a look of solid land rather than water.

By the time we returned to the hostel, Wildman and the others were asleep. I tucked myself into a top bunk in a room of snoring, tired men.

August 6, 2001, to Poplar Ridge Lean-to, 11 miles

We left the hostel early and hiked across a footbridge over the Sandy River and through dense woods to begin the approach to Saddleback Mountain. In about two miles we encountered Piazza Rock, an enormous flat-topped granite boulder cantilevered out from a cliff, about the size of a small house – a surprising sight in this heavily forested area, I thought.

The beginning of the ascent was gradual and steady. We stopped once at a brook to fill our water bottles; it would be the last water for the next six miles and was an added weight of three pounds. That water was a welcome respite for the rest of the ascent, but I was hot and thirsty when I finally reached treeline. But the thirsty climb was worth the effort; on the summit of Saddleback on this magnificent day, I could see for miles in every direction. Katahdin was almost visible in the north and Mt. Washington was clearly visible in the south.

I loved hiking above treeline, particularly in Maine. I suspect it was the feeling of being completely alone in a remote, safe, unspoiled wilderness of relatively easy hiking (once you were up) and expansive views. No matter how hot the day, the breeze above treeline was always cool. On this day, the above-treeline hike extended for almost three miles. With the wind in my face and then at my back, I practically skimmed the peaks, surrounded by views of green mountains and blue lakes in every direction below, and blue sky and white clouds all around me, above. I loved it.

It was a little disappointing to come to the end of the open expanse of barren bedrock and glacial erratics scattered about the summits of Saddleback and The Horn. I spent the remainder of the afternoon descending to the Poplar Ridge Lean-to, where we had agreed to meet for the night.

Jed had already set up his tent by the time I arrived, and the lean-to was full of Canadians not eager to share their space. I pitched my tent on a rocky piece of dirt, and chatted with the group of thru-hikers assembled around the fire ring. Wonder and Wildman arrived just at dusk and pitched their tents nearby.

The evening was calm and humid, with a hint of rain. Wildman, sipping some LLBeam, bemoaned the fact that he had lost his rain fly.

"How about me joining you if it starts to rain tonight," he suggested, as I hung up my pack for the night.

"How about you making friends with the Canadians," I replied, zipping my tent with finality. Wildman was Wildman. I didn't want him in my space overnight.

Luckily, the night was dry, and I never was put to the test.

August 7, 2001, to Stratton, Maine, 22 miles

Everyone was up early, ready to hike the peaks of Lone Spaulding and Sugarloaf mountains. The maps forecasted a day of significant climbing; the early morning heat and humidity promised a day of thirst, sweat, and toil. I drank some cappuccino instant breakfast and Tang, filled my water bottles with extra water, and hiked out.

The initial descent to Oberton Stream was a long climb down to a canyon floor, and then a long climb back up to the sparsely wooded summit of Lone Mountain. I hiked by myself most of the way, enjoying the solitude, trying to ignore the sweat dripping into my eyes and down my back. By nine o'clock the straps of my pack were soaked and slippery, my tank top and shorts clung to my body, and I reeked with the odor of stale sweat which had one advantage: the bugs left me alone.

In the early afternoon, reaching the northwest shoulder of Spaulding Mountain, I decided to take the side trail a tenth mile to the wooded summit. I sat with my back against a tree to eat some lunch and wondered, for the millionth time, what on earth I was doing climbing mountains with thirty pounds on my back in the middle of a heat wave. Unable to answer my own question, I drank some water, re-strapped my wet pack to my wetter body, and hiked on, thanking aloud every stir of breeze that floated past me. I had discovered that whenever I thanked the breeze for cooling me, it increased in velocity, volume, and cooling power. Sometimes I shouted my thanks through the forest and sometimes I wondered if anyone but the wind heard me. I didn't care at all. The sacrosanct custom of keeping my voice soft and tones pleasing, learned in childhood as lessons in becoming a woman, were thrown to the wind, literally, as I shouted my gratitude – to the wind, the sun, the rain for their powers of cooling, heating, cleansing me. The hiker's way of going native, I assumed. But thanking and praising, rather than grousing and complaining, made an enormous difference to my hike; I kept doing it.

I met up with Jed near the trail crossing to the summit of Sugarloaf Mountain. On a clear day, the view from Sugarloaf, the second highest peak in Maine, was said to be outstanding. On this humid day of shimmering heat and hazy skies, the view would probably not be worth the climb. Jed and I decided to follow the relocated AT and hike on. We split up and agreed to meet at the base of the mountain, the South Branch of the Carrabassett River, and camp overnight.

For me, the descent seemed to take forever. A rocky ridge walk at first, I thought I would be down in about an hour. However, the rocky ridge walk turned into a steep, rocky descent over which I had to pick my way. My estimated hour's descent took almost twice as long and I didn't reach the river until almost six o'clock.

Jed was waiting for me on a rock in the middle of the river; he was stretched out, propped against his pack, and looking at his map. I was tired, hot, and thirsty – eager to find a camping place to stop for the night.

"Ya know," Jed said when I drew near, "we can take this old gravel road and get to Stratton tonight. It's only a couple of miles. How 'bout it?"

I really would have preferred to camp. There were several level, pine-covered tent sites near the river, and I wanted to stop there and hike on in the morning. But Jed really wanted to push on.

It was a long walk ahead of us. Luckily, before too long a pickup truck came by and gave us a ride to town. Jed sat in the truck bed with our packs; I sat in the cab and tried to make polite conversation with the driver. Too much, I thought, at the end of a hard day.

Stratton, Maine, turned out to be a main street with a dilapidated-looking wood frame hotel full of migrant workers on one side of the street and an only slightly less dismal hiker hostel on the other. There was a No Vacancy sign in front of the hiker hostel. I groaned when I thought about the pine forest next to the stream that we had passed up, and looked back at the hotel, our last option: the tired-looking men on the porch were sitting on the floor, batting at mosquitoes, and passing a bottle around.

We started toward the hotel when someone called out from behind the screen door of the hiker hostel. "If you're looking for bunks for the night," he rasped, "I've got two upstairs."

We turned around and followed him up the stairs and into a bunkroom. It was lined with a dozen beds, each fitted with clean white sheets, a wool blanket, and a pillow. At the end of the room, in front of a screened window, a large fan on a tall pedestal whirred quietly, moving the hot humid air in breathable gusts. Despite the No Vacancy sign, we were the only guests.

Jed and I quickly chose our beds, stowed our gear, splashed water on our hands and faces, and went across the street to the only eatery still open. In fact, the restaurant was about to close but agreed to feed us leftovers from the menu: roast chicken, mashed potatoes, toast, gravy, strong coffee and homemade apple pie. We ate in silence with total concentration on the food.

After dinner, I went back to the hostel, took a quick shower, and fell onto my bed in a stupor, exhausted. Everything hurt – especially my feet. In fact, my feet hurt all night. Getting up in the middle of the night, stepping out onto the bare wood floor, and trying to descend steep stairs to the bathroom was almost more than I could manage. My feet just would not bend; the soles and heels and the tops of my toes were numb from too many miles in stiff, unbending boots. To restore circulation to my toes, I had to rub them with alcohol, every morning and evening, stretching the tendons and massaging the pads of hardened skin and calluses whenever I took off my boots. This night, it hadn't helped.

August 8, 2001, Stratton, Maine, 0 miles

In the morning, going downstairs with knees bent at a forty-five degree angle and ankles that would not allow my feet to arc forward, I realized that I had developed a hiker profile: I shambled. I was in good company with my scarecrow-like shuffle, but I wondered if I had done permanent damage to the tendons and small bones of my feet. Under all that swollen flesh, nothing was very responsive. In fact, my feet were a mess.

We spent our time that day retrieving our packages from the post office, doing laundry, and shopping at the general store across the road from the hostel. I bought a "Welcome to Maine" tee shirt to wear instead of my hot rain jacket while my laundry was churning. The clerk in the general store loaned me a pair of scissors to cut out the neck and sleeves of the shirt, and I created a tank top on the spot. Stepping behind a stack of boxes in the back of the store, I put it on.

Outside, flies buzzed in the dusty glare of the noonday sun. The raised wooden sidewalk along the street was deserted. I watched, amazed, as a pickup truck drove up to the store and the driver jumped out and hustled past me, leaving the motor running and the truck door ajar. Several minutes later, she came back out, arms loaded with full bags, hopped back into the truck, revved the motor, and sped away. Had I just witnessed a heist, I wondered? In rural Maine?

I poked my head back into the store. All seemed just as I had left it: the middle-aged woman behind the counter smiled at me but continued to talk with the only other customer. No ruffled hysteria or cries for help. All was well in the middle of the day in the middle of the week in the middle of the summer, in the middle of Maine.

Later in the day Wildman and several others hiked into town. A thunderstorm broke the heat of the day while we were all eating dinner, reminding us of the stormy Fourth of July feast we had shared at the Knotty Pine Motel in Vermont. Wildman couldn't quite remember that occasion. Replenished with a new supply of LLBeam, he seemed to be headed for similar cloudy memories tonight. I couldn't imagine how he could hike with a hangover. I could never have hiked his hike; I could barely hike my own, stone sober.

August 9, 2001, to Little Bigelow Lean-to, 15.5 miles

The morning began in the rain. Jed and I ate a greasy breakfast of eggs, bacon, and toast and headed to the trail crossing. He was in a funk and wasn't talking to me or anyone else.

We hitched a ride with several other hikers and I reluctantly entered the wet and dripping woods to begin the climb up Bigelow Mountain, three thousand feet in six miles. Behind me, Jed hiked sulkily, pushing me to hike faster. Aware of the strained silence, I asked him if something were wrong.

He refused to talk and, brooding, picked up his pace and hiked on.

As it turned out, I hiked by myself most of the day. The sun came out about midmorning and the day turned lovely, though still humid and hot. At least, in the mountains, there is usually a breeze, I mused, remembering to thank its cooling caress over my sweaty brow and back.

When I reached the summit of the west peak of Bigelow, Jed was nowhere to be seen. I had expected him to be on his cell phone, talking to Amy, as was his usual custom. I called George and sat on my pack overlooking the twenty-two mile reservoir of Flagstaff Lake, shimmering blue and silver in the dazzling sunlight below. We chatted about the events of the morning. When I mentioned Jed's puzzling behavior, he suggested that perhaps I had hurt Jed's feelings.

"When you're tired," he reminded me, "you can be abrupt with people." This was George's nice way of saying I had probably said something thoughtless without realizing it.

That I could be opinionated, I knew only too well; it was my mother's legacy. She had had a razor-sharp wit and sharper tongue that lashed out, often unprovoked, to stun its target. By her standard, I was a milquetoast. But that was no excuse, and I wondered if George could be right. Putting one foot in front of the other in sheer determination just to make it to the next destination, it was possible, I supposed, that one of those feet had landed in my mouth.

I hiked on, wondering what I might have said that morning to hurt Jed's feelings. Hiking with bad feelings between people only made a tough situation tougher, I reflected. I wanted to clear up whatever it was that was bothering Jed, and I wanted to be done hiking.

Jed was finishing his lunch when I reached the Myron Avery Lean-to a bit later. He was with a thin young man named Metro, whom he had known earlier on the trail. Metro was from New York City and talked as fast as he hiked – which, I soon discovered, was fast. He reminded me of a late-night comedian: wickedly funny, smart, a good storyteller, and outrageously irreverent.

Metro was recounting a recent trip that had taken him off the trail to a wedding in Italy. His words were spilling out so quickly, I could hardly follow the story. I was relieved when both he and Jed hiked out together while I was still eating. Jed seemed to be in better spirits, but he was still not talking to me. I wondered if I would ever find out what had been bothering him that morning.

After lunch I hiked to the east peak of Bigelow. This peak is also called Avery Peak, and, like the lean-to I had just left, was named for Myron Avery, who, with Benton McKaye, is considered to be one of the founding fathers of the AT. The views from the peak were stunning, and I hiked on with a lighter heart.

The hike to the next lean-to on Little Bigelow, I estimated, would take about four more hours. I expected to reach my destination by dinner and hiked steadily all afternoon.

When the four hours became five, however, I began to grow a bit concerned: I had not yet begun the descent of Little Bigelow, and I knew that once begun, that descent would take at least an hour. I picked up my pace, weary of hiking and wearier still of trying to catch up to Jed. I began to fret. Had Jed been speaking to me earlier in the day, I grumbled to myself, I would have known his plan for stopping tonight. As it was, I would just have to keep hiking until I found him – not easy over steep, rocky terrain at twilight.

An hour later, I was still looking for Jed and the shelter; I felt sluggish and muddled, like I was walking on rubbery legs through a nightmare of Jell-O. I bonked.[17]

I sat down on a log, drank some water, and ate an energy bar to wait for my head to clear. Bonking, I knew, caused hikers to consistently either over- or under-estimate the last miles to the shelter and either arrive disoriented and confused, or miss the shelter altogether. I decided to hike for another fifteen minutes and then camp whether or not I found Jed or the shelter.

17. Bonking, or hypoglycemia, is a condition known well by endurance athletes; it occurs when the glycogen stores in the brain and muscles are depleted by over- exertion, especially in conditions of extreme heat and humidity. The most common characteristics of 'bonking' are irritability, disorientation, indecisiveness, combativeness and/or lethargy. Ingesting a rapidly absorbable carbohydrate such as a sports drink, sugar cube, or energy bar and water can relieve the effects of bonking.

With more clarity and firmer muscles, I picked up my pack and reset-tled it on my back. I hiked on. Over the next rise I found the shelter.

The shelter was full and all the tenting spaces were taken; Jed, Metro, Wonder, Wildman and several other thru-hikers were camped nearby. I found a spot in a pine grove, set up my tent, and went down to the stream for cooking water.

The stream was wide, cold, and swirling with runoff from a small cas-cade upstream. I would have liked to shower under the waterfall but was aware of contaminating the drinking water for all the other hikers. I con-tented myself with a side-of-the-stream splash, filled my cooking pots, and climbed back to my tent site.

Jed met me at the path back to my tent and said he had taken my food bag up to the fire ring where the others were gathered for dinner. Guessing he was trying to make amends, I followed him back to the fire ring, cooked, and listened to the conversation around me. After dinner, back in my pine grove, I fell asleep on top of my sleeping bag, listening to the shouts of laughter that punctuated Metro's stories.

Around midnight, I woke to a brisk wind rushing through and filling up my tent. Looking up, I could see the tops of the pines overhead sway-ing and whipping against the sky. The moon and stars were bright and I looked for dead branches that might fall in the wind. Seeing none, I crawled inside my sleeping bag and slept without a rain fly under the cool mountain stars. It had been a difficult day of tiring hiking and misunder-standings, but I had made a decision. In the morning I would be out of the mountains and hiking on my own, at least for the next few days.

August 10, 2001, to Pierce Pond Lean-to, 18 miles

When Jed was ready to leave, I told him to go ahead without me; I was still tired from yesterday's climbs and did not want to be rushed. By the time I left camp, everyone else had gone and the rain had started.

The hike would be eighteen miles over fairly level terrain past Flagstaff Lake, West Carry Pond, and East Carry Pond. With the exception of two minor elevations of fourteen hundred and sixteen hundred feet, respec-tively, it looked like an easy day.

The rain eased off, but for most of the morning the weather was over-cast, humid, and windy. I loved the change in the barometric pressure; it energized me, somehow. Young children, I had observed for years, were much more lively when the barometric pressure dropped; so too was I on this morning of lower atmospheric pressure. Perhaps it was hiking at only twelve hundred fifty feet above sea level, or maybe it was hiking on my own with no one to hurry me along. Whatever the reason, I had more energy, and when I reached West Carry Pond, I decided to cool off with a swim.

Ditching my pack on shore, I tore off my boots, shirt, and shorts and ran into the water. It was perfect – cool and silky against my hot, sweaty, body.

I walked on along the Arnold Trail, thinking about the legacy of the trail and its stories. When I reached East Carry Pond, I took another swim. Wonder ambled through the woods and joined me. We hiked together after that.

Along the way, I learned a little more about Wonder. Both his parents, he told me, had graduated from Gettysburg College, a few years after George and I did, and both his parents had joined the Peace Corps after graduation, just as I had. However, he didn't know much about their stu-dent life during the early 1960s. Reminiscing, I filled him in on the ide-alistic days when John F. Kennedy was first in office, before the divisive-ness of the Vietnam War changed campus life forever.

The miles under my boots disappeared quickly that afternoon, with lively conversation and easy terrain. Wonder was a good hiking compan-ion; his pace was more in tune with mine. He didn't mind breaking his stride to jump in the water for a cool swim, or taking a nap under the shade of a stately pine tree. He wasn't concerned about doing miles, though he still hiked with purpose and discipline. I liked that.

Late in the afternoon, Jed caught up with us about a mile from the Pierce Pond Lean-to, our destination. He had been lost, he said, and had spent the day bushwhacking. I was glad I hadn't been hiking with him; bushwhacking through dense underbrush filled with mosquitoes would have frustrated me today. His feeling of accomplishment for rediscover-ing the trail had lightened his mood, however, and I was glad to see him, though I was still wary; I didn't know what provoked his mood swings, or how to interpret them.

Pierce Pond Lean-to was full of young Boy Scouts and their leaders when we arrived. Luckily, the troop only used the shelter fire ring for cooking; the boys pitched their tents in the woods behind us. They were noisy and full of questions about hiking.

Rather than deal with them, Wonder and I went for another swim. Noting the age of the teenagers, I swam well away from the clearing in front of the shelter, trying to be discreet. The leader, unfortunately, was not as considerate; when I was ready to climb out of the water, he brought several of his charges over to my shoreline to wash their pots and pans. He insisted on talking to me while they worked. I tread water, shivering, held captive by my good manners. Finally, the Scouts took their pots and went back to their tents; their leader begrudgingly moved on.

Jed, Wonder, Metro and several other hikers were back at the shelter, affording me the privacy I needed to haul myself out of the water and pull on my long underwear and shorts. Reflecting on backcountry manners, I decided that the Boy Scout leader needed to learn a few.

That night, those in the shelter were a merry band of cohesive hikers. The smell of Katahdin was in the air. In the morning, we would be hiking to a twelve-stack pancake and sausage breakfast at a nearby fishing camp. After that, we would cross the Kennebec River by canoe ferry, pick up mail drops in Caratunk, and hike on to Pleasant Pond at the end of the day. It promised to be an easy day of good eating, level hiking, and pleasant company; a short hike of only ten miles.

That night I dreamt about a never-ending supply of pancakes: stacks and stacks from a magic cooking pot that never ran dry. I'm not sure if it was the magic pot theme from the children's stories of Strega Nona and Johnnycake-Ho, or my insatiable hunger for blueberry pancakes that fueled my dreams, but I awoke in the morning famished and ready to eat.

August 11, 2001, to Pleasant Pond via Caratunk, Maine, 10 miles

The day was stunning: blue sky, rifting breeze, bright sun, and lots of good, nourishing food. It began with a short walk from the lean-to to Harrison's Pierce Pond Camp, where we sat at picnic tables on a

screened-in porch of the main lodge to wait for our pancakes. The camp
has several cottages and a children's log cabin playhouse set on the edge
of the pond in a pinewoods. Mainly vacationers and anglers use it. On
this morning, we were the only guests for breakfast. We were a high-spir-
ited group, laughing and clowning while we ate our allotted dozen pancakes with maple syrup, sausages, orange juice, and coffee, hoping the
cook would miscount and add a bonus pancake or two to each dozen. My
stomach seemed to be bottomless; I could have eaten twelve more.

After breakfast Metro, Wonder, and I hiked together to the shore of
the Kennebec River, wide, blue and benign-looking in the quiet morning
sun. We sat on low brown rocks in tall grass waiting for the canoe to pick
us up and ferry us across to Caratunk. The ferry is the official AT route
across the river. In the past, hikers crossed the Kennebec by holding their
packs overhead and stepping over slippery rocks, in strong currents,
through unpredictable water levels. Water release from upstream dams
made fording particularly hazardous when water levels were high. After a
thru-hiker drowned in 1985, the Appalachian Trail Conference and
Maine AT Club established a canoe ferry to eliminate the ford. While we
waited our turn to board the canoe, we signed forms releasing the clubs
from responsibility in case of accident. Metro, a lawyer, read the form as
a legal document and gave us permission to sign.

"A bureaucratic hiccup for safe passage," he said.

The ferryman in the stern of the canoe was named Muscrat; as his
helper, in the bow, I was surprised to see Jed wielding a paddle.

At Caratunk we dropped our packs at the hostel and hustled up the
street to the post office to pick up our mail drops before the Saturday
noon closing time. Back at the hostel, I spread my new supplies on the
lawn and reorganized my pack while the hostel owner prepared giant-
sized cheeseburgers with lettuce, tomato and onion for our lunch. With
ice-cold Coke and ice cream sandwiches from his freezer, I barely noticed
the hot afternoon sun overhead.

After lunch, we all sat under the trees on the hostel lawn, reading magazines, talking, and sleeping. Jed went back to the post office to talk to
Amy on the outside pay phone. I sat under a spreading shade tree, listening to wind chimes on a nearby porch. I painted a watercolor of the white

frame house across the street, brilliant with purple nasturtiums and pink and red geraniums shining in the glare of the afternoon sun. It was a long, lazy, quiet respite.

In the late afternoon Wonder, Metro and I gradually gathered our gear and began to head out of town. We agreed to meet at the Pleasant Pond Shelter six miles farther. Jed was still talking to Amy when I left; he said he would catch up.

The lean-to was near the shore of Pleasant Pond, a quiet lake of small cottages and motorboats. It is said to be the second-cleanest lake in Maine; chest-high in the water I could still see my feet on the bottom.

I pitched my tent on a grassy piece of land in the woods, away from the shelter near the shore. Wonder, Jed, and Metro soon joined me. We had a swim before dinner, then cooked by the shore, watching the sunset of pink, orange, purple and blue streak in soft, lingering rays across the sky. Listening to the low mournful cry of loons, I watched the bright pin-pricks of stars gently replace the afterglow. Mosquitoes, unfortunately, invaded my reverie; I slapped my way back to my tent, crawled inside, and fell asleep to the gentle sounds of the night. I loved the Maine woods.

August 12, 2001, to Bald Mountain Brook, 16 miles

The day started with Jed calling to me to come out and watch a hawk eat a chipmunk. I unzipped my tent, stuck out my head, and, luckily, missed it.

It was a sultry, dewy early morning, and my tent was wet from dew on the outside and condensation on the inside. Even my sleeping bag was wet where my feet touched the tent roof. I shook everything out, keeping it off the long wet grass as best I could, and started walking with Jed, Metro, and Wonder.

We walked around Pleasant Pond and began a fairly steep twelve hundred and fifty-foot ascent to the summit of Pleasant Pond Mountain, through old growth spruce and fir forests. The wet needles overhead smelled wonderful; under my feet they provided a soft, cushiony carpet, a welcome relief from the hard rocks and snaking roots of the past few weeks.

The four of us were strung out along the trail, and I hiked alone or with Wonder or Metro off and on most of the day. Jed was way ahead.

Hiking in the afternoon sun, it took longer than I anticipated to reach the open summit of Moxie Bald Mountain, because the trail was lined with blueberries, ripe, sweet, and thirst quenching. I ate as many as I could hold and put some in an empty water bottle for dinner. Wonder, I discovered later, had done the same thing and had a similar cache for his breakfast.

When I reached the lean-to where we had agreed to stop for the night, Jed was waiting for me and wanted to continue hiking. The day had not been particularly strenuous, but I was ready to camp. Monson, the next day's destination, was only fifteen miles ahead. We would reach it by midafternoon, well before the post office closed, if we stopped now. But Jed insisted that we continue a few more miles, and I gave in.

Reluctantly, I followed him around a pond, through more spruce and fir forests, and across the rocks of Bald Mountain stream. We passed several pine groves that would have been perfect for camping, but Jed wanted to keep hiking, so I struggled, weary and hungry, to keep up with him.

We hiked about an hour longer, until both my resources and the suitable camping places disappeared. It was growing dark and I was exasperated; we seemed to be crashing through underbrush on a forever walk to nowhere.

Finally, Jed found an area that would do, he thought, and we pitched our tents in branch-strewn pinewoods, trying to avoid the roots on the forest floor.

After some black beans, rice, and blueberries, I felt better but was still tired and drained. Why, I wondered, did Jed not accept that my limits were real limits? When I told him I couldn't hike any farther, he seemed to take it as a challenge to push ahead rather than a request to stop and refuel.

> "One of the differences between men and women hikers, I've come to realize, is that women hikers can admit to being tired; men hikers see fatigue as weakness, something to be ignored. In fact, men deal with being tired by bragging about how much they did that day, and how much more they will do tomorrow. For men, the contest is the essence of the effort, and their metaphors are either of war (the trail is the enemy to

beat), or of competitive sports (they will whip the ass of that mountain). For women, or, at least me as a woman, the trail is a physical challenge to experience and manage, using resources of intelligence rather than physical strength. Knowing when to admit to fatigue and how to deal with it seems not only prudent, but also necessary.

Or maybe it's only the difference between Jed and me."

Nine more days until we would summit Katahdin, and I wanted to go home tonight. I did not share Jed's excitement about reaching the final destination, the final mountain.

For Jed, Katahdin meant not only the end of this long distance hike, but also the end of long distance hiking for the next few years. After Katahdin, he planned to settle down, and lead a more conventional life, he said. Getting to Katahdin was an end and a beginning, for him.

For me, Katahdin was a two-thirds mile marker, another big mountain to climb. I was resigned to reaching it, to climbing it, and to continuing on through the southern portion of the trail to Springer Mountain, Ga., but just thinking about what lay ahead exhausted me.

August 13, 2001, to Monson, Maine, 12 miles

The next morning we were up and out early; Jed was eager to reach Monson and pick up his mail drop, do his laundry, and find a grocery store.

"I'll catch up with you," I said. My feet and legs still hurt from yesterday's hike, and I was tired. Very tired. I hadn't slept well and could see no point in rushing to Monson just to pick up a mail drop a few hours early.

I hiked by myself through dense forest, fording the West and then the East Branch of the Piscataquis River without having to take off my boots. About midmorning I sat down on a log to eat some peanut butter and honey. Two hikers came loping by: ET and Waco.

"Hey!" I greeted them with enthusiasm. "Great to see you. Heading in to Monson?"

"Yeah," Waco answered. "But we're in a real hurry – can't stop. We'll talk in Monson."

I kept sitting on my log, eating my peanut butter, wondering what the big hurry to get to Monson was all about. As far as I knew, Monson was important only because it was the last place for a mail drop or resupply before entering the Hundred Mile Wilderness leading to Katahdin. Symbolically, I knew, it was important; but realistically, I didn't expect much more than a few hiker hostels, a post office, and a general store. Monson didn't even have a restaurant; hikers ate at the hostels. What was the big fat deal, anyway?

Two hours later, hiking at my normal pace, I passed two hikers taking a break: ET and Waco again. They hadn't gone very far, very fast, after all.

"See you in Monson," I called as I hiked by. They looked up and waved.

When I reached Monson, Jed was talking on the only pay phone in town, outside the general store. As I walked by, he handed me the phone and I said hello to Amy, and then continued on down the street to the B&B where he had booked us for the night. I was relieved that we were not staying at a hiker hostel.

The B&B was an old Victorian house that had been remodeled into a living room, bathroom, hiker kitchen, and three well-appointed bedrooms upstairs and a Laundromat downstairs. It was clean and comfortable, well run, and more like a traditional bed and breakfast than a typical hiker hostel. Jed and I were the only guests and I was thankful to stow my pack upstairs, find the shower, throw my filthy clothes into a washing machine, and relax on an Adirondack chair in the back yard overlooking Lake Hebron.

Unlike the two hiker hostels in town, Shaw's and the Pie Lady's, our B&B did not serve food. However, downstairs next to the Laundromat, a large freezer filled with homemade meals was available for hikers to purchase and cook for themselves. Bacon, English muffins, eggs, orange juice, and fresh fruits and vegetables were also available. It was more fresh fruit than I had seen in a month and I simply stared at the bananas and oranges. Bob, the owner, invited me to help myself. I did.

As I had predicted, Monson had a small town main street and was the last resupply point for northbounders on their way through the Hundred Mile Wilderness to Katahdin, and the first town for southbounders just beginning their trek. The town supported hikers in the summer and snowmobile enthusiasts in the winter. There was no other industry. It was backwoods Maine, and I loved it.

Jed decided to take the next day as a zero day and rest for the hundred miles ahead. I was surprised that he wanted a day in town, but I did not argue. I was too tired and wanted some time to repack my food and send a small package on to a fishing camp halfway through the Wilderness.[18]

August 14, 2001, Monson, Maine, 0 miles

I spent my unexpected zero day cooking, eating, and sitting in a chair by the shore of the lake with my watercolors, journal, and a paperback book. I watched the early morning sun streak shadows across the water, the noonday sun reflect a mirrored glare of brightness, and the evening sun set in a pink and orange gloaming that merged into the black surface of the water in tiny ripples. What a misnomer, I reflected; my zero day had been far from empty. Like Leo Leoni's Frederick, who used his time to gather beauty rather than grain for the long winter ahead, I had used my time to rest my body and spirit, to gather the beauty and peace of backcountry kindness, and to renew my depleted stores of energy.

The trail ahead would pass through extensive logging forests, winding through relatively flat lake country between mountains and across streams. Katahdin would be at the end, a five-mile climb of over five thousand feet. But, with renewed energy from my day of rest, I thought I could do it. I began to look forward to the hike.

In Massachusetts, Megg and I had laughed about the aphorism: "When the going gets tough, the tough get going." At the time, the trail had not been that tough, for me.

But in Maine, the trail had gotten tough – and then, even tougher. As I closed my eyes on my zero day in Monson, I made a decision:

"My resolve for the next nine days is to hike at my own pace, without apology or resentment, agree to meet Jed at the end of

---

18. The Hundred Mile Wilderness is wildernesses only in the sense that it is remote; logging roads provide accessibility to outside towns but hitching to these towns is difficult. Food for the entire expanse needs to be carried in. However, Jed knew of a camp that would accept mail packages, for a small fee. By sending a food package to the fishing camp, we could save carrying four days supply of food, about eight pounds of extra weight.

the day, but go no farther unless I feel really equipped to do so. I need to conserve my energy and be tougher, mentally and spiritually, than I have been in the past few weeks. With fewer physical reserves to draw on, I need to hike smart. The going's gotten tough – I'll need to be tougher."

12. The Tough Get Going – The Hundred Mile Wilderness

"a woman can't survive by her own breath alone..."
Joy Harjo, What Moon Drove Me To This?

Monson, Maine, to Katahdin, 124.4 miles

August 15, 2001, to Long Pond Stream, 15.1 miles

Jed and I arranged for a shuttle to take us back to the trailhead to begin the Hundred Mile Wilderness. ET and Waco had not taken a zero day in Monson and had hiked on. We planned to meet Metro and Wonder near an old gravel tote road fifteen miles into the Wilderness. A former thru-hiker was hosting a three-day beer and spaghetti bash there. Also, in Monson Jed had run into Ranger Bob, who I had last seen with his girlfriend, Kathryn, in Manchester, Vermont. Kathryn had agreed to slack all of our packs and meet us at the end of the day. I gratefully gave her my pack, heavy with resupply, and entered the Wilderness unencumbered.

The day's hike was relatively level, through deep valleys and along low slate ridges and quarries. Jed and I hiked in silence under tall old growth pines all morning, fording streams and skirting small ponds.

Around lunchtime, climbing through a pine grove, I heard the unmistakable sound of falling and gurgling water directly ahead. It turned out

239

to be Little Wilson Falls, the highest waterfall on the AT and one of the highest in Maine. On this day, however, only a few thin streams of water slipped over the hundred-foot drop from the flat rocks at the top to the slate canyon below.

When Jed and I reached the edge of the water, the trail turned abruptly and descended deceptively through the woods to the base of the falls. From the top, however, it had looked as though the trail continued straight across the water, a shallow flat-topped walk to the bank on the other side. The stream appeared benign until it suddenly disappeared and dropped stealthily to the rocky floor below.

Jed and I sat down on some rocks at the edge of the stream to fill up our water bottles and have lunch. Wonder was upstream, filtering water and eating a sandwich. I lay back and drowsed in the midday lull, my back against a warm flat rock.

Quite unexpectedly, I heard someone approaching, walking heavily, and clattering with every step. A young hiker under an enormous pack with cups, bottles, and pots and pans hanging from his straps was striding straight towards me, head down, eyes on his feet. He looked neither left nor right but continued straight ahead, stepping into the water to slosh across the slate rocks to the other side, totally unaware that the white blazes had turned downstream, through the woods. He strode brazenly to the middle of the falls.

Numb with disbelief, I froze. It was like watching a child run into the middle of a busy highway, oblivious to the traffic approaching from both directions. The danger of the hiker's situation whizzed through my mind, accompanied by the realization that I would not be able to stop him if he lost his balance. It was a long way down and those rocks would be unforgiving.

Never more aware of my own insignificance in the face of overwhelming natural phenomena, I shouted as the scene slowed and the hiker gained a rock ledge midstream. At last, he woke up. He looked around and down. Below his feet, just beyond the small ledge, the slate floor dropped away and the water disappeared, down. The hiker shook his head as though to clear it, struggled over to the rock ledge, and sat.

When he saw me watching him from my bank, I motioned that the trail turned and went down stream. He nodded, but continued to sit on his ledge, recovering and embarrassed, I think, that he had been observed.

Late in the afternoon, I caught up with Jed and Wonder at the beer and spaghetti bash; they had already joined the other hikers assembled on the cabin porch for the appetizer: lobster bisque. Someone gave me a tin cup and I ladled delicious, pungent, satisfying soup from a large black pot.

As we ate and drank beer, other hikers drifted in. The last to arrive was the hapless tinker from the top of the falls. Today was his first day out, he said, and he was heading south to Georgia. He clattered his overloaded pack onto the porch floor and admitted that he had been in a daze on the top of those falls.

"I didn't see the blaze change," he explained. "I thought the trail went right over top 'til I saw you sitting there. Thanks."

I remembered my first few days out and the befuddled state I had been in when my body was trying to adjust to the pace and my head was trying to register all the requirements of the trail.

"It's okay. We've all been there. Have some soup," I offered, nodding towards the pot, closing the subject from further discussion. He seemed grateful to accept both gestures.

The woods were quiet and deep, and I was glad to pitch my tent and crawl inside. In the morning we would begin climbing again. Jed was already talking about hiking a bit faster to reach Katahdin two days sooner than we had planned. I fell asleep repeating my resolve: to hike at my own pace without apology or resentment and to go no further each day than my body felt equipped to go.

August 16, 2001, to Chairback Gap Lean-to, 11.1 miles

The day was hot and dry. The first ascent, up Barren Mountain, was tedious, even with the views of the Bodfish Intervale, Lake Onawa and Borestone Mountain as a reward. I was too hot and footsore to appreciate the views; water was my main concern. There had been no water resupply before the summit and I was thirsty.

About a mile past the summit of Barren Mountain, I took a side trail to Cloud Pond, a small mountain tarn. Hiking the Lake District in England, I had encountered my first tarns: unspoiled pools of sparkling clear water formed by the scouring action of a glacier. Cloud Pond was like these tarns. I set my pack down and drank my fill. It was delicious and my last opportunity for water for the next five miles of climbing and descending in the hot afternoon sun.

Filling my bottles and splashing my face with the clear, cold, glacial liquor, I hiked on. Jed had pulled ahead of me, but I wanted to conserve my energy by keeping a steady pace.

The smaller peaks of Fourth Mountain, Third Mountain, and Columbus Mountain, though only about seven miles, took most of the afternoon to cross. Many pointless ups and downs, Dare's PUDs, kept me focused on the trail that was littered with rocks. At least the rocks were dry, I thought. In wet weather they would have been treacherous. Today was just one (more) of those days when the hiking just wasn't much fun, but there was nothing to do but keep moving and try not to think about thirst.

Looking at my map late in the afternoon, I discovered that the water source for the Chairback Mountain Lean-to, where I would meet Jed, was at the base of the next five hundred-foot climb. There would be no water for cooking at the lean-to; I would have to lug extra water up and down the next mountain, two miles, to the shelter.

My guess was that Jed would choose to hike past the shelter to the west bank of the Pleasant River, seven miles farther, rather than carry water for cooking up the mountain.

It was getting late; I knew I could hike two miles to the next shelter, even with extra water, but I was not so sure about another five miles after that. I decided to fill my bottles and cooking-water bag, drink my fill before I started, and decide whether to stay or move on when I reached the lean-to. Maybe Jed would be waiting for me.

It was a long, slow climb. By the time I reached the lean-to, my head was throbbing from exertion and I felt weak, dizzy, and dry. Despite drinking a lot of water before beginning my ascent, my body was over-heated and I had begun to dehydrate. My energy sagged.

Jed was not at the lean-to. The only one at the shelter was another woman about my age, a section hiker; she had not seen Jed hike through. I sat down to rest and think about my options.

To catch up with Jed, I would have to continue climbing – two hundred fifty feet up Chairback Mountain – and then stumble four and a half miles down in the twilight and set up camp in the dark. The prospect was not appealing; I was too hot and thirsty, too tired. And, I forecasted ruefully, when I finally reached him at the river, he would probably only ask what had taken me so long. I decided to stay put.

As I was settling into the shelter, Ranger Bob and Kathryn hiked through; they planned to camp three miles farther, off a side trail near a small pond. Kathryn looked longingly at my sleeping bag stretched out on the shelter floor. This was only her first day out and she was tired, but Ranger Bob wanted to continue, so she hiked on.

I asked them to send a message to Jed, with anyone who passed them, so he would know not to expect me that night. The grapevine on the trail, I knew, would confirm my whereabouts to him by morning, but to make sure, I also called Amy on my cell phone and told her of my change in plans. I knew she would be talking to Jed and would relay my location.

I pulled out my rice and beans, lit my stove, and settled down to enjoy the evening. It pleased me to have decided to honor my own body and stop for the night. It was a turning point for me, I knew, and though I felt unnerved to be discontinuing my hike with Jed, I experienced an extraordinary sense of freedom, as well. Our interactions had become more and more strained and his comments to me or about me often left me feeling bruised and disrespected.

By dropping behind him tonight, I knew I would probably not be able to catch up with him, and that he would not wait for me. He would be free to hike even faster so he could reach Katahdin and summit with ET and Waco after all.

I would have to get to Katahdin on my own and would have to climb it alone. It was sad, in a way, but I was relieved more than worried by the change in events.

"I have an itinerary, I'll stick to that... I can hike at my own pace, reclaim my hike, and do it my way!"

August 17, 2001, to Logan Brook Lean-to, 20.7 miles

The day began with overcast skies and rain in the air. The steep rocky climb up and then down Chairback Mountain was unremarkable. Although those rocky ledges had seemed formidable the night before, in the morning I scaled them with ease. Beginning to feel better about being on my own, I congratulated myself for making the wise decision to stay at the lean-to. My bravado was short-lived, however; I promptly lost the white blazes marking the AT and, for the first time in a long time on the trail, I had a feeling of panic. All of a sudden it was crystal clear: no one knew or cared where I was; if I became lost, no one would miss me for at least a week.

Turning around to retrace my steps, I spotted a white blaze directly behind me and realized that the trail continued one hundred eighty degrees behind my back. Sobered, I turned again and hiked on, filing the moment of panic as a caution to remain vigilant for the white blazes. Hiking with Jed, I had grown lazy about watching for them.

It began to drizzle; I pulled out my pack cover and raingear and covered up just before a deluge drenched me within minutes. It was not the kind of rain that looked like it would stop any time soon. I slogged on.

At midmorning I reached the West Branch of the Pleasant River, a wide, knee-deep stream separating me from the large strand of towering white pine trees known as the Hermitage. Even though it was pouring, I decided to ford the river in wading shoes rather than my hiking boots. My boots, I knew, would be soaked inside and out within a few hours, but I wanted to preserve my dry socks for as long as possible. I sat under a pine tree on a log and changed my footgear. A young woman ranger, the first person I had seen all morning, approached from the woods and joined me.

She sat on the log and chatted with me for a few minutes while I drank a water bottle full of cappuccino instant breakfast drink. In due course, I hoisted my pack, grabbed my boots under my arms, and forded the river without falling. It felt better to have spoken with some-one; at least someone would remember my whereabouts, I thought, if I didn't turn up at Katahdin in a week.

Wet, but refreshed, I hiked on. I had read that one of the most out-standing natural features along the AT could be seen from the Gulf Hagas Trail, a five-mile loop trail just beyond the ford of the river. However, on this rainy day of lonely walking, I decided to save that for another time and keep to the AT. I wanted to try to make it to the far side of White Cap Mountain before stopping for the night.

When I reached the Sidney Tappan Campsite in the late afternoon, I was happy to keep walking. Situated in a clearing of long grass, the ground was soft and soggy; a nice place to camp on a clear night, but a long, wet night of cold food and no company tonight, I thought.

The sleeves and pant legs of my rain gear stuck to my skin and water sluiced down my face and hands in rivulets, but there were three peaks to climb before the next shelter: the partially open summit of West Peak, the wooded summit of Hay Mountain, and the open summit of White Cap Mountain. Resolutely, I put down my head and kept climbing as the day grew darker, the clouds thicker, and the wind fiercer.

When I reached the bare rock summit of White Cap Mountain, rain pelted my crouched body in horizontal sheets. Hunched against the wind, even with my heavy pack on I was nearly blown sideways several times. The views of Katahdin, only seventy-two miles north, were com-pletely obscured; I could barely see my feet in front of me, much less dis-cern any potentially outstanding views. I struggled across the rocks, wind filling my lungs, rain stinging my eyes. Feeling like the last survivor at the edge of the earth, I hiked on.

Arriving at the shelter just before dark, I was exhilarated. The hiking conditions had been far from ideal and the hike was much longer than I normally would have done with Jed, but I was neither tired nor discour-aged. In fact, because the decision to keep moving had been mine, and because I had been able to stop during the day to refuel and reconnoiter as I wished, I was not exhausted. It had been one of the most physically and mentally demanding in a series of taxing days, but I felt invigorated and confident rather than disheartened and spent.

To my delight, under the dry and welcoming pine log roof of the lean-to, I found Wonder cooking his dinner. As soon as I settled into a dry corner of my own, Ranger Bob and Kathryn straggled in. The four of us cooked together in the dripping dark shelter, a circle of headlamps around the flames of our small camp stoves. I was far from alone and felt warm and safe.

"My parents are meeting us at the logging road tomorrow night," Ranger Bob said. "They're camping at the Jo-Mary Campground, bringing my brother to hike with Kathryn and me for the rest of the week. There'll be plenty of food, showers, and laundry. You're welcome to join us for the night."

Wonder and I both said we'd give it some thought. As I drifted to sleep I thought about my day.

> "I hiked seventeen miles in the rain today, forded a river, climbed three mountains – White Cap at dusk, in dense fog, pelting rain, fierce wind – and pushed on to the shelter without a mishap. Nice to have Wonder and the others here – a cozy umbrella in the rain."

Friday, August 18, 2001, to Jo-Mary Campsite, 15 miles

The morning dawned fresh, sunny, breezy and clear. As I hiked, I noticed the first red maple leaves of fall, plastered on rocks and roots at my feet. The change of seasons was in the air, and I felt a surge of energy that matched the briskness of the breeze. Striding with long steps, swinging my poles at my side, I hiked alone, smelling the difference in the earth, trees, and sunlight; it felt like a day in early fall. It was a day from my childhood when we closed the cottage on Laurel Lake, packed our cedar pillows and outgrown summer sandals into the family car, and drove back to Connecticut, excited to begin a new school year. This day had that same aura of excitement for only good things to happen: a new day, a new season, a new teacher, a new pair of school shoes. It was a good day to be alive.

> "The hike was on mostly level ground today, through huge pine forests, on soft pine paths, beside lakes and rocky streams.

I forded several rivers, but didn't need to change shoes. I ran into Wonder, Ranger Bob, and Kathryn off and on all day. No one was in a hurry but I couldn't help hiking fast – it just felt so good to be moving!"

I loved hiking in this wilderness.

In the early afternoon I stopped for lunch on a sandy beach next to a quiet body of water. The beach was sheltered by a ridge of gravel and large boulders separating it from another beach on its other side.[19]

The water was cool, the breeze fresh, and the sun was pleasantly warm on my back. Leaning against my pack, I watched the reflection of the mountains, clouds, and sky on the mirror-like surface of the lake. I wanted to remember this day, this hour, this moment. I let out a breath of air and rejoiced in the opportunities hiking on my own afforded me:

a woman can't survive
by her own breath
 alone
she must know
the voices of the mountains
she must recognize
the foreverness of blue sky
she must flow
with the elusive
bodies
of night winds
who will take her
into herself
look at me
i am not a separate woman
i am the continuance
of blue sky

---

19. Known as an esker, the ridge separating the beaches was once the bed of a river flowing within a glacier, literally left high and dry when the glacier retreated. With the retreat of the ice sheet, the beaches are the former stream sediments from the glacial river.

i am the throat
of the mountains
a night wind
who burns
with every breath
she takes
– Joy Harjo[20]

Ranger Bob and Kathryn hiked in for lunch just as I was leaving the lake. I decided to accept Ranger Bob's invitation of the night before; my clothes could use a laundry, and I was tempted by the thought of his mother's cooking. More to the point, however, I wanted to accept Ranger Bob's hospitality – his version of trail magic. Thinking about giving and receiving, I wondered how I would repay the trail when I completed my journey. There was no doubt in my mind that some sort of stewardship to the trail community would be high on my list of priorities in the years to come. In contrast to the attitude of entitlement of some of the hikers I had met along the way, I was consistently awed by the dedication and hard work behind every section of the trail I hiked. From the thoughtful and helpful information in the data books and maps, to the placement of logs, stepping stones, iron handgrips, and paths to beautiful viewpoints, the AT thus far had been an awe-inspiring affirmation of volunteerism, conservation, and generosity of spirit. In some manner, I resolved, I would help that tradition continue. For now, it was enough to accept an invitation to a camp shower and hot meal, appreciating the gift as I received it. I agreed to meet Ranger Bob and Kathryn at the logging road and ride to the campground to stay overnight with his family.

Walking through the deep soft needles of the forest path, I was enchanted by everything around me. No harsh weather, demanding elevation changes, melting heat, or annoying bugs impeded my trek. This hike was my reward for southern Maine; it was perfect.

About midafternoon I was startled to find a wooden outhouse almost on the trail. Not much farther, I discovered the Cooper Brook Falls

20.Harjo, Joy, "Fire," from How We Became Human, WW. Norton & Co., NY, 2002, p.25.

Lean-to, sitting on a ledge overlooking a cascade, with a natural pool at its base. Several hikers were splashing and shouting in the naturally bubbling swimming hole, one of the finest I had yet to see. I was tempted to stop for a swim but was neither hot nor tired. In fact, I was enjoying my solitary stroll through the pine forest and didn't really want to break my mood with boisterous hikers. I hiked on.

Before the appointed meeting hour, I reached the logging road and sat down to wait for Ranger Bob and Kathryn. Wonder emerged from the woods and sat down to wait with me. He had decided to pass up the campground for a solitary backcountry campsite on another shore of Jo-Mary Lake. Wonder continued to impress me with his determination to hike his own hike; he remained personable and gentle but never capitulated to peer pressure or gave up his hiking vision or purpose. I admired him for his steadfastness. He always affirmed my own.

Ranger Bob and Kathryn arrived just before a vehicle pulled up to the side of the gravel logging road. Ranger Bob's family spilled out and graciously accepted me into their fold for the night. They drove us to the campground where their trailer was parked for the week.

Accustomed to backcountry camping, I was not prepared for the campground: an oval footprint of trailer-sized patches of hard dirt along the southern shore of Jo-Mary Lake. Connected by a gravel road to a recreation center-laundry-camp store-bath house, it was noisy with families large and small, barking dogs, and blaring radios. Next to the recreation center, a large generator belched power for the garish lights strung around the covered picnic area and camp store complex.

My brain shuddered as I tried to block the amplified noise from my ears. No wonder Wonder had opted to hike to a backcountry campsite. He knew what I had forgotten: campsites accessible to vehicles bring the city to the woods. The Jo-Mary Campsite was an abrupt change of pace in the isolated backcountry. It spoke to the folly of trying to force twenty-first century conveniences into a nineteenth century setting. In converting energy for the people from the city, the generator alone was enough to shatter the silence and destroy the very essence of the peace they sought. Their loud radios, dogs, children, and gasoline-powered engines did the rest.

Taking the jolt of the campground in stride, Kathryn and I pitched our tents and headed to the shower/laundry house to wash up. While we were gone, Ranger Bob's mom fixed a large meal of ham, potatoes, vegetables, and fruit and served it up in plastic dishes on a picnic table covered with a vinyl cloth. By the light of a gas lantern, we sat at the table and talked until weariness drove the women inside the camper to wash dishes so the men could use the table to spread out their maps.

A slice of American camping life, I mused, writing in my journal by the light of my headlamp. I had pitched my tent behind the trailer, on the edge of the lake. Listening to the mournful cry of loons in the distance, I tried to ignore the voices of the men at the picnic table, and the campers at the next campsite. I fell asleep thinking about Katahdin.

> "I can hardly believe I've come this far, that Katahdin is so close. I'm glad it's not the end for me, that I still have the southern portion of the trail to hike; I'm not ready to end my adventure yet, though I will be glad when this part of the trail is over."

August 19, 2001, to White House Landing, Maine, 10 miles

The first thing I saw in the morning when I unzipped my tent and poked my head out was a beached red canoe on the lakeshore in the foreground, and the table top silhouette of Katahdin, shimmering and silent in the distance beyond.

To the Indians, it was known as "Kette-Adene" – the "greatest mountain." A massive, isolated, granite monolith, Katahdin had finally emerged – from fantasy to reality, overnight. When I had pitched my tent in the early darkness the night before, blinded by gasoline light, I had no idea I would be sleeping under the protective aura of this quiet giant. Behind the mist rising from the lake, Katahdin had emerged this morning, as though called up from a witch's cauldron, mysterious, solid and strong. I couldn't wait to reach her and couldn't imagine how anyone could come this far and not dare to climb her. I was bewitched by her inscrutability.

After the promised stack of Aunt Jemima pancakes, Ranger Bob's dad drove us back to the trailhead to continue hiking. It was good to be back on the trail, away from the dust and noise of the campground.

The morning was sunny and mild and the hike one of fording streams, crossing logging roads, and circling the western end of Lower Jo-Mary Lake. When I passed Wonder's option for the previous night, I was struck by the contrast in our two choices. Wonder's, a former fishing camp on the shore of the lake, offered a bed of soft needles and ferns under soaring red pines; it was solitary and isolated from other campers. Next time I would sleep there, I decided, though I did appreciate the hospitality that Ranger Bob's family had provided.

Continuing, I followed a short side trail to a sandy beach on Lower Jo-Mary Lake for a brief morning swim. The water was cold and refreshing and I floated in naked privacy, luxuriating in the stillness of the water, reconnecting with the natural landscape.

Calmed and refreshed for the day ahead, I climbed a slight incline of four hundred feet through the woods to the top of Potaywadjo Ridge. So gentle was the rise I was not certain that I was actually climbing or descending until I passed the lean-to on the other side. I crossed Twitchell Brook and took a small side trail to the shore of Pemadumcook Lake. There was Katahdin again, across the lake, in brilliant midmorning sunlight, now less than forty-eight trail miles away.

The view was magnificent and I could feel my excitement and anticipation rise as every step drew me closer. With luck, the weather on the day I climbed would be similar to that of today: clear, sunny, warm, and cloudless. However, I knew there were only a handful of perfect climbing days on Katahdin in any given summer, and most climbs were done in less-than-perfect weather. Occasionally, hikers were even prevented from climbing until clear weather conditions on the rocky summit prevailed. Sometimes hikers had to wait several days at the ranger station below, postponing the end of their adventure and the culminating climb.

My window for climbing Katahdin was not wide; George and Amy would meet me in five days. Tonight I would be only forty-three miles from the ranger station at the base: two days of hiking twenty-two miles each day. That would leave me three days to wait at the base for good climbing weather. Certainly one of those days would be decent.

I was not worried about climbing Katahdin and decided to not worry about weather conditions that were beyond my control. Katahdin would wait for me and I would climb her. I had no doubts now.

Walking through the tall green woods, I relaxed and began to look for signs to the trail to White House Landing, my destination. Another former fishing camp, the Landing is now operated as a wilderness retreat on the far shore of Pemadumcook Lake, a short boat ride from the trailhead. Since this detour for a mail drop resupply had been Jed's idea, I did not know how to reach the camp. However, when I stopped to look at my map, a southbound hiker named Bluebird came through the woods. She had just come from the White House Landing and gave me specific directions, but neglected to mention that the trail to the boat launch traversed soggy, marshy lakeshore and doubled back parallel to the AT for more than a mile. I wondered why the trail followed such a circuitous loop but slogged on, curious and a little skeptical about ever finding the camp.

The moose horn tied to a tree was unmistakable; it was hanging in a small clearing just large enough for a motor boat to dock and pick up or discharge passengers. A sign posted on the tree read: "Blow horn and wait. The boat will come."

Feeling a bit foolish, I squeezed the bulb of the horn, looked across the sparkling empty lake, and took off my pack, prepared to wait. One thing I had perfected on my odyssey was how to appreciate a long quiet wait with nothing to do but watch, listen, daydream, or sleep, letting my body and mind enjoy the unavoidable, legitimate rest.

On this sunny Sunday afternoon, my wait was only a few minutes.

Boarding, I braced myself on my pack in the bow and watched the shoreline whir past. We sped across the lake. The air streaked past my face and took my breath away; it had been a long time since my last motorboat ride.

White House Landing was well named. The setting that awaited me was a collection of white weathered buildings: a bunkhouse for hikers, a small cottage for hikers who wanted privacy, a bath house, a latrine, several cottages for families, and one large building with a wide front porch – the main lodge/kitchen/dining room for everyone. Rustic and remote by any standard, the camp looked sparse, clean, and comfortable. I knew my resupply had arrived when another hiker greeted me and told me that Jed had been there the night before and had left some instructions about what to mail back home. The midday pizza and burgers had been served to the hikers in residence at the camp, and the proprietor and his family were about to take a siesta.

Since the lodge was closed after lunch, the main door to the lobby was locked. I could see my package on the floor inside, but could not retrieve it; nor could I access the clearly labeled freezer of Ben & Jerry's ice cream just inside the door.

Hot and weary, I sat down on the porch and waited. I fantasized about ice cream, deliberating on the flavors I would choose, wondering how many pints I could eat in one sitting. I thought it might be several.

To my left, another hiker was lying on a hammock strung between two white birch trees: Metro. He had hiked in earlier that morning and was sleeping off a huge lunch. Even thinner than I was, Metro ate only Snickers bars when he could not find restaurant food. He had tossed all his dehydrated food into the hiker box in Monson; today had been his first meal since the spaghetti and beer bash outside of Monson five days earlier.

Sharing Metro's sentiments about trail food, my cravings were for fresh oranges, bananas, tomatoes and corn on the cob. Dehydrated food tasted nasty, but to me, Snickers bars were worse.

When the camp store opened, I retrieved my food package and bought a pint of Ben & Jerry's. Sitting on the front porch, I ate it all. Then I weighed myself on the UPS scale: three pounds lighter than the last time on a scale, six pounds if you discounted my hiking boots. But, other than weariness after a long day's hike, my body felt fine, though my temper was quick and emotions close to the surface.

For the remainder of the afternoon, I swam in the lake, relaxed in the sun, took a solar shower, and refurbished my food bag. Only three or four days until the end, I kept only my least offensive food and donated the rest to the hiker box. A southbound hiker could stock his entire hike from donations in this hiker box, I thought. Everyone had taken the same opportunity to lighten his food bag, knowing the end was within a few days' reach.

Early in the evening, we all gathered again in the dining room for a dinner of personalized hamburgers. Mine was loaded with extra lettuce and tomato, so full that I had to open the bun to parcel in bites, open-faced.

Lazing on the porch after dinner, someone suggested we take the canoe and paddle across the lake to look for the resident moose that came to feed about this time of night. Metro and another hiker agreed to paddle the canoe; I volunteered to sit in the middle and seek the moose.

Gliding over the purple and pink lake of reflected clouds and sunset sky, I lazily trolled my fingers in the cool water. Even talkative Metro fell silent in the long slow stillness of our paddle down the lake, listening and watching for moose on shore. The hikers in the kayak pulled ahead of us. Our canoe was alone in the twilight, a silhouette against the waning light, blending into its own reflection on the water below. Loons cried mournfully to each other across the water, and the air grew cooler. Metro guided the canoe along one shoreline, then another, searching for moose. We looked and listened, hushed and vigilant. No moose.

We turned the canoe around. Upstream a dog began to bark, tentatively at first, then with increasing frenzy. A minute later we heard something crashing through the underbrush along the shoreline, and then the higher yelps of a frustrated, captured dog.

Two campers and their dog had discovered our moose. The dog had begun to chase it, but was held fast by the owners who feared for his life, the weight differential between the moose and the dog being substantial.

The campers told us that the moose had smashed through the bushes straight at them, but their dog had scared it into the woods.

"That was our resident moose your little yappy thing scared," Metro chided sardonically. "Maybe you should let him go. Maybe the moose will eat him."

Metro wasn't kidding. Disappointed, we paddled back to the wilderness camp. I had seen a lot of moose tracks in the past few weeks; I had carried my share of moose turds through the White Mountains; I had heard the sound of a moose crashing through the woods. I would have loved to see a moose eat that yappy little dog and drop her bones in the mud.

We arrived at camp in the dark. No generator-driven string of lights greeted us. Silently we beached our canoe and slipped up to the bunkhouse to find our sleeping bags. Overhead, the wind pushed puffy clouds to reveal the stars shining in clumps and patches. Tomorrow it will rain, I predicted without really thinking about it; the air was growing heavier. Glad to be under a roof for the night, I crept into my bunk and zipped up my sleeping bag. Loons and the brushy sound of wind against the trees were the only sounds in the black, still night.

August 20, 2001, to Rainbow Stream Lean-to, 16 miles

As predicted, the morning dawned wet, misty and threatening rain. Metro and several section hikers met me at the boat launch after breakfast with covered packs and bodies suited in rain gear. As always when saying goodbye to a nice place, faced with hiking all day in the rain, I was filled with melancholy. Sitting in the stern of the boat, I concentrated on looking for the elusive moose along the shoreline as we whizzed down the lake back to the AT trailhead.

The section hikers were heading south. Metro and I waved goodbye to them as we disembarked and headed north. Two more days to Katahdin – or maybe three, depending on the weather. In this morning of rain and fog, a clear climb in three days seemed iffy.

Metro and I hiked the first seven miles together, fording several streams. Metro told me a bit about himself. He was a disenchanted lawyer, most recently from New York City, escaping the pseudo-sophisticated life of a thirty-something bachelor. Quick-witted and entertaining, he also had a quieter, more reflective side that matched this morning of thick gray clouds and dripping branches. As we hiked the two miles along the western shoreline of Nahmakanta Lake, we talked about real estate and the history of the logging and fishing industry in rural Maine.

I was glad that the joint purchase of all that I could see around me would preserve the beauty and seclusion of the area in perpetuity. Metro was more inclined to think in terms of land-development values, though he eschewed private development and exploitation. We both appreciated the privilege of walking through this quiet, remote, and still-wild landscape.

There was only one real ascent to the day. Nesuntabunt Mountain was a climb of about seven hundred feet in a mile and a half. Ascending to the ledges at the summit of Nesuntabunt, I was able to see the expanse of Nahmakanta Lake stretching below. However, rain and fog prevented a view of Katahdin, only sixteen air miles from the lake.

Descending the northern slopes of Nesuntabunt, I wandered through a stand of old growth red spruce and white pine, marveling at the girth of some of the trees.[21] The forest was magnificent and calm, but I was ready to be finished with my hiking for the day. The weather was still cloudy and wet and, hiking alone, all I wanted to do was get to the next campsite, pitch my tent, eat, sleep, and hike to Daicey Pond, the lean-to closest to Katahdin for AT thru-hikers. With good weather, I would be able to climb Katahdin the day after tomorrow. I couldn't wait.

Crossing a stream later in the afternoon, I met a hiker called Gravy Train, also headed to the campsite eight miles farther. We had both started our thru-hikes on the same day and would probably finish at Katahdin on the same day. However, Gravy Train had started his thru-hike in Georgia, eight hundred miles south of my starting point in Shenandoah, Virginia; he was moving much more quickly and efficiently than I. He averaged twenty-five miles a day to my fifteen, started earlier in the morning, hiked later into the evening, and traveled with a pack that was ten pounds lighter than mine. We walked together for a few minutes before he pulled ahead, tall and lean with a stride three times my own.

As I neared the Rainbow Stream Lean-to early in the evening, the rain that had been threatening all day finally began. Hustling to the lean-to, I decided to wait it out, and hike on to the campsite after dinner. Gravy Train had the same idea; he was cooking under the roof of the lean-to when I ducked in.

The lean-to was tucked into a grove overlooking a noisy stream with its own sluice on the rocks in front. Loud rushing water from the stream and the steady drum of rain on the tin roof overhead made me feel warm and lethargic. Gravy Train decided to stay overnight in the shelter and tried to convince me to do the same.

21. This ten-acre old growth stand is within the AT corridor; some trees are at least one hundred forty years old. The average diameter of the red spruce is seventeen inches and the white pine is twenty-three inches.

"We can get up at five o'clock," he said, "and be at the campsite by the time you would hike out if you stayed there tonight. And you'll be dry instead of wet tonight."

He had a point. Setting up camp in the rainy dark night was my second least favorite thing to do; my first was to break camp on a rainy morning, after a wet hike the night before.

"Besides," he added, "today's my birthday. I'm twenty-six today."

How could I refuse? I agreed to stay the night and hike out with him early in the morning. I spread out my stuff, dug around in my food bag, and found something to commemorate the occasion. Instead of cake and ice cream, we celebrated the day with instant chocolate pudding – lumpy, thin and only vaguely resembling a treat.

It rained all night.

August 21, 2001, to Daicey Pond, 22.5 miles

Gravy Train and I were up and out by five forty-five. By seven o'clock we were at Rainbow Stream campground, shouting for Metro to get up and get moving. He poked his head out of his tent, cursed the rain, and told us he'd catch up. We kept going. There's nothing like a steady morning rain to keep your hike on track, I thought. At the rate we were hiking, we would reach Daicey Pond Lean-to by dinnertime.

Today was the day ET and Waco had planned to climb Katahdin. I wondered if Jed were with them and if all three were waiting at the base for better weather. It didn't look like a good day to climb to me; I was glad I was not close enough to have the option.

Metro eventually caught up with us and we hiked together most of the morning. Gravy Train wanted advice on marriage and Metro, recently divorced, had plenty to say. The time passed quickly. In the late morning, we stopped at the Hurd Brook Lean-to, encountering two elderly women hikers. The women were eager to know how we liked the stone stairs leading to the shelter. Their questions surprised me because I had noticed how easy the stairs were to maneuver. The rise of most stone steps was usually much too wide. These particular steps were just right for me, carrying a pack and shifting my weight to alternating legs as I stepped up or down. Metro and Gravy Train were noncommittal, but I waxed eloquent about the steps.

The women were most appreciative. They had been responsible for designing and helping to build the steps and had constructed them for women as well as men to transcend. For me, the trail had been a series of revelations like this: shelters, privies, paths, steps – all were built to the measure of the stride and strength of tall men, rather than the generally shorter women. It made me wonder, again, if the trail would have been easier for me if all design considerations had taken a woman's body and strength into consideration. The placement of these stone steps was only one example of how to accommodate to hikers who were fewer than six feet tall.

As we hiked out from the lean-to, a young couple approached us through the woods. The woman greeted me with evident surprise and delight: "Leslie, we were just talking about you. How great to see you," she gushed.

This young woman's recognition was bewildering. Completely out of context, I could not begin to remember her, and she did not give me the usual social hints about her identity or the circumstances of our knowing one another.

After a few awkward attempts, I finally gave up and asked her to tell me who she was: one of the stylists from my beauty salon in Ohio, hiking for a week in the wilderness. The encounter was a jolt. It reminded me that I would be back in my old life in just a few days, to help my staff organize for a new school year. Weary as I was, I was not quite ready to be back in civilization either.

Metro and Gravy Train hiked ahead, anticipating the West Branch of the Penobscot River and the camp store at Abol Bridge with its promise of food. Hiking alone for the first time all day, I thought about the days and weeks ahead. After Katahdin, George and Amy would meet me in Millinocket, and we would drive back to Ohio together. My schedule was to check in at work, reorganize my food parcels for the southern eight hundred miles to Springer, buy some new boots, clean up, and begin hiking again. Megg and Jim planned to bring Nemo to Ohio to celebrate his second birthday, when George and I would observe our thirty-seventh wedding anniversary. After the family weekend together, George would drive me back to the trail in Virginia to finish my journey.

The thought of being with my family again made me tearful. Even though I was doing what I wanted to do, I missed them terribly. The young men who had befriended me on my odyssey had helped take my mind off my loneliness, but I missed my daughters, my friends, and my husband. I was eager to rejoin them in a celebration of birth, marriage, and the completion of twelve hundred hiking miles. And I was impatient to finish my hike; I was bone tired, footsore, and drained.

Hiking through a forest of large hemlock trees and huge boulders, I fought back tears of self-pity. Cold rain pelting on my hood didn't help. The camp store at Abol Bridge couldn't come too soon.

When I reached the gravel parking lot next to the camp store, Wonder, Metro, and Gravy Train were sitting at a picnic table, eating soggy sandwiches in the rain. My appetite had been set for a hot dog or two, but the camp store offered only pre-wrapped sandwiches in the refrigerated case, nestled snugly against open containers of bait. The bait looked better than the sandwiches, I thought. The coffee was hot, though, and sipping it between bites of slimy cheese and gray meat, I joined the others out in the rain and ate my lunch.

Katahdin, from the Abol Bridge over the West Branch of the Penobscot River, was hidden behind the mist, clouds, and rain. We hiked out, eager to reach Daicey Pond by evening.

The afternoon's hike took me across several streams on stepping-stones, footbridges, and fords, around the shore of Pine Point, and along the streambed of Nesowadnehunk Stream, with its many quiet pools and spectacular falls. I hiked alone most of the time, losing the trail in one boulder-strewn stream for a long ten minutes, finding it again with the help of Gravy Train when I encountered him, also lost, retracing his steps downstream.

Late in the afternoon, I crossed the boundary of Baxter State Park and entered the environs of Katahdin.[22]

22. Acreage for the park was originally purchased and donated to the State of Maine in 1931 by former Governor Percival P. Baxter. The terms of the gift stipulate that the land be used for public park and recreational purposes and kept in the natural state as a sanctuary for wild beasts and birds, with no further construction or development of roads or ways for motor vehicles. Thus, the number of visitors and activities within the park are highly regulated. Thru-hikers register at Daicey Pond Campground and are permitted to camp or stay in lean-tos before and after their ascent of Katahdin.

As I forded the Nesowadnehunk Stream, passed Big Niagara Falls and then Little Niagara Falls, my excitement mounted. I had hiked almost twenty-four miles today, in the rain and fog, and I had almost reached the base of Katahdin. The Hundred Mile Wilderness was behind me, as was the most difficult two-thirds of the AT.

Tomorrow, if the weather cleared, I would climb five miles to the summit of Katahdin (5,267'), with four thousand feet of elevation change. According to the guidebook, the climb should take between three and four hours. Metro and Gravy Train would wait until later in the week to climb – Metro with his brother, Gravy Train with his father. Climbing tomorrow, I would be climbing alone. The thought thrilled and terrified me.

Bursting out of the woods, looking to register for the night, I was stunned to see several cars parked in the grass. What were cars doing in the wilderness? Walking a little farther, I realized the state park campground was accessible to a limited number of vehicles. Unlike the Jo-Mary Campsite, however, the cars at Daicey Pond were parked away from their tent sites; their campers were nowhere to be seen.

Hurrying, I found my way to the ranger station to register for the night and found Wonder sitting on the lawn, surrounded by flowers. He was planning to climb in the morning.

"Let's hike the four miles to Katahdin Stream together," he suggested. "The weather is posted by seven o'clock – we can get daypacks when we register. I want to climb by myself, but we can meet at the Katahdin sign on top."

"Sounds perfect," I replied, relieved and pleased. "I'll be your official photographer."

The sign on the summit, "Katahdin, Northern Terminus of the Appalachian Trail," is the goal for traditional thru-hikers. Touching the sign marks the end of the journey. Meeting Wonder at the sign on Katahdin and having him there for me was a gift I was glad to give and receive. Wonder was wonderful. I was pleased that I would see him at the top.

When I signed in for the night, the ranger asked my real name. Learning it, he said, "Oh, I have a note for you. You won't like it," and handed me a piece of paper torn from a notebook.

The note was from Jed:

Leslie,

I climbed today. Based on what I encountered, I would strongly suggest that you do not attempt to climb Katahdin. It took ET, Waco, [and me], two and a half hours to get to the summit. I believe that you would need at least five to six hours in good weather. Please consider this before you make your decision.

Amy and I can come back with you at sometime and I can help you up. But I would strongly discourage you from attempting to climb now. See you in Millinocket. Jed.

I was flabbergasted! I read the note again. What on earth was wrong with Jed? Had his climb today been that hard? If he and the others had climbed in two and a half hours, in bad weather, why would it take me five or six hours in good weather? I asked the ranger if the climb held some hidden dangers that he thought I could not meet.

Looking me over, the ranger said, "Well, you've hiked this far... you look fit to me. Lots of people climb Katahdin – kids, grandmothers – all kinds of people. If the weather's good, you should be fine."

"That's what I think," I replied, scratching my head, still puzzled. "I can always turn back if it seems too much for me," I added, though privately I thought: "Fat chance!"

Later, at the shelter, I showed the note to Metro and Wonder. Metro suggested I climb and never mention it to Jed.

"When I was getting my divorce," he said, "I got all kinds of crazy notes from my wife... they got more and more bizarre. I went ahead and did what I needed to do and didn't let her stuff bother me."

Wonder thought maybe Jed was feeling guilty because he had hiked on and climbed without me.

I didn't know what to think, but I was not about to let Jed's assessment of my hiking ability keep me from climbing. In fact, I was beginning to think that his impatience and unclear communication when we hiked together were partially responsible for my past weariness and exhaustion. Hiking on my own through the Wilderness, I had been full of vigor and good spirits, even though I had been tired at the end of every day, even though my feet hurt and my body was too thin, even though I could not get enough nourishment no matter how much or how often I ate.

"If the weather's good, I'll be climbing tomorrow," I declared. As I settled into the shelter, it began to rain again. Gravy Train opened an umbrella (his Go-Lite raingear) and we cooked at the picnic table.

A reporter from the Associated Press walked in and sat down opposite me. He was writing an article about land use, he said, and wanted to talk to some thru-hikers.

Welcome back to civilization, I thought, bemused by his appearance and questions, in the rain, at the base of the sacred Katahdin. We talked while I cooked; he talked while I ate. Later that month, a friend of mine sent me the article: "Citizens Worry About Accessibility of Maine's Wilderness Kingdoms." The article ended with:

> "AT hiker, Leslie Mass, 60 of Powell, Ohio is glad to be in Maine. In busier New Hampshire, she said, hiking Mt. Washington with so many others had felt like riding a 'convey-or belt.'
>
> So she lays down her walking sticks, hangs sweaty socks over a branch, and fires up a camp stove. Two hares streak back and forth, hunting stray morsels in the flickering light.
>
> In some ways, she sees the world as a traditional conservation-ist: We must protect more wildernesses. Owners ought to be stewards.
>
> But, at the end of today's trail, even she moderates her views. "I understand that people have to have jobs, and they have to have vacations," she says, "And we have to share the land."

August 22, 2001, Katahdin, 14 miles

At five o'clock in the morning, the woods were misty and wet, but it was not raining. Trying not to wake Gravy Train and Metro, I packed up my gear, ate some granola and instant breakfast, and met Wonder, sitting on a log near his overnight tent site. We crept out of camp and hiked the three and a half miles to Katahdin Stream as the sky cleared from dark to light.

The weather posting at the ranger station predicted a forty percent chance of showers and thunderstorms on Katahdin, a Class II day. We agreed it was good enough to climb. Stowing our heavy packs with the ranger, we put our lunch and raingear in daypacks, snapped photos of each other on the footbridge over Katahdin Stream, and began our separate ascents, agreeing to meet in a few hours at the summit.

In spite of myself, because of Jed's dire warnings, I felt a little apprehensive. The terrain ahead must be very difficult, I thought, because the first two miles below treeline were certainly no harder than anything I had yet encountered. In fact, the canopy of tall trees, the bubbling water of Katahdin Stream, and the fifty-foot cascade crashing through the trees beside the trail were good company. "In beauty will I possess again," I chanted as I hiked. Passing several groups of day hikers, younger but less fit than I, I decided to forget about Jed and enjoy my day. The trails, so far, seemed well graded and carefully designed. Thousands of people climbed them every year; several dozen were climbing them this morning. If I were to meet an unassailable obstacle, I could always turn back; so far, nothing of the kind had presented itself. I kept climbing.

Just before treeline I passed The Cave, a small slab of overhanging rock that could serve as a shelter in bad weather, I supposed. It was the beginning of the boulder scramble.

The ascent grew steeper and the boulders considerably larger. Strapping my poles to my daypack, I began climbing on all fours plus my backside, grabbing tree roots, securing toe holds in rock crevices, and pulling myself up however I could. The air was clear but still misty; it didn't feel as though it would rain. I relaxed into the climb and began to enjoy myself. I felt like a child again, scrambling up the rocks on my hands and knees.

At treeline, the climb became even steeper, and slower. Hikers ahead of me carefully picked their way across the sides and tops of ten- and twelve-foot-high rock face. But unlike other boulders I had climbed in New Hampshire and Maine, these boulders had iron bars welded into the rocks to grab, step, and pull up on. The difficulty was not in the climb, but in the wait to climb. It was a slow process, but everyone was cheerful and patient, offering encouraging words and a helping hand when needed. I encountered only one couple, an older woman and her woefully out-of-shape husband, returning as I climbed. The Hunt Spur had proved too much for them "this time," they said. I surmised that they had climbed Katahdin before and that "this time" was a post-illness attempt to recapture something from their past. Respectfully, I watched them descend. They were a dignified example of wisdom, I thought.

After the Hunt Spur, the climb never got any harder. In fact, it was fun. The air was cool and growing lighter, though not yet completely clear, and occasionally I could discern sunlight just beyond the mist. With only a daypack on my back, I wished I had had lighter trail shoes on my feet. My boots were stiff and hard to maneuver on the rocks; trail shoes would have been more fun, I thought.

About midmorning, I reached the Gateway (4,550'), the edge of the plateau. The flora was low-growing and adhered to the rocks, lichen-like. Before, behind, above, below, all around me there were rocks and more rocks, covered with low clouds and mist, softened by clumps of hardy grass and scaly-looking brown ground cover. The wind in my ears and mist on my face lent an aura of other-worldliness; I was, once again, alone on the top of the gray, misty, fog-swirling world.

At mile 4.6, I reached Thoreau Spring (4,627'), named for Henry David Thoreau, who climbed Katahdin in 1846 from the West Branch of the Penobscot River. The spring was actually a disappointment: a small puddle of water wetting the dirt between several rocks. I snapped a photo and hiked on. Baxter Peak, the summit, was only a mile away, across the tableland.[23]

Ascending from the tableland, my steps grew wider, lighter, and jauntier. I passed several other hikers, all headed to the summit. The clouds began to lift and, from time to time, I could glimpse clear valleys and lakes below me, illuminated briefly by sun before becoming quickly covered again by clouds. I anticipated that the clouds would disappear when

---

23. Thousands of years ago, the continental glacier planed off the top of Katahdin, leaving a flat tableland of rocks and boulders rising toward the south.

I reached the summit; the sun would shine to reveal Pamola, the deity of Katahdin.[24]

Shortly after eleven o'clock, the clouds did lift and I walked onto Baxter Peak (5,267'), the highest point in Maine. Wonder was there to greet me with smiles and hugs and a round of applause. I was surprised to see several dozen other hikers, as well; families, children, former thru-hikers back for another go, and Ranger Bob and Kathryn. Most had ascended different trails, some much more difficult than the AT. We were a giddy group.

Ranger Bob, Wonder, and I gathered behind the "Katahdin" sign at the summit. Wonder lit a sparkler, Ranger Bob waved a small American flag, and I held up the little red Elmo that had been strapped to my pack since Shenandoah. Kathryn snapped our group photo, and then took individual victory poses. The day-hikers surrounding us applauded and congratulated us with cheers.

Too excited to eat lunch, I split my last Hershey bar four ways and we toasted each other with treated water and the stale candy. The sun made a brief appearance before the clouds and mist once again closed in. I never saw the shattered mirror effect of the lakes and green-mantled forests below, described so vividly by my trail guide. Next time, I thought, pulling my jacket around my body. The wind was picking up; time to descend.

Sharing hugs all around, Ranger Bob, Kathryn, Wonder, and I said goodbye: Kathryn and Ranger Bob to descend along the trail to Abol Bridge, Wonder to follow another trail to Bangor. With a sly grin, Wonder gave me a parting affirmation. "Tell Jed to 'eat my turds,'" he said, lifting his hiking stick in salute.

Bold for Wonder, I thought. I had never heard him reprove anyone.

Picking up my day pack and repositioning Elmo in the straps, I began my descent on the AT, back the way I had come, to exchange packs at the ranger station and hitch a ride to Millinocket.

24. Katahdin has been described as an enormous flat fishhook. To the Native Americans, Pamola, the projecting point of the rounded dome (4,902') was the deity of Katahdin. In awe of Pamola's wrath they never dared venture too near the mountain. Until 1804 when Charles Turner ascended Katahdin for the first time, Native folklore held that Pamola would destroy anyone who dared approach. Turner survived as did Thoreau, forty years later. Today, Katahdin is the destination of thousands of hikers and climbers each year with many trails leading to its summit and surrounding basins and Knife Edge.

Back at the gateway to the boulders, the sun reappeared. Taking advantage of a patch of light, I sat with my back against a rock to absorb the beauty of the moment: green and gold below, as far as I could see; crisp air and brisk breeze on my face and knees; sunlight in my eyes and warming my shoulders. What a day.

I had been right to hike, right to climb, after all. It was the perfect culminating experience for this part of my journey. I knew that whatever lay ahead, I would be able to do it. I would do it my way, and that was okay.

I had gained a lot during my summer's foray into the unknown. I had become reacquainted with my soul and hiked a memorial to my father, through his sacred New England cathedral, the mountains of New Hampshire and Maine. My father and I had walked a thousand miles together.

The next part of the journey would be for me, alone. I would do it in my time, at my pace, and with my needs at the forefront.

I put my poles away and nearly floated through the sunlight, arms outstretched, feet barely touching the rocks. When I reached treeline, though the sun was still bright, it began to rain. Under the trees, I didn't even get wet. The sun caught the drops of moisture on the leaves in front of me, making the woods sparkle. It felt like the magical illustrations in a 1920s children's book of fairy stories. It would not have surprised me to see a wood nymph fly by or beckon me to follow her through the shimmering woods to her cave. It was a thrilling, childlike fantasy in the mysterious iridescent forest.

All too soon, I passed the cascade that had kept me company this morning and began to follow the water of Katahdin Stream back to the campground, returning to civilization. Checking in at the ranger station, I found a note from Wonder:

Gotta Hike!,

I took another trail down and then hitched here, so I somehow managed to beat you down. If I do get a hitch to Bangor, I won't see you or Jed. Give him a 'hello' for me. Congratulations – this was our day!

– Wonder

I would miss Wonder.

Trading in the daypack at the ranger station, I discovered Elmo was gone. He had been strapped into my pack since Nemo gave him to me on the first day of my hike. It was fitting, I supposed, that Elmo would jump out on Katahdin. I remembered the sunlit rock where he and I had stopped on the slope above. He got out, I knew, when I realized that I would be all right on my own from that point on. Anthropomorphic reasoning, but somehow it pleased me to think of Elmo amid the wildflowers and wild grass in a rock crevice on Katahdin. He was probably waiting for the next apprehensive hiker, I thought. Thanks, Elmo.

I hoisted my heavy pack and walked to the parking lot to hitch a ride to Millinocket. Most of the day-hikers were still descending Katahdin and, not wanting to wait for them to return and take a chance on a ride, I walked to the gravel road at the campground entrance. It would be a long walk to Millinocket, twenty miles south, if no one came by, I thought.

As I crossed the road from the campground, an enclosed pickup truck rumbled in from the north and shuddered to a halt at my stuck-out thumb.

Peering in the passenger window, I saw a middle-aged woman in the driver's seat. She opened her door, jumped out, and came around to open the back of the truck and stow my pack. Papers, boxes, old batteries, clothing, and large sacks of mulch took up most of the space. We wedged my pack and poles on top, slammed our doors, and scrunched off down the road together.

"I'm Nancy," she introduced herself.

"Gotta Hike!" I replied automatically. "I mean, Leslie," I amended, readying myself for civilization. "I just finished the first two-thirds of my thru-hike."

Nancy was impressed.

"I've never known a woman to do it before," she said. "As many years as I've been driving this road, I've never seen anyone like you."

Then Nancy told me about herself. She had a camp forty miles up the road and every Tuesday night drove from her convenience/truck stop job on the Connecticut/Massachusetts state line to spend her day off at camp. She was headed back to Connecticut. My lucky day.

"Nancy and I talked like old friends – I enjoyed her company, bumping along the gravel, then paved, road to Millinocket. When she dropped me off, I thanked her, said it was nice to meet an independent woman. She gave me a big hug. I invited her to join me for Chinese food, but she declined.

"Gotta drive, Gotta Hike!" she said with tears in her eyes. My eyes welled up, too. I'm not sure why. It was a nice encounter."

I called George, Amy, and Megg from Millinocket. They were relieved to hear from me and were full of congratulations. I was tired and sore but proud of myself. I was proud that I had walked the last twelve hundred miles, proud that I had come through the Hundred Mile Wilderness, and proud that I had climbed Katahdin pretty much on my own.

In Millinocket, I chose a regular motel on the highway rather than the hiker hostel in town; I wanted to escape the tall tales and thru-hiker bravado reverberating within its walls, and savor my success in a long, hot bubble bath.

August 23, 2001, Millinocket, Maine, 0 miles

When I woke up in the motel at six o'clock the next morning, I took another hot bath. Climbing out of the tub, I glanced in the mirrors along the bathroom walls. The body that greeted me was appalling: wrinkled skin draped over sharp bones, swollen, toenail-less feet, scratches, cuts, and scrapes on each shin, and a fist-sized purple bruise on the cheek of each buttock. I looked like an undernourished chicken too skinny to be roasted, only good enough for soup.

I looked like a survivor of a concentration camp.

My first stop of the morning was McDonald's for yogurt, fresh fruit, and orange juice. I noticed that McDonald's in Maine also served lobster rolls; dinner, I thought. Next I stopped at an outlet clothing store for a new pair of shorts and a tee shirt to wear to the laundry. The only clothes that fit were from the pre-teen pajama department.

The day was another Maine scorcher. As I walked down the highway to the Laundromat, I decided to stop at the hiker hostel to say goodbye to Waco, ET and anyone else still there. Jed, I expected, would surface at my motel later in the day; we were expecting George and Amy in the morning for a ride back to Ohio.

There was no one I knew at the hiker hostel, but the owner showed me around. It was a nice place, but couldn't come close to the privacy and bubble-bath opportunity afforded by my motel.

Walking up the road, I passed an outdoor market of fresh vegetables and bought a melon, two ears of corn, a quart of strawberries, and a tomato. Next, I stopped at the drug store for some Band-Aids, and at the grocery store for orange juice and cottage cheese. My lunch would be a feast of fresh vitamin C, potassium, and calcium. Salivating, I arrived at the motel and discovered Jed waiting on the doorstep, looking clean and civilized, wearing town clothes and a new haircut. He gave me a hug and we escaped to my air-conditioned room to wait for George and Amy.

We spent the afternoon drowsing and talking in climate-controlled air. Jed talked about his meaningful summit of Katahdin but did not ask me about mine. I had decided to follow Metro's advice and forget that Jed had advised me to keep Katahdin for another time. I was still buoyed by the success of my climb; Jed's puzzling behavior no longer seemed relevant.

In the early evening, we went to McDonald's for supper. Remembering the lobster roll, I ordered two, with blueberry pie for dessert. Alas, McDonald's is still McDonald's, even in Maine. The lobster roll was dripping with grease and the blueberry pie was glutinous blue sugar wrapped in an elongated fried dough case.

Jed and I talked a bit over dinner about the last few weeks of our hike together. He told me that others saw me as flaky and goofy, romanticizing and idealizing the trail.

Nothing about my experience had been romantic or idealized, I assured him. For me, it was plain hard work that never got any easier.

We never resolved our difference of opinion.

When we returned to the motel, Amy and George called to tell us they were ahead of schedule and would arrive before midnight. Elated, we ran back to the grocery store before it closed and bought a bottle of wine, crackers, and deli cheese. Jed bought flowers for Amy and booked another motel room. We awaited their arrival in our separate rooms. I spent my time in yet another long, hot bubble bath.

When Amy and George arrived, dazed from twelve hours in the car, we toasted Katahdin, their trip, and our return to civilization. It was amazing, to me, that only a few hours ago, our worlds had been completely separate. My feet had been so firmly on the trail, I had almost forgotten the priceless ties that bound me to my family. They had been with me, supporting my journey in spirit, but now, here they were, ready again to receive me in person.

The exertion of the past few weeks, the past few days, and the past few hours, finally caught up with me. I was totally exhausted, overjoyed, and overcome. That night, for the first time on the trail, I cried myself to sleep. I didn't know why. I was happy and proud of myself; I was grateful for all the help and support I had received; I was eager to continue my hike. But I was so glad to be in George's arms again, so glad to be really safe, warm, and almost-home again, I couldn't help but weep.

That night, with the whir of air-conditioned air masking the quiet of the dark, I surrendered to a long, dreamless sleep.

Ohio Interim

August 24, 2001 to September 15, 2001

Returning home, asleep in the back of the Odyssey while George drove, I tried to prepare myself to re-enter my old life. At first, I only wanted to sleep, eat, and sleep again. Opening school and reorganizing mail drops for the next phase of my hike was the last thing I wanted to do.

"What happened to you?" one of my teachers greeted me when I walked into our first meeting before classes started. "We expected you to come back robust and healthy – looking like a mountain climber. You've disappeared," she cried, shocked at my emaciated appearance.

"I guess I lost a little weight," I replied, somewhat abashed by her enthusiasm.

"How was your hike – was it wonderful?" she pursued.

"It was a lot harder than I expected it to be – but, yeah, it was great. And I'm tired."

In fact, I was very, very tired. So tired the first week that, after meetings at work each day, I went home to sleep for several hours before rousing myself to be sociable, briefly, with my family. I felt as though I had been very ill and had just returned, out-of-touch and dazed, from several months in the hospital. My body was stiff and sore and I did not want to be bothered with visitors, phone calls, mail, or social obligations. I wanted to rest, eat fresh fruit and vegetables, and be left alone. I did not want to talk about my hike.

By the second week at home, however, I felt more like interacting with the world that I had left behind. More rested, I spent some time shopping for new gear and, anticipating hot days and cold nights during the southern portion of my journey, replaced my summer hiking clothes with a pair of zip-off long pants, a long-sleeved turtleneck shirt, and a new pair of boots.

271

To avoid losing more body weight, I also packed larger portions of protein and complex-carbohydrate meals: for breakfast, homemade granola, instant milk, Tang, and hot tea or coffee; for midmorning snacks, instant breakfast drink and dried fruit; for lunch, homemade ten-grain bread, peanut butter and honey, a Hershey bar with almonds, and Gatorade; for afternoon snacks, high protein energy bars; for dinner, dried vegetables and meat added to each portion of beans and rice, polenta, cous cous, or noodles. My treat at the end of the day was a combination of hot chocolate, decaffeinated coffee, and powdered milk: a bedtime mocha latte.

During my third week at home, I began to feel more like my former, energetic self. Although busy with last-minute work details, I felt much more sociable, regained some body weight and, the Sunday before I was to leave again, organized a combination birthday and anniversary party at our home. Our house was full of family and good cheer until the morning of September 11, when the World Trade Center and the Pentagon were attacked, and our entire world and sense of well being changed.

It was hard to concentrate on preparations for hiking after that. Frustrated by my inability to do anything constructive to help, I was reluctant to leave my family to do something as frivolous as hiking. However, everything was in place for me to finish the southern portion of my trek, and everyone expected me to go.

I decided to leave the next weekend as planned. George and I loaded the Odyssey once again and began our drive to the trailhead at Rockfish Gap, Virginia, for the last eight hundred miles of my journey. Our mood was subdued, but hopeful.

13. On the Trail Again... and Off

"... to catch a terrorist... you work with your community and you look for people who don't belong."
Gene Voegtlin, legal counsel for the
International Association of Chiefs of Police[25]

Rockfish Gap, Va., to Pearisburg, Va., 196 miles

September 15 and 16, 2001, to Seeley-Woodworth Shelter, 20.5 miles

Not only were the nights in the South colder than I expected, they lasted longer. Poking my head out of my sleeping bag at six o'clock in the morning of my second day back on the trail, I saw only the pitch black of the empty shelter. Burrowing back inside, I tried to fall back to sleep, but it was too cold. Resigned to packing my gear wearing gloves, hat, and all my clothes, I began a new ritual of planning my day inside my sleeping bag, looking at my map by headlamp.

25. As quoted in the *New York Times*, 2/9/03.

The first two days were fairly easy. The trail south of Rockfish Gap ran almost parallel to the Blue Ridge Parkway, crossing and re-crossing the highway, winding back through woods of dappled shadows and quiet sunlight for almost twenty miles. There had been only three significant elevation changes: Humpback Mountain, the Three Ridges, and The Priest. To my Maine and New Hampshire-hardened legs, I was surprised at how easy the climbs were; the ascents and descents were graded in long, zigzagging switchbacks, and even the three thousand-foot climb from the Tye River to the top of the Priest seemed effortless. My steps were quick and sure. But, in contrast to the previous May when I began my hike north from Rockfish Gap, it was now late summer in the southern mountains and, though the trees were still green, the air was cool and the night sounds included the sharp crack of falling acorns. Most significantly, however, the tranquility of walking in the woods à la Sainte Terre,[26] just a few days after September 11, was now marked by emptiness and total silence. The accustomed sound of commercial air traffic overhead had ceased, and there were no other hikers. I was alone. Deer, squirrels, and barred owls were my only company.

September 17, 2001, to Brown Mountain Creek Shelter, 15.8 miles

The first hikers I met had been awakened before sunrise, as had I, by the roar and vibrating aftermath of a formation of military jets just over our heads.

"Are we at war?" they asked anxiously. "We haven't heard any news in days. What's happening?"

Before rejoining the trail, I had bought a tiny FM radio receiver with earplugs and could, at the proper elevation, pick up news from National Public Radio. "No, not yet," I assured them, "though the president seems to be headed that way, getting ready to invade Afghanistan for harboring the terrorists he thinks are responsible for the attacks."

Away from the constant barrage of media coverage, stripped of hyperbole and headlines, the events of September 11 seemed more frightening than when they had occurred. Then, my family and I had watched the

26. In the Middle Ages, according to Henry David Thoreau, those who walked in the woods, asking for charity under the pretext of going à la Sainte Terre—to the Holy Land—were true saunterers (walkers).

television coverage of the events as they were happening. Like everyone else with access to the media, we had drawn together and kept vigil, reassuring each other that we would survive and that life would return to normal, in time.

But driving back to the trail, through Sharon, Pennsylvania, the site of the third plane crash, I was reminded that the Appalachian Trail was but a narrow corridor of trees, hills, and mountains, parallel to the megalopolis of the eastern seaboard. On the trail, I was secluded, but not excluded, from the events that had shattered the country's security.

War was familiar territory for my husband. Born in Rumania at the beginning of WWII, he had emigrated with his mother, grandparents, and extended family across Hungary, Austria, and Germany under the bombing of American aircraft. He knew, as a small child, what it was like to run for cover, or dive into a ditch for protection from an unseen enemy. As an older child in postwar Germany, he learned how to find, or go without, food, clothing, and schoolbooks. He knew, from the adults around him, the terrifying reprisals and irredeemable losses of war. For my family, rhetoric of retaliation for the terrorist attacks was reactionary, dangerous, and callous, particularly in the midst of the bravery and sorrow for those families dealing directly with the tragedy.

In the woods, I could, and did, think about these things. They unnerved me. The day before, the only station I could find on my radio was from nearby Lynchburg, Virginia, the home of Jerry Falwell, one of the most outspoken voices of the religious right and chancellor of Liberty University. Falwell had just issued a statement holding homosexuals, feminists, and abortion rights supporters, among others, partially responsible for the terrorist attacks.[27]

The discussion on the radio was about whether Falwell's comments were defensible. I was dismayed to hear the assenting voices of many listeners calling to express their opinions. To me, their remarks sounded bigoted, but when their opinions began to be linked to xenophobic patriotism, I began to worry.

27. "I really believe that the pagans, and the abortionists, and the feminists, and the gays and the lesbians who are actively trying to make that an alternative lifestyle, the ACLU, People for the American Way—all of them who have tried to secularize America—I point the finger in their face and say, 'You helped this happen.'" Jerry Falwell in the Washington Post, Sep. 14, 2001.

Walking alone, not far from the audience whose prejudices had been inflamed and then sanctioned in the name of patriotism, I began to wonder if I would be safe in these southern woods. My roots were deeply planted in the north and, as ET had been ill at ease in Yankee territory, my experiences south of the Mason-Dixon line had been limited to fiction.

Like the sudden notice of fall I had detected in Maine several weeks ago, Virginia's change of seasons was not far behind. The leaves were beginning to lose their intense green hue and easily broke off when I passed through them. The thick underbrush had grown sparse and wilted, and many of the gurgling streams of summer were now bone dry.

Late in the morning, I came out of the woods and crossed Tar Jacket Ridge, a two-mile hike across open meadows covered with a scrubby type of privet shrub known as coral berry. Studded with early fall flowers and long green grass, this open space was a forecast of the balds of southern Appalachia, ahead. I was eager to see them.

The southern balds are wide, grassy, treeless domes, open to full views all around. They appear suddenly at the top of graded climbs and rise up, like the hairless crown of a man's head, above a fringed-ring of woods encircling the mountain below. Unlike the high peaks of New Hampshire or Maine, however, meadows of wildflowers rather than krummholz signal the end of treeline on a bald, and rather than fragile alpine vegetation, balds are covered with natural pastureland, wildflowers, low-growing shrubs, and a scattering of rocks.

I approached my first bald, Cold Mountain, under a sky wispy with high clouds and sunshine. Able to see in every direction, my mood lightened; I sat on a low rock, sheltered from the breeze, took out my journal and watercolors, and began to paint.

> "Now this is more like it. A warm sunny day, views of mountains in the distance, classical music on my earphones, and time to enjoy it all – shoes off, back against a rock, feet extended to the grass – no worries about terrorists."

When I pulled out my food bag, I congratulated myself on its refurbished contents. Munching a newer version of *The Sandwich* and reading my trail guide, I wondered if this Cold Mountain might be the Cold Mountain of the Civil War novel of the same name.[28] Squinting my eyes, I pictured the nineteenth-century homesteads that must have been below, and could still see some remnants of the stone walls that had kept their hogs and cattle grazing inside these higher, warm-weather meadows.[29]

While my watercolors dried, I lay full length in the sun and dozed until a shift in the wind startled me awake, urging me to continue my hike.

The trail descended through an old orchard of gnarled apple trees and wormy free-fall, and then into the woods again. I picked up several apples as I walked, bit into one, and savored the tart juice that quenched my thirst. Stowing a few apples in my pockets for later, I climbed the next elevation. It was disappointing and didn't live up to its name, Bald Knob. At over four thousand feet, I expected a bare expanse and wide view of the valleys below. Not bald at all, this knob was covered with thick shrubs and dense woods. I kept on walking.

In the late afternoon, I reached Brown Mountain Creek Shelter. As in the previous three nights, the shelter was cold, dark, and empty. The mice were my only audience as I set up camp, pulled out my stove to cook, and wrote in my journal while the water boiled:

> "Really enjoyed my hike today but, with the country on the brink of war, I find it incongruous to be here, relaxing in the sunshine, thinking about a bygone era, wondering about the change of seasons. I wish those hikers I met this morning were at this shelter tonight; I enjoyed our conversation today.
>
> I feel so sad and powerless. More than anything I want to understand. How can we have come so far in our civilization and still not know how to live together, conserving our

28. Frazier, Charles, Cold Mountain, Atlantic Monthly Press, New York, 1998. That Cold Mountain was in North Carolina, considerably south of this Cold Mountain, in central Virginia.
29. Though cattle and hogs no longer graze on Cold Mountain and Tar Jacket Ridge, the Appalachian Trail Conference and the US Forest Service keep the summits clear with a program of combined burning and mowing.

resources, and sharing our wealth? I wonder what would happen if we put even half of the money we allot to defense into peace – and addressed the wants and needs of those frustrated by hunger, fear, and hopelessness? Can't we help them make their voices heard without resorting to bloodshed? We certainly can't help them by hating and retaliating with more violence. How can we learn to live together in peace if our method is one of war?"

That night, in the dark lonely shelter, my troubled thoughts returned. I stowed my gear, turned out my headlamp, and burrowed into my sleeping bag. The nearly-full moon shone through the trees, casting shadows on the hard-packed dirt around the shelter. The air was cold and dry. Listening to the plaintive call of a barred owl, "Who cooks for you… who cooks for you…" I tried to arrange my bones in a comfortable position on the unyielding planks of the shelter floor. Cold and uncomfortable, I willed myself to sleep.

September 18, 2001, to Johns Hollow Shelter, 18 miles

In the morning, I waited to crawl out of my warm sleeping bag as long as possible, but it was still dark when I pulled on my boots and lit my stove to heat water for coffee. The sun had barely begun to streak across the sky when I began hiking a short time later. It was too cold to sit still.

Passing Pedlar Dam with the sun behind me, I watched my shadow on the cement path before me. My shadow was one-dimensional and flat, a bit like I felt, I mused. I skirted the southern end of the Lynchburg Reservoir and climbed west, through a forest of virgin pine and hemlock, over a thousand feet in less than two miles, to the summit of Rice Mountain. Tall trees, rich brown soil, sunshine, and warming temperatures began to revive my spirit.

"In beauty may I walk… Through the returning seasons may I walk."

About noon, I discovered the Punchbowl Mountain Shelter, nestled beside a small pond in a clearing of tall trees. I sat at the picnic table to read the shelter register while I prepared *The Sandwich*. No one had written in the register for several weeks, not even weekend hikers.

The setting was beautiful and tranquil. I sat next to the pond, watching the breeze tickle the tall grass, and listened to insects buzz in the warm noontime air. It would have been a good shelter to stay in overnight, I thought, and speculated that if I had been hiking with a partner, I might have spent the afternoon relaxing by the pond, writing and painting, and taking it easy. But, though not in a hurry, I needed to keep moving. Melancholy was my partner today.

As soon as I finished lunch, I hiked on. The ease of the trail and the climbs continued to surprise me. The ascents were gentle and gradual and before I quite realized it, I had reached the summit of Bluff Mountain, the site of a small monument to a young child lost there in 1891. His epitaph read:

"This is the exact spot Little Ottie Cline Powell's
Body was found April 5, 1891,
After Straying from Tower hill School House Nov. 9
A distance of 7 miles,
Age 4 years, 11 months."

According to legend, the child had missed the turn back to the schoolhouse when he had followed some older boys to the woods to fetch wood for the stove. His father, a preacher, had placed an ad in the local paper: "blue eyes, fair complexion, light hair. He is intelligent," and a search party of over one hundred people had looked for him. He was found five months later, three and seven-tenths miles as the crow flies, with his hat still on his head.

The woods were neither harsh nor forbidding, but I was not comfortable. I thought about Little Ottie Cline Powell as I hiked. I wondered how long it would take someone to find me if I were to need help here. I had passed only two couples in four days, and had spent every night in a shelter by myself. Where was everyone? The weather during the day was warm and sunny – perfect for day hiking. Were people avoiding the park because of the terrorist attacks? Surprisingly, I was uneasy; I felt isolated, alone, and vulnerable.

Continuing to hike, I reached the rock cliffs of Big Rocky Row about an hour later and for the first time saw the James River snaking its way between the mountains below. On this warm, sunny afternoon, it looked lazy and untroubled, a silver ribbon on a green and blue carpet.

Sitting on the rocks, I ate a snack and tried to get a signal on my cell phone. The hiking had been so easy, I was two days ahead of schedule. My plan to meet a friend at the footbridge across the James River needed to be adjusted and I needed to let her know my new schedule.

Mary had been one of the women behind my original plan to recruit thru-hike participants from the AYF Summer Seminars for Women. That plan had been abandoned when no one signed up, but Mary had been an enthusiastic supporter from the beginning. A former bookseller, Mary had inherited a mountain in nearby Villamont, Virginia, and was eager to meet me when I hiked through her part of the Blue Ridge Mountains. She had promised to clean me up, feed me, and maybe hike a little, too. I was looking forward to our few days together.

Descending from the rocks in the late afternoon, I reached the shelter where I would spend the night. Like the other shelters all week, the Johns Hollow Shelter was bare. I thumped my pack on the wood floor, looking for any signs of life, but the shelter was deserted.

By now, my settling-in routine was well-practiced: I spread out my sleeping mat and bag on the shelter floor, hung my pack on a peg under the shelter roof, suspended my food bag from a tuna can/string above my head, went to fill my water bottles at the closest source, and splashed my face and hands with water. Back at the shelter, I changed into my long underwear, fleece shirt, gloves, and hat, took down my food bag, lit an Esbit fuel cube under a pot of water, chose a dehydrated meal to add when the water boiled, and read the trail register while I waited.

When the water boiled, I blew out my fuel cube, re-hydrated my dinner, waited for the steam to disappear, dipped my plastic spoon into the pot, and ate until every speck was gone. Lighting my fuel cube again, I filled my cooking pot with more water, ate a Hershey bar with almonds, and waited for the water to boil. Adding cocoa, instant milk, and instant decaf coffee to my water bottle, I poured the boiled water from the cooking pot into the water bottle to make my mocha latte, swishing the water as I poured to clean the pot. This was my trail version of elegant dining and after-dinner dishwashing. It was enough.

Carrying my drink to my sleeping mat, I zipped myself into my sleeping bag, strapped on my headlamp, opened my journal, and, sipping my warm drink, began to write about the day's happenings. During the long days of the New England summer, my routine had been the same and I was usually asleep before nightfall.

Since returning to the trail in the South, however, I discovered that nightfall came much earlier, and I needed something to read during the long, dark solitude. Otherwise, the melancholy that seemed to dog my steps all day was in danger of crawling into my sleeping bag with me all night.

That night, for the first time, I wrote:

> "Hiking suddenly seems trivial and self-indulgent... this is too isolating. It doesn't make sense anymore. Maybe I should continue my hike in the spring."

September 19, 2001, to Thunder Hill Shelter, 18 miles

At six o'clock, too cold to stay zipped into my sleeping bag, I pulled on my hiking clothes and quickly broke camp. By first light, I was ready to hike. Stamping my boots to awaken the circulation in my cold feet, I strapped on my pack and headed out. The new James River footbridge was less than two miles away, and I was eager to cross it.

In years past, the bridge across the James River for hikers was shared with motorists on the highway and/or trains along the riverbank. In 1998, a six hundred twenty-five-foot pedestrian bridge downstream from the highway bridge was completed and dedicated in memory to Bill Foot, a former thru-hiker, member of the Appalachian Trail Conference Board of Managers, and the driving force behind the bridge's construction.

My map pictured a trail relocation to reach the footbridge, but I could not find the white blazes leading to the trail. They just disappeared. I walked to no avail, down the road to the highway crossing. Retracing my steps, I tried to cross the railroad tracks behind a tall wire fence, knowing that this could not possibly be the entrance to the trail, but trying anyway. Frustrated with my inept rendering of the map, I cursed myself for not knowing where I was or how I could regain the white blazes. Once again, I was reminded of how little I really knew and of how far from home I really was.

Exasperated, I hiked along the highway, and eventually found the blazes to the trail leading to the new pedestrian bridge. Somehow, my first attempt had taken me east of the relocation across the river; I had been following the old AT, which crossed on the highway. I consoled myself about the detour and was ahead of schedule anyway. What did it matter that I needed to retrace my steps on this beautiful morning in the Blue Ridge Mountains of Virginia? Self-chastised, I hiked on.

The trail took me along the bank of the James River gorge and then ascended by a series of switchbacks through ten miles of the James River Face Wilderness. Fall wildflowers of purple and golden aster, blazing star, and red berries were just beginning to show their colors, and the ferns lining the path were tinged with brown, losing their summer feathery green. It was peaceful hiking under the blue hazy sky and warm breeze at midmorning.

The major ascent of the day, seven hundred feet in a mile, was not as difficult as the guidebook would have me believe, and I reached the rocky, wooded summit of High Cock Knob in less time than I expected. There was nothing to see, but it was time for lunch.

Pulling out my food bag, I cut a slab of bread, smeared it with peanut butter and honey, and thought about the hike ahead. I would reach the shelter about six o'clock, I thought, and would give Mary a call to confirm our meeting place in the morning. She would be driving from her home in Washington, D.C. to ferry me from the trail. I was looking forward to her company. Mary was one of those women I admired for being her own person. Some lines from a small book by Patricia Lynn Reilly might have been describing her:

> *"Imagine a woman who believes it is right and good she is woman.*
> *A woman who honors her experience and tells her stories.*
> *Imagine a woman who authors her own life.*
> *A woman who trusts her inner sense of what is right for her.*
> *Imagine a woman who has grown in knowledge and love of herself.*
> *Who remains loyal to herself. Regardless."* [30]

30. Excerpted from Imagine A Woman In Love With Herself, by Patricia Lynn Reilly, with permission of Conari Press, an imprint of Red Wheel/Weiser, Boston, MA and York Beach, ME USA. To order please call Conari Press at 1-800-423-7087.

Mary was one of those women and I liked to imagine myself as becoming like her.

As I ate, I thought about the remaining weeks of my hike. My family seemed far away. The trail was empty. I missed the sense of community I had found on the trail during the summer. I hadn't realized that my flip-flop hike would put me so out of step with the thru-hiking community. Or perhaps it was a sign of the times. Perhaps the aftermath of September 11 had taken its toll on the trail as well as in the towns and cities across the country. I didn't know. But I wasn't sure I wanted to continue my hike. It seemed trivial, an exercise to meet an expectation that was no longer relevant. Other concerns claimed my attention, though I had no compelling reason to abandon my hike and return home. I felt like a stray dog, prowling the alleyway after the trash trucks had made their weekly rounds, the last remaining guest at a party where even the hosts had gone to bed. Out of step with both the trail and the world at home, my feet were planted in neither place.

Continuing with this train of thought, I picked up my pack and began to hike on. The afternoon sky had begun to cloud over and the wind blew from the northwest. Quickening my steps, I climbed the next ascent, looking forward to reaching the shelter before early evening.

The shelter was empty except for a sign posted inside: "No Water," and directions for a stream two miles farther up the road, crossing the Blue Ridge Parkway. Since my water bottles were nearly empty, I stowed my pack in the shelter, picked up my water bottles, and hiked out to find water.

When I reached the stream, the source was dry. Tonight, I realized, I would not cook, and in the morning I would need to wait, without water, until Mary drove in from her mountain to pick me up for our day's hike.

By the time I returned to the shelter, it had started to rain. I spread out my sleeping bag under the shelter roof, rooted through my food bag for something edible, and set my cooking pot on the picnic table to catch some run-off for breakfast.

Watching the rain from the edge of the shelter, I felt like a cloud was swallowing me, but rallied enough by seven o'clock to call Mary to confirm our meeting place. Through the static of my cell phone, I could barely make out her voice. She had just arrived at her mountain home and was busy cooking dinner for herself and her eighty-three-year-old cousin, Frank.

"Where are you?" she asked.

"Thunder Hill Shelter, about a mile from BRP 76," I shouted back, hoping she had heard me.

"Frank and I will come get you right now," she insisted. "You're right down the road from us."

Since my present circumstances were not very tempting, I agreed. Quickly I re-packed my gear, put on my rain pants and parka, strapped my headlamp to my head, and started out to the Blue Ridge Parkway to meet my rescuers.

It was pitch black. The rain had settled in for a long, thorough soak, and visibility on the Blue Ridge Parkway was obscured by swirling fog and rain. When I reached the trailhead, I sat down on my pack, turned off my light to conserve the battery, and waited. No cars drove by. Being alone in a foggy downpour at a shelter was one thing, I thought. Sitting on all my belongings, at the side of a dark, deserted road, was quite another. But I was neither anxious nor frightened. I knew Mary would find me; it was just a matter of waiting. I waited.

Eventually, I saw the reflection of light coming towards me from the south. I quickly turned on a light to mark my presence. The car pulled over to the side of the road, and stopped.

Mary jumped out to give me a hug and a helping hand with my wet pack. Frank greeted me as though it were the most normal thing in the world to pick up a sixty-year-old woman in the middle of the parkway on a dark rainy weekday night in September. They were both in high spirits and of good cheer; I felt warmly welcomed as I crawled into the back seat and settled my pack.

We careened around dark, curvy mountain roads, spewing gravel onto the low trees and shrubs, and shuddered to a stop in the garage of Mary's mountain homestead, *Bryn Aval.*[31] I had never seen this hot rod side of Mary, an alto in the National Cathedral Choral Society. It surprised and tickled me.

31. Bryn Aval is a corruption of the Welsh 'Bryn Afel' which means Apple Mountain. Mary's Welsh grandfather named it, as he had an apple orchard there, but decided he didn't want to live on an 'awful mountain,' so changed the spelling.

The original homestead had burned to the ground when Mary was a child, but the mountain had been in her family since the early 1900s. At one time it had been a self-sufficient dairy farm and orchard. Now it was a vacation retreat, used by Mary and her extended family whenever they could steal away from their professional lives lived elsewhere. The low cinderblock home features large plate glass windows and doors facing southeast towards an expanded mountain view of the Peaks of Otter.

While Mary put the finishing touches on dinner, I showered and tossed my clothes into the washing machine. Then she, Frank, and I dined on macaroni-hamburger casserole, garlic toast, fresh salad, and wine – much better than my anticipated cold supper at the shelter. More than anything, however, I loved having Mary and Frank's company. They were the first people I had really talked to in almost a week; I was starved for conversation. The isolation I had felt at the close of every day, in empty shelters with only the night sounds for company, had begun to leave its mark on me. As much as I liked hiking by myself, at my own pace, I missed the camaraderie of other hikers at the end of the day.

September 20, 2001, to Apple Orchard Mountain, 6.7 miles

It was still raining in the morning, but Frank had agreed to lead us on a wildflower walk on the AT, through the Guillotine, to the summit of Apple Orchard Mountain, familiar trails to him since boyhood.

Frank had grown up hiking the Blue Ridge Mountains and had many stories about the days of the trail before the Blue Ridge Parkway was constructed in 1929. He told me about a giant poplar tree, eighteen feet in circumference, which had been destined for removal when he was a young teenager. Frank had been part of the delegation that helped persuade those in charge to move the highway around the two hundred-fifty-year-old tree and build a retaining wall, so that its roots would not be disturbed. The tree stood for sixty more years, and had sheltered a gentle curve along the Blue Ridge Parkway until its demise from storms and wind only a few years ago. The stone retaining wall can still be found, however, and is the only wall of its kind on the parkway.[32]

Frank had hiked the AT in the Blue Ridge Mountains on his honeymoon in the early 1950s, and again with each of his four children as they

32. Frank Smith, Montvale, Virginia, personal communication.

grew to adulthood. He knew the name and history of every flower, every species of tree, every mountaintop, and graciously shared his enthusiasm for them with me.

In the rain and fog, we hiked through the Guillotine, a boulder suspended about twelve feet off the ground between a narrow cleft of rock, and continued to the top of Apple Orchard Mountain. Frank said that on a clear day, the Natural Bridge of Virginia, eight miles to the north-northwest, was visible from the summit. I took his word for it; on this day we could see nothing but fog.

By midafternoon, wet and hungry, we drove to the coffee shop at the Peaks of Otter Lodge for lunch of chicken sandwiches and French fries. Frank showed me the remains of the rescued giant poplar tree, now a jagged stump, before we drove back to his house to look at old scrap books and trail memorabilia from the earliest days of the AT in the Blue Ridge Mountains. I particularly enjoyed a notebook he had written as a young Boy Scout, advising hikers on equipment and best practices. The illustrations were cut from old magazines and catalogues; the fire-building and tree-cutting methods were sketched in black ink. Frank was a man from my father's generation, with my father's recollections of camping life during the Depression. It was interesting to look at the Blue Ridge AT through his eyes; his lens looked way back in time. I felt humbled by his knowledge and privileged to share his memories.

September 21, 2001, Black Rock Overlook
to Bobblets Gap, 18 miles

The day began with bright sun streaming in the windows, startling me awake. Mary was already up, baking chocolate chip cookies. We ate a trail breakfast from my resupply that George had sent to her house, picked up Frank, and drove to the trailhead at Black Rock Overlook. I planned to hike to Bearwallow Gap, meet up with them again at five o'clock, walk three miles farther to Bobblets Gap, and then treat us all to the All You Can Eat (AYCE) seafood buffet at the Peaks of Otter Lodge.

As we entered the trail to Cornelius Creek Shelter from the parkway, a yellow cab pulled away from the side of the road. Behind the cab was a fifty-ish woman surrounded by plastic grocery bags, a backpack, and an assortment of full trash bags.

Frank groaned and whispered, "I'll tell you about her later."

Curious about all her stuff, I asked her if we could help her carry everything to the shelter. She accepted without hesitation and Frank groaned again, "The ranger won't thank us for this," he whispered.

We all picked up several bags and followed the woman down the trail to the Cornelius Creek Shelter, about half a mile from the trailhead.

The shelter was unoccupied but the woman looked around for level ground to pitch her tent. I assumed that she was planning to spend the weekend camping and hiking, but something about her demeanor puzzled me. She seemed a little disorganized, to my trail-honed eyes, and, though grateful for our help, not particularly friendly.

After we left her, Frank explained his not-so-subtle whispers. That, he said, was Peggy, a well-known character in these parts. She calls herself Margaret Windsor and claims to be part of the British Royal family, kidnapped at age two, and brought to this country by the Kennedy family. For the past ten years, he said, Peggy had been frequenting the shelters along the Blue Ridge parkway, getting chased out by park rangers when they discovered her presence.

That would explain the plastic garbage bags full of stuff, I thought. Peggy is homeless and, undoubtedly, harmless. Remembering myself sitting by the side of this same road, in the middle of the rain the night before last, it occurred to me that Peggy and I were not that different. To an outsider, we probably looked the same. The things that separated us, I realized, were our relationships with other people: family, friends, authority figures – and some differences in brain chemistry and life experiences. "There, but for the grace of God, go I," one of George's frequent maxims, crossed my mind. I wondered what Peggy would do when the rangers found her this time. According to Frank, she would only go inside in the worst winter weather, and then, not for long. These woods were her year-round home.

I hiked all day by myself, with the promise of the early fall foliage beginning to turn from deep green to yellow, brown, and red. It was an easy sixteen-mile hike, especially with only a daypack and lunch on my hips. I enjoyed the solitude, knowing there would be people happy to see me and hear about my hike at the end of the day.

At Bearwallow Gap in the late afternoon, I sat in the grass to wait for Mary and Frank. My friends arrived in one car; they had left the other car three miles farther at the trailhead to Bobblets Gap and intended to hike with me to the other car.

We hiked slowly in the gathering dusk, enjoying the evening shadows. When we realized that our pace was falling behind the shadows, however, Frank decided that he would wait for us at the next overlook. Mary and I hiked on, sometimes parallel to the parkway, for another two miles, talking all the way. When we reached Bobblets Gap, we picked up Frank and continued on to the Peaks of Otter Lodge for dinner. I was sweaty and dirty, but after I zipped on the extensions that changed my shorts to long pants, washed my face and hands, and combed my hair in the ladies room, I looked a little less like Peggy and a little more like myself.

True to thru-hiker style, in the dining room I loaded my plate with crab legs, shrimp, corn on the cob, rolls, and fresh salad, topping it off with several peach cobblers, a southern treat I had just discovered. Although I had re-gained some weight in Ohio, I was still much thinner than my normal self, and hungry most of the time. Our candlelit AYCE buffet, served with a bottle of wine and good conversation, was more like my old life than my trail life. I appreciated the difference.

Riding back to Mary's mountain through swirling mist and evening fog, I was glad I was a passenger around those steep hairpin curves that disappeared into darkness. When we reached Bryn Aval, I found my way to bed without even turning on the light. Civilization was beginning to look better, I thought. It was comforting to curl up under a pile of quilts, surrounded by walls, a roof, and friendship on all sides. I slept well.

September 22, 2001, to Trout Creek, 7 miles

Mary woke me early the next morning to show me the sunrise. Outside her dining room windows, overlooking the Peaks of Otter, the sky was streaked with pink and gold; the air was fresh and cool. It would be a good day to hike.

Frank had convinced me to change the order of my hike this day so that I could slack the Dragon's Tooth, a giant columnar stack of rocks on top of Cove Mountain, in order to enjoy the climb without a heavy pack.

He and Mary would meet me at the end of the day, he said, and we would have supper at The Homeplace Restaurant, a thru-hiker tradition of family-style AYCE feasting in nearby Catawba. Bowing to his experience and expertise about the trails in this area, I was happy to follow his advice.

En route to the trailhead, we stopped at the Catawba post office to pick up my next food drop, but it had not yet arrived. With apologies for delay, the postmistress cautioned me that my package might not arrive for three more days. Since I had access to a car and Mary's gracious hospitality for the next two days, this delay did not worry me, but I wondered how the interruptions in the mail service would affect the rest of my hike. Hitching from the trail to remote towns with meager resupply resources this late in the hiking season, timely arrival of mail drops would be crucial. Mail delivery had never been a problem before September 11, but I might not be so lucky in the weeks ahead.

The Dragon's Tooth, like Mt. Moosilauke, the Whites, and Katahdin in the northeast, is a very popular climb and, though rugged and difficult, the trail is well graded and moderate. On this Saturday morning, I passed other day-hikers on their way to the summit. Happy not to be carrying a heavy pack, I was able to bound ahead of them without stopping to rest.

The most impressive feature of the climb up Dragon's Tooth, I thought, was the stone staircase leading across the steepest rocky area near the summit. The stairs were designed to look like natural rock-fall but were placed so that average hikers could mount them without undo strain. Rock stairs are controversial in some circles of AT maintenance and construction, the dispute being one of function versus a wilderness look of happenstance. These steps approaching the Dragon's Tooth were successful in both wilderness design and hiker-function, I thought; I made a note to tell Frank about them at the end of the day.

When I reached the summit, I took a side trail another hundred feet up to the top of the rocks, to dangle my legs over the edge and say I did it. The climb was steep but much less frightening than the Knife-Edge in Pennsylvania or the West Peak of Baldpate Mountain in Maine. Without a heavy pack, it was an energetic rock scramble to a good view and exhilarating feeling of accomplishment.

Later, I sat on a lower rocky ledge below the tooth for about an hour, eating lunch, writing in my journal, and enjoying the afternoon sun. Reluctantly, I hiked out to the trail crossing at Trout Creek, a leisurely descent of five miles south, to meet Mary and Frank at the agreed-upon time. On our way to The Homeplace, I marveled at the view of the Dragon's Tooth from the valley below. It looked quite impressive. Had I known how impressive, I might not have climbed to the top to dangle my feet over the edge.

The Homeplace is a rambling white farmhouse with porches, rocking chairs, and swings on three sides, with pastures and white fences all around. We sat on the front porch to wait for a table in one of the many dining rooms. A favorite gathering place for families and friends, the food is aromatically, deliciously southern, served on long board tables set with pitchers of lemonade, iced tea, and hot biscuits and butter to appease hungry appetites before the main course is brought in.

Dinner of fried chicken, vegetables, mashed potatoes, grits, and gravy, in addition to a side order of Virginia ham or roast beef, was served family style by a squadron of middle-aged women in aprons parading around the dining room. The food kept coming for as long as there were hungry mouths to appreciate it and, though I never figured out their method of knowing, dessert magically appeared when we could eat no more. The women wound their way between the tables with huge trays of warm peach cobbler and dripping vanilla ice cream; we found we could manage just a bit more.

Although I did not see any other thru-hikers, either on the porch or inside the dining rooms, I didn't feel out of place in my hiking boots and trail clothes. After three nights in a clean bed, with hot showers and freshly laundered clothes, my usual hiker's aroma had been pleasantly distilled. I looked almost presentable, I thought, and enjoyed the early evening dinner and my companions immensely.

Later we drove to find the trailhead in Troutville so Mary could meet me there at the end of the next day's hike. Frank helped me map out my hike for the next few days, involving a complicated series of trailhead meetings that would allow me to continue without missing any part of the trail. I was humbled by his kindness and eagerness to assist me. Mary assured me that she had planned to spend her weekend ferrying me around the mountains, and Frank insisted that it was fun for him to talk about the trail and re-experience it with someone as eager to hike as he had been before his health kept him on the sidelines. It was a good arrangement for all of us; I was deeply grateful for their kindness and friendship. I would miss them when I rejoined the trail. Their company was a welcome respite from loneliness, trail food, and my own thoughts.

September 23, 2001, Black Horse Gap to Troutville, Va., 14 miles

The next day was a long, meandering walk amid the changing colors of early fall. Reaching my destination long before Mary was due, I sat in the long meadow grass overlooking rolling farmland neatly divided by fences and tree rows, and wrote in my journal:

> "My hike has taught me that I want to be out in the country where it's quiet and beautiful, but comfortable and hospitable. I want a place where George and I can be together, to welcome the girls and their families, with us at the center, not them.

I've decided to meet George in Pearisburg, Va., next Saturday. Mary helped me clarify why. "It's important 'hike your own hike,'" she agreed when we talked about why I was hiking, "but does that definition ever change?"

It was like having a light bulb flash in my eyes. Of course the definition changes. At first, hiking my own hike meant hiking a flip-flop hike, starting in Virginia, going north to Maine, then hiking south from Virginia to Georgia. My initial plan was to do it all at one go. After hiking by myself for long stretches, meeting and leaving family and friends, finding a place for myself in the hiking community, learning how to keep both feet in that community, helping my daughters reclaim another part of themselves, and memorializing my father's life, I'd done what I came out to do, and then some.

> "The part of my hike that is just for me is about to begin. But being on the trail right now, with our country terrified of terror, is not the time to begin it. I want to be at home right now.

I can't quite explain the emptiness I feel, walking alone across these meadows, through the woods – everything deserted and waiting. It's too isolating. Completing the hike is still important to me, but I want to do more than just finish it 'doing miles.' I want to complete the trail with joy and a sense of freedom, not fatigue and a sense of loss. I'm a little sad when I think about not hiking every day, but I know that the trail will be there in the spring, ready for me to begin hiking again with a new definition of 'my own hike.'

I am satisfied with my summer's hike. It taught me some things I didn't think I had to learn about my body, my mind, and the spiritual connection I feel to the natural world around me. It taught me that hiking alone is not as hard as I thought it would be, that hiking with women can be a lot of fun, and that hiking with men presents its own set of challenges. I learned that my body is efficient and wonderfully resilient, but that I have to respect and accept its limits, without apology or shame. I re-discovered the connection between my will and my ability to succeed, and I learned that my compassion for others, including myself, does not tolerate a bully.

I'm glad I came out on the trail again, even for such a short time. I'm fully capable of hiking, physically, and mentally. I can endure the loneliness, the hardship, the uncertainty. I feel good about this decision to leave the trail until spring. I can trust the inner strength of what is right for me. I have grown in knowledge of myself and I remain loyal to myself. Regardless."

September 24, 2001, to Campbell Shelter, 18 miles

Before daybreak, Mary and I were packed and ready to leave the mountain; she back to Washington, D.C. to sing in the Service of Remembrance at the Kennedy Center, me back on the trail south until I would meet George. He and I had talked the night before and agreed to meet the next weekend in Pearisburg, to spend some time together before we returned home.

My heart sank as I stepped out of the door. Rain. After four beautiful days of sunshine, warm temperatures, and clear sky, I would have to hike McAfee's Knob and the rocky cliffs above Tinker Creek in the slippery, foggy rain. Damn.

Mary dropped me at the McDonald's in Troutville, and I sloshed my way into its jarring interior, brash with glaring fluorescent light against the soft misty gray of the morning outside. Anticipating that my mail drop would, indeed, be at the post office in Catawba in the morning, I carried only a day's supply of food; I ordered breakfast.

Looking at my reflection in the windows of McDonald's, I felt disconnected; neither the scene around me nor the woods awaiting me appealed to my senses. Nevertheless, as soon as I finished eating, I hoisted my pack and set out across the slick parking lot, shimmering with taillights of drivers stopping at the take-out window on their way to work. How far apart our lives were, I thought, as I crossed the road and entered the woods. Did I really want to leave the woods for that?

I hiked all morning across low pastureland, roads, and finally, back up into the mountains. I had been looking forward to hiking in Annie Dillard's neighborhood, and seeing through her eyes the beauty that lives everywhere, that she wrote about in *Pilgrim at Tinker Creek*. I yearned for Annie's sight and her ability to articulate what she saw:

> "Then one day I was walking along Tinker Creek thinking of nothing at all and I saw the tree with the lights in it. I saw the backyard cedar where the mourning doves roost charged and transfigured, each cell buzzing with flame. I stood on the grass with the lights in it, grass that was wholly fire, utterly focused and utterly dreamed. It was less like seeing than like being for the first time seen, knocked breathless by a powerful glance."[33]

I have experienced light like that, suddenly blazing the trunk of a tree, briefly holding the world captive before melting into the air, disappearing as only a memory of brilliance and hope. However, on this day of rain

33. Dillard, Annie, Pilgrim at Tinker Creek, Harper Collins, 1974, p. 36.

and fog, the beauty of the woods was in the moldy wet smell and slippery leaves, not in the light. I resigned myself to hiking, shroud in raingear with the view all about my feet.

Hiking along the crest of Tinker Mountain, I began to hear the dreaded rumble of thunder in the distance. The last thing I wanted was to be on exposed rock crest in a thunderstorm. I pushed myself to be off the crest before the storm hit. As in other potentially dangerous situations, however, I was not frightened – only aware that I needed to have a strategy in case the storm broke before I could reach the safety of a shelter or cave. Although hungry, I didn't dare stop. I continued to push on, hiking fast.

In a gap about half a mile north of the Lambert Shelter, it began to rain harder. The wind picked up and the birds stopped singing. I knew from past storms that when the birds stop singing, it's time to run for cover.

I was in the woods when the full force of the storm hit. Soaked in minutes, I put my head down and just kept hiking. I knew the shelter was not far, and promised myself a long, relaxing lunch break when I reached its safety.

Within minutes I saw the blue blaze indicating the side trail that led to the shelter. I almost ran through the woods, and when I reached the shelter, threw my pack onto the floor and climbed up after it. Under my rain gear, my clothes were soaked from perspiration. Otherwise, I was fine.

The shelter was empty and dark. I pulled out my headlamp and food bag, took off my boots and socks, and began to assemble a *Sandwich.* Watching the rain from under the roof, munching my sandwich, I was surprised when three young hikers came running in. They were south-bounders – very wet southbounders following the go-lite hiking method. For rain gear, this threesome wore only nylon running shorts and trail shoes; the young woman wore a running bra. Their philosophy was to hike in as little as possible, putting on dry clothes whenever they stopped or were in camp. All three were shivering from the rain, wind, and cold.

They spread a tarp on the shelter floor, took off all their wet clothes, and changed into dry ones. We chatted while they fixed lunch for themselves. The couple was on their honeymoon; their friend was someone they had met on the trail. Friendly and full of energy, the three settled onto the tarp and began a game of Hearts, inviting me to join them. Preferring to relax while I waited for the storm to clear, I declined.

Even though it was still early afternoon, the southbounders planned to stay at the shelter overnight, whiling away the afternoon with card games and sleep. I appreciated their invitation for company, but was eager to hike on. I wanted to finish the climb to the Tinker Cliffs before the next storm hit. I was scheduled to meet Frank at the Catawba trailhead in the morning; I had miles to go before I could sleep.

By the time I left the shelter, the downpour had become a drizzle and the wind was quiet. Although the birds had not yet resumed their chatter, I decided to take my chances on the cliffs. As I ascended the Tinker Cliffs, the rain stopped altogether and the clouds began to lift. The Catawba Valley, Gravely Ridge, and North Mountain stretched ahead of me and into the far distance. Ribbons of mist rose from the valley floors to the slice of clear sky just above the mountaintops. Shadows from a sun I could not see patched the trees and fields in the distance below.

The rocks under my feet were wet, but not dangerously so. I was thrilled that the storms had gone elsewhere, leaving me a clear view of Annie Dillard's valley, once a tundra environment, home to mammoth, mastodon and early native tribes.

For the next five miles, I hiked through woodlands of changing color, from green to gold to deep auburn. Fall seemed to have descended with the rain; the air held the pungent odor of rotten wood and wet bark.

In the late afternoon, I reached the wooded setting of the Campbell Shelter, on the crest of a hill overlooking the trail. The woods were more open here, and though the shelter was empty, it looked clean and secure, a good place to spend the night.

Inside the shelter, I hung my pack and hiking poles on a peg and went out to find water. It was piped and clean; I carried more than enough back to the shelter for dinner and breakfast. Sitting on the floor of the shelter, looking out into the wet, empty woods, I was glad that I had decided to hike on by myself this afternoon. It occurred to me that had this been last summer, I probably would have stayed at the other shelter with the young hikers, just for the company. Somewhere in the last twelve hundred miles, I had lost my fear of being the only one in the shelter at night. Not only did I pitch my tent in the woods by myself, I had ceased to be spooked by empty shelters in the middle of the woods. I trusted the trail and the trail community, even though I couldn't always see them, and knew I would come to no harm when other hikers were around.

As I cooked my ration of bean threads, vegetables, pasta, and hot chocolate, the rain began again, first slowly, then with more conviction. The rest of the night, dry and almost warm under the shelter roof, I listened to the rain. Eating the last of Mary's chocolate chip cookies, I wondered how the Remembrance concert had been received at the Kennedy Center and wished, for a brief moment, that Mary and I could trade places. As confident and secure as I had begun to feel on the trail, I was beginning to think in terms of being home.

> "I'm glad that it's raining – it helps me stay centered. When the southbounders came into the shelter this afternoon, dripping and dirty and making the best of it, I realized again that I was ready to put an end to this phase of my hike. It isn't just any companionship that I crave; it's the relationships with my own family and friends that I miss. The sudden reality of the World Trade Center tragedy has wormed its way into my heart. Right now I need to be with the people I love and who love me. On the trail, I am too dependent on the kindness of strangers. To them, I am an outsider. That doesn't feel right to me. I'm gratified to know that I can still do a twenty-mile day without strain; in fact, I'm hiking better than I did at the end of the summer. I'm more experienced, better rested, and better nourished. But I still want to stop; I just don't have the heart for hiking right now."

September 25, 2001, to Laurel Creek Shelter, 21 miles

The day began an hour earlier than my usual rising time because I misread my watch and rose at six, rather than seven o'clock. Normally, the pitch dark would have kept me in my sleeping bag until sunrise, but I didn't want to be late for my meeting with Frank, a three-mile hike from McAfee's Knob, which was a mile away. I was eager to see the Knob in the early morning light, so I struggled to break camp and be on my way before the first birds began to chatter.

A large anvil-shaped slab of rock overlooking the Tinker Cliffs and the valley below, McAfee's Knob is one of the most photographed rocks on the trail. By the time I reached it, it had stopped raining and the mist rose from the valley floor in tall, singular columns to a clearing sky above. McAfee's Knob was as dramatic as I expected it to be, jutting out into space, carved out underneath like a huge comma punctuating the clouds rising above it.

I sat on the edge for a few minutes, alone in a universe of slowly swirling air. I'm just a speck, I thought, a tiny dot on the edge of a rock, briefly poised and balanced before someone or something else takes my place. I matter because I am part of the universe – small but not invisible – important to a few, for that brief moment in time when we are all swirling together. It was exhilarating and sobering to be on that rock, at that hour, in that space, watching the shadows overtake the valley.

The chilling wind moved me, reluctantly, on.

When I hiked off the mountain to the crossroad that marked Catawba, Frank was waiting at the trailhead. It was good to see him. He took me to the post office, helped me rearrange my gear, and suggested we go to the general store across the road for sandwiches.

A white clapboard structure with a creaky screen door, the general store looked like a Wyeth painting. Elongated squares of sunlight slanted on the wide, bare floor, uneven from years of boot traffic. Shelves lined with tobacco products, small tins of peas, soap powder, and cellophane-wrapped baked goods looked old and sad. The sandwiches and the woman behind the counter looked dejected.

Although we were the only customers, I had the feeling we were imposing on the storekeeper's hospitality; she wanted us to pay for our food and disappear. We escaped to the car and drove to the trailhead to eat and say goodbye.

I hiked out a little after noon, anxious about hiking seventeen more miles before dark. The brisk breeze and clear sunshine helped; it was good for hiking, but not for stopping.

I hiked up Brush Mountain, a fifteen hundred-foot ascent in three miles, past a monument to Audie Murphy, the most decorated soldier of WWII and a movie star of my adolescence. The monument marks the site of his death in a plane crash in the 1950s – a beautiful, but lonely spot to die, I thought. I continued along the crest of the mountain for another few miles before descending into Craig Creek Valley, and then up again to the crest of Sinking Creek Mountain. The woods all around me, with only occasional views out into the valleys, kept me focused on hiking steadily, pushing myself to reach the shelter before dark.

By six o'clock, tramping through rhododendron thickets still wet from yesterday's rain, I began to wonder if I might have missed the shelter. I remembered that the last two miles of the day always seemed the longest, and reassured myself that the shelter would soon appear, but I was worried. Glancing to my right, down in a gully, I thought I saw the ruins of an old farmhouse. Without a tent, it would do if I couldn't find the shelter, I thought. It looked pretty spooky, though, and I hiked on, quickly.

Crossing a country road, I was surprised by a pickup truck rushing up from behind me at full throttle. As it drew closer, I realized it wasn't going to share the road with me. In fact, it swerved right at me. Astonished, I looked up to see three young men, yelling at me through their open windows. I rushed to move way over into the grassy berm. Over the roar of their exhaust, I caught the words "lesbo freak" as they sped by, a large American flag decaled to their tailgate.

The twilight was shattered. At first I thought they were drunk. Then I began to wonder at their audacity. Those yokels had tried to run me off the road! Granted, I probably did look different to them, but how did that give them permission to do that? And what was the taunt, "lesbo freak"? Did they think I was a lesbian because I was hiking? If I were a lesbian, did that make me an okay target for harassment on a deserted country road in southern Virginia? And what about that flag on the back of their truck?

I began to wonder, again, at the power of people like Jerry Falwell with their messages of intolerance. Had they given these bullies permission to act out their narrow-mindedness under the guise of patriotism? Was this the new American way?

More eager than ever to find the shelter, I hurried to re-enter the woods, as far away from the road as I could get, adrenalin pumping through my body, strengthening my stride.

By seven o'clock, with twenty minutes of daylight remaining, I found the shelter. It was empty, but looked safe and welcoming to my anxious eyes. I took off my pack, walked out for water, and returned to cook and make camp just as the stars began to rise above the trees, followed within the hour by a sharp, crisp moon.

The shelter was cold. I spread out my sleeping mat and bag on the floor and strapped my pack to a post in the center of the shelter, using it as a backrest while I ate and wrote in my journal. The night sounds were comforting, though I was still unnerved by my encounter on the road. When I thought about my decision to leave the trail until spring, I knew I was not leaving out of fear of the trail. If anything, the trail was safer than town, I thought. Yet... the pickup driver's senseless taunts left a sour aftertaste.

September 26, 2001, to Pine Swamp Shelter, 18 miles

In the morning, it was too cold to do anything but break camp quickly and hike out, dressed in all my clothes, including long underwear. The air was more like November than September. I was glad I had warm clothes.

The day promised to be dry, and I had plenty of energy. The initial ascent, up Kelly Knob, a steep, seven hundred-foot climb, seemed easy. Nothing like a tail wind to push me up the mountain, I thought for the hundredth time. Once I reached the crest of the Knob, it was a quick two-mile walk through the woods before the gradual descent into Johns Creek Valley. I crossed another country road in the valley, and though I didn't expect another pickup truck, was relieved to discover the road deserted. All was quiet except the bird song in the early morning air.

Continuing, I began to gradually climb again along switchbacks to the summit of Salt Pond Mountain and Lone Pine Peak, and then across five miles of almost-level woods to Wind Rock, overlooking the Stony Creek Valley to the east. The woods were dense and quiet.

Reaching the Bailey Gap Shelter in the late afternoon, where I thought I would stop for the night, I discovered that the nearest water was two miles north. Rather than backtrack, I decided to continue four miles farther to the next shelter. With two hours of daylight left, I was certain I could make it and be settled before nightfall. I hiked on.

Pine Swamp Shelter was visible from the trail and faced a creek. Built of cold, dark stone, the shelter was dirty, damp, and dark inside, but it had a fireplace on the back wall between the bunks at each end, and a hard-packed dirt floor. Although I was the only inhabitant, I claimed space for my gear and body on one of the bunks near the fireplace. Judging from the trash and mice droppings, it looked like it had been a long time since that fireplace had held a fire, I thought.

At the picnic table in front of the shelter, I cooked, ate, and listened to a bird somewhere in the trees.

It was, by far, the coldest night I had spent on the trail. During the night, I got up twice to do jumping jacks on the floor of the shelter, just to warm my body before zipping myself back into my bag, hoping I had generated enough heat to let me rest a few more hours. Maybe I should have tried the fireplace, I grumbled to myself at the darkest hour before dawn.

In the morning, I was up at first light, shivering in all my clothes, eating granola with hot milk, and drinking hot instant breakfast mix to take the chill off my bones. I began hiking as soon as my chores were finished, and hoped the day's hike would be warmer than the night's sleep.

September 27, 2001, to Pearisburg, Va., 21 miles

The walk was quite nice, through tall hemlocks and dense rhododendron, along Stony Creek for a short distance, then up, along switchbacks, to the Pine Swamp ridge and the top of Peters Mountain. The sun and wind competed for my attention all morning; it was so cold I didn't even take off my gloves and hat until eleven o'clock.

Nevertheless, I enjoyed walking through the old orchards and overgrown meadows along the crest of Peters Mountain, and hiked in and out of woods at an elevation of thirty-five hundred feet, along the Virginia-West Virginia line, for almost ten miles. Passing through a thicket of raspberry bushes in the late morning, I finally met another hiker, a young man wearing a large gold cross around his neck and carrying a staff in one hand, looking like one of Thoreau's Saunterers. He was heading north and assured me that the Rice Field Shelter, my destination for the night, did, indeed, exist, though it had been eliminated from my trail guide. We didn't talk for long; he was heading for the shelter I had left early that morning and was hiking at a slower pace than mine. I hoped he would be warmer at that shelter than I had been. I encouraged him to use the fireplace.

At midday I ate lunch on a power line cut overlooking valleys and mountains to the east. The sun overhead was full, but the wind from the north was brisk and steady; it was too cold to linger.

About three o'clock, ascending the crest of a steep meadow, I discovered the Rice Field Shelter hidden behind a wooden stile in a patch of trees at the far edge of the field. More like a bald, Rice Field was studded with gray rocks and alive with a wide band of long green grass and black-eyed susans, blowing and ruffling in the wind. Beyond this swaying mound, valleys and mountains stretched green and gold, joining the horizon and pale blue sky miles and miles away.

This was the shelter I had been searching for all summer. It was newly built of clean wood, with a sturdy picnic table, compost privy (with toilet paper), sleeping lofts, and the open vista of meadows, wildflowers, and rolling mountains in the distance. It would have been the perfect place for an afternoon of painting, reading, or writing, and an evening watching the sunset and waiting for the lights from the valley to merge with the stars on the horizon.

It was a tempting place to spend my last night on the trail except for two things: 1) there was no water, which could have been manageable if it had not been so 2) cold! On the open meadow, even in the full sun, the wind was frigid and too strong to ignore. I considered wrapping up in my sleeping bag to read in the sun, but it was just too exposed, too cold, and would be too long until morning. I knew it would be foolish to stay overnight in this weather, without water or the possibility of hot food. Reluctantly, I decided that I should move on. Pearisburg was only seven miles farther and, if I left shortly, I could reach it by dusk.

But it was hard to leave the shelter, knowing that I was saying good-bye to the trail until spring. I felt that I was leaving a good friend, my companion of the past four months. I knew I would miss the trail in the dark months ahead.

I pulled out the shelter register and wrote the prayer that had sustained me for so long:

In beauty may I walk
All day long may I walk
Through the returning seasons may I walk...
In beauty will I possess again
Beautifully birds
Beautifully joyful birds.
On a trail marked with pollen may I walk
With wildflowers about my feet may I walk
With dew about my feet may I walk
With beauty before me may I walk
With beauty behind me may I walk
With beauty above me may I walk
With beauty all around me may I walk.
In old age, wandering on a trail of beauty
Lively may I walk.
In old age, wandering on a trail of beauty
Living again may I walk.
It is finished in beauty.
Gotta Hike! 2001-'02

I continued on my way. By signing my name and date, 2001-'02, I committed myself to finishing my thru-hike during 2002.

When I came off Peters Mountain it was nearly five o'clock; I could hear and smell the town of Pearisburg long before I could see it from the trail, which ran parallel to the New River. The closer I came to Pearisburg from the pristine meadow above, the less beautiful the woods became. Instead of rocky paths and trimmed underbrush, the paths became cluttered with loose dirt, roots, and litter. Tangled bushes branched over the trail, chin high, making it hard to see my feet and the rocks under my boots. Metro would have called these hostile woods "bad karma," I thought, and agreed. It was as though the people living in the valley had never been on the mountain behind them, and had lost touch with its beauty, treating it as a dumping place for their trash.

As I descended into the valley, I was deafened by the noise rising up to greet me: the Celanese cigarette-filter factory crashed and belched smoke, creating a horrendous background racket; semis with diesel engines clanked and cranked, dump trucks backed and beeped and rumbled; workers hammered a steady "rat-a-tat-tat" with motor-driven tools; sirens, engines, and aircraft all conflated into one echoing din of artificial noise above, below, and around me. And the stench. Chemicals, raw sewage, exhaust, gasoline, hot tar, and an odor I couldn't identify pervaded the air. It was a valley in the shadow of hell, an awful reminder of civilization, in stark contrast to the quiet isolation of the woods in the mountains I had just left. Overwhelmed, I wanted to flee.

Instead, I crossed several intersecting highways, glaring and treacherous in the late afternoon light, and walked to the office of the "Rendezvous otel" just off the tarmac across the road from the trail. This will be where I pick up the trail in the spring, I thought, casting a rueful eye at my surroundings.

I rang the desk bell several times. Finally, an unshaved man in dirty jeans, boots, flannel shirt, and baseball cap came out from the back room. I thought he was drunk, but then realized it was his accent, not drink, that slurred his words. He gave me a key to a room, a cinderblock rectangle with a bed, nightstand, lamp, telephone, straight back chair, TV, and bathroom. It was warm, clean, and only for one night. It would do.

Ignoring the flags on the pickup trucks parked in front of the other rooms, I stowed my gear and walked up a long, steep hill on the side of the highway, looking for food. At the top of the hill, I found an Italian restaurant on the edge of a parking lot of the Magic Mart shopping strip below. In my big dirty hiking boots, I climbed the stairs; with my calloused, grimy hands, I opened the door.

Inside, I found a candlelit sanctuary of white tablecloths, gleaming silverware, and a large hearth for wood-fired pizzas. The owner greeted me at the door and escorted me to a table overlooking the West Virginia mountains through a plate glass window at the back of the dining room. From my table, the strip shopping mall disappeared.

The owner brought me a glass of wine and suggested I try the fresh seafood stew, salad, homemade bread, and cheesecake. I was stunned by his gracious welcome. The food was delicious. And all the while, as I watched the mountains disappear into a reflection of myself in the window, I listened to a tape of Italian opera arias, broadcast softly over speakers hidden in the ceiling.

It was the best I could have wished for on my last night of the trail. At the end of my meal, I thanked my host for welcoming me back to my real world; George and I would come here again in the spring, I decided, for my first night returning to the trail. There are many good ways to celebrate beauty, I reflected, even in little towns impoverished by the twenty-first century economy and scarred by ignorance.

September 28, 2001, Pearisburg, Va., 0 miles

The next morning, looking for a cup of coffee to accompany my granola, I met Brenda, the wife of the motel owner. She had bought some mums for a dollar each and wanted to plant them around the sign on the front lawn of the motel. She found a cup of coffee for me and I offered to help her plant the mums.

We dug a dozen holes around the "Rendezvous otel" sign, arranged the flowers by color, and stuck them into the ground, tapping the dirt all around to keep them from slipping sideways. Growing up in these mountains, Brenda said, she had never planted flowers before. Up in the mountains, they just grew, she said.

I was doubtful that these mums would "just grow," and suggested that she keep them watered and mulched so that they could take root and maybe bloom again next fall. Brenda was delighted with our work; I thought the flowers gave that poor dispirited sign a more hopeful look.

While I waited for George, Brenda and I sat on tilting metal lawn chairs, vintage 1950, and sipped a second cup of coffee, talking in the cool morning sun. Brenda told me about her girlhood in the mountains, living with her grandparents on a small farm surrounded by cousins. Except for her accent and the southern location, she could have been describing my childhood summers in New Hampshire.

When George drove up in the Odyssey to pick me up a little later, Brenda and I were swapping stories and recipes like old friends. Just before I left, she disappeared into the motel, asking me to wait a minute. George and I sat in the Odyssey, warm in the sun, and waited for her to return. She came out of the motel office holding a small cardboard box. Inside she had placed a selection of her home canned vegetables: corn, string beans, cucumber pickles, beets, applesauce, and fresh raspberry jam.

"I just want you to have these," she said, with tears in her eyes. "You've been good to me."

I hadn't been aware of doing anything except planting flowers and talking with her. But I was touched with her gift. It helped counterbalance the redneck pickup truck with the brazen American flag of not so many days ago.

"We'll be back in the spring," I reassured her, hugging and thanking her with tears of my own.

George and I drove away, into the winter to wait for spring.

In beauty will I possess again...

14. Back in Ohio, Again

Over the winter, in the full swing of classes at the university and responsibilities at home, I didn't spend a lot of time thinking about the trail, though I did put my photographs in order, with captions and annotations from my journals, so that I would have something concrete to show for the four months I had been hiking.

Everyone, I found, was very interested and full of questions about my journey. They congratulated and admired me for the miles I had walked, the hardships I had endured, and the weight that I had lost. It was fun to share stories about some of the people (and critters) I had encountered, but talking about the trail usually left me dissatisfied with the conversation, as though I had not really communicated the experience.

Most of the time, I felt somewhat disconnected from the concerns, routines, and social gatherings that my friends and I had once enjoyed together. One friend commented that I hadn't really "come back" yet. My focus, she said, had turned inward; I had become a loner.

I noticed some differences in my attitude and demeanor, as well. When I returned to my workplace, my patience for the excuses of undergraduates who forgot to hand in assignments or needed extra time to meet their responsibilities was low, and my tolerance for long meetings characterized by rambling words and posturing had evaporated. My expectations, I realized, had become leaner, and my behavior more efficient and task-oriented.

In addition, I needed to spend part of each day outside, preferably in the woods.

I discovered that unless I expended a certain amount of physical energy running, hiking, or swimming every day, I became out-of-sorts, irritable, and a little depressed.

I could no longer listen to television newscasts or the car radio; I kept up with world events by reading the *New York Times* or Internet news services. George was amused when I began our Sunday morning read-athons with a round-trip jog of eight miles, just to pick up the newspapers. I didn't need the excuse, but did need the run.

Most significantly, I realized, without giving it much thought at all, I had developed a core of self-confidence on the trail that permitted me to listen to my own assessment and intuition about people and situations. Sometimes that put me out of step with the social expectations around me.

On one occasion, running on the beach near our home in Florida, I was stopped in my tracks by the taunt, "Oh Babe!" as I ran beside the water. I turned around and confronted the three young adolescents coming up behind me.

"That was pretty rude," I said.

"I didn't say anything," one boy replied

"It was him," another boy said, pointing to his friend in the middle.

"That was pretty rude," I repeated, directing my words to the tall boy in the center. "I don't like it. Please don't do it again."

"I didn't say nuthin'," the tall boy replied, smirking.

I ran on down the beach.

An hour later, returning from my run, I had to pass the same three boys, now lying on towels surrounded by other sunbathers.

As I ran by, I heard it again, "Oh Babe!"

This time I walked over to the threesome and looked directly at the young man responsible for the taunt.

"That's still rude," I said. "I told you before and asked you to stop."

"There's nuthin' wrong. You're s'posed to like it," he replied.

"Well, I don't. Women don't. Besides, I'm old enough to be your grandmother. It's disrespectful. Women don't like to be disrespected."

The tallest boy's two friends giggled, embarrassed, and hid their faces in their towels as I turned to leave.

My tormentor, lying on his stomach, head just inches from my feet, looked up at me and jeered.

"There's nuthin' you can do about it," he sneered. "I can say whatever I want... *bitch*," he added in an undertone.

His eyes and mouth were open and wet. He looked up at me, triumphant and fearless.

I realized, in a flash, that he was right. There was nothing I could do about it. I turned to go. But then, in an instant of indulgence, before I could stop myself, I lifted my running shoe and kicked a large foot-full of sand right in his face, directly into his open eyes and wet, leering mouth.

He gasped and sputtered and yelled, grabbing desperately at his eyes and spitting into the sand. His two friends rolled over in disbelief and uncontrolled laughter. They couldn't have been a better audience.

I walked away, vindicated, thinking about the ad for Atlas Body Building on the back page of my brother's 1950s comic books.

"Let him be humiliated in front of his friends," I thought. "Maybe it'll teach him something."

Later, I was a little chagrined that I had acted on impulse. In our culture, as in many others, women have learned to ignore mocking whistles from gawking men. I should be above that sort of thing. My actions had surprised him, and me. Still, I was glad I had confronted him, hoped that he had learned something, and was certain that I would do it again. I was no longer afraid to be a strong woman.

So, the next spring, returning to the trail seemed natural and effortless. Without much comment or explanation, I re-packed my backpack, re-packaged my food drops, and re-worked my itinerary south, to Georgia.

By the time the first buds of spring had unfurled into leaves and classes were finished for the term, my body, mind, spirit, and sense of social responsibility were ready to get back on the trail. I was eager to resume my trek of six hundred eighteen miles, from Pearisburg, Virginia, to Springer Mountain, Ga., and finish the odyssey that I had begun twelve months earlier.

My plan was to complete the entire 2,164 miles of the AT by the end of June 2002, one year and one month from the time I began.

15. Spring: A New Beginning
Pearisburg, Va., to Damascus, Va., 158.9 miles

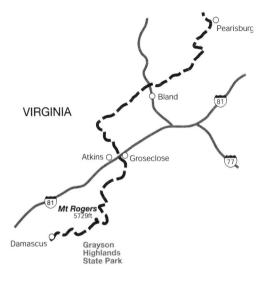

May 19, 2002, to Woods Hole Hostel, 10.5 miles

Pearisburg in May was even colder than Pearisburg had been at the end of September. An unseasonable temperature drop had settled in the mountains. When George and I returned to the Rendezvous Motel, I was wearing all my cold weather clothing, plus a nubby outer vest over my fleece jacket. My thought was to send the vest home with George, but a taste of late evening air convinced me I might need it until my first post office visit later in the week.

One of my students had decided to accompany me. A tall, strong, athletic nineteen-year-old, Stephanie had done a lot of hiking with her older brothers and mother, she said, and was eager to do something a little more daring this summer; she wanted to hike all the way to Georgia.

I thought she would be up to the physical challenge, and talked with her about the mental stamina and flexibility the trip would require. I knew from my own experience that while each day would be different, the hike each day would be the same in two important ways: it would be hard work, and it would not get any easier.

Stephanie was eager to be responsible for her own gear, food, and itinerary, and I agreed she could join me on the condition that we each hike our own hike, at our own pace, and plan to meet at the end of the day at a designated shelter or camp. I was impressed that she would want to hike with me for six weeks, more or less on her own; I was willing to give the idea a try.

The Rendezvous Motel had not changed much over the winter months. The "M" in the sign out front had been reinstated, but the mums that Brenda and I had planted with such hope had not survived. Brenda had also disappeared, and the Italian restaurant, sadly, had suffered a fire during the winter; its doors were closed and looked like they would not re-open. George, Stephanie, and I had dinner in a nearby town the night we arrived, but it wasn't what I had envisioned. Not surprisingly, I was disappointed.

In the morning, saying goodbye to George was easier than it had been the summer before; we both trusted the trail and my ability to deal with it. Both of us knew, now, what to expect of the weeks ahead, and we were both confident that I could do it. I had learned something about the nature of his support during my hike last summer. It was the support of a scaffold, assisting but not intruding, helping me reach a higher level as I stretched towards my goal on my own.

I would meet George again in two weeks at our fortieth college reunion. Ingrid, a classmate from South Carolina, would pick me up near Damascus, Virginia, drive me to Gettysburg for the weekend, and deliver me back to the trailhead at the end of the reunion. Stephanie would spend that weekend hiking with her mother.

After George snapped our photos at the trailhead, Stephanie and I were on our own. We hiked straight up, two thousand feet in two miles, to the top of Angel's Rest, a rocky overlook on northern end of Pearis Mountain. It was my first climb in more than seven months, but it felt good to be extending my muscles and testing my aerobic stamina again. I climbed with the technique that had worked best for me the preceding summer: keeping a steady pace, using my poles to push me forward, not stopping until I reached the top.

On the summit of Pearis Mountain, I waited for Stephanie on a rock ledge, looking eastward towards Blacksburg. Sheltered from the brisk wind, I was warm enough to strip off my jacket and vest and enjoy the strong morning sun. Stephanie was not far behind.

After a break to catch our breath, we hiked along old woods roads another five miles, through an area profuse with rhododendron and azalea bushes almost ready to bloom. In another week, I predicted, their glossy green leaves would be resplendent in brilliant pink, purple, orange, and red splotches. This year I hoped to see some of the magnificent color that Earl Shaffer wrote about in *Walking With Spring,* his account of the first end-to-end thru-hike in 1948.[34]

When it was time for lunch, Stephanie and I stopped at Doc's Knob Shelter to eat, out of the wind. I had provisioned my food bag with the same kind of food I had planned to eat the previous fall: dehydrated dinners, homemade granola, half-loaves of ten-grain bread, small plastic containers of peanut butter and honey, and snacks of dried peaches, Hershey bars, and energy bars. To drink, I stayed with Gatorade, Tang, instant milk, instant breakfast cappuccino, and hot chocolate. I had deliberately avoided these foods all winter.

This spring I had remembered the terrible cravings I had had on the trail for meat, corn, tomatoes, bananas, and orange juice. I dehydrated and included some of each in my food bag, this time acknowledging, wryly, the gastronomic rule of the trail: "Trail food is *fuel* and one shouldn't expect it to taste good."

Stephanie wasn't very hungry when we stopped, but she was very tired. We rested until it was too cold to sit still any longer, and then decided to hike only three more miles to the Woods Hole Hostel at Sugar Run Gap, a half-mile east of the trail. The hostel promised a bunkhouse, solar shower, and hot breakfast for $3.50; I thought it a good option for this cold, first night out. Stephanie thought so too.

We discovered the hostel was an old log cabin, built in 1880 and renovated by Tillie and Roy Wood in the 1940s, when Roy had been studying a herd of wapiti, the elk indigenous to this area. Before his death, Roy had been an assistant to the Secretary of the Interior during

34. Shaffer, Earl, Walking With Spring, Appalachian Trail Conference, Harper's Ferry, W.Va., 1983.

the Carter administration; his summer homestead spoke to his respect and love for the natural environment and its inhabitants. His wife, Tillie, now in her eighties, carried on the tradition of offering food and lodging to hikers, and was in residence with several of her friends when Stephanie and I arrived.

We knocked on the door of the cabin to introduce ourselves and pay our respects. Tillie invited us to sit by the fire and get acquainted. We chatted, southern style, as perspiration trickled down my back; I had forgotten the southern custom of small talk, endearingly, eternally elongated well beyond my Yankee expectations of good manners.

The interior of Tillie's cabin was as dark, warm, and cozy as the bunkhouse, our home for the night, was stark, cold, and forbidding. Stephanie and I climbed a steep ladder to the loft and spread our sleeping mats and bags on the dusty, wood-plank floor. There were several other hikers already established when we emerged from the loft to cook our supper. All but one of these hikers were Stephanie's age, and they had been heading north for over a month; they were full of themselves and the hardships they had already endured on the trail. The other hiker, Fahrtin' Jack,[35] was a section hiker going south. It was his third day on the trail. Jack and Stephanie were easy prey for the northbounders and their tales of pluck and fortitude.

After dinner, it was too cold to do anything but crawl into sleeping bags and read or write before sleep. Writing in my journal in gloves, hat, and vest, in the glow of my headlamp, I settled into the quiet descending all around us.

All of a sudden, Stephanie sat bolt upright and screamed, slapping at her sleeping bag, waving her arms in the air.

"Something's crawling on me. Get off. Get off," she shrieked.

Mice. I hadn't even heard them – but then, they never had bothered me. Tonight, they were bothering Stephanie. I tried to reassure her that they weren't interested in her – only her food, which we had hung downstairs on an upside-down tuna can suspended from a cross beam. Stephanie settled down a bit, but then said,

---

35. I was a little startled, as was Tillie, by Fahrtin' Jack's trail name. He explained that Fahrtin was a play on the German word, 'fahrt', meaning travel, so Farhtin' Jack meant Travelin' Jack. He said we could call him Jack.

"I don't think I'm going to go on with you tomorrow. I called my mom from the cabin. She's going to pick me up when Tillie and the others go for food in Pearisburg... they said I could ride in with them."

I was stunned. I thought Stephanie had enjoyed the day. The hiking hadn't been very hard, and except for the very first ascent in the morning, the terrain had been relatively level and uneventful. What about hiking to Georgia?

"It's just too hard," Stephanie said, "and not at all what I expected it would be."

I knew better than to try to change her mind.

> "I think her decision might be a bit premature, but, if this isn't her thing, maybe she should just end it before she gets hurt. It makes me wonder – is this hike really so out-of-the-ordinary?"

Fortunately, in a week I would acquire two other hiking partners: Mary Clare, a friend from the AYF Summer Seminars for Women, and Forrester, a friend from my university community in Ohio. These women did not know each other, but planned to meet me in Atkins, Virginia, and hike with me through Mt. Rogers National Recreation Area and Grayson Highlands State Park.

Until my friends joined me, however, I would be on my own again. I was surprised the prospect did not bother me; I really had become comfortable hiking by myself. I looked forward to my friends' company, but I had learned not to count on it.

May 20, 2002, to Jenny Knob Shelter, 21.5 miles

In the morning, seven hikers gathered around Tillie's dining room table and, holding hands, sang grace before beginning the hearty breakfast she and her friends had cooked for us. The morning sun shone through the cabin window at my back and the fire in the living room hearth warmed my cold hands and feet as I ate.

A photo of all of us on the front porch after breakfast shows seven shivering hikers in an array of warm-weather gear. Stephanie, having decided to go home, looked relaxed and cheerful; she was relieved, I think, and I was reassured that she was not embarrassed or ashamed to have changed her mind about hiking with me.

I hiked out in early morning sun, five miles across the wooded crest of Sugar Mountain, at right angles to Pearis Mountain, our hike the day before, and ate a late morning snack at the Wapiti Shelter at the base of the mountain on Dismal Creek. The Wapiti Shelter had an unfortunate reputation among hikers. Originally it had been located farther down Dismal Creek, close to a road. In 1981, two hikers had been murdered at that location,[36] and though the perpetrator was eventually caught and imprisoned, the shelter was subsequently torn down and moved to its present, more remote, setting. In the bright morning sun, I was not aware of any resident ghosts, but I knew Stephanie would not have been comfortable here the night before. If the mice in Tillie's loft had spooked her, this shelter would have really unnerved her, I thought.

Most of the day, I hiked by myself. I was eager to reach Lickskillet Hollow, two miles beyond the creek; I liked the sound of its name. To me, it shouted "southern Appalachians."

All afternoon, I passed thru-hikers heading north; they made the trail seem less desolate than I remembered from the previous fall. This was thru-hiker season, and most of these hikers had started in Georgia and were planning to finish at Katahdin in September or early October. I almost envied them their hike north, but kept my focus on my southern journey, instead.

Hiking alone, I found, was a joyful experience this spring. Being by myself did not bother me at all; in fact, I fully enjoyed it. As much as I had looked forward to Stephanie's company, I was rather relieved that I would not have to watch out for her in the weeks ahead. That she had made the decision to stop as soon as she knew this was not the experience for her was impressive; I was glad she had the courage to act.

I hiked along a creek on an overgrown woods road below Brushy Mountain, climbed a ridge by switchbacks, caught a glimpse of Big Walker Mountain and valley from a viewpoint, and reached the shelter just by dinnertime. It pleased me that I had hiked more than twenty-one miles and still had energy to spare.

My shelter-mate was a woman about my age, doing a section hike of southern Virginia and, like me, was hiking alone. She reminded me of Dare, the only other woman my age that I had met, so far, hiking alone.

36. Reported in "Hikers' Killer Going Home", Roanoke Times, September 26, 1996.

Before I left Ohio, I had emailed Dare for some advice about rejoining the trail after a seven-month hiatus, a similar experience to hers. She told me that I didn't need any advice. "You already know you can do it," she said. "Now just relax and enjoy it."

Mountain Mama was full of advice and offered it freely as she watched me set up camp.

"Why don't you drape your tent over your sleeping bag inside the shelter," she suggested. "That will keep you warmer – it's going to be another brutally cold night."

It made sense to me.

Later in the evening, Fahrtin' Jack arrived and set up his tent behind the shelter. He had left Tillie's later than I had, and reported that Stephanie had caught a ride to Pearisburg and would meet her mother at the Rendezvous Motel. I wondered, briefly, what Stephanie's mother would think of the Rendezvous, and then, reassured that all was well, let Stephanie slip from my mind.

Jack, Mountain Mama, and I cooked, ate, wrote in our journals, and went to bed. About midnight, I woke up with the sense that something was wrong.

Feeling around under the tent draped over me like a tarp, I discovered that my down sleeping bag was soaked. The tent had trapped the condensation from my body; I was warm, but would be in a soggy bag by morning if I continued with Mountain Mama's method. She must have had a synthetic-filled bag, I thought. Though heavier than goose down, synthetic bags can get wet and not lose warmth. Goose down can't. Reluctantly, I traded warmth for the drying power of evaporating condensation and removed my tarp covering, exposing my wet sleeping bag to the elements. I snuggled back inside my bag, warm enough to stay alive, but not really warm.

May 21, 2002, to Bland, Va., 13 miles

In the morning, my feet felt like blocks of ice; the temperature had dropped to twenty-seven degrees and my sleeping bag was coated lightly with frost. The sky was overcast and looked like it might snow. In May? Luckily, I had only thirteen miles to hike before I could find hot food in town; I had a mail drop at the post office in Bland, Virginia. I left early, before Jack and Mountain Mama were awake.

The quiet of the early morning woods pleased me. I hadn't realized how much I would miss the silence of the woods until I returned home over the winter. Ours is not a noisy home, now that our children are grown and there are just two of us. However, once I returned to Ohio, wherever I went, I found noise all around me. Background blare greeted me everywhere – grocery store, shopping mall, dentist's office, gas station, gym, park, airport, ice cream stand, train station, telephone hold button, beauty salon, stable, theatre, concert hall, sporting event – nowhere, it seemed, could I escape background music and advertising. In addition, each location had its own unique set of sounds – motors, drills, horns, announcement systems, bells, sirens, and people's voices – loud, louder, loudest. We all lived, I realized, in a din of echoes; it was much noisier than it needed to be, and certainly much noisier than I wanted it to be.

In civilization, I couldn't hear the birds, or the wind, or the rain. I couldn't hear my own breath, even when I ran. Out of the woods, there were so many competing vibrations, I couldn't feel my own heart beat. What had happened to the sound of silence?

One of the things I had missed most, and was happy to return to in the spring, was the quiet of the woods – which wasn't quiet at all, just not artificially raucous.

All morning, I hiked along the wooded crest of Brushy Mountain to the summit of Brush Mountain and then to a gap on Brushy Mountain. It seemed that Brushy, or Brush, Mountain went on forever until I read there are nine Brushy Mountains and four Brush Mountains in Virginia, and the trail crosses several of them. At least I wasn't going around and around the same mountain, I thought, relieved. I hiked on, across a steeper part of Brushy Mountain and the crest of Brushy Mountain, lush with rhododendron, and then across two branches of Kimberling Creek.

In the early afternoon, I reached the overpass of Interstate 77 and the road to Bland, my post office destination. Following the white blazes painted on the bridge and on road posts, I kept walking, up a steep asphalt hill to a dirt road that eventually re-entered the woods. There I met some northbound hikers also headed for the post office in Bland. They had not yet encountered the town; I had missed it.

I turned around. We all hiked back to the road and hitched a ride three miles into town.

Our driver dropped us at the post office and I retrieved my mail drop just as a school bus stopped across the road and discharged its passengers: twenty-five kindergartners on an end-of-the-year field trip. I was surrounded by five-year-olds, all wanting to know about my pack and whether I had any candy. The postmaster bailed me out; he had a basket of candy waiting for everyone – children and hikers alike.

That was about the best part of Bland.

While the kindergartners were inside learning about the post office, I squatted outside in the gloomy, cold damp, repacking my food bag and trying to keep my gear dry. Somehow I had managed to throw away my plastic container of peanut butter and honey, and there were no grocery stores in Bland.

But there was a pizza parlor where I met the northbounders for lunch. They were still able to eat pizza; I wasn't,[37] and ordered a hot cup of coffee, instead.

The northbounders and I traded tidbits about the respective trails ahead: I told them about Tillie's hostel, they gave me the scoop on the next shelter.

"If you can," they advised, "stay in Bland tonight. The closest shelter is twelve miles south, and the roof leaks."

I had a tent, but wasn't eager to add another twelve miles to the thirteen I had already hiked. And it had begun to rain. The postmaster told me about a motel across from the interstate, a mile down the road. I decided that another cold night, in the rain (or snow), would probably be better spent in that motel.

The Big Walker Motel was on the crest of a hill overlooking the interstate, across the road from a Dairy Queen truck stop. By the time I had checked into the motel and taken a hot shower, it was time for dinner. I walked down the hill to the DQ, shopped the convenience store shelves

---

37. After a certain number of miles, eating greasy pizza in small towns loses its appeal. The northbounders had not been on the trail long enough to disdain pizza; I had lost my taste for it somewhere in New Hampshire.

for something to replace my peanut butter and honey, and ordered some hot dogs for dinner. Outside, it was still raining, but inside the air was steamy and warm. It tickled me to think that this truck stop seemed welcoming; I never would have noticed it had I been on a road trip.

Just as I finished eating, Jack walked in. He had also decided to stay in the motel overnight. We agreed to get up early and hitch back to the trail together in the morning.

> "Jack talked my ears off in the DQ – so much so that I left my bag of deviled ham & processed cheese slices – peanut butter replacement – behind. When I ran down the hill (again) to recover them, they were gone … I had to buy a whole brick of Colby cheese to replace my replacement. I'd forgotten this survival part – about having to be hyper-vigilant in towns where there are so many distractions to claim your attention.

> Even with the hard parts, though – like losing the trail into town, worrying about hitching, losing my peanut butter and then its replacement, being cold and hungry and not in control of town things – I'm having a great time – eager to keep meeting people, eager to continue and move on to the next adventure. I'm ready to take on the world. This is more like it."

May 22, 2002, to Chestnut Knob Shelter, 22 miles

In the morning, the world outside my window was painted white; frost covered everything. I was happy to get dressed within the warm walls of the motel.

Jack and I walked the mile back into Bland and then two miles along the road. When a Mercedes sped by, I stuck out my thumb and smiled. The car stopped. Jack was dumbfounded. "How did you do that?" he demanded, hustling to the car.

Our driver was Motel Man and his wife, Caroline. I had met Motel Man the day before, at a rocky viewpoint; we had both been taking a break. He had told me then that he was finishing a section-hike of the trail that he had started many years ago. This year, his wife was helping him by shuttling him back and forth to the trailhead each day, so that he didn't have to camp in the cold. He only had this one section of Virginia to complete, he said, and he would be a "2000 Miler."

This morning, Motel Man would take us to our trailhead, dropping us off where I had finished my hike the day before. It was a very good way to begin the day.

Motel Man, Jack, and I hiked together for the next four miles, through dense underbrush, to a wooded road crossing. At the road crossing, we met a trail angel – someone from my hiking past.

In the back of his station wagon, our angel had a supply of fresh sandwiches, bananas, orange juice, and a box of small, lightweight New Testament bibles, wrapped in Ziploc baggies. The baggies touched me; this trail angel knew about hikers.

Chatting with our benefactor, I discovered he was a preacher delivering for his church, which was just down the road if we cared to visit or needed anything.

As we talked, something about the man struck a familiar chord. My association was a summer Sunday morning in a restaurant, surrounded by jovial, well-fed patrons, reminding me of home. I put the pieces together and asked:

"Were you in Kent, Connecticut, last summer, doing some missionary work?"

"We certainly were," he said. "Have we met?"

I told him about my hike of the summer before, coming into the town of Kent, on a beautiful Sunday morning, eating breakfast in an upscale café surrounded by people who reminded me of my family and my childhood, and about learning, at that place, how to avoid being homesick. I remembered meeting him, remembered how cheerful he had been, and how affirming his acknowledgement of me had been. I thanked him for that, and, accepting a banana and a Ziploced-New Testament from his ministry, thanked him again. He was pleased to be remembered for his beneficence.

Jack and I left Motel Man and headed south for five miles, through dense green woods on well-graded trails, crossing six or eight streams. Jack talked the entire time, but it was interesting to learn more about him. He had been in the world of young Washington D.C. assistants, working his way up the bureaucratic ladder when September 11 convinced him that something in his life was amiss. He chucked it all, he said, and was returning to school at the age of thirty-eight to become a special education teacher. His two-year program would start midsummer; he was hiking, now, to prepare himself for graduate school.

We stopped about noon in a sunny clearing, next to the last stream crossing of the day, and again met Motel Man, heading north. His was a circuitous route and I doubted that I would see him again, though we exchanged addresses for a Florida reunion sometime when we were both in winter residence. He was a nice, nice man, I thought. Seventy-eight and still hiking!

After lunch the hike was hilly, somewhat rocky, and reminded me of the terrain in New York. We began a steep, fifteen hundred-foot ascent of Garden Mountain, hiking steadily and warming up enough to take off our pant legs and extra shirts. It was the first time I had hiked in a tee shirt and shorts since the previous fall.

By five o'clock we still had five miles to go – across a cliff and some rock outcroppings to the top of a high knoll, then down and uphill again, and along interminable switchbacks to the open summit of Chestnut Knob, an overall ascent of more than four thousand feet.

ET had prepared me for the switchbacks in southwestern Virginia; he thought they were wonderful. Switchbacks did take the steep grade out of the climb, I had to admit, but they increased the total mileage by half. I would have preferred a steeper, shorter climb. However, although I was beginning to tire, I was not spent, and made sure that I stopped several times to refuel with high-energy snacks and fluid replacement as we climbed. Jack continued to talk, passing the time with observations about lightweight hiking. By the time we reached the summit of Chestnut Knob, he had almost convinced me that my pack was too heavy.

The Chestnut Knob Shelter, a rehabilitated fire warden's cabin, was an enclosed stone structure overlooking a valley surrounded on all sides by mountains. Green and unspoiled, this valley, affectionately known as God's Thumbprint, had been inhabited for more than seven thousand years, first as hunting ground by native tribes, then settled and farmed by German homesteaders in the eighteenth century. About three hundred people, descendents of the original settlers, still live in the valley and pride themselves that they have kept further development out. There is only one gas station, one general store, one paved road and only a scattering of farms throughout the entire 20,000 acres.

I pitched my tent on the edge of a meadow of long grass overlooking the valley, surrounded by the colorful tents of other hikers gathered at the fire pit adjacent to the stone cabin. The cabin was full of hikers, too, already settled into the sleeping lofts. These hikers were out of the wind, but their perch was damp and cold. I looked forward to the coziness of my tent, sure that I would be more comfortable than the cabin-dwellers.

As darkness fell, I joined a hiker named Red Wolf who was tending a roaring fire in the fire ring. He told me that he was spending the week at the cabin, keeping a warm fire for thru-hikers.

Red Wolf was from Savannah, Georgia, and had discovered the Chestnut Knob when he thru-hiked in 1979. I listened as he poked sticks into the fire and told me his story.

His liver had been damaged, he said, from a contaminated blood transfusion. He knew when he thru-hiked that he needed surgery, but was determined to complete his hike before "goin' under the knife."

The first transplant had been unsuccessful. His body withered, he said. He couldn't get up the energy to walk across a room, never mind hike a mountain. Discouraged and fearful, he agreed to a second transplant attempt.

"I had to get my body ready for that second transplant," he said. "Like doin' a thru-hike… it wasn't easy."

He vowed that when he recovered, he would return to Chestnut Knob, hike to its bald summit, and keep a fire burning for tired, cold, thru-hikers who happened to pass by on their "Walk with Spring."[38]

Red Wolf spoke quietly, and I had to listen closely to his words, drawled in a thick southern intonation difficult for me to follow. But I understood his mission. He was one of Thoreau's Saunterers, giving alms to those who followed in his footsteps. His alms were courage and inspiration, and the will to keep going that he had found through long days and nights in a bare hospital room, remembering his hike on the AT.

38. The reference to Walking with Spring is to Earl V. Shaffer's book of the same name. A venerated and much loved trail hero, Earl had just died, on May 5, 2002.

"They told me I would never hike again," he said, "but I walked all the way up this mountain." He repeated, in awe, "...the most beautiful place I've ever been... these're the most beautiful people," he said, gesturing his arms in a wide circle to include the sleeping hikers and tents.

Red Wolf and I sat by the fire, listening to the quiet snap of burning wood, looking up at the stars and bright moon in the cold sky above. It was a most beautiful place, with the most beautiful people.

I counted thirteen lights dotting the valley below; only thirteen farms in God's Thumbprint, and one bright soul on His Wrist above, I thought. I would not meet another like Red Wolf.

May 23, 2002, to Crawfish Gap campsite, 16 miles

The day began with breakfast on top of Chestnut Knob, watching the mist rise from the valley. Red Wolf and I watched the morning emerge from the sky. It looked like a miracle.

Descending the Knob, I was the only person hiking for miles around; I loved the quiet. I tried to monitor my pace and find my own rhythm, listening to the meadow sounds around me. It was a relief to not have company. Fahrtin' Jack had hiked out early and planned to go another twenty miles to the next shelter. I did not have to meet Mary Clare and Forrester until the next afternoon; I had plenty of time to hike the twenty-four miles to our meeting place in Atkins, Virginia. I wanted to take my time and enjoy the peace of my own company.

> "One thing that has changed for me since my hike last summer: I no longer need to listen to music or books on tape or other people when I am alone. I'm content, no, I prefer, this solitude. I prefer fashioning my pace to become one with the rhythm in my surroundings. I find I walk in a reverie and have to wake up when I come in to a shelter full of people. When that happens, I'm not rude, just not ready to be social.
>
> At lunch today, I came in to the Knot Maul Shelter, which is right on the trail. There were several friendly young hikers

there. I shook hands all around, and then sat down at the picnic table to eat. Quietly, I began to talk to a young hiker from Maine… but I needed an extra bit of time, at first, to get my social bearings. Later I thought about what a change this was for me. As a woman, I have been socialized to keep the conversation going and make sure that everyone feels included. But after being on my own in the woods for so long, with only my own thoughts for company, I no longer respond to those old social roles. Sometimes I don't even join the conversation. My walk in the woods has given me permission to withdraw and not participate."

After lunch, I continued on my own again, ascending the low hills above the north fork of the Holston River, descending and then crossing the river over a low-water bridge, and walking on bog bridges along the banks of the river, through rhododendron thick with nascent blooms. The afternoon was warm, sunny, and tranquil. When I reached the wooded crest of Big Walker Mountain in Tilson Gap, my thoughts were calm and uncluttered. I had reached a peace of perfect understanding and harmony with the dirt under my feet. I felt the "earth remembered me." I was glad to be back on the trail.

In the late afternoon, I found a clear, level area with a fire ring next to Reed Creek, and decided to camp overnight. I pitched my tent off to the side of the clearing, listening to the birds and insects set up their evening ritual. The stillness of the air delighted me. Sitting by the fire ring, eating beans and rice and chocolate, I was warm and happy.

By the time of the first white stars overhead, I was asleep in my tent. It had been a lovely day.

May 24, 2002, to Atkins, Va., 6 miles

I rose with the sun and ate a leisurely breakfast, leaning against my pack at the edge of the fire ring. The temperature had warmed and the day promised to be sunny and mild. I had only six miles to hike to meet Forrester and Mary Clare later in the day.

I hiked in harmony with my surroundings, climbing seven hundred feet to the crest of Gullion (Little Brushy) Mountain the first mile, and then descending and ascending gradually across the saddle and between meadows and woods for the rest of morning. The ridges and farms across the valleys were, I knew, part of the historic Great Valley of the Appalachians.[39]

By noon, I had reached Davis Fancy, once a large property located at the headwaters of the middle fork of the Holston River. I climbed a small hill to an overgrown cemetery, a collection of crumbling stones and two thriving maple trees enclosed by a split rail fence. I climbed the fence, set my pack against a tree, and walked over to read some of the headstones:

Aghizel, son of FG and MF Davis Died Dec. 4, 1883;
aged 14 mos & 16 days
Lizzie M wife of FG Davis born Nov 27, 1859 died April 29, 1883
Harold P. Davis, born June 2, 1808, died Apr.7, 1886
Anne wife of Harold P. Davis born Oct 1, 1816, died July 29, 1837

It struck me that none of the women had their own identity – not even a surname – only the relationship: "wife of." And they died young; probably in childbirth.

Resting against one of the trees, I pulled out my watercolors and began to sketch. My only companions were the joyful birds, the rustle of grass and leaves, and the memories within the old stones.

The afternoon passed quickly. By the time my watercolors dried, I was ready for live company.

I hiked out to the trail crossing at U.S. 11 and booked a room at the Village Motel for the night. Forrester and Mary Clare would arrive by

39. The Great Valley of the Appalachians is a chain of linked valleys west of the Blue Ridge that extends from the Hudson River in New York to the hill country of Alabama. It was a crucial transportation route, called the Warrior's Path when the Iroquois used it to raid and dominate other tribes as far south as Tennessee. Later it became a key route to the interior for migration and settlement—the Great Wagon Road from Pennsylvania and the Piedmont of the Carolinas and Georgia for the Irish Protestant, German, and English settlers moving west towards Kentucky and Ohio.

dinner time; we would hike out together in the morning for a week-long trip, crossing Mt. Rogers National Recreation Area. I was looking forward to hiking with women again.

May 25, 2002, to Partnership Shelter, 12 miles

My friends arrived in plenty of time to sample the home cookin' at The Barn, the only restaurant within walking distance of our motel. I ordered pork chops and fresh salad, saving one of the chops for my next day's dinner of instant rice and beans.

We spent the evening looking at maps, eliminating superfluous items from our packs, and resting up for an early morning start. Forrester quickly acquired her trail-name, Digger, for the good-natured but furious searches she made to the bottom of her pack for items invariably located elsewhere.

In the morning, after a breakfast stop back at The Barn, we hoisted our refurbished packs, parked Digger's car in an out-of-the-way clearing, and hiked across overgrown railroad tracks to the top of a meadow and an old apple orchard overlooking the Great Valley below. Stopping to catch our breath and take off extra clothing, I congratulated my new hiking partners on successfully completing their first ascent. Both women had been a bit apprehensive the night before, wondering what this day would bring. They were relieved, they said, that the first climb had been manageable and they had been equal to its challenge.

We continued through the woods and reached the clearing to the Settlers Museum of Southwest Virginia. The restored schoolhouse on the edge of the property was furnished with a potbelly stove, rows of double desks, slates, inkwells, and McGuffey Readers.[40] Walking to the schoolhouse through the woods gave me a feel for the isolation and promise of rural education in the nineteenth and early twentieth century. I had spent my elementary school years in a four-room rural school, with two grades per room, and had begun my professional life teaching in multi-grade classrooms, following the tenets of John Dewey and the Progressive Education Movement, with roots in the one-room schoolhouse tradition.

40. The Settlers Museum of Southwest Va., founded 1987, is a functioning 1890-era farm on 275 acres and includes apple orchards, kitchen garden, granary, root cellar, wash house, farm shop, visitors center, and a restored one-room school house.

This schoolhouse reminded me, nostalgically, that lessons from the past were not necessarily out of date.

My friends and I gathered on the porch of the schoolhouse in the bright morning sun for a snack and a break, then hiked on through hardwood forests scattered with rhododendron and laurel thickets. Digger had grown up in the Virginia countryside, riding horseback on trails through these woods, along the streams, and into the hills. She was hiking home.

We followed her up the crest of Glade Mountain to the top of a wide, wooded knoll on Locust Mountain, and then along the wooded ridges of Brushy Mountain for the rest of the day. The air was heady with the fragrance of honeysuckle, and we hiked in and out of purple rhododendron, orange fire azalea, violet flox, and pink mountain laurel all afternoon. The weather was glorious, with sunny, mild, blue sky, white clouds, and a cooling breeze. The path was relatively easy. For the first day out, it could not have been a better experience, and both Mary Clare and Digger hiked well.

Our destination was the Partnership Shelter just inside the Mt. Rogers National Recreation Area, a distance of twelve miles. We reached it by five o'clock, hot, thirsty, and ready for a shower. The shelter obliged us and provided a sink, privy, picnic table, two sleeping lofts, piped water, and a warm-water shower built onto the deck of the shelter. It was very luxurious; not at all like any shelter I had experienced thus far.

We took full advantage of the amenities, then pitched our tents and cooked at the picnic table. It would have been possible to order pizza delivered to the shelter, but we elected to eat trail food and lighten our packs, instead.

The stars came out crisp and sharp in the dark mountain sky. We burrowed into our tents and listened to the whir of insects in the cool evening air. It was easy to sleep on the soft grassy beds under our tents. The trail had not let me down today – the well-bred countryside of southwestern Virginia was putting on a good show for my friends. It was fun to have company.

May 26, 2002, to Raccoon Branch Shelter, 12 miles

The weather was still fine and warm; it promised to be another beautiful day for hiking. We started about eight o'clock with the goal of completing eight miles by noon. We almost made it.

One of the hardest things about beginning a hike, I think, is learning how to listen to your own body and discover the pace that works best for you. This includes stops for resting and eating. Too many stops can be counterproductive, as muscles stiffen up when they are not moving, hastening fatigue and soreness; too few stops to replace nutrients, including water, depletes the muscles, causing them to slow or cease moving efficiently.

During our second morning out, we stopped a few times, briefly, to fill our water bottles and snack. Remembering my discomfort when I ignored my own needs and tried to keep up with Jed's pace last summer, I encouraged Mary Clare and Digger to experiment until they found their own stride. Mary Clare discovered that a slow, steady pace and many breaks to cool off with water kept her energy level up and fatigue down. Digger liked hiking a bit faster, especially climbing up; she discovered descending on rocks needed a slower pace.

I liked keeping the same pace, up or down, and kept moving, no matter how steep the climb. This earned me the nickname "Mountain Goat," but kept me from falling on descents or losing steam halfway up a hill.

We agreed to hike within hollering distance of each other, but not necessarily together, and meet up at designated stopping points for snacks, water, lunch, or a gorgeous view. Mary Clare liked to consult her map, and Digger used a trail guide; neither was afraid to hike alone in the woods.

This system worked well and no one got lost, hurt, overtired, or grouchy. Again I noted the difference between men and women hikers: men competed with each other to conquer the trail; women cooperated and hiked in relationship to each other and the trail. I was much more comfortable hiking with women.

Just after midday, we reached the South Fork of the Holston River in Rye Valley and looked for a shaded place to spread out our packs and have lunch. We found the perfect retreat next to the water, under a stand of pine trees. We took off our boots, splashed our heads in the stream, and relaxed on the soft pine needles in the shade of tall pines.

The Sandwich never tasted so good. We all stretched out and napped after lunch – a satisfying interruption to a good hike.

We may have overdone the snooze. Climbing twelve hundred feet in four miles after lunch would have been easier if we had not rested so long, we decided. Or perhaps we overdid the peanut butter and honey. Whatever the cause, we all felt a bit sluggish until we found our trail legs for the steady climb to High Point, and then another half-mile to the Raccoon Branch Shelter.

By late afternoon, the heat of the day had turned heavy, and the sun had disappeared behind gray clouds. I expected rain before sunset and hastened my pace.

When I reached the shelter, two older men had already claimed space in the shelter. They were drinking beer and cooking at the fire ring. I walked over to the stream, ostensibly looking for level tent spaces but really trying to decide if we should stay near the shelter or move on. My companions, I knew, would be eager to stop soon, and I thought it might rain before we reached the next camping area.

On the other hand, I wasn't sure about the men at the fire ring.

Putting down my pack, I walked over to the picnic table, and introduced myself. They responded in kind. Blue Jeans and Bishop were hiking at a slow pace, catching rides whenever possible, thinking they might make it to Maine by September. Today they had only hiked a mile from the road crossing; hence the beer. I wasn't sure they would make it to Maine this season, but decided they were harmless.

When Mary Clare and Digger hiked in, we set up camp next to the stream. The rain held off and we cooked around the fire that the men had built. Mary Clare had enough energy to talk social policy with them long into the night. Digger and I opted for our tents and some quiet time.

May 27, 2002, Old Orchard Shelter, 11.7 miles
The morning was sunny but grew increasingly overcast, still, and humid as we hiked up and out. We left Blue Jeans and Bishop by their fire ring, smoking some early morning pot. I really doubted that they would make it to Maine; they didn't seem to have the drive.

Although the trail followed an old railroad bed and ascended gradually for most of the morning, our pace was a little slower than it had been the day before. My partners were stiff and sore. We hiked through thick woods, and by late morning, began the ascent of Hurricane Mountain, hearing thunder in the distance. My goal was to climb at least halfway up Hurricane Mountain by lunchtime so that after lunch the climb wouldn't seem so daunting.

We found a good picnic spot in a level, clear area about a third of the way up, and settled back to enjoy a break. I was a little concerned about impending rain and didn't want to linger, knowing that the climb to the crest of Hurricane Mountain would seem longer after lunch, especially in the rain. Luckily, the trail after lunch was on an old, well-graded logging road, and the thunder, which continued to rumble in the distance, never produced a storm.

The crest of Hurricane Mountain marked the beginning of the Blue Ridge Plateau; for the next forty miles we would not descend below three thousand feet. The grassy balds of the south, beginning with Grayson Highlands State Park, were just ahead. Grayson Highlands State Park is 4,822 acres of grassy balds and outcroppings of pink and red volcanic rock, and features two herds of wild ponies that graze across the balds. Among hikers, the wild ponies are the park's biggest draw. Digger, a horsewoman, was particularly eager to see the ponies; I couldn't wait to reach the balds.

By late afternoon, all of us were ready to find a campsite for the night. When we emerged from the woods to an open grassy area overlooking Mt. Rogers to the west and Graves Mountain to north, we had found our spot; the Old Orchard Shelter was nearby, full of thru-hikers heading north, and a small tent was pitched at the edge of a pine grove, next to a fire ring stacked with wood and small kindling.

Digger and I set up the tents while Mary Clare built a fire and made tea. When I went for water, I stopped at the shelter to introduce myself to the hikers, a formal courtesy practiced by long-distance hikers, even if they never see each other again. I had discovered early on that knowing who was camped nearby was not only civilized, it was a safety-check. I trusted my intuition on meeting hikers, and would not hesitate to move on if I felt any discomfort or bad vibes emanating from them.

In addition, meeting hikers who are heading in the opposite direction was a good way to gain pertinent trail information. The hikers at this shelter were full of information about the Grayson Highlands. They had hiked under the storm and, unfortunately, missed the ponies.

While I chatted, Digger and Mary Clare went to the stream to wash up and rinse out their clothes, something I had long ago stopped doing, preferring to control my sweatiness by splashing water on my hands and face whenever possible and ignoring the smell of sweat, smoke, and dirt on my clothes and pack. I looked grubby, but did not consider myself dirty. I never wanted to take a chance on getting my clothes wet; wet clothes wouldn't keep me warm if the weather suddenly changed.

We cooked by the fire ring between our tents and then sat by the fire, watching the flames as the sun set quietly across the hills directly in front of us. The evening was mild, though the air was chilly away from the fire. A full moon rose above the clouds while we talked quietly, and the fire burned down. For the second day of hiking, my friends were doing well, but it had been a hard climb in the dark woods. I was looking forward to the next day's hike on open balds, in the sun. I hoped for good weather and lots of ponies.

May 28, 2002, to Thomas Knob campsite, 11 miles

The day dawned sunny, mild, and clear, but my hiking mates were moving slowly. They were slow to get up, slow to get their stuff together, slow to eat, slow to break camp, slow to hike. Without pushing, I wanted to keep them focused on our destination so that they would not deplete their energy too soon. I knew our day's hike would take us over exposed balds, with wonderful views, and wanted to get there before afternoon when the weather could change suddenly.

Mary Clare earned her trail name, Weather, that day, by predicting that the atmospheric conditions would be fine for watching the ponies, and then an alternate spelling, Whether, for her ability to suggest alternatives.

Weather, Digger, and I hiked all morning, ascending to the ridge crest of Pine Mountain by switchbacks, crossing fence lines and open fields, eating mountain blueberries as we went. By midmorning, we reached a corral for cattle and horses between Pine and Stone mountains. Known as the Scales, the area is crisscrossed by fences and stiles, and holds cattle grazing in open pastures. We continued our ascent to the crest of Stone Mountain, and then began a gradual descent to the footbridge over the east fork of Big Wilson Creek. By then, Weather had fallen once and Digger had wrapped her ankle too tightly, causing it to swell. She was limping.

We sat on rocks by the Wilber Creek bank, in the sun, and ate lunch. Digger soaked her ankle in the cool rushing water while Weather and I rested. Eventually, we hiked out and climbed, gradually, to our reward – the crest of Wilburn Ridge, an exquisite green bald with views for miles in every direction. Far off in the distance we could see tiny dots moving across the hillside: the wild ponies.

I grabbed my camera and picked up my pace, with Digger and Weather right behind me. The afternoon was sunny, warm, and quiet. A soft breeze stirred the air.

Drawing closer to the ponies, I stopped to let them come to me. One white pony with a russet-colored head and splotchy neck markings ambled over; I took off my pack and sat down while the pony investigated. Digger and Weather joined me. Soon other ponies surrounded us, inching closer and closer, nuzzling our packs and licking our hands. They liked our salt.

Digger knew just how to talk to the ponies. They milled around her, and us, for almost an hour. It was a breathtaking sight under the enormous blue sky: ponies and people connecting in gentle harmony with each other, alone in the wilderness at the top of the world.

Reluctantly, we had to hike on; we still had five miles to go before we would reach the shelter. The wind had picked up, the temperature fell, and the lovely white clouds overhead grew puffier.

We hiked on with the beautiful panoramic views of Stone Mountain behind and the crest of Pine Mountain and Mt. Rogers ahead, through brilliant green meadows and over large flat rocks. As we came up and through a rocky pass, we discovered the second herd of wild ponies, this one much larger, on the other side. We left them alone and hiked on, over more rocks, through Fat Man's Squeeze, a narrow tunnel in the rocks, to the rocky summit of Pine Mountain.[41] The view, on this afternoon of gathering clouds, was of four states: North Carolina, Tennessee, Kentucky, and Virginia.

The descent through a rhododendron grove was gradual and the hiking almost level, though the rocks made it difficult for Digger's sore ankle. I was relieved when we came off the exposed ledges and began to hike under limited tree cover; the clouds overhead had continued to amass and I didn't trust them.

We finally pulled into the Thomas Knob Shelter a little past six o'clock. The shelter, a log cabin on top of a rocky ledge, faced the trail, with its back to the valley below. It was windy, rocky, barren, dark, and full of thru-hikers already settled for the night. We decided to camp further downhill, out of the wind, and found a small grove of pines off the trail just below the shelter. We set up our tents and Weather started a fire while Digger and I went for water.

Digger had decided that she would call her brother and ask him to meet her a day earlier than originally planned. He lived nearby and would not mind taking her to her car so that she could come back for Weather and me the following day. This would give her more time with her brother and less stress on her sore ankle.

I was a little startled, but not surprised at this change in plans. It had been a good hike, I thought, and, except for Digger's uncomfortable ankle, no one had been hurt, frightened, or disillusioned. That the hike had been harder than my friends anticipated was not unexpected either. In fact, I thought they had done really well; except for my daughters, they had been the only women, so far, who had actually joined me on the trail for anything longer than a day hike.

> "What is it that makes this whole experience so hard, I wonder. Perhaps it is being so tired most of the time and having to deal with so many details: food, water, bodily aches and pains, keeping clothes dry, keeping warm, staying healthy, being

41. Pine Mountain (5,526') is the third-highest point in Virginia and the highest point on the AT in Virginia. It is higher here than the summit of Katahdin or the Franconia Ridge in New Hampshire and is the highest point between Hump Mountain in North Carolina and Mt. Washington in New Hampshire.

organized and always being alert for weather changes, uncertainty, and the unexpected.

It's all so difficult. I wonder how the early settlers managed? Well, they weren't trying to live in two separate worlds at once, and they were more accustomed to living outdoors and enduring hardship.

I no longer expect the hike to get any easier; the challenges just change. So far, I've been able to meet whatever has come my way, but long-distance hiking is hard."

I fell asleep listening to the wind rustling through the trees above and the mountain passes below, with the songs of crickets as accompaniment.

May 29, 2002, to Lost Mountain Shelter, 13 miles

The three of us broke camp early and hiked out through sparse woods, skirting the summit of Mt. Rogers, the highest point in Virginia, and descending gradually to an open bald of green grass, rocks, light breeze, and brilliant sunshine. We left Digger sitting on a rock overlooking the parking lot where her brother would pick her up later in the morning. She had a cell phone, plenty of food, and an air of confidence about her; I was reassured that she would be fine. We would meet the next day at the trailhead crossing near Damascus.

Weather and I hiked on, across the parking lot and into the woods to follow the trail ascending and skirting the summit of Whitetop Mountain to Buzzard Rock, the high point for us, at over five thousand feet.

We sat out of the wind and watched hawks circle above while we ate our trail food and drank in the beauty all around us. It was a typical southern bald with open meadows scattered under the crest below us, magnificent, unspoiled, and quiet.

The trail descended sharply, nineteen hundred feet across small rocks and boulders and through scrubby brush bordering the fields on all sides. With the wind at my back, I felt like I was flying down the trail; it was as exhilarating as any climb in the White Mountains, and higher and greener than the Franconia Ridge, one of my favorites the summer before.

We hiked companionably the rest of the afternoon, reaching the Beech Mountain Road about four o'clock. Digger had told us that she wanted to return to Virginia someday, and had been looking for property for her horses. When we crossed the Beech Mountain Road, Weather and I thought we had found just the place: an abandoned farmhouse surrounded by fields and woods, close to the trail but otherwise, in the middle of nowhere. We thought it would suit Digger's purposes quite well.

Behind the farm we ascended a wooded ridge and reached the Lost Mountain Shelter near the crest of Lost Mountain by late afternoon.

There was one other inhabitant, a lone woman with a shaved head, appropriately named Buzz. Weather and I looked forward to having a shelter experience of women that night, and set out our sleeping bags on the floor next to Buzz before cooking the last of our trail food.

But our hopes for a women's shelter were short-lived. As we finished eating, a young man hiked in, an actor from the Barter Theater in nearby Abingdon, Virginia. The Barter Theater had begun as a cultural outreach to the southern Appalachian people during the Depression. In those days, barter bought a ticket to the production. The actor, an intriguing young man, entertained us with stories and scenes from his favorite roles.

Not long after his arrival, a group of brash young hikers burst into our sanctuary. They had been hanging out in Damascus since the end of Trail Days,[42] they explained, and now needed to "do miles" to catch up with the rest of the thru-hikers. I had planned to avoid Trail Days and I wish I could have avoided these hikers. Loud, inconsiderate, and boisterous, they took over the picnic table and shouted insults at each other and boasted about their amazing hiking ability well into the evening.

Buzz, Weather, the actor and I disappeared into the shelter to avoid them. It was the first night in a long time that I used earplugs and burrowed deep in my sleeping bag, trying to block out their noise and confusion.

May 30, 2002, to Highway 58, near Damascus, Va., 10.2 miles

Weather and I were up and out early. We planned to meet Digger at the highway crossing and didn't want to be late. She had promised to

---

42. Trail Days is a yearly, three-day festival of AT hikers in nearby Damascus, Va. It was first held in 1987 as a commemorative event for the 50th anniversary of the AT, and includes such activities as a hiker reunion and talent show, exhibits, street dances, live music, and a hiker parade.

bring us ice-cold Coke and 7-Up; that was as much incentive to hike out as we needed.

We hadn't hiked long before the AT joined the Virginia Creeper Trail[43] to cross Laurel Creek on the former railroad trestle. As I walked across the bridge, looking down at the water below, I wondered what it was like to cross this five hundred-foot expanse, high in the mountains, in windy, icy conditions. Even on a beautiful summer morning, it looked scary.

We continued through the woods to the crest of a ridge overlooking Beech and Whitetop mountains. The view was beautiful, but our focus was on reaching the trailhead and meeting Digger. Five minutes before the appointed time, we approached the trailhead crossing the highway. I looked up and saw Digger's black Durango pull to the side of the road. Digger jumped out and ran down the trail towards us, ice-cold drinks in hand. I was amazed at her timing, our timing, and the precision of the meeting. It was remarkable to me, still, that I could emerge from a trailhead in any weather, at any time of the day or night, and be met by the person who had agreed to meet me at that exact location, at that exact time.

We hopped in the car and drove away. Digger's brother had picked her up, as planned, and taken her back to retrieve her car. Her foot was no longer swollen and she was eager to see the property that Weather and I had picked out for her.

By car, the abandoned farmhouse with its collapsed barn and forlorn looking "For Sale" sign looked less appealing than it had the day before. We got out and looked around, but soon drove on to the motel where I would meet my college friend Ingrid later in the day.

At the motel, Digger and Weather cleaned up, repacked their car, and were about to leave when a taxi drove up and deposited two disheveled hikers onto the gravel – Blue Jeans and Bishop. They had not walked far since we had last seen them, but they were ready for a motel rest.

It was fun to see them again at the end of our trek, a full circle for Digger and Weather, a night's stopover for me. Ingrid would arrive later

---

43. The Virginia Creeper Trail follows an old railroad grade for thirty-four miles from Abingdon, Va. to the North Carolina state line. The train that serviced this route, the Creeper, got its name from its slow progress over the mountains from North Carolina to the sawmills at Konnarock, above. The Creeper carried passengers until the 1950s and continued freight service until the 1970s. The Forest Service acquired the railroad's land and easements for the Creeper Trail, now used by hikers, bicyclists, and horseback riders from North Carolina to Damascus, Va.

in the evening; in the morning we would drive to Pennsylvania to meet George and the rest of the class of 1962 for our fortieth reunion at Gettysburg College.

I spread all my gear on the front lawn of the motel to air and dry out in the late afternoon sun, and went inside to clean myself up. One look in the motel mirror told me that the task would involve some major scrubbing.

I set about making myself glamorous – well, cleaner than I had been on the trail. By morning I had to be ready to face my classmates. I would be leaner, trimmer, and less well-manicured than they, but I was eager to reconnect and share our latest news. I hadn't seen them since our meeting in Pennsylvania the summer before. We had some catching up to do.

16. My Own Hike – At Last

Damascus, Va., to Hot Springs, N.C., 170.6 miles

VIRGINIA

Damascus

NORTH CAROLINA

Watauga Lake

TENNESSEE

Laurel Fork Gorge

Erwin

River

Roan High Knob
6285ft

Nolichucky

Spivey Gap

Big Bald
5516ft

French

Hot Springs

Broad River

June 3, 2002, to Vandeventer Shelter, 22 miles

The reunion was all I had expected it to be. Transported back in time, I took both feet off the trail and, for a weekend, re-acquainted myself with the dreams and dreamers of my youth. The weather was hot and sunny and our campus, dry when we were undergraduates, flowed with alcohol and never-ending conversation. It was fun to remember and be remembered, and lovely to stay in a modern hotel with soft, thick towels and subtle air conditioning.

At dinner Saturday evening, I was honored to receive the "Rehabilitated Foot Award" for having walked the most miles since graduation. I tried, but no one accepted my offer to hike the remaining 453 miles with me. If anyone thought my journey eccentric, I didn't notice, or care. Most of my classmates seemed envious and full of admiration.

That pleased me. And on Monday morning I knew I would be on my own again. The thought of hiking by myself didn't bother me at all; in fact, I looked forward to it.

Early Monday morning, Ingrid drove me to the trailhead to begin the final leg of my journey. She would continue her drive to her home in South Carolina; I would continue my trek to Georgia. She would reach her destination by evening; mine would take until the end of the month. I much preferred my journey, though I was grateful she had interrupted hers to facilitate mine.

After the hubbub of the reunion weekend, with its social chatter, clinking glasses, and renewal of friendships long dormant, being back in the quiet, soaring woods was a relief. The pace of social life, with its multiple changes of clothing, had been draining. I was glad to resume a simpler demeanor and quickly lost myself in the task of finding the next shelter.

Today I would walk twenty-two miles with a six-day supply of food and three pounds of water on my back. Although the load was heavy and the temperature well above eighty degrees, I was happy to be able to set my own pace and walk in quiet.

I looked forward to the last part of my hike, the part that would be just for me. From this point on, I would not meet anyone from my other life; I had no schedules to honor except my own. I hoped to finish at Springer Mountain by June 30 so that George and I could continue on to Florida for a week at the beach before returning to Ohio to resume our other lives.

Looking at my trail guide, my goal would be possible if I hiked sixteen miles a day for the next twenty-eight days. Although I didn't know the details about the terrain ahead, I did know about my body and my ability to hike. Barring unforeseen circumstances, I knew I was fit enough and determined enough to accomplish such a hike.

And I was determined to enjoy myself, my way. This meant I would stop when I felt like it, stay in town when I felt like it, hike alone when I felt like it, hike with a partner when I felt like it. So far, I had often accommodated to others on the trail, even when that meant ignoring my own needs. Now, I knew, my need was to hike my own hike. I could, at last, listen to my own cues and follow them.

As I walked through the woods, I surprised myself by hiking faster than my usual pace. Even with a heavier pack, I was moving at a steady three miles per hour; it felt right.

At the first shelter, when I stopped for a midmorning break, I met a couple about my age. They told me about a hiker hostel two days south: "Kincora is a wonderful place to be," they said. "The owners are really nice people."

I filed the information in the back of my mind and hiked on.

The trail in this section follows the ridgeline of Holston Mountain, and then crosses to the narrow crest of Iron Mountain via Cross Mountain, in the pattern of the letter H. For me, it was a carefree walk in the woods until I reached a marker for the grave of Nick Grindstaff just past the summit of Iron Mountain.

Set back from the trail in a patch of long grass, the ruins of an old stone chimney mark Nick's last resting place. "Uncle Nick Grindstaff / Born Dec. 26, 1851, Died July 22, 1923 / Lived alone, suffered alone, and died alone." His epitaph was chilling and sad, I thought. Was his fate the consequence of a solitary life, I wondered? Perhaps relationships are the ballast one needs for balance. Perhaps I should not be too quick to slough them off.

I hiked on, through mature woods, following the ridge crest along a series of switchbacks and was surprised, late in the afternoon, when I reached the Vandeventer Shelter on a cliff facing the trail, with its back to a view of Watauga Lake and the valley below.

I was as far removed from the social repartee of my college reunion as it was possible to be. The shelter was quiet. Even though I shared it with two men, they were not talkative. The setting discouraged small talk. Sitting on the rocks overlooking the valley, we cooked our dinners and listened to the breeze flutter the leaves in the trees behind us. A lone motorcycle circling, and a dog barking somewhere in the distance, were the only interrupting sounds from the valley below. I could once again hear the insects.

As the valley settled down for the night, we on the mountaintop did the same. I missed George but I was happy to be back on the trail – tired, sweaty, smelly, but content.

June 4, 2002, to Kinkora Hostel, 17.3 miles

A whippoorwill woke us in the morning. It would be a beautiful day. I decided to call the owners of the Kinkora Hostel to inquire about lodging for the night. Not only did Bob, the owner, welcome me, he suggested that his wife, Pat, meet me at noon and slack my pack to their hostel so that I could meander through Laurel Gorge that afternoon and enjoy the falls without a pack.

If I hustled, I could be at the trailhead by eleven o'clock. I hustled.

The Watauga Dam is an impressive structure, particularly early in the morning, with no one else around. Completed in 1949, the dam is 320 feet high and 840 feet long, creating Watauga Lake, a body of water spreading indolently through the Cherokee National Forest. Thru-hikers are the only ones allowed to cross the dam and, on that beautiful summer morning, I was the only person for miles. Although the sun had not been up for long, it was hot, and the shadows were strong on the asphalt and concrete under my feet. I would be glad to return to the soft dirt and tree cover of the mountains, I thought.

My plan to meet Pat worked like clockwork. I arrived at the trailhead with enough time to eat a snack and organize my pack for slacking. Pat arrived about eleven fifteen with some fresh water, a daypack, and some good advice about the trail ahead. It was hot – above ninety degrees – with steady sunshine and no breeze.

"Unseasonable," Pat said.

I sweated my way up Pond Flats, over four thousand feet, and sweated my way back down again. My reward was Laurel Fork Gorge.

After the glaring yellow heat of the morning and the sticky, grimy climb of the afternoon, the gorge was like a cool blue oasis of gently burbling water, tall sheltering trees, and fragrant blooming rhododendron and mountain laurel. The earth smelled damp and cool. For three miles, I walked between wooded slopes rising steeply and uninterrupted to the mountaintops sixteen hundred feet above. When I reached the streambed, I looked up to see rocks and cliffs soaring vertically on either side of me. I followed the rocks to the base of the crashing falls. There I found a young couple on their honeymoon, taking pictures of each other by the water. I offered to take a photo of them together, then sat down to take off my boots and soak my feet in the icy water. I would have plunged under the falls, as well, but, aware of the young couple, resisted and cooled off instead by ducking my head and feet in the rapids and drinking my fill from the flow.

Examining my feet, I was surprised to discover hot spots on the bottoms of both. Hot spots signal blisters; it had been a long time since I had dealt with blisters. But, I had spent the weekend softening my calluses and painting my toenails so that I could wear sandals rather than hiking boots with my little black dress, and I had walked almost fifty miles since then, in very hot conditions. My feet were telling the long, hot, sweat-pounding story; I would need to tend to them more carefully at the hostel.

June 5, 2002, Bear Branch Road to Kincora Hostel, 20 miles

Kincora, in Celtic, means "kinship of the heart," and the owners, Bob and Pat Peebles, were perfect stewards. Tucked in at the end of a dirt road, the hostel is a wooden structure with showers, laundry facilities, bunks, lounge, and kitchen; it was built to accommodate hikers, and is rustic, comfortable, and sensible. When I arrived, my pack was waiting for me on the porch, with a note to find a bunk and help myself to whatever I needed.

I needed a shower and some blister supplies. Later, with several other hikers, Bob drove me to town and I stocked up at the local pharmacy. My feet were a mess; the hot spots I had discovered at the falls had filled with water and become large, sore blisters on the soles and heels of each foot. A pharmacy in the middle of the mountains had just what I needed: sticky gauze tape, Second Skin, and knee-sized Band-Aid squares. I hoped that these bandages would adhere to my feet so that my blisters could heal as I walked. I didn't mind the pain, but I did not want to risk infection. And my cache of supplies had been expensive: twenty-four dollars for bandages. I was appalled.

In the morning, Bob, who was also a maintainer for the trail I would hike that day, offered to drive me twenty miles south to Bear Branch Road so I could slack back to Kincora for another night at the hostel. Tomorrow he would return me to the trailhead to continue my hike south. He was going to Bear Branch to work on the trail, anyway, he said, and it would be no trouble.

I was happy to oblige. The hostel was a friendly place at the end of the day. Buckeye, another hiker from Ohio, was a guest as well. He would be hiking on from Bear Branch in the morning, and we tentatively agreed to hike out together. But first, I had twenty miles of forty-five hundred feet of elevation change and considerable scrambling to accomplish.

Bob dropped me at the trailhead at Bear Branch Road under threatening gray skies. The temperature and humidity were still high, and I was glad to be carrying only food, water, and a rain jacket. I had forgotten to pack my map, however, and was inconvenienced without it. I relied on my maps to plan each day's hike. With a map, looking at the squiggly-lined contours of different colors, I could plan my food, water, and rest stops for the day and use my watch to gauge my mileage, checking elapsed time against the map to determine where I was and how long it would take me to reach my destination. This system worked well for me. I was always surprised when I met hikers who did not use a map or trail guide. Even more puzzling were the women hikers who merely followed their partner's lead, never inquiring or knowing where they were going.

Thinking back to when I had first hiked with ET and, following his lead, climbed down Mt. Williams in the wrong direction, I remembered how that experience had taught me to gather as much information as possible about the trail ahead, and trust my own judgment and knowledge rather than rely on someone else to do my thinking for me. It was a lesson that kept me in good stead as a hiker, safe and able to use my energy to hike well rather than complain or resent the terrain.

Through pine woods and pastures, I hiked across a summit with good views of White Rocks Mountain (west), Beech Mountain (east), and Hump, Little Hump, Yellow Mountain, Grassy Ridge, Jane Bald, Round Bald, and Roan High Knob (south, southwest). I would climb them all in the days to come. These were some of the magnificent southern balds and, remembering my experience on Cold Mountain the previous fall and Grayson Highlands the past week, I couldn't wait.

Except for the heat and uncertainty of having no map, the hike was not too difficult. I was grateful for the soft pine needles underfoot and the fact that I carried only a light day pack. The blisters on my feet reminded me with every step that I needed to step lightly and be gentle. I passed the day in solitude, crossing wooded spurs, seeping bogs, pine-covered ridges, streams lined with rhododendron thickets, and the boggy remnants of a moonshine still.

In the late afternoon, sweating profusely, I began a climb almost straight up along a newly cut dirt road. The trail followed this road to the abandoned fire tower on White Rocks Mountain, and veered off into the woods just before the summit. Peeved at the absurdity of climbing straight up, I continued to follow the road to the top, just to see where it went. The climb was not worth the view. And then it started to rain.

Descending through pine forest and meadows, I was glad that the day was over. I was happier still to be returning to a hostel where I could shower, cook indoors, and sleep enclosed in four dry walls. It rained all night.

June 6, 2002, to Overmountain Shelter, 8.7 miles

True to his word, Bob drove Buckeye and me back to the trailhead at Bear Branch Road to continue our hike south. Buckeye was also headed to Springer Mountain, but did not expect to reach it until mid-July. We agreed to hike over Hump and Little Hump together. I was looking forward to the climbs, twenty-five hundred feet in the first five miles, but was disappointed that the day had started with rain; clouds might obscure the view from the tops of Hump and Little Hump.

We began our climb in dense woods, via switchbacks that made the ascent seem effortless. By noon we had reached Doll Flats, the beginning of the pastureland leading to the summit of Hump Mountain. A resident longhorn steer watched our approach from his vantage point alongside the trail. His head was crowned by two horns, a spread of at least a yard. I was relieved that he left us alone; he outweighed me by fifteen hundred pounds and probably could run faster, even with those horns.

Continuing to the top of Hump Mountain, I was thrilled with the open land all around me. Although there were some trees on the perimeter of the summit, most of the expanse was covered with grass, low-growing vegetation, and a scattering of flat rocks. Buckeye and I were the only hikers in sight; we had the bald to ourselves.

Settling behind a set of large rocks, I sat down to assemble some lunch. The wind had picked up and the sun peeked sporadically through the clouds to warm my bare skin. Buckeye and I took advantage of the elevation and used our cell phones to call home.

By the time Buckeye was ready to hike again, the clouds in the west had turned from wispy white to light gray. The wind from the west was strong and, though we were headed south, I was anxious about our speed. Buckeye hiked more slowly than I and seemed unconcerned about the weather.

Looking around for potential cover in the event of a sudden storm, I saw nothing but open space, wide hills, and grass in every direction. Then I heard thunder.

Over my right shoulder, I saw a sky full of billowing gray clouds, blowing in our direction. Buckeye had disappeared behind a knoll. I wondered if he had heard the thunder.

Slipping out of my pack, I ran back to find him and urge him to move a little faster. Behind the rise I found him, loping towards me more quickly than I thought he could.

I ran back to my pack, quickly fastened the straps, and joined him in a race across the open hillside. The other contestants in our marathon, heralded from the west by fierce wind and dropping temperature, were a bank of dark black clouds, rumbling thunder, and quick flashes of lightning.

Buckeye and I dashed across the peaks, thrashing through wet under-brush and scratchy thickets of nettles, and scrambled off the trail at the first stand of trees taller than our own heads. We had gained the first lap and outrun our opponents, briefly.

Under the protection of the trees, we rested on our packs, waiting for the herd of clouds to catch up. The wind decreased and brought cold drops of rain, but the thunder seemed to be farther away. Looking at our maps, we figured the shelter in Yellow Mountain Gap to be less than a mile away, through the woods. If the storm rested between the balds, we thought, we could make it to the shelter before it resumed its fury. We decided to go for it.

Protected by raingear and pack covers, we set off through the woods. Within minutes, we could see the shelter in the distance, an old red barn on the far side of a meadow, overlooking the mountains all around. I didn't like the look of that open meadow, five hundred yards between the woods and the shelter, but picked up my feet and headed directly towards it anyway.

The grass leading to the barn was long and wet, and the path open and exposed. Buckeye and I ran across the meadow, wind and rain buffeting our rain hoods and legs. I had forgotten about my throbbing, raw feet; blisters were nothing compared to the anger overhead.

We made it to the barn as the first bolt of lightning and crash of thunder met in unison over the barn roof. Rain poured down in furious sheets, coming in through wide gaps in the old siding, making wide circles of wet on the muddy shelter floor and sleeping lofts above.

Two other hikers, protected from the rain by an overhang in front of the barn, greeted our turbulent arrival. They were a couple from Florida, and had hiked in from Roan High Knob an hour earlier. The rickety old barn was a safe haven for all of us. We settled in to wait for the storm to pass.

An hour later, it was still raining, but the thunder and lightning had disappeared into the distance, south. The next shelter, almost two miles away, had no water or privy, the couple told us. In the rain, it seemed pointless to hike on; I decided to stay for the night, and spread out my gear on a dry patch of floor in the loft above. Buckeye had already committed himself to staying and was stretched out on his sleeping bag, enjoying the sound of the rain on the roof overhead.

Later in the evening, I sat at the picnic table listening to birds chirping and calling through the valley, and sketched the view in front of me: silhouettes of dark mountains with wisps of clouds rising in streams and streaks between them, joining the band of night above. I was embraced by solitude.

"Even though I'm not quite warm, not quite dry, not quite comfortable, I'm glad to be in this remote place, accessible only by foot. The solitude, the stillness of the hour, the quickly rising and changing mist, the breathtaking isolation of the wilderness above, before, and behind the mountains, can only be accessed as a Saunterer."

That night, under dripping eaves, I slept with restless mice and snoring hikers. I didn't mind their company. They afforded me solitude without loneliness.

June 7, 2002, to Clyde Smith Shelter, 12.4 miles

Buckeye and I hiked out in hopeful sunshine through the wet grass and continued through dripping trees and shrubs, over a small knob, through several sags, and up to the Stan Murray Shelter. Although we had been hiking for only a short while, Buckeye dropped back at the shelter to take a catnap. He wasn't feeling well.

I hiked on alone, climbing steadily through the soaking woods, squishing my feet in wet boots, trying to ignore the pain that shot through my feet with each step. As soon as I reached the crest of the northern end of Grassy Ridge, I stopped on a flat rock to look at my feet in the open air. The shelter had been too dark to really see my blisters, but in the early morning sun I would be able to assess and, hopefully, tend to them.

The sole of my right foot and inner heel of my left were stark white, soft, and painful. The skin was ripped, exposing jagged holes of puckered tissue underneath; the expensive Band-Aids were scrunched uselessly at the edge of each wound, worm-like. Opening my pack, I pulled out the last of my gauze tape and wrapped it around each foot, securing the ends with duct tape. Putting on my least wet socks, I re-laced my boots, and sat for a minute, gathering courage for those first few steps of the next nine miles. Tying the old pair of wet socks to my pack, I set off. The pain from my feet was just bearable; I hiked on.

Following the crest through open fields, passing over the open summit of Jane Bald, I forgot my own misery. Jane Bald, I had read, was named for a woman who had died there of milk sickness, a disease caused by drinking the milk of cows poisoned by eating snakeroot. Imagining Jane's misery, I accepted my own. To help me, the rhododendron and flame azaleas were in full bloom across the bald, under a wide blue sky and bright warm sun. From the ridge I could see mountains in all directions and the wind whipped the socks on my pack dry.

As I descended into Carvers Gap and crossed the park road, I met several other hikers just beginning their climb to the bald behind me. They were energetic and friendly, eager to see the rhododendron at the top of the ridge.

I climbed in the opposite direction, through dense balsam and red spruce growth, and skirted the summit of Roan High Knob, an elevation of over six thousand feet. I had timed my visit perfectly; this was the peak of the rhododendron bloom in the high elevations, and because it was still too early in the day for many visitors, I had the natural gardens to myself.

I continued my climb to the site of the old Cloudland Hotel, built by John T. Wilder as a resort in the "land of sky, of magnificent views above the clouds where the rivers are born."[44] The hotel was dismantled in 1919 and now all that remains of the Clouldland are an old stone chimney and fireplace, a signboard of old photographs, and the still-magnificent view. I saw it through eyes nostalgic for past glory, and then hiked on.

Looking for a place to eat lunch, I hiked along the top edge of cliffs overlooking Roan Mountain to the south, Ripshin Ridge to the north, and Unaka Mountain to the west. Suddenly exhausted, I gave up my lunch search, sat down on the edge of the trail, pulled off my pack, and fell into a sound sleep. A group of young campers woke me as they ascended the trail, almost stepping on me as they hiked by.

I moved from the edge of the trail, pulled out some food and water, and after lunch, was able to hike on with renewed energy.

The rest of the afternoon passed without notice, through a continuing corridor of open woods splotched with rhododendron and laurel in full bloom. When I reached the blue-blazed trail to the Clyde Smith Shelter, my feet screamed at me to stop. Bob Peebles and his crew had recently rebuilt this shelter and I was eager to see it.

Bob was proud of the shelter's design: a waist-high counter along the front for cooking, benches along the sides for sitting, and everything pro-

44. From a sign at the site of the old hotel.

tected by an overhanging roof. The inside sleeping area was roomy, light, and dry. I set up camp, stripped off my boots, and gingerly tried to revive my shriveled, weeping feet. They always hurt the most and looked the worst at the end of the day. Would they never heal, I wondered?

> "I may not have any company in the shelters after this – except for section hikers. The northbounders have all passed through. The trail seems to inhabited by large groups of young campers. I expect I will see the same sort of hikers in the Smokies – but probably no more thru-hikers… I guess I'm the first of the southbounders this year."

June 8, 2002, Curley Maple Gap Shelter, 20 miles

It was cold again in the morning. I packed quickly and set out at first light. It was too cold to tarry and because I wanted to hike twenty miles, I pushed hard all morning. It was a hike up knobs, across ridge crests, and down steep rocks; then up, across, and down steeply again, all day. The colder temperature helped me hike quickly, and I was determined to stay well hydrated. I made a point of drinking my fill at every stream and carrying a full supply of treated water between water sources. My sudden need for sleep on the edge of the trail the day before, I thought, had been the result of dehydration rather than lack of food. Today, hiking through the Iron Mountains, there were plenty of streams and, as long as I treated the water, I could drink continuously all day. Even my feet felt better; I enjoyed my hike.

In the afternoon I crossed Little Bald Knob, Unaka Mountain, and the grassy, sunny bald of Beauty Spot. Most of the day, however, I was under tree cover in the woods, and though the sun was strong, it never got too hot. Towards the end of the day, my feet began to burn again, so I kept myself busy thinking about a book I could write about my journey. It occurred to me as I was walking, that in order to follow my dream, I had learned how to focus on immediate, attainable goals, and scan the path for rocks, roots, and slippery spots while at the same time looking up for the white blazes to guide my way.

I had learned to listen to the birds and wind and leaves around me, and to be aware of my surroundings and alert to any dangers or unexpected events. I had learned to be in tune with my body and its needs for water, food, rest, and energy boosts.

Now that I was close to my destination, I realized that somewhere along the way, my journey had become metaphor for living, and had helped me understand the life I had lived thus far.

> "I thought, today, that the first seven hundred miles or so I was preoccupied with my physical needs and fears of being lost, frightened, and alone. The next seven hundred miles, I worked on relationships with people – the people I hiked with, my parents, my daughters, and my husband. This last seven hundred miles I have become more confident and have been free to think more creatively about new goals, dreams, and plans for the future. As I did in my young adulthood, I am once again looking forward, not back, and I am eager to hike on."

June 9, 2001, to Spivey Gap, 15 miles

I was full of energy the next morning when I hiked out early to pick up my mail drop at Nolichucky Johnny's.[45]

Johnny and his wife, Charlotte, ran their hostel as a business and provided a shower house, bunk house with private and semi-private rooms, covered picnic/cooking area, and an outfitters supply store. When I shopped in the store for bandages, Johnny looked at the pattern of blisters on my feet and suggested I try new sole inserts for my boots. Then he offered to slack me from Spivey Gap, ten miles south, back to his hostel for the night. I agreed that a light day of only ten more miles with just a daypack might be helpful to my feet, and took him up on his offer. Charlotte drove me to the trailhead in her truck.

As we drove, she asked me why I was hiking south at this time of year. I explained that I had left the trail after the events of September 11 the

45. With the permission of hostel owners, it is possible to use their address for mail drops. This is particularly helpful if your arrival is on a weekend when the post office is closed, or if the hostel is near a trail crossing. Nolichucky Johnny's hostel is sixty feet from the trail; I arrived on a Sunday morning.

previous fall because I had not felt comfortable in the small towns near the trail. She thought for a minute, then said:

"We knew you wasn't a terrorist, but you wasn't one of us."

That was exactly right. I had felt excluded from the town communities that usually welcomed hikers, particularly after I was nearly run off the road near Pearisburg. Back on the trail this spring, I had not had that experience at all. In fact, southern hospitality this spring had been even more welcoming and helpful than I had experienced in my northern birthplace the summer before.

Upon reflection, I realized that when people feel threatened, as we all did after the events of September 11, they turn inward to exclude outsiders – any outsiders. Charlotte had expressed what I had felt intuitively at the time, but did not understand until now. I had been right to heed my feelings then. This spring I felt completely comfortable both on the trail and in the small towns; life had returned to normal for most of us, and the community of the Appalachian Trail was once again welcoming, strong, and inclusive. This spring, a middle-aged woman hiking alone was not an outsider.

I thought about these things as I hiked from Spivey Gap, through tall pinewoods, back and forth around the sharp ridges of No Business Knob,[46] and stopped at the shelter of the same name.

As I stretched out in the sunshine to read the shelter register, a slim paperback publication fell out of the plastic bag holding the notebook. It was written by a woman named Peace Pilgrim, and described her nine-year journey of twenty-five thousand miles, "walking coast to coast for peace." In her early sixties when she began, she had been inspired by walking in the woods one night, she wrote, and quite suddenly was overtaken by "a complete willingness, without any reservations, to give my life to God and to service." She prepared for her journey by hiking the Appalachian Trail in 1952, the first woman to do an end-to-end flip-flop hike, then gave up her money and her name, and, dressed in pants and a tunic lettered with "Peace Pilgrim" on front and "25,000 Miles on Foot For Peace" on the back, began her trek.

---

46. No Business Knob, the story goes, was named by a man who tried without success to climb it when it was overgrown with thick underbrush; he reckoned he had "no business" on that knob.

I marveled at her journey, averaging twenty-five miles a day, sometimes walking all night to keep warm if there was no shelter available or the night was too cold. She carried only a comb, a folding toothbrush, and her current correspondence, and wrote and spoke as she walked, arguing against war and showing the way for peace.

As I read about her life and mission, I thought about Peggy, the vagabond woman living in the shelters in the Blue Ridge Mountains of Virginia whom I had met the previous fall. Peace Pilgrim had probably been mistaken for someone like Peggy, I thought, especially during the 1950s and '60s, before the peace movement gained momentum during and after the Vietnam War.

It was not hard to imagine why either woman preferred the simple life of walking in the woods to the complexity of contemporary life and its problems. I didn't identify with either woman, but I could appreciate the simplicity each sought and could fully understand the mission for peace. Now, more than ever, the wrong-headedness of war as a solution to personal, national, or global problems was clear to me. But I had no idea what to do about it; becoming a peace pilgrim, hermit, or eccentric wanderer did not seem to be the answer, for me.

I continued my hike through the late afternoon sunshine, and stopped at the top of Cliff Ridge overlooking the Nolichucky River two thousand feet below. A train of more than sixty open coal cars snaked its way through the gorge and across the bridge over the Nolichucky. This freight train had discontinued its passenger service several years ago and effectively cut off modern transportation to the small community of Lost Cove, N.C., four miles south. Because the rail line was the only passage possible through the narrow gorge, the town was, eventually, abandoned. How easy it was to forget these rural, mountain communities, I thought, as I watched the train slowly disappear, its mournful whistle fading in the distance.

June 10, 2002, to Hogback Ridge Shelter, 14.2 miles

The next morning, in clothes freshly laundered by Charlotte and new boot inserts provided by Johnny, I returned to Spivey Gap to continue my trek. My sleep in the valley had been interrupted all night by the rumble and whistles of trains; I was glad to be returning to the mountains.

The morning was warm and sunny. I entered the woods and climbed right away, through a stand of white pine and hemlock trees, then through hardwoods, to a promontory called High Rocks, where I could see Little Bald ahead of me, and No Business Knob, behind. For most of the day, I would be traveling the state line between North Carolina and Tennessee.

When I reached the wooded summit of Little Bald, I walked along the ridge to begin the climb up Big Bald. Coming up through the woods, looking ahead, I saw its crest. It was solid yellow – a carpet of wildflowers as far as I could see, reflecting the sun back to the sky. Wordsworth's daffodils must have looked like this, I thought, and laughed when I thought of my fifth-grade teacher, making us memorize his poem about daffodils.

These yellow flowers made me feel like dancing and shouting, as well. It was a magnificent show across the bald, framed by the distant view of mountains over the rim: Mt Mitchell, the highest peak in the eastern U.S., and Mt. LeConte, Coldspring Mountain, the Unaka Mountains, and the Nantahalas, my destination in a few days.

Before I left Big Bald, I met two other hikers, heading north. We sat in the sun and talked for a few minutes while we ate lunch. Directly across from us, a resort development scarred the view. It was a reminder of civilization pressing closer and closer, and spoiled the natural look to the beauty all around. When a small truck drove over the crest of the bald and stopped near our resting place, that civilization grew even closer: a middle-aged couple and their dog climbed out to gaze at the view before them. The woman told me they were from Atlanta and had just purchased a summer home "down there," pointing to the development across the mountain. She wanted to see her new home from the mountain, she said. I wondered how many yellow flowers their truck tires crushed as they sped over the bald to the viewpoint. Their intrusion irritated me. I quickly packed my food bag and moved on, surprised by my reaction to their sense of entitlement and seeming disregard for the privilege of stewardship.

Walking through the tall cool woods after lunch, I followed an old woods road for several miles. When the trail follows old graded roads, it's easy to become lost in daydreams and forget to watch for white blazes. I knew better, but did that very thing; after about two miles, I became aware that I had not seen a blaze in quite some time and began looking ahead and behind me as I walked. Nothing. No blazes on either side of the trees. Reluctantly, I turned around and began retracing my steps back up the mountain, looking for blazes off the side of the old road indicating that the trail had turned into the woods. Still nothing. Almost at the top of the bald, I finally found a blaze, going north. Reassured that I was still on the trail, I turned around and again headed south, careful, this time to watch for blazes. It was unusual to have so few trail markings, with so much distance between. I made a mental note to be more vigilant in the future. Irked with myself, I traveled on.

By late afternoon, my feet hurt. Each step brought a sharp pain directly to my brain. There was nothing to do but keep hiking. I longed for the shelter and finally found it, set in the woods near a stream.

As soon as I pitched my tent and made camp, I took off my boots to tend to my feet. On the edge of each old blister, a new blister had formed, red, angry, and painful. So painful, in fact, that I was unable to put any weight on the bottom of either foot to walk across the campsite without boots.

That night I slept with my sleeping bag unzipped at the bottom, exposing my feet to the cool evening air. My feet throbbed all night; I hoped that meant they were healing.

June 11, 2002, to Jerry Cabin Shelter, 14 miles

The next morning, ignoring my newly bandaged, still-sore feet, I hiked out through woods and high grass heavy with dew. As soon as I reached a higher elevation I called George on my cell phone; our early morning conversations were still one of the high points to my day. This morning, sitting on my pack, looking out through the woods and underbrush, we talked for a long time, uninterrupted. When we hung up, I felt renewed and energetic and barely noticed my feet.

In the late morning, ascending the slope of Coldspring Mountain, I passed the graves of two civil war soldiers, relatives divided by loyalties to each side of the cause, killed at the same spot. Not much farther, on another grassy knoll, I saw a small stone memorial for a 1968 thru-hiker, whose ashes had been scattered there after his death. The beauty of both resting places sobered me; on this sunny summer day, serenaded by a chorus of birdsong, they seemed particularly peaceful.

At lunch, I stopped to fill my water bottles at a shelter and discovered, to my amusement and his dismay, a naked hiker taking a bath in the woods.

He saw me winding down the trail to the stream before I saw him.

"Hey, wait!" he shouted at me. I looked up to see an outstretched arm and leg on either side of a tall tree, and heard the man's outraged plea behind its bisecting trunk.

"It's okay," I hollered back. "I'm only coming for water. I won't peek."

He was an old man, I gathered, from his voice and obvious distress, and I didn't want to upset him further. But I did need water, so I continued to the stream, filled up my bottles, and left him alone.

When I reached the shelter, the hikers sitting around the picnic table asked me if I'd seen "grandpa." I chuckled, said, "not really, but he knew I was there," and left it for him to elaborate. The hikers were a family from Florida and Texas, spending their vacation hiking and camping in the backcountry.

By the time I reached the shelter in the late afternoon, my right heel had a red ring around the edge of its main blister. I cleaned it as best I could, doused it with tea tree oil, and bandaged it with a clean gauze pad; it was the best I could do until I reached more sophisticated medical help. I busied myself with cooking and camp chores, chatted with the young couple who hiked in to the shelter after me, and fell asleep listening to crickets and other dark night sounds in the woods. Except for my throbbing feet, I was comfortable and content, surrounded by fresh air, lulled by the natural rhythm of the earth.

June 12, 2002, to Rich Mountain fire tower, 18 miles

I knew when I looked at my map early the next morning that the challenge of the day would be after lunch, along a long slow climb of eleven hundred feet to the top of Spring Mountain, so I planned my stops accordingly.

I passed most of the morning in a forest dense with rhododendron and mountain laurel, walking along a ridgeline with no view. I was not interested in taking any side trails to fire towers or promontories, even to see the Great Smoky Mountains. Today, my feet hurt and I concentrated on hiking just to get there.

At lunchtime, I sat on the trunk of a felled tree, extending my legs downward towards the ravine below, my back against my pack, and rested. I was hot and bored more than tired or hungry and had stopped just to have something besides trees, woods, and sore feet to occupy my attention. However, the tiny bugs swarming my head, shoulders, and *The Sandwich* made me itch; I hiked on shortly, sweat dripping down my back and into my eyes.

When I reached my destination in the late afternoon, even though my feet hurt, I continued for several more miles to a spring and campsite near the Rich Mountain fire tower. It was a lovely spot to spend the night: a level grove of tall trees with a fire ring, log bench, wooden counter between two trees, a clothesline, knobs on the trees to hang my pack and food bag, and a soft carpet of pine needles under my tent. Except for the constant swarm of bugs around my eyes and neck, I had the site to myself. It felt quite luxurious.

Under the soaring pines and a canopy of stars, I fell asleep listening to bugs hit the netted roof of my tent. In the morning I hoped to reach Hot Springs before noon to pick up a mail drop and get medical attention for my blisters. I thought an antibiotic might be in order for the infection developing on my right heel.

Only 274 miles to Springer, I thought as I drifted off to sleep. I'm almost there.

June 13, 2002, to Hot Springs, N.C., 9 miles

I filled my water bottles at the spring below the campsite and hiked out early. Within two miles, the trail crossed a road and I met a man named Elmer and his dog, Rufus.

I had heard about Elmer from northbounders on the trail. A former Methodist turned Buddhist, university chaplain turned innkeeper, Elmer ran a commune-like organic farm and hiker hostel in Hot Springs. This late in the hiker season, I wasn't sure that he was still accepting hikers, but, as we chatted in the early morning sun, he assured me that I would be welcome at his hostel.

"Go up to the back door and ask for Sonja," he said. "She'll find a room for you. And there is a clinic right across the road for your feet," he continued, noting my discomfort as I limped towards him.

What a kind man, I thought, as I left him to his morning and continued with mine.

I re-entered the woods, cooler under the trees, and ascended across the southern slope of Mill Ridge with sweeping views of mountains ahead of me. The air buzzed with activity: a group of thirty teen-aged campers and their leaders were resting in a pine grove around the next bend in the trail. I was surprised to see so many people hiking in one group. How could they follow the code of low impact camping with so many people, I wondered. I chatted with their leaders, briefly, and asked them the same question.

The leaders seemed unconcerned and unaware of the damage sixty booted feet all tramping to the same destination, at the same time, could do to the trail environment. I tried to make my point about "leave no trace hiking"[47] without offending or embarrassing them. Thinking about our conversation later, I realized that I had adopted a proprietary kinship for the trail and wanted to protect it. I never would have confronted these campers a year ago, I thought. It never would have occurred to me.

Continuing along the trail, I came to the famous rock outcrop called Lovers Leap Ridge, named by the Cherokee for one of their maidens who, forsaken by her lover, jumped from its crag to the French Broad River gorge, a thousand feet below. The view of the gorge, now, is a sprawling tangle of railroad tracks, industrial buildings, and houses baking in the heat – incongruous to that simple Indian story.

As I hiked into town from the trail, I passed a large sign announcing, "Famous mineral baths of Hot Springs," but saw no hotels, resorts, or spas to authenticate its claim. The typically aging town was sleepy and

---

47. The principles of Leave No Trace ethic include: travel only on foot, stay on the footpath, pack out waste, travel in small groups (four to six is ideal), camp in groups of ten or less, take only pictures, leave only the lightest footprints, use a small stove instead of a fire, stay on trail lands, use campsite privy or dig a small hole, wash (dishes, self) away from water, respect other hikers and wildlife by traveling quietly.

hot, tucked into the gorge next to a maze of railroad tracks. I hoped my stay would not be too long.

After I picked up my mail drop from the post office, I headed across the street to the clinic. They would not, of course, prescribe an antibiotic without seeing my feet. When I removed my boots and unpeeled my socks, the nurse attending me gasped in disbelief. My right foot was fiery red with little lines snaking up my ankle; the left was puckered and raw-looking, but not infected. After that, it was not hard to get a prescription for an antibiotic to fight the infection. But the nurse strongly advised me to keep off my feet until the infection began to heal. I decided to stay overnight at Elmer's Sunnybank Inn and walked up the street to talk to Sonja.

She was washing the old-fashioned wood floor in the back kitchen, but interrupted her mopping to show me to an upstairs room and a downstairs shower. I cleaned up, borrowed some clothes, limped down the street to the laundry, and ate lunch in a vegetarian café while my clothes were being washed.

Later, back at the inn, Elmer suggested that I take advantage of the hot springs and mineral baths at the edge of town, to heal my feet, he said. At sunset, I walked back to the edge of town and for ten dollars, purchased an hour-long soak in a wooden tub of heated, swirling hydrotherapy. Relaxing in the fading light of early evening, it was nice to be by myself, just doing nothing. I deliberately did not think about how much nicer it would be if George were there with me.

After the spa, I re-bandaged my feet and walked back through town, stopping at an outdoor restaurant for a glass of Pinot Grigio and a candlelit dinner of a fresh tomato and greens salad, and Littleneck clams in white wine sauce over angel hair pasta. Not bad for a trail town, I thought, enjoying my food and watching the other diners. On the way back to the inn, I called George from a pay phone in a gas station parking lot and we talked while I watched the clouds over the mountains drift towards the town. I told him about my clinic visit and that I was weighing their advice to take a zero day in the morning. He convinced me to stay over by saying that my insistence to hike "sounded like an addiction." He was right; a day of rest was the smart thing to do. I went to bed reconciled to waiting out the day with my feet up and inert between Epsom salts soaks.

During the night, the clouds drifting into town collided to produce a thunderstorm. Tucked under the covers in my old Victorian bedroom, I didn't hear a thing. I was surprised to wake to dripping trees, gloomy skies, and cool damp air. It would be a good day to curl up with a book and watch the rain swirl by.

June 14, 2002, Elmer's Sunnybank Inn, Hot Springs, N.C., 0 miles

After a family-style breakfast, I soaked my feet and talked to several other hikers. Later, I sat upstairs on the sheltered back porch and looked at my maps, soaked my feet some more, and read from the voluminous collection of travel, hiking, and philosophy books on every landing, along every hallway, and in every nook of Elmer's turn-of-the-century home. Train locomotives and coal cars kept me company, whistling shrilly as they rumbled deafeningly through town. During the glory years, six passenger trains a day had stopped at the depot in Hot Springs; today, cars filled with coal and freight roll through the town, but do not stop.

Jumping from outer to inner travel, my reading that morning ranged from early town history to a discussion of the personality profiles of Appalachian Trail thru-hikers. I read that one psychologist, in a study of more than eight hundred hikers, discovered that the overwhelming majority of them were Introverts, as contrasted to the population at large, who were Extroverts. Introverts, he explained, took energy from the inner world of ideas, feelings, and images, and preferred to see the world in terms of possibilities.

No wonder I felt so at home on the trail, I thought. I had always known myself to be an Introvert. Now I could relax and claim my place among introverted thru-hikers. What a relief.

Picking up another book, I discovered something else that resonated with me in light of my experience on the trail. This author talked about the rhythm of thinking generated by walking, and the mind as a landscape of ideas and images that only a walking pace could traverse.

Hiking the trail in the past year had certainly been that for me. Walking had given me the time and opportunity to think and to travel the inner landscape of my mind as I traversed the outer landscape of the soaring, majestic, and mundane – more than two thousand miles of thoughts, experiences, and arrivals. I was more and more grateful for the enormous privilege that had been granted to me to dream, to think, to learn, just by walking.

Later that afternoon, I walked to the U.S. Forestry Service office for the required permit to hike in the Smoky Mountains National Park, and paid a visit to the outfitter on my way back. Dave, the outfitter, kindly trimmed the insoles that had been inserted into my boots; the insoles, we discovered, had caused the most recent set of blisters and, once trimmed, made it possible for me to hike without further damage to my feet.

17. The Great Smoky Mountains and Nantahala

Hot Springs, N.C., to Georgia State Line, 166 miles

June 15, 2002, to Davenport Gap Shelter, Tenn., 22 miles

After my last breakfast with Elmer and his family of hikers-turned-farmers, I hiked out to the trailhead. I regretted that I could not spend more time at Elmer's hostel and learn more about him; his life fascinated me. But, my short stay started healing my blisters, enlightened my mind, and refreshed my spirit. I was ready to climb to the grassy bald summit of Max Patch and continue my trek south, to Davenport Gap, the gateway to the Great Smoky Mountains National Park.

The wind on the summit of Max Patch was brisk when I reached it, but I was in top hiking form, hiking at a brisk pace all day.

Most of the hike was in the woods with only slight elevation changes, and I met no one until Brown Gap, where a troop of Boy Scouts and their leaders had set up camp. I had been impressed with the Boy Scouts all along the trail; they were unfailingly polite, considerate, and knowledgeable. These Scouts were no exception; we talked about the trail while I treated some water and ate a snack. I felt good about sharing the woods with them.

After I left the Scouts, I climbed again, steeply, up the eastern slope of Snowbird Mountain to its west peak. As I emerged from the woods, I noticed the ground had become deeply rutted and scarred, as though some giant had thundered by, pulled out the vegetation, and flung it to the side as he lumbered across the bald. At the top, under a stunning blue sky, a white cement structure, its flat, circular cap resting like an upside-down mushroom, broke the natural curving line of the land. This was an airplane tracking system, built by the Federal Aviation Administration in 1964, but it looked like an alien UFO that had cut down everything in its path, leaving the slope and crest of the mountain with only broken sticks, felled trees, dead branches, and scrubby underbrush struggling to prevent further erosion. The structure seemed a blatant disregard for the environment – such a contrast from the respectful conservation practiced by the Boy Scouts. My hope for the future of the environment lay with the Scouts.

Descending the other side of Snowbird Mountain, through sparse timber, I followed wooded hillsides for the remainder of the afternoon, and crossed the Pigeon River late in the day. The Pigeon River is less than a mile from the boundary into the Great Smoky Mountains National Park, and I was eager to reach the park, a milestone in my journey south. For the next seventy-two miles, between the Pigeon River and the Little Tennessee River, I would be hiking along the crest of the Smoky Mountains, the master chain of the southern Appalachians, on trails maintained by the National Park Service and the Smoky Mountains Hiking Club.[48]

Hiking across the mouth of Tobes Creek, I ascended by switchbacks past a large rock formation at the foot of tumbling cascades, filled my

48. The land for the national park began to be acquired in 1928; by 1935, 400,000 acres had been purchased by public and private donations and the Great Smoky Mountains National Park was formally dedicated in 1940, by President Franklin Roosevelt. Today, over 900 miles of trails crisscross the park. These trails are open to foot travel by hikers and horses, but not dogs. The National Park Service also maintains sixteen shelters (thirteen along the AT) and 98 campsites in the park. Shelter space along the AT is limited to one overnight stay for twelve to fourteen people, and, except for thru-hikers, is available only by reservation.

water bottles, and continued to climb along the State Line Branch, following the sound of rushing water until I came to an old dirt road. There I encountered several northbound thru-hikers, debating about where they should spend the night.

I wondered why they had passed the last shelter as they descended Cammerer Mountain; the shelter was less than a mile behind them, and my destination for the night.

When I reached the shelter, several thru-hikers and some teenaged boys from South Carolina, on a five-day hike through the Smokies, occupied it. The boys had reserved their space, but the thru-hikers had not. The shelter was crowded and as ugly to the eye as it was to the ear. A gray chain link fence, from ground to roof, stretched across the front of the structure and provided access through a heavy metal door. Every time the door opened, the air shook with a metal clanging and scraping sound. To me, it seemed a cumbersome way to protect life and property. Surely an educated shelter-public did not need to be caged from the wildlife.

The teenagers and their leaders turned out to be good company. They built a fire, cooked, and told stories about their adventure so far. After being by myself in so many shelters, it was novel to have so much company. I hadn't experienced such a crowd since the White Mountains in New Hampshire.

June 16, 2002, to Tri-Corner Knob Shelter, 14 miles

In the morning, before most of my shelter mates were awake and bustling about camp, I got up quietly, pulled my gear outside the shelter to pack without disturbing anyone, ate, and hiked out just as the birds began their cheerful exchange overhead. I knew I would miss the birds when my journey was finished.

The first four miles were straight up, four thousand feet along the slope of Mt. Cammerer to a spur on the Tennessee side of Sunup Knob. Traveling south, the view to my right (west) was of Tennessee, that to my left (east), North Carolina. Whichever direction, I discovered, the scenery was spectacular – green conifer growth below, blue sky and sunshine, above.

The day was cool, clear, and perfect for hiking – not rainy or smoked in by clouds as I had expected from the name, Smoky Mountains. All day

I walked along a ridge through spruce-fir forest, and noted the damage to the trees from the insect attack of the balsam wooly, and from wind blowing so strong that whole trees were uprooted and felled sideways, exposing their undergrowth as a vertical wall of tangled roots and dirt.

I passed only two other hikers, all day; they were going north. But even though I was by myself, I did not feel alone. It was easy to tell that the trails were well used, and well populated. In addition to the white blazes marking the AT, wooden or metal signs at each trail crossing, in each gap, and at every lookout announced the location and approximate distance to the next sign. There were so many signs, I put away my guidebook and map and just followed the trail, stopping to note my progress by reading the signs. It was a "no-brainer" way to hike, I thought, and definitely easier than trying to figure out the confusing contours of a topographic map.

When I reached Deer Creek Gap, the view of Mt Guyot, Luftee Knob, Balsam Corner, and Mt. Sterling was on the North Carolina side, across the mountains. Above the mountains, dark clouds were gathering, occasionally blocking the sun and casting everything in shadow. Not wanting to be caught again on a ridge in a thunderstorm, I hiked faster. The Tri-Corner Knob Shelter was only three miles south, just behind Mt. Guyot Spur, the highest point on the AT in the eastern Smokies. I reached it within an hour and decided to make camp, even though it was only five o'clock. I debated about whether to hike on to the next shelter, Pecks Corner, five miles south. However, that shelter was off the trail by half a mile, and the clouds overhead had become even darker and gloomier. I amused myself by painting a watercolor of the shelter from a downed tree three hundred yards away. It had rained before I reached the shelter and everything sparkled and dripped in the after-rain stillness.

By dinnertime, two groups had hiked in. One group was comprised of two men and four teenagers from Hawaii; the other was a group of self-proclaimed computer geeks from Alabama. None of the computer geeks had any experience in backcountry camping; it was their first night on the trail. The teenagers and I showed them how to light their stoves and set up their gear inside the shelter. The Alabamians drawled their appreciation and comments about life in the backwoods. Their lack of skill with anything except computers was somehow endearing. I enjoyed their dry humor.

After dinner, the temperature dropped way below Alabamian or Hawaiian standards; the boys gathered wood for a fire and soon the fire ring sputtered with wood smoke on wet logs. Eventually, a small fire did ignite and burn with cheer, if not warmth, but by then, I was tucked into my sleeping bag behind the chain-link barrier, safe from bears and other predators, and asleep in minutes. I slept soundly, but in the morning, the Hawaiians and Alabamians claimed to have heard all kinds of mysterious night noises.

June 17, 2002, to Gatlinburg, Tenn., 15 miles

The next morning was cold, gray, and damp, but it wasn't raining. I was glad for my warm gear, and for the first five miles hiking, wore it all. All morning I hiked at over six thousand feet, through heavy mist and cloud cover. I was disappointed not to be able to see the view of the headwaters of Eagle Rocks Creek when I reached the Eagle Rocks.

My destination was Gatlinburg, Tenn., via Newfound Gap, where I had a mail drop waiting for me at the Happy Hiker Outfitter on the edge of town.[49] I planned to spend the night in town and hitch back to the trail in the morning, to climb Clingmans Dome.

Continuing through the woods, I hiked at over five thousand feet all morning, through gaps and across ridges. By the time I reached Porters Mountain, where the trail followed the crest of a jagged range known as the Sawteeth, I was hot; the sun was high and the mist had burned off. I stopped at the first water I found, and patiently held my bottles to a seeping crack in the rock. Filling the bottles took a long time.

When I passed the side trail to Charlies Bunion, a group of young hikers scrambled ahead of me over the rocks to be first to climb the knob. I was too hot to care about the view from this climb and did not want to climb on rocks with twelve-year-olds; I passed the bunion by.

49. There is only one main road in the park. It bisects the park from east to west, connecting Gatlinburg, Tenn. and Cherokee, N.C. During the height of the summer, this road is clogged with traffic; off-season it is a winding, solitary corridor through the mountains. The AT crosses this road at Newfound Gap, approximately halfway between Gatlinburg and Cherokee. Most thru-hikers hitch a ride from the parking lot at Newfound Gap and pick up their mail drop in either Gatlinburg or Cherokee.

By early afternoon, I reached the Icewater Spring Shelter, situated in a grassy patch of meadow, just right for a break. I sat in the sun and took off my hot boots. My feet were healing nicely. I wriggled my free toes and stretched out on the grass to eat lunch. Several hikers wandered off the trail to look at the shelter. One couple with two young children came to reminisce; they had been thru-hikers ten years earlier and now, married, were eager to hike again with their children. Finally, a troop of Boy Scouts hiked in, and when they discovered how much of the trail I had already hiked, asked to interview me for their PowerPoint presentation.

I was surprised there were so many people in and out, until I looked at my map and discovered the shelter was only three miles from Newfound Gap directly below, and was the first stopping place for all the hikers from the parking lot enroute to the view from Charlies Bunion.

After lunch, I re-bandaged my feet, repositioned my pack, and hiked down to Newfound Gap, through a tall green forest and a southwest view of Clingmans Dome, my destination in the morning. It was an easy hike, and I reached the gap within an hour.

Emerging from the cool green woods to the glaring, noisy, parking area at Newfound Gap was shocking. The lot was full of cars, parked and moving in the roadway; people in summer clothes were everywhere, and the air was white hot. Coming from the woods, even though I had seen more and more people all day, I was stunned and dazed by the confusion. I ducked to the side of the road leading to Gatlinburg and stuck out my thumb.

Within two minutes, a bright pink Geo Tracker with its canvas flaps buckled and tidy stopped to enter the roadway. I called in to the driver, "Can you give me a lift to Gatlinburg?"

The driver pulled to the side of the road and I hopped into the backseat with his ten-year-old daughter. He and his wife sat in front and, as we sped down the roadway, they shouted to me from the front seat, their words lost in the wind streaming by. I finally was able to understand that they were from New Orleans, were staying outside of Gatlinburg in a large RV park, and had rented the little pink car for the day to see the Smoky Mountains. They were having a wonderful vacation and couldn't believe their luck at meeting a hiker.

There was a steady lane of cars ahead and behind us down the mountain, but, with the wind whipping at the canvas flaps and against my face and body, we seemed to be speeding out of control. It was the joyride from hell, though no one but me probably thought so.

At the edge of town, the Tracker dropped me off in the parking lot of the Happy Hiker Outfitter and I found my mail drop without further adventure. That night, I stayed in a low-budget motel with a discounted thru-hiker rate. I would only be in town overnight and had no interest in seeing the sights in Gatlinburg. If it hadn't been so late in the day, I would have hitched back to the trail. Instead, I took a shower, washed my clothes, and had dinner at a nearby restaurant: two pork chops, salad, corn, applesauce, and ice cream. Not bad for $6.95, I thought. But I was lonely in town and eager to be gone in the morning.

June 18, 2002, to Spence Field Shelter, 22 miles

At seven o'clock, the tourists in Gatlinburg were still in bed. I stood on the road at the edge of the park, thumb in the air, looking apprehensively at each car that passed. I continued to walk as I hitched, hoping someone would stop before I hiked all the way back, by roadway, to Newfound Gap.

I continued to hitch, continued to hope, but in half an hour only a handful of cars had passed me, and none were interested in giving me a ride. Finally, several miles later, a beat-up old luxury car swerved to the side of the road and stopped. I had a quick flashback to the pothead driver in Killington, Vermont last summer, and was pleasantly surprised when an older, affable man reached over to the passenger door and turned the door handle.

He was a taxi driver, going to pick up an early hiker fare at a trailhead west of Newfound Gap, and would be glad to shuttle me to their pick-up point. Relieved and grateful, I settled in to enjoy the ride.

My benefactor had lived in the area all his life and had a lot to tell me about the trails in the Smoky Mountains and the town of Gatlinburg. By the time we reached the trailhead to pick up his hikers, he told me that he would take me farther, to my trailhead, if his hikers didn't mind.

We arrived at the hiker's trailhead before the hikers did, and I listened to more stories while we waited for them. Soon a small car pulled in to the space next to us and a young man and woman got out. They were our hikers, James and Diana.

James and Diana did not mind dropping me at my destination at all. In fact, they were envious of my hike and told me some of the impressive places they had hiked, and alerted me to the beauty of the hike I had ahead of me on the other side of Clingmans Dome. Employed as chefs at a nearby country club, James and Diana hiked, they said, every time they had a day off. James' descriptions of their hikes were surprisingly poetic, keen, and crisp. I liked his enthusiasm and the way he used words to describe what he saw and felt as he hiked.

We shook hands at the trailhead and hiked on in separate directions, James and Diana to their car north, me towards Fontana Dam, south.

It was a beautiful day to hike in the mountains. The early mist in the valley cleared to bright sunshine, clear views, and comfortable hiking temperatures by midmorning. The time passed quickly as I hiked along the crest of Mt. Mingus through the woods, and then along the state line ridge to the summit of Mt. Collins, Mt. Love, and finally, to the summit of Clingmans Dome (6,643'), the highest mountain on the AT.

The summit of Clingmans Dome, like the summit of Mt. Washington in New Hampshire, has buildings and parking lots and can be reached by car along a paved road. The observation tower at the top, however, is less elaborate than the complex on Mt. Washington. On this clear summer day, the view from the tower was magnificent: wave upon wave of green, dark green, and deep blue mountains as far as I could see, blending into the clouds overhead like the surface of a turbulent ocean tossing and licking the prow of a ship.

The afternoon's hike was strenuous, ascending and descending elevations between five and six thousand feet. I saw few other hikers, and most of the day I just walked, looking at the views on either side, sometimes both sides at once, lost in the beauty of the day.

James' poetic enthusiasm earlier that morning had reminded me again of the spirituality found in the present moment. Though I was eager to reach my destination, I did not want to blinker my senses to the beauty along the way. I wanted to be as open and receptive to the majesty all around me and see it as vividly and poetically as James had, preserving it in memory: *In old age, wandering on a trail of beauty, lively may I walk.* The trail, and the people on it, continued to teach me. *In old age, wandering on a trail of beauty, living again may I walk.*

In the late afternoon, I crossed a rocky, dirt road looking for the path to the shelter at Spence Field. Half a mile later, I was glad to be there; it had been a long, though beautiful, day and I was ready to rest.

Two men, section hikers, were settled at the shelter, and had already finished eating when I hiked in. I inquired about water and they told me that it was back down the slope along that dirt road I had passed on my way in. I looked at their abundant water supply. Chivalry, apparently, was dead; the men kept their supply to themselves.

I set down my pack, picked up my water bottles and cooking water bag, and hiked back out, half-mile to the road, another quarter mile to the water, and then back up again, retracing my steps to the shelter, an extra mile and a half at the end of a very long day. I remembered why the logistics of the trail sometimes outweighed its beauty. Finding water at the end of the day, coping with bugs, dirt, hunger, and fatigue, not to mention weather and fear — all these had to be figured into the equation of beauty. Keeping a balance, I decided, was the best I could do. The trail would never be easy, no matter how much I learned or how hard I tried. Beautiful, yes. Easy, no.

Spence Field Shelter was another old, stone cage, and even though there were level places around the shelter where I could camp, the two men convinced me to stay inside, for fear of bears. The rigging for hanging our packs and food bags was very elaborate, as was the chain-link cage.

I didn't mind obliging their request, and locked myself in for the night as soon as I finished stowing my gear in a patch of woods, out of reach of the tallest critter.

June 19, 2002, to Fontana Dam, 16 miles

No bears or other visitors interrupted the night. I was up and out of the shelter by seven o'clock, walking through sparse woods and open meadows still wet with morning dew. The land sloped gently and, dotted with the silhouettes of trees, seemed enchanted in the hushed and mysterious early light.

My hike was a continuous ascent and descent, from gaps to knobs to gaps again, covering more than eleven trail miles, all above four thousand feet until the end of the morning. I left the crest of the Great Smokies and turned south along a spur ridge to Shuckstack Mountain.

I could see Clingmans Dome over my left shoulder as I walked along the ridge crest south. A cool breeze blew at my back, making the noon-day heat bearable.

When I reached an old road leading to the fire tower on Shuckstack, I met a couple sitting on the side of the trail, eating lunch. They invited me to join them and said they would watch my pack while I ran up the road to the fire tower; the view should not be missed.

It seemed churlish to refuse their trailside hospitality, though I doubt-ed that anyone would be interested in my sweaty pack or its contents. Slipping my pack to the ground, I thanked them and hiked a quarter mile up the hill to see the view from the fire tower.

My experience with fire towers, thus far, had been ambiguous: they always seemed flimsy and unsafe, and to see anything at all, had to be climbed, dizzyingly, breathlessly, swayingly, to a small, usually crowded apex, reached by crawling through a hole in the upper floor. Sometimes the view wasn't worth the climb.

This tower had the usual missing railings and floorboards, but the view, as I climbed, was worth it: the crest line of the Smokies from Thunderhead to Clingmans Dome, Hangover to the southeast, the Nantahala mountains to the south, Fontana Lake below, and the Little Tennessee River, meandering west, serene and simple in the early after-noon sun. The wind at the top of the tower was breathtaking, as well, so after I snapped several panoramic pictures, I was happy to return to earth and *The Sandwich* waiting for me below.

The guardians of my pack were professors from a nearby college. They told me something about the history of Fontana Dam and Village, five trail miles away.[50] It was possible, they said, to take a shuttle from the

50. Fontana Dam is part of the TVA system built on Little Tennessee River during WWII for hydroelectric power. The dam itself is four hundred eighty feet high, the sixth highest in the US, and the lake it creates is twenty-nine miles long and forms the southern boundary of the Great Smoky Mountains National Park. Fontana Village, at the base of the Yellow Creek Mountains, is three miles from the dam and originally housed TVA construction workers. In 1946 the village was leased to a private company to provide for public recreation.

dam to the village and stay overnight at the lodge for a reduced hiker rate that also included an AYCE dinner and breakfast buffet.

All the way down the mountain I considered whether I should stay in the village. The AT shelter on the shore of the lake had a reputation as the "Fontana Hilton," and I knew I would be able to have a shower at the visitor's center at the dam, not far from the shelter. However, I was curious about the village and wanted to see it, as well.

When I approached the dam from the woods, I was surprised to see that it was deserted, having expected a parking lot full of cars, tourists, and bustle. As I crossed the dam, I saw only a handful of cars in the parking lot, and only one couple strolling on the bridge.

Out of the woods, the heat was oppressive and the white concrete of the dam dazzled my eyes. I decided to shower at the visitor's center, catch the shuttle to the village, and then return to the shelter for the night. It would mean carrying my pack to the village, but that would save steps in the long run.

As I reached the visitor's center, the shuttle was just leaving for the village, so I took advantage of the timing and postponed my shower until later.

It seemed like a long ride, over the winding country road, and the village, when we reached it, barely lived up to its name. Along the side of the road, on a hillside, a covered wooden boardwalk connected several buildings: a post office, general store, and a restaurant that was closed. Across the road, a large baseball diamond led up another hill to the outfitter and recreation center.

Several northbound hikers were on the boardwalk in front of the post office rearranging their packs. They told me that the post office had just closed, but, since I did not have a mail drop or anything to send on, it wasn't a problem for me. I did wonder, however, where everyone was. Other than the hikers and the clerk in the general store, no one else was about, and there was not much fresh food at the general store. I bought some grapes and an ice cream cone and went across the road to the outfitter to inquire about the shuttle back to the dam.

The clerk at the outfitter assured me that someone would take me back to the dam in about half an hour. As I sat down to wait, it occurred to me that the recreation center might have a shower. When I asked, the clerk said, "Sure," and pointed to the shower room through some glass doors.

Ten refreshing minutes later when I emerged from the shower, the clouds outside the glass doors were black. A thunderstorm had blown into the valley, and we were in for our share. As this information registered, the hikers from the post office walked in.

"We can stay at the lodge, have dinner and breakfast for twenty dollars," they said. "With a storm coming in, what do you think?"

I agreed, but didn't want to wait for a shuttle back to the trail in the morning; I had a significant climb of two thousand feet in two miles, first thing, and wanted to get an early start.

"That's no problem," the clerk said. "You can hitch a ride from the night watchman, going off duty at six a.m."

Another rumble from the clouds overhead convinced me. The two northbounders and I settled into the minibus and the driver shuttled us to the lodge, in the center of a cluster of cabins a mile away.

The other hikers were Hiep, from Vietnam by way of California, and Dave, from Arkansas. We met up again in the dining room for the AYCE buffet. Hiep reminded me of Metro, my friend from the Maine woods; he talked as fast, with so much energy and wit I could hardly keep up with him. He had just finished hiking the Pacific Crest trail and expected to finish the AT by mid-October. If he hiked as fast as he talked, I thought, he would have no trouble reaching Katahdin before it closed for the winter.

I slept well under a solid roof, listening to the rain blow around the buildings. It had been a good few days in the Smokies, but I was glad to be heading south, out of the national park system. Because of the volume of hikers through national parks, the regulations and precautions were necessary, I supposed, but also intrusive. I much preferred hiking in less traveled areas, without the elaborate bear bag cables, camping in my tent rather than a caged shelter, enjoying the quiet by myself or with just a few other people.

I had read all the park signs and respected their system, but I was happy to be on my own again, on Frost's "road less traveled." I looked forward to the Nantahala and Blue Ridge Mountains of North Carolina and north Georgia – wilder, more rugged hiking – and then to reaching my destination.

June 20, 2002, to Locust Cove Gap, 18 miles

The difference between hiking in the Smokies and in the Nantahala National Forest was immediately apparent.

The night watchwoman picked us up at five forty-five and dropped us at the trailhead before six o'clock. At that hour, after a rainy night, the air was dark, wet, and cold. A photo shows the three of us, me, Hiep, and Dave, packed and suited up, ready to hike into the gloomy, dripping forest – me heading south, they heading north.

Waving goodbye, I turned and climbed the stone steps into the woods, alone with my pack, poles, and wits, to find my way to Georgia. I wondered, briefly, if the bears that everyone feared in the Smokies knew that I was now across the boundary of the National Park system; I hoped I would not encounter an early morning marauder, as I had on a similar wet morning in New Jersey a year ago. I didn't feel any braver now – only luckier.

As anticipated, my first climb was straight up, from seventeen to thirty-seven hundred feet in two and a half miles. I was surprised to reach the high rocks past Walker Gap in only an hour and a half. Though I could not yet see the sun, the woods were light and fresh; it would be a good day to hike.

Wondering for the thousandth time how the early morning could be so cold and the day following it so hot, I stopped to take off my hat, gloves, and fleece and pare down to tee shirt and shorts. The morning passed quickly. I encountered only a bobcat on the slope of Tommy Knob. I could see him watching me from the trail ahead and kept a significant distance between us. It felt like we were sharing the trail, if only briefly; I thanked him for his company before he disappeared into the forest. It was nice to be back with the animals, I thought, away from the intersecting trails and signposts of the Smokies.

By noon I had reached Brown Fork Gap Shelter, where I stopped for water and a snack. Another hiker at the shelter told me that he had begun the trail at Springer Mountain in April but had quit after the first week because the weather had been so cold. He was back, hiking south to his getting-off-place, taking his time. Having just retired, with the rest of his life to hike, he wanted to enjoy it.

I couldn't help agreeing with his point of view. There were many ways to hike the trail, I had discovered, but taking one's time to enjoy it seemed the best way of all. If I were to do it again, I would do it in smaller pieces, and not have a schedule. However, this close to the end of my journey, I needed to stay on task. After lunch, I left him at the shelter and hiked on. I was eager to reach the Nantahala Outdoor Center for a mail drop the next day.

The afternoon was sunny and warm, and though I could not see much of the sun through the woods, I did catch glimpses now and then. It was not strenuous walking, but the continuous ups and downs were tiring.

About four o'clock, as I reached the crest of a ridge, I started to hear thunder in the distance, coming from the west. The trees were still quiet, the sun overhead still bright, but I didn't trust the clouds in the higher elevations, though I could not see them through the trees. The next shelter was five miles farther, over Cheoah Bald, and I knew I didn't want to be on a bald in a thunderstorm. I decided to head for the next gap with water and stay overnight if a storm materialized.

Locust Cove Gap, at thirty-seven hundred feet, is an open depression between two wooded slopes, with several level places for camping and a water source two hundred feet below. When I reached the gap, I could finally see dark, dangerous-looking clouds overhead. The wind had picked up and birds were chattering warnings through the trees. I dropped my pack and went down the slope for water. The woods were charged with energy.

Scrambling back up the hill to the clearing, I watched the trees overhead, now bending to the wind, whipping their leaves backwards. The thunder was closer, and louder; I knew I didn't have a minute to spare.

Unzipping the bottom of my pack, I said a quick thank you to my earlier organization: my tent and raingear were easily accessible without opening the top of my pack. I pulled out my tent and began to assemble the tent poles. The wind was fierce and grabbed the edges of my tent, billowing the fabric, trying to wrestle it out of my hands.

On my hands and knees, I quickly assembled my tent. A loud crack of thunder directly overhead opened the clouds. Without looking up, I threw my pack inside the tent and crawled in as the first hailstones hit the roof. I wanted to inflate my air mattress inside, so that I could avoid lightning if it hit the ground and traveled towards me in a stream.

The storm seemed to be blowing directly at me, through the gap between the shoulders of the knobs on either side of me. I had scanned the trees for loose branches when I initially dropped my pack, but by the time I set up my tent, the wind was blowing too hard to know if it was really safe.

Under the flimsy roof of the tent, I inflated my air mattress, pulled myself into a crouch position, and ducked my head onto my knees. The hail continued to batter the roof and thunk against the ground. A wide stream of water rushed along the side of my tent, barely a foot away. Thunder roared, lightning flashed and then flashed again. I had never been so close to a thunderstorm. My body tingled from the vibrations in the earth and sky. I felt like I was at the very center, the bulls-eye in the target for Zeus' fury. I was at the mercy of the elements that were way beyond my power to control. Once again, I knew I was but a tiny speck in the universe – and not a very important speck, at that.

The storm raged for over half an hour. My body cramped from its crouched position and eventually, I sat down, and then lay down, still curled, on the air mattress. I had not heard any trees breaking or falling, and though it was still raining hard, the hail had grown smaller and finally stopped altogether. Eventually I could hear the thunder move away from directly overhead, but I was still worried that lightning might strike in the clearing in front of my tent.

The rain continued for another half hour, but the storm moved on. I dozed, listening to the rain and receding thunder, not really asleep. Eventually, the rain ceased and a patch of sunlight hit my tent roof and startled me fully awake. I unzipped my tent and crawled out to check for damages. The pack cover and water bottles that I had left outside were covered with dirt and wet forest duff. The ground swirled in muddy streams, rushing downhill past my tent.

But the birds resumed their singing and the sun made diamonds of the drops of water clinging to leaves and grass. It was a miracle. Only the dripping trees belied any change from the hot, sunny afternoon I had come to expect along the two thousand miles of my summer journey. By now it was six o'clock and I didn't feel like breaking camp to hike over Cheoah Bald to the next shelter.

I found a wet log, instead, and sat down to cook supper and write in my journal. It would be an early night; I was tired from the adrenalin rush of the early morning climb, the bobcat, and the drama at the center of a late afternoon thunderstorm.

I called George and told him about my adventurous day. He was impressed that I had known what to do. I was impressed that I had lived through it. I knew that whatever I had done would have been for naught if a tree had fallen or lightning had struck. I had only hung on and hoped for the best. Never had I felt so vulnerable.

That night I hung my food over the highest branch I could reach with the rope I used for such occasions. Any hungry bear would find this laughable, I thought, as I tied the rope to a nearby tree. My system was not quite as elaborate as that used in the Smokies, but it would do for the night. I wasn't afraid of losing my food bag to a bear.

June 21, 2002, to Nantahala Outdoor Center, 10 miles

In the morning, the bear bag was hanging where I left it the night before, unmolested and nearly empty. I would pick up more food at the Nantahala Outdoor Center later in the day, so the bag held only breakfast, lunch, and snacks. I had perfected, it seemed, the art of carrying only what I needed between food drops and had learned to take advantage of package pickup other than the U.S. Post Office.[51]

After breakfast, I broke camp and hiked twelve hundred feet up to the ridge crest of Cheoah Bald. On the way, I encountered a huge blowdown, perhaps from the night before. The tree had stood on the slope above the

---

51. The AT passes through the middle of the Nantahala Outdoor Center (NOC) on the Nantahala River. The NOC provides a number of services to hikers, kayakers, and rafters, including a base camp for overnight stays, restaurants, an outfitter, and parcel post service.

trail and had been knocked over so that its trunk and many leaves lay across the path, heading down. It was impossible to climb over the tree and impossible to climb the slope above it. I could only descend to the place where the branches had more space between them.

It took some time to navigate, with my pack, and then regain the trail. I knew the storm had been a fierce one and I was grateful, once again, that nothing had blown down on me. Until they fall, tall trees seem graceful and benign; on the ground, they are heavy, awkward, and wide spreading. It would be hard to escape a tree falling in your direction, I thought, especially in the woods where navigable paths are narrow and underbrush dense.

The morning passed quickly as I hiked through hardwoods, descending, ascending, and then descending again along switchbacks to the railroad tracks and finally across the bridge into the Nantahala Outdoor Center.

Here, my expectations were once again upended. I expected a bigger Nolichucky Johnny outfitter and hostel. I found, instead, a large complex of buildings, busses, cars, and crowds of shrieking young people, rafting in the white water under the bridge, gathered in groups at the snack bars, and walking together with too-full packs, setting out on backcountry adventures.

The sun was hot and I was eager to retrieve my mail drop from the outfitter, find a restaurant for lunch, and be on my way. But the outfitter could not locate my parcel and suggested I try the business office, several buildings away on the other side of the campus. The business office could not find my food drop, either. They suggested I try the central receiving area, in yet another corner of the sprawling complex. It was Friday afternoon and the office workers were eager to close for the weekend. If I could not find my mail drop, I would have to hitch a ride to Bryson City, thirteen miles east, and find a grocery store; the outfitter had only expensive short-term resupply, and not enough to last until my next mail drop, five days away.

I walked back to a building where I had begun my package hunt. The volunteer inside suggested that I reserve a bunk at their base camp for the night, leave my pack with her, and go find something to eat while she tried to locate my food drop. I appreciated her helpfulness, though I didn't want to spend the night. However, my options were limited at that point, so I unstrapped my pack, left it behind her desk, and headed to the restaurant across the parking lot.

The volunteer found my package back at Central Receiving while I was eating. Though they were closed for the weekend, someone would come open the building so I could find it.

By the time everything was located, it was past five o'clock in the afternoon. I dragged myself up a steep hill to base camp and found a bunk in a complex of tiny rooms next to a large reception hall. A church group from South Carolina had rented the reception hall for the weekend.

A young botanist named Plantman and I were the only hikers there. Plantman had been hiking for a week, collecting information for the Appalachian Trail Conference about non-native plants that were encroaching the trail. He wanted some help reorganizing his pack. With his research equipment and donations from helpful supporters, he had been carrying more than eighty pounds of gear over the Georgia/North Carolina mountains.

Feeling like his grandmother, I tried to help him sort out his stuff. We trimmed his pack by at least twenty pounds by eliminating the padded cases for his equipment. Then we started paring his clothing and food. I remembered how over-packed I had been when I first began my trek and tried to help Plantman think in terms of multiple uses for everything he carried. By the end of the evening, his pack weighed less than half its original weight, a respectable forty pounds.

He went to dinner with the church group and I repacked my own gear. Within a few minutes, someone rapped loudly on the screen door of my room. It was a man from the church group, hoping I would join their fellowship for dinner. Even though I wasn't hungry, it seemed boorish to refuse, so I climbed the stairs to the reception hall and joined them.

There were about thirty adults and teenagers in the group, sitting at long tables, eating sumptuously. More interesting than the menu, however, was the social stratification of the assembly. The men sat together, talking loudly about their days' adventure on the river. The teenaged boys sat with the men and listened. The women also sat together, but were more mobile than the men. Whenever anyone needed or wanted any-thing, one of the women would jump up and get it. The teenaged girls stayed in the kitchen, with a few older women, serving, washing dishes, and cleaning up.

When I came in, dinner was almost over. Plantman called to me and I joined him, not realizing, initially, that I was flaunting a social rule.

I listened to the talk around the table as I ate my salad. One of the men was talking about his job as a spokesman (sic) for the Wild Turkey Federation of America. He explained that it was a conservation group whose purpose was to save the species from extinction by sowing fields with wheat, corn, and grain, collecting huge flocks of wild turkeys in one place. He was passionate about his work, and very proud.

Since I was eating his food, I merely listened, but when I innocently asked him if wild turkeys continued to be hunted, he only stared at me. Finally, he said,

"Well, ma'am, that's why we're feedin' them."

His concept of the word "conservation" had never occurred to me.

After dinner, several men brought a huge wooden cross, in pieces, up the stairs and through the door of the recreation center. Others pushed back the tables and assembled the benches in a row. Our hosts invited Plantman and me to worship with them.

We begged off.

Later, in my bunk, I fell asleep to singing and praising that lasted long into the night. The soft strains of "Amazing Grace" and "Abide With Me" wafted through the screened windows and under my door, curling like smoke and evaporating in the darkness of my tiny bunkroom, coloring my dreams with sadness.

I went to sleep knowing I was in the South.

June 22, 2002, to Burningtown Gap, N.C., 13 miles

At dawn when I visited the bathhouse to brush my teeth, I met one of the churchwomen of the night before. She was hot-rolling her hair and applying makeup. Our eyes met in the mirror. We couldn't have been more different, but a flicker of mutual understanding passed between us: isn't this make-up stuff silly, especially in the woods. We smiled. I thanked her, again, for the evening meal and the fellowship, and bid her a pleasant good day.

Plantman and I walked down the hill to the restaurant overlooking the trail. I wished him luck with his research, and he told me several more ways he intended to lighten his pack. I had enjoyed our brief meeting and conversation, but was eager to hike out. I left him taking samples of Boston ivy planted in a box on the side of the trail, technically a non-native plant, and technically, encroaching the AT.

It was another hot day climbing up, down and across ridges, through the woods, searching for water. I passed several groups of young people, hiking into or out of the Nantahala Outdoor Center, and climbed another fire tower at Wesser Bald. On the tower I met two well-dressed couples my age, relaxing after their short climb from the parking lot below. We chatted, briefly, and when I inquired about the nearest water supply, they offered me theirs.

"We're hiking right back down to our car," they insisted. "Please drink as much as you want."

I accepted their water, with thanks, and drank it on the spot. I noted the similarities in our manner and spent the rest of the afternoon dreaming about retiring in the Nantahala Mountain Range. I loved the trees soaring all around me. They reminded me of the trees in New Hampshire around my childhood summer cottage on Laurel Lake. I wondered if George would like it here as much as I did; the location, halfway between Ohio and Florida, would make sense for us, and I could feel at home in these woods. Maybe we could find some land here, and do trail maintenance in retirement, I mused.

I hiked on, considering what it would be like to live in these mountains. I climbed the west side of Rocky Bald, Black Bald, and Tellico Bald, and then around the west side of Copper Ridge Bald before descending into the gap and the shelter where I planned to spend the night. The shelter sat on a rocky slope just above a shallow, bubbling stream. Both the stream and the shelter were infested with mosquitoes. I filled my water bottles and decided to hike on and look for a level place to camp, away from the bugs. I continued another mile before coming to Burningtown Gap, an open grassy site of a former orchard. I set down my pack and went to find water. The source was dry, but I had filled up at the shelter and thought I would have enough until morning. I returned to camp and set up my tent.

As I was about to start cooking, someone appeared suddenly through the woods. It was a bearded young man, a section hiker, he said, going to the next shelter. He asked me if I needed anything. It was such an unusual question from a fellow hiker, I responded truthfully.

"More water would be nice," I said. "The source here is dry."

Without skipping a beat, the hiker handed me his full water bottle, insisting that he could get more at the shelter I had passed earlier.

I agreed and accepted the water. Then the hiker asked me what the best part of my hike had been.

It was another unusual question, from a hiker passing by, and I replied that I loved walking in the woods. That was true, but the first answer that had occurred to me was, "meeting people like you." Afraid he would misunderstand, I talked about walking in the woods, and then included the spontaneous acts of kindness from people I met along the way, who generously offered food, water, shelter, or a shuttle without any need for repayment or even thanks. This natural kindness on the trail had been the rule, not the exception, and I had experienced it both north and south. That generous spirit affirmed the American people, for me, and gave me hope for the future of our country.

I also told him I liked the long stretches of time the trail had given me to think and still be moving, physically, towards a goal. It had been tiring, and hot, and sweaty, I said, and the camping and not-really-comfortable sleeping accommodations had grown old. Occasionally I had been frightened or unsure of myself, but more often I had been surprised at how capable and competent I was. I had learned a lot about my body, I told him, and how it functions best, and I learned that it was okay to be an introvert and heed my intuition and intelligence. I learned that I have good judgment and can get along on my own if I have to, I added. All that learning – that was the best part of the trail, for me, I concluded.

Later, I thought he might have been asking about the scenery.

June 23, 2002, to Franklin, N.C., 16 miles

I had been awakened during the night by rain hitting the roof of my tent. I groaned and turned over; maybe it would be gone by morning.

In the morning, everything outside my tent was soaked: pack, food bag, trees, grass, and trail. Everything inside my tent was damp: clothes, sleeping bag, boots, maps, journal, and me. There was nothing to do but wriggle into my clothes, rain gear, and boots, pack up my sleeping bag, mat, and books while crouching inside the tent, and shake out the worst of the wet before stowing the tent in the bottom section of my pack.

When I rescued my food bag from its protective tree branch, it was heavy with rain and five days' resupply. I tried to ignore the water running down my sleeves, making my hands slippery. This was not my favorite way to begin the day. I hiked out.

Within an hour, I was as wet inside my raingear as I was outside. When I came upon a group of young hikers from the NOC camped by a stream, I noted their plight. Sitting around their campsite, in the rain, they were wet and miserable. I knew how they felt, but thought I was better off moving than they were, sitting.

In about an hour, I climbed seven hundred feet and reached the stone tower at the summit of Wayah Bald. It had a roof over its upper floor and I quickly scrambled up to have some breakfast. My granola was soggy and the powdered milk lumpy, but at least I was out of the rain, if briefly, to enjoy the break. I called George and reported the rain. He sympathized but I could tell by his voice he wouldn't have traded places with me for the world.

I stopped to read the information panels on the graded path from the parking lot to the tower. I was always moved by these tributes to the men responsible for creating and maintaining the first trails and fire towers. It would surprise and please them, I thought, to know how many people enjoyed the results of their vision and hard work.[52] Standing in the rain, surrounded by fog overhead and puddles underfoot, I thanked them.

The rain continued for the rest of the morning and into the afternoon. By early afternoon, I had reached the summit of Siler Bald and took a side trail down an old logging road to the Siler Bald Shelter to eat my lunch. The shelter was nice. Situated on the edge of a field, it had a large

52. The stone tower at the summit of Wayah Bald, the John B. Byrne Memorial tower, was named to honor the first supervisor for the Nantahala National Forest, who came to the fire tower in 1933 and died a year later of injuries incurred from poisonous gas during service in France in WWI, from descriptive panels at the tower, 2002.

overhanging roof, counter space for cooking, and benches – all under cover. I suspended my tent and rain gear around the shelter, hoping to dry out some of it, and ate a leisurely, relatively dry lunch. Sitting with my feet up, back against the side of the shelter, I listened to the rain on the tin roof overhead. It sounded twice as loud and four times as fierce. But I was dry and able to relax, wring out my wet socks, and figure out what to do next.

The hiker who had given me water at the campsite the night before had also told me about hitching to Franklin and then catching a free shuttle back to the trail. The members of the Nantahala Hiking Club, he said, were dedicated to helping hikers, and the motel at the edge of town would give me a list of people ready to shuttle me back to the trail. I decided to keep my options open and hiked out, into the rainy afternoon.

By midafternoon, I reached Winding Stair Gap and the trail crossing over a paved highway, U.S. 64, into Franklin, N.C. As I came out of the woods, the rain stopped and the sun made a brief, welcome appearance. Hoping this meant the weather would clear, I hiked on another three miles, across a slight rise through the woods to Wallace Gap and the trail crossing of Old U.S. 64 to Franklin. By this time, the sun had disappeared again, and the clouds overhead looked gray and gloomy. Kicking myself for passing up an opportunity to hitch into Franklin at the new highway, I began to cross the old paved road.

A pickup truck drove by and stopped. The older man inside asked if I would like a ride into Franklin. Looking him over for possible danger, I decided to take a chance on the trail manners of the people of Franklin and accept.

I hopped into the cab and he turned the truck around and drove me to the outskirts of Franklin and the nicest, newest, cleanest Microtel I had ever seen, up the hill from an AYCE Shoney's restaurant. My ride apologized for not being able to take me back to the trail in the morning, but told me to call anyone on the NHC list at the motel desk. Someone would be sure to come for me, he said.

Now I knew I wanted to retire in the Nantahala Mountains; I could join the NHC and shuttle tired, wet hikers back and forth to the Microtel, I thought.

I checked into the motel and immediately took my wet gear to the side entryway at end of the building. I tied my bear bag rope around the pillars of the portico, hung up my clothes, and spread my sleeping bag and tent on the bushes and grass. The sun came out again from behind huge purple, white, and pink clouds, cleaning the view, as does a soft cloth to a smudged mirror. The wind was brisk and strong; my gear would be dry in no time.

I sat with my back to a pillar and watched the clouds rolling across the sky. Almost at the end of my journey, a night in a clean, dry motel appealed to me. The room was the size of a cabin on a well-appointed ship; it met my needs perfectly. I called several people on the NHC list of members willing to shuttle hikers and lined one up for eight o'clock the next morning. It meant a later start to my day than usual, but a start with dry feet and gear and stomach full of fresh food would make the twenty-mile hike easier.

At dinner I met an interesting couple, Bobby and Glenda, from Cordele, Georgia. We were all waiting for a table at Shoney's, and when a table became available, the hostess asked if we were together. Chuckling, I invited them to join me, and they graciously accepted.

They had just driven in from southern Georgia, they said, for a mountain respite from the heat. Bobby was a Pentecostal preacher and had recently purchased the family homestead from his eleven brothers and sisters and, planning to farm in his retirement, had restored its log cabin house and barns. He intended to give away all of his produce to whoever needed it. Glenda talked about her grandchildren and Bobby talked about the farm. I loved listening to their soft southern accents and the gentle way they interacted with each other and with me. They were interested in my hike, but equally interested in telling me about themselves.

When we parted after dinner, I felt that I had brushed shoulders with Jimmy and Rosalind Carter. Glenda and Bobby seemed the same sort of down-to-earth, genuinely kind, intelligent people.

June 24, 2002, to Standing Indian Shelter, 20 miles

At eight o'clock sharp the next morning, Charlie McLaughlin of the NHC pulled his pickup truck to the front of the Microtel and I climbed into the cab. Talkative and friendly, Charlie told me about the hiking club as we drove back to the trailhead. It was a beautiful morning. After the steady rain of the day before, the blue skies were a welcome sight.

My goal was to hike twenty miles, over Albert Mountain to the shelter at Standing Indian Mountain. Looking at the map, I saw a crosshatch of other trails that could be used in bad weather to eliminate miles and climbs to my destination. But the weather today was perfect for hiking and climbing mountains; I did not anticipate thunderstorms until late afternoon, if then. I would climb Albert Mountain before noon and would probably be at the shelter on Standing Indian Mountain by the time any storms hit. Besides, I wanted to hike the AT, not the loop trails, though they would be good day hikes on another vacation.

All morning, through the woods, I daydreamed about living and hiking in these Nantahala Mountains, working on a trail maintenance crew, helping preserve the beauty of the trails. Somehow, the scale of these mountains and the ruggedness of these trails appealed to me more than any I had encountered. The trail maintainers and hikers I had met here made be think that George and I would be welcomed into this community; we would feel at home in these woods.

By midmorning, I reached the summit of Albert Mountain and climbed the fire tower to look out over the Little Tennessee River Valley below and the Blue Ridge mountains to the east. Above, I noticed, the clouds were gathering again for some threatening weather. After my thunderstorm experience in the high mountains a few days before, the look of these clouds made me wary. Remembering the crosshatch of alternate trails, I was reassured, but did not tarry, climbing down over rocks the trail guide forecast to be worse than they actually were.

After the rocks of New England, the rocks in the south were easy to navigate, and my legs and ankles, by this time, were tough and agile. In fact, now that my blisters were almost healed, my body felt better than it ever had. Well nourished, rested, and strong, I was no longer plagued by fatigue, dizziness, or disorientation at the end of the day, as I had been the summer before. I had never felt better or more in harmony with my body and my surroundings, experiencing a calmness that came from self-confidence and respect for the universe and my place in it.

Peace Pilgrim wrote about the inner peace that comes from walking, as the precursor to global peace.

> "All of us can work for peace. We can work right where we are, within ourselves, because the more peace we have within our own lives, the more we can reflect into the outer situation… peace within ourselves [is] a step toward peace in our world."[53]

Physically, intellectually, socially, and spiritually, I understood Peace Pilgrim's simple message and hoped I could remember that feeling of oneness and harmony when I was back in the complicated world of business, family, and social interaction. With all the hardships of the walker's life, its reward of inner peace was sweet.

Continuing my walk, through tall trees and grassy understory, I entered the southern Nantahala Wilderness Area and ascended Little Ridgepole Mountain, leaving the Nantahalas for the Blue Ridge. The sun came in and out through the trees, making the hike pleasant, dry, and effortless. I stopped for lunch in the woods, bypassing the Carter Gap Shelter, and met other hikers on and off throughout the day. By late afternoon, I again heard thunder in the west, though the sun still shone through the trees. Alert to the possibility of another late afternoon storm, I listened attentively, but none of the other storm signs were present. The birds and wind were calm, the sky was clear; I predicted the thunder would blow elsewhere and calmly climbed to the summit of Standing Indian Mountain, the highest point in the trail south of the Great Smokies. I was eager to see where I would hike in the next few days.

The view at the top was green, placid, and welcoming. In five days, I would be on Springer Mountain.

Standing Indian Shelter was empty when I reached it, but when I returned from filling my water bottles at the stream, a group of teenaged girls and their leaders had hiked in for the night. They were learning how to function as a group and quickly took over the shelter with their packs, gear, and food. I was happy to give up the space, but their leaders insisted that the girls make room for me in the shelter.

---

53. Peace Pilgrim, Steps Toward Inner Peace, Friends of Peace Program, Somerset, California, p.4.

That night, nine of us were tucked in together, warm and giggling in the dark, quiet woods. It was the first time in two thousand miles that I had been in an exclusively female shelter. The emphasis of the leaders was on sharing and cooperation, and the girls worked well together gathering wood and water, building a fire, cooking, making camp, and getting along in general. I enjoyed their company. Their camp songs reminded me of my camp days as a child and with my own daughters, at Camp Miniwanca in Michigan, the home of my Summer Seminars for Women.

Life had a way of coming full circle, I mused as I fell asleep to the girls' singing. A circle of women at the end, as at the beginning of my hike, seemed appropriate and complete.

18. Springer

"It is finished in beauty."

North Carolina/Georgia State Line
to Springer Mountain, Ga., 83.8 miles

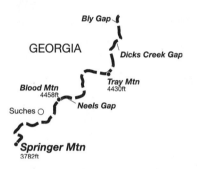

June 25, 2002, to Deep Gap Shelter, 21.5 miles

Even without the wooden sign posted on a tree, I would have known I was in Georgia: the soil turned to red clay almost immediately, the humidity edged up a notch, and the bugs swirled in front of my head like a tiny black smoke screen. But I was thrilled to finally be there. I sat down in the first available shade, under a deformed tree with a trunk horizontal to the ground, bench-like, under its spreading, leafy branches. The sun was steaming hot.

Mixing the last of my cappuccino packets into my water bottle, I shook the concoction until the lumps disappeared, toasted the state of Georgia, and drank the entire bottle in one long gulp. When I finished, with foam at the corners of my mouth and dripping down my chin, I admitted to the insects, flowers, and trees around me that it really did taste slimy. It was the last faux cappuccino energy potion I would ever have to drink.

The trail in Georgia was true to its reputation: not always well marked, with many short ups and long gradual downs that made the hot, humid hiking tiring. Along one cool patch of trail, I almost stepped on a brown, yellow and white-patterned snake at least a yard long, stretched in front of me. My hiking pole hit the ground next to its tail before I realized the camouflaged copperhead was not part of the sun-dappled path. It coiled and spit; I backed away and went uphill, around a large rhododendron thicket, and rejoined the trail ten yards away. It was the first snake I had seen since the rattlers in Pennsylvania, though I was sure I had passed others that had not been disturbed enough to coil. Unruffled, I walked on.

I reached the high point of my hike at midday, shared a quick sandwich with the no-see-ums buzzing around my head, and continued my up-down-up trek for the rest of the afternoon, through Bull Gap, Buzzard Knob, Cowart Gap, and Little Bald Knob, all the way to the road crossing at Dick's Gap. I had a food drop waiting for me three and six-tenths miles from the trailhead in Dick's Gap. Unfortunately, I would have to hitch a ride in the late afternoon heat to retrieve it, and then hitch back to the trailhead at dusk.

The highway was hotter than I was. Though there had been no rain, a wavy curtain of moisture rose from the black asphalt in the late afternoon sun. It would be a long, hot walk to the Blueberry Patch Hostel; chances for a hitch seemed slim.

When I started to walk, my boots left imprints on the softened tar. I walked for ten minutes before a car came zooming down the road and braked to a sudden stop. Three high school students on their way home from summer school offered to take me to a driveway where they thought they remembered seeing a sign about blueberries.

I wondered just how this adventure would turn out as we squealed away from the roadside, spitting dirt and gravel into the air, looking for the hostel.

It was a long three miles without another house, driveway, or car. I had my doubts about the Blueberry Patch, and wondered how on earth I would ever get back to the trail. The teenagers were friendly, however, and indeed, almost respectful. They didn't call me ma'am as good southern manners would require, but they did try to be helpful, and I appreciated their intentions.

As the driver accelerated, one handed, he turned his head to the back seat to ask me a question.

"One thing I never understood," he said. "How come you hikers can go two thousand miles, but three miles down the road you need to hitch?"

It was a strange phenomenon, I admitted. I had never met a hiker who didn't try to avoid the road walk towards town.

"Walking in the woods," I tried to explain, "is very different than walking on the road. The road is dangerous, and noisy, and hot, and hard on the feet – it's just no fun."

But my teenaged driver could not see the difference. To him, walking in the woods was all that I described a walk along the road to be – hot, tiring, dangerous, and no fun.

We sped on, down the winding asphalt and eventually spotted a small sign reading "Blueberry Patch" at the end of a long driveway. With jellied knees, I thanked the young men for their lift, and walked down the deserted driveway to the shed adjacent to the sagging frame hostel fifty feet away.

My package sat in a dusty sunbeam, surrounded by discarded boxes, old clothing, and the abandoned parcels of earlier northbound hikers. I quickly opened it up, refilled my food bag, and left a contribution for the hostel owners for their trouble. Once I got back to the trail, I would still have three miles to hike; it seemed an improbable undertaking at the end of the day.

Hoisting my pack, I walked out to the end of the driveway to either hoof or hitch back to the trailhead. Looking around the curves in both directions, however, I knew it would be hard for anyone to see me, let alone stop, on this narrow road without a shoulder.

The angels were once again with me, however. As I stood at the end of the driveway, a car came down the road and pulled in next to me. It was the owner of the Blueberry Patch. He had been expecting me to pick up my package, he said. Apologizing because the hostel was not open this late in the thru-hiker season, he offered to take me back to the trailhead.

Gratefully, I hopped into his car, relieved and thankful that I didn't have to hitch, or walk those long miles back to the trail. It was the last time I would have to try to hitch a ride, the last time I would have to count on the good graces of a local Samaritan to help me on my journey.

I knew I would not miss the drama or tension of these spontaneous acts of kindness. I had been lucky. The Trail Angels had been watching out for me, and I was glad I didn't have to rely on them much longer.

Back on the trail, I hiked up Powell Mountain, across the crest of a ridge, and then down through McClure Gap and Deep Gap to the Deep Gap Shelter. It was a relief to be in the woods again. No matter what my young drivers had thought, hiking in the woods could not be compared to walking along a highway. No matter how hot, tiring, or uncomfortable, walking in the woods was a release from the complications of civilization and a quiet infusion of energy from the life in abundance, all around. In beauty will I possess again.

At the shelter, I set up my gear in the loft, pulled out my stove, and selected dinner from my newly refurbished food bag. A section hiker had strung up his hammock between two nearby trees and kept me company while I ate my gourmet beans and rice with instant chocolate pudding for dessert.

Two more days until Neels Gap; four more days until Springer. Four more days. I still could not believe it.

June 26, 2002, to Blue Mountain Shelter, 15 miles

When I awoke the next morning, my socks were wet. I had hung them on an outdoor clothesline overnight and, for the first and only time on the trail, had forgotten to bring them in; an overnight rain had soaked them through. It was a bad beginning to a gray, overcast, and humid day.

My first climb of the day was seven hundred feet in less than a mile to Kelly Knob, the highest peak between the North Carolina/Georgia state line and Tray Mountain ten miles south. The trees and underbrush were wet from the night's rain, and my boots were sopping within minutes from the long grass at my feet. *"With dew about my feet may I walk,"* I reminded myself, but I was drenched within half an hour of leaving the shelter, and knew it would be a long day of ups and downs with wet feet and no view.

I looked, instead, at the *wildflowers about my feet* and followed the trail through Addis Gap, Sassafras Gap, around the east side of Round Top, and across The Swag of the Blue Ridge, the lowest gap in the area. Under gray skies and intermittent rain, I followed a broad ridge crest and then began some more ups and downs before beginning the ascent of Tray Mountain. Unfortunately, covered with dripping trees, there was no reward at the top except getting there.

Descending Tray Mountain, I reached an old mountain road and spring, and, by lunchtime, a grassy area known as the "cheese factory." The cheese factory was once a remote farm operated by a transplanted New Englander; today it is a level open area near the bank of a bubbling brook. I thought I could relax and rest awhile, but as I opened my pack, so did the clouds, forcing me to quickly cover my pack and run for a laurel and rhododendron thicket in the woods. Under the boughs of dense, waxy leaves, I sat on my pack and listened to the rain, munching a slab of ten-grain bread.

After lunch, there were only two more mountains to climb before I could stop for the night: Rocky Mountain and Blue Mountain, both above four thousand feet. With soggy feet in wet boots, I dreaded the terrain. Today had been a hard hike, probably the most tedious I had yet to experience.

The terrain in the north Georgia mountains is legendary among thruhikers. Because most thru-hikers begin their trek in Georgia and are not trail-seasoned until they reach Virginia, their hike in the north Georgia mountains tends to be clouded by exaggeration and inexperience. That notwithstanding, I was prone to agree; the ups and downs had lived up to their bad reputation. Trail-hardened as I was, I thought these Georgia mountains were tough.

With these thoughts, I climbed to the top of Rocky Mountain. It was long, slow, and steep and I concentrated on just putting one foot in front of the other until I got there. The descent into Unicoi Gap was even steeper, and when I reached the road crossing at the gap late in the afternoon, I was ready to rest. By then it had stopped raining, and the sun was almost out.

I sat down on my pack, took off my boots, and wrung the water out of my socks. Unfortunately, I had nothing dry as a replacement. A northbound hiker, crossing the road, came over to say hello and take a break while I tended to my feet.

As we talked, a car pulled across the road. The driver parked, but did not get out of the car. At first, I paid no attention. Then, I realized the driver was watching us. His behavior made me uneasy. I glanced up at the car from time to time and finally, when the driver, a middle-aged man, got out and started towards us I quietly said to the other hiker, "Let him think we're together and don't tell him anything."

I had never before seen this hiker, a young man in his early twenties, but I did not trust the man in the car across the road. I did not want that man to see us leave in two different directions, me south, the other hiker, north.

The man came over and asked us who we were and where we were going. We were noncommittal and busied ourselves getting ready to hike out, together. We weren't very friendly and the man started to tell us about the hiking he hoped to do someday – but his talk just didn't ring true, to me. Something about him was not quite right. The other hiker and I hoisted our packs and headed, together, back up the trail, away from the road, north.

After a few minutes, the man got back in his car and drove away. The northbound hiker waited while I hiked into the woods to ascend Blue Mountain, a thousand feet up, south. Then he resumed his hike into the woods to ascend Rocky Mountain, a thousand feet up, north.

I never saw that hiker again and don't really know who he was. But I had trusted him, immediately.

This was the only time on the trail that I had been suspicious of anyone I met, but the man at the road crossing gave me the creeps. I had learned to trust my intuitions, implicitly, and the other hiker, true to the unwritten code among hikers, heeded my signal and united with me.

When I reached the crest of Blue Mountain and began the narrow rocky descent along the top of the ridge, I looked up to see a couple approaching me.

"Hey, Gotta Hike!" the man greeted me.

"My gosh, this must be Wednesday," I replied, completely surprised to see them again.

It was James and Diana, the poet and pastry chef from my hitch in the Smoky Mountains.

"Our day off," James explained, and then went on to alert me to the flaming azaleas just ahead; he was still waxing poetic about the flora and fauna around him. Diana seemed a bit disheartened by the wet, but nothing seemed to dampen James' enthusiasm for hiking. Good for him; I applauded his perseverance.

Someday, James and Diana would walk the entire trail and probably love every minute of it. I was delighted to see them again; they brought sunshine into an otherwise tedious, soggy day.

A few minutes later, I reached the trail to the Blue Mountain Shelter and hiked in for the night. I was eager to eat, rest, and sleep. But more than anything else, I wanted to hang up my socks and dry them out before morning. My blisters were almost healed, but hiking in wet boots and socks could flare them up again. I would do almost anything to prevent that.

Some section hikers at the shelter had built a fire by the time I arrived. I set my boots and socks on the rocky rim of the fire ring, close to the blaze, and willed them dry by bedtime. That night, hoping to use my body heat to complete the drying process, I slept with the damp socks inside my sleeping bag, next to my skin.

In the morning, both the socks and I were damp.

June 27, 2002, to Walasi-Yi Hostel, Neels Gap, Ga., 17 miles

The day began with a descent from Rocky Knob to the Chattahoochee Gap, the headwaters of the Chattahoochee River. With a name like Chattahoochee, I thought, I had to be in Georgia. I felt like I was walking in a book. Somehow, the names in the Georgia mountains told stories all their own. Today's story would have the profile of a steady heartbeat, up and down at regular intervals with a few level places to rest. The names of Wolfpen Stamp, Hogpen Gap, Wildcat Mountain, Levelland Mountain, and Bull Gap made me wonder about the people and circumstances that had created these names. They sounded rugged, self-sufficient, and rough; so did the day ahead.

I hiked into a misty morning that promised to be hot. I met no one on the trail until almost noon, near Hogpen Gap. I had already hiked eleven miles by then and had begun to look for a place to sit down and take a break, have lunch, and take off my boots. Crossing the gap, I looked up and saw a short, silver-haired man dressed in a green shirt and khaki shorts, holding a small pail, brushing white paint in a 2x6 rectangle onto the side of a tree.

I couldn't believe it. I must have seen at least ten thousand of the twenty-two thousand white blazes painted on trees, rocks, posts, and bridges between Georgia and Maine, and wondered as many times who had painted that blaze and how they had done it. I had convinced myself that the painting was done in the dead of night, under the light of a full moon, by a band of silver-haired leprechauns dressed in green and brown, to blend in with the trees. And now, on a hot summer day, I had found my leprechaun. At full noon. Oh well, I thought, the leprechauns in Georgia might have something better to do in the full of the moon.

Not to let the moment pass, I pulled out my camera and took a quick photo.

My leprechaun's name was Craig Lyerla, and his green shirt bore the letters GATC (Georgia Appalachian Trail Club). He told me that he sometimes used a homemade template to keep the edges of the blaze straight because this was a wilderness area and he could only use non-power tools to keep the trail maintained. He had been maintaining this section of the trail, from Hogback to Tesnatee Gap, since 1978, he said, and was proud of his section of the trail. Everything had to be done by hand, he explained; even blowdowns had to be cut up and removed without chainsaws. Remembering the huge blowdown I had seen after the thunderstorm in Nantahala, I was impressed with the challenge of his task. Keeping the trail clear with only a meager set of hand tools could only be a labor of love and deep respect for the wilderness. I was glad he could not defile these woods with gasoline engines and loud, offensive machinery.

After that, the climb up Wildcat Mountain was easy, so I hiked a little farther before stopping for lunch. At the top of Cowrock Mountain, I looked down into the gorge and the steep rock face of the mountain below me. I made a *Sandwich*, drank a liter of Gatorade, and leaned back on my pack, feeling like the queen of the heap surveying my kingdom.

After lunch, I continued down a ridge crest and climbed back up another ridge, through steep, scrubby rock, reaching an open campsite with exquisite views. I would have loved to camp there, but knew I had to push on to Neels Gap and the Walasi-Yi Hostel before it closed at six o'clock.

I hiked on, crossing an open rocky area and the summit of Levelland Mountain, descended into Bull Gap, and, within forty-five minutes of closing time, reached the archway of the Walasi-Yi Hostel and outfitter in Neels Gap.

My last mail drop, a shower, and empty bunkhouse awaited me at the hostel. I quickly repacked my food bag and went to the bunkhouse to spread out my gear and relax. It had been a long day. Another thunderstorm was rolling in and I was happy to be in an underground shelter. That night, I had the bunkhouse to myself.

June 28, 2002, to Gooch Gap Shelter, 16 miles

Even buried within the thick stone walls of the Walasi-Yi hostel, I could tell that it was raining when I woke up the next morning. In the dark, empty bunkroom, I rolled over and went back to sleep until seven o'clock. By eight o'clock, I was up, packed, and ready to hike into the dismal, gray rain.

Crossing the road, I began a gradual, then steep ascent by switchback to the top of Blood Mountain. Blood Mountain is known for the red hue of the lichen covering its rocks, but it was named for a battle between the Cherokee and Creek Indians that was so fierce, legend says, that the mountain ran with blood.

The morning showers worsened into furious wind and pounding rain. As I hiked onto the open rock summit, I felt, once again, like the only person in the world. I picked my way across gray rock in dense fog, with the wind in my face, blowing me backwards. I thought, suddenly, of the evening I had struggled up the slope of White Cap Mountain and battled my way across its windy summit, trying to find my way, on my own, to the shelter. This morning, the gray, windy, ethereal circumstances were similar, but the spark of confidence, newly ignited within me then, had matured to a steady flame. Then, nearly to Katahdin, I had awakened to the knowledge that I could persevere, feel my way, and trust my good judgment to get me through.

Picking my way across the rocks of Blood Mountain on this morning, in similar weather conditions, I was stronger, wiser, and more tenacious. Springer Mountain was only twenty-eight miles away. I was almost there.

It rained and blew hard all day. The sun tried several times to make an appearance, but I had learned not to trust the sun on a rainy day until the birds began to sing, full throated. My rule was: if it's been raining, and the sun peeks out but the birds don't sing, keep your rain gear on; you'll be sure to need it soon.

It was a long climb in hot, wet raingear.

By lunchtime, I had crossed Bird Gap, reached the shoulder of Turkey Stamp Mountain, crossed Horsebone Gap, ascended and descended Gaddis Mountain and Granny Top Mountain, and climbed to the rock outcroppings of Big Cedar Mountain. In the rain, it was slippery, wet, and cloud covered – there was no place on the trail to sit down and have a *Sandwich*.

When I reached a parking area with a signpost under a shingled roof, however, I knew I had found the perfect place for lunch. I sat down, dug into my pack, and cut a thick slab of bread. Two hikers emerged from the woods as I was about to take my first bite.

The hikers were Ben and Jorge, a graduate student from California and his uncle, a filmmaker from New York City. They looked hungrily at my *Sandwich*, but declined my offer to share, though I had plenty to spare. Ben and Jorge were also heading south to Springer, and were eager to find the next shelter. I sat under my roof and watched them disappear into the rain.

Licking the honey from my fingers, I finished my lunch, stowed my food, and followed them into the dripping woods. Ben and Jorge had not gone far and were at a streambed filtering water when I walked by. We hiked on together, ascending and descending, looking for the trail to the Gooch Gap Shelter.

At the Walasi-Yi Hostel, the caretaker had told me a new shelter had just been completed to replace the old one at Gooch Gap. It was about two miles beyond the old one, he said, and might not be marked from the north. I passed the tidbit of information on to Ben and Jorge. In the rain, a new structure with a solid roof would be far superior to an old, leaky CCC-built shelter, I told them. I planned to find it.

The trail markings were confusing, but when we found the old shelter it was indeed an original CCC model: moss-covered stone, dark, damp and smelly, with a rotten, leaky roof and wet flooring. Ben and Jorge were ready to stop, but something about my self-assurance, they said, made them listen to my suggestion that we hike on and find the newer shelter.

"If it doesn't exist," I promised, "we can always come back here – this shelter won't be going anywhere."

We hiked on, along the side of Gooch Mountain to the top of Horseshoe Ridge, and crossed a footbridge across a creek. And then, just like in the movies, the sun came out, the birds began to sing, and the clouds faded to wispy white and lifted to reveal a bright blue sky. At the end of the footbridge, we saw the new Gooch Gap Shelter.

It was beautiful: a three-sided wooden structure with a sloping overhang, upstairs sleeping lofts, counters, benches, and a picnic table in a clearing surrounded by tall green trees and mountains in the distance. Down one short path was a state-of-the-art compost privy, down another, a healthy-looking burbling brook.

We quickly slipped out of our wet packs and gear and settled into the dry, pine-scented shelter. Jorge brewed gourmet coffee and I shared slices of the bread they coveted. We dined in elegance under the soft evening breeze at the Gooch Gap palace. From the shelter site, we could see Springer Mountain, just fourteen miles away.

June 29, 2002, to Springer Mountain, 14.3 miles

My last day on the trail dawned misty, but clear. Too excited to sleep late, I was up and ready to leave by seven o'clock. My shelter mates, a little slower, promised to meet me at the shelter on Springer Mountain by evening. They said they would take my picture when I crossed the top.

I hiked in the quiet green morning in beauty. I walked along old forest roads, through gaps, across the summit of Sassafras Mountain and near the summit of Hawk Mountain, listening to the sound of birds through the trees. The ascents and descents were gradual and, though I was watching for the Army rangers on reported maneuvers, I only saw trees and wildflowers, red dirt and tangled underbrush.

As I descended Hawk Mountain, I heard the unmistakable sound of rushing water through the woods. I hurried to find the Benton MacKaye Trail along the side of a large creek, and followed it, under soaring hemlock trees, to Long Creek Falls.

After the hot sticky morning, the cool dark woods next to the falls was like entering an air conditioned movie theatre from the bright afternoon sun: the only thing visible, until your eyes adjust to the light, is the scene in front of you. In this cool green forest, my eyes focused on the bright crashing cascade at the end of the path. As my eyes adjusted, I was surprised to see other people at the falls, posing and snapping pictures in front of the spray.

I sat on a flat rock overlooking the water to eat my last *Sandwich* and was tempted to duck under the falls to cool off. Looking at the well-dressed people around me, however, I realized my skinny-dipping days in cool mountain streams would need to wait for my next hike into the backcountry. One of the trade-offs for the comforts of civilization, I sighed, was propriety.

Beginning to chill and growing tired of the deafening roar of the falls, I put away my food bag, picked up my pack, and hiked out, retracing my steps back to the AT.

I followed the ridge crests and descended alongside Long Creek to Three Forks, where three mountain streams converge to form Noontootla Creek. Following an old abandoned road along Stover Creek, through a magnificent stand of hemlocks, I began my last ascent, the climb to the top of Springer Mountain. I was almost at the end of my odyssey.

It was fitting that I crossed, and then followed, the Benton MacKaye Trail, contiguous to the AT through the hemlocks, for this last portion of my journey. Benton MacKaye, more than any other dreamer I had met or heard about on the trail, most reminded me of my father. I thanked them both for their separate dreams of the Appalachian Trail. They had passed their dream to me, and I was grateful.

As I hiked through the rhododendron thickets up the side of Springer Mountain, I realized that without acting on my dream, it would have never come true. My mother had taught me how to be active. I thanked her for that.

Nor would it have been possible for me to hike if my daughters, Amy and Megg, had not grown into the capable young adults they had both become. I thanked them, too, as I walked.

Remembering all the people who had helped me along the way, I thanked the university women who helped me train. I thanked all my friends who sent me CARE packages.

I thanked the roofer who whittled my first walking stick, and the many trail angels who came after him, always emerging to sprinkle their trail magic just when I needed it most.

Finally, I thanked George, my wonderful partner, for encouraging me to act on my dreams to make them come true. His support had been steadfast and constant; he had believed in me. Without him, I knew my hike would never have been possible.

It had been a long trek. The planning, logistics, training, expense, arranging and rearranging of schedules and priorities – all had been complicated and full of effort. The actual, everyday, uphill and downhill walking, pulling and pushing on my trekking poles, lugging a heavy pack, watching where I put each foot, keeping my eyes open for white blazes, blue blazes, signs, snakes, and bears, keeping my ears open for weather changes, other people, and animals, being vigilant every day, all day, and every night, all night, had been hard.

Learning how to operate a camp stove, cook in the rain, set up a tent, set up a tent in the rain, take it all down without getting my clothes and gear wet, and keeping my socks dry, had been tough.

Learning how to hitch a ride, sleep in a hostel, sleep in a shelter, and be self-sufficient, independent, and non-dependent, had been difficult.

Learning to listen to my body, my thoughts, my intuition, and my needs, had been liberating.

It had all been an exquisite education in patience, forbearance, endurance, and courage. I was glad I had the opportunity to accomplish what I set out to do. And I was glad it was almost over.

I would miss the tall green solitude of walking through the trees with only the birds, insects, rustling leaves, and unseen wildlife for company.

But when I reached the shelter on Springer Mountain, two-tenths mile from the terminus of my hike, the heavens once again opened and a thunderstorm rumbled in. I would not miss the sudden thunderstorms!

I ducked into the shelter, shaking my head in disbelief. A thunderstorm for the final curtain? As I waited for the storm to pass, Ben and Jorge hiked in. We cooked dinner under the overhanging roof of the shelter and they toasted my near-completion of the trail by clicking their plastic bottles of treated water with mine.

When the last of the thunder rumbled over the mountains and the birds resumed their song, I picked up my poles and walked the final two-tenths mile to the bronze plaque on the top of Springer Mountain. The plaque, placed on a flat rock by the Georgia Appalachian Mountain Club in 1959, shows a hiker, with a pack, stepping up to the task, ready to take on the world.

A tortoise under a brown and amber shell appeared at the edge of the plaque just as I lifted my foot for the final step. She under her shell, and I under my pack, crossed the finish line, together.

I turned around to the view behind me as Jorge snapped my picture, a portrait of joy.

The curtain of mist from the late afternoon storm lifted on a stage of blue-green mountains stretching as wide and as far as my eye could see, as deep as my spirit could hold. The trees glistened with jewels and sparkled in the recovering light.

I sat on the rock and called George on my cell phone. I was too happy to cry.

"In beauty I have walked
All day long I have walked
Through the returning seasons I have walked
In beauty I have possessed again
Beautifully birds
Beautifully joyful birds.
On a trail marked with pollen I have walked
With wildflowers about my feet I have walked
With dew about my feet I have walked
With beauty before me I have walked
With beauty behind me I have walked
With beauty above me I have walked
With beauty all around me I have walked
At my age, wandering on a trail of beauty
Lively I have walked,
In old age, wandering on a trail of beauty
Living again I will walk
I have finished in beauty."

                     – Gotta Hike!
                     – Va.-Maine – Va.-Ga., 2001-'02

Epilogue

In June 2003, my friend Lura and I finally hiked the AT together. My goal was to fill in the missing sixty-four New Jersey miles from June 2001, when I had yellow-blazed the trail, so that I could rightly claim that I had, indeed, walked the entire AT and could legitimately qualify as a *2000 Miler*. I particularly wanted to hike the relocation over the boardwalk and pedestrian bridge that spanned the wetlands of Vernon Valley, and was eager to hike with Lura, to fulfill the promise we had originally made to hike part of my AT journey together.

"How did you do this for two thousand miles?" she asked on our third day out. "No amount of reading or working out in the gym could have prepared me for actually carrying a pack up and down over rocks and through streams, and then setting up camp at the end of a tiring day, sometimes in the rain, when my resources were at their lowest," she said.

Annie Dillard, in writing about the tenacity of weasels, described what I knew to be true about myself and hiking the trail. No matter how tough the terrain, no matter how hungry, cold, hot, or tired my body, no matter how lonely, scared, and bruised my spirit, I had hung on, and did not let go of my dream.

I reminded Lura that she was also tenacious. A survivor of breast cancer, she had also hung on through adversity, though of a different sort.

But a long distance hike on the AT was somehow different, she said.

"A long distance hike is not the same as a day or weekend loop hike. Hiking over an extended period of time, to a destination, takes discipline. It's more a vocation than a recreation. You needed the tenacity of a dream to sustain you."

I agreed. An end-to-end thru-hike takes more than superb physical conditioning and mental stamina to hike it. It takes more than a sense of adventure to fuel it. It takes more than time, energy, planning, support, trail angels, humor, and money to sustain it. Hiking the AT, from beginning to end, requires all those things. But it also requires what my mother would call "stick-to-it-ive-ness" – an unwillingness to give in, an ability to endure and press on, tough, dogged, opinionated, and persistent, no matter what.

I guessed I had that tenacity. I had been well-named, *Gotta Hike!*

On the last day of our hike together, Lura and I sat under the pedestrian bridge next to Pochuck Creek and toasted our friendship and our fulfilled promise to hike together. Later, crossing Wawayanda Creek, we played "Pooh Sticks" on the footbridge, throwing sticks into the water upstream, then dashing across the bridge to discover which stick led the downstream race. We were silly and light-hearted, enjoying the day and the pace of a leisurely walk.

My hike had been a wonderful journey and had consumed my attention for the better part of four years. Now it was time to let it go. Unlike the weasel in Annie Dillard's description, more than instinct to hang on would guide my next steps.

"Reach high, for stars lie hidden in
your soul. Dream deep, for every
dream precedes the goal."

– Pamela Vaull Starr

This is a true story, as experienced by the author.
Some names have been changed or altered to maintain
the privacy of certain individuals.